Hippocrene Concise Dictionary

Nahuatl-English
English-Nahuatl
(Aztec)

Hippocrene Concise Dictionaries

Arabic	Japanese *Romanized*
Armenian	Kurdish
Azerbaijani	Ladino
Bemba	Lithuanian
Bosnian	Nahuatl
Bugotu	Neo-Melanesian
Byelorussian	Norwegian
Catalan	Pilipino
Chinese Pinyin	Polish
Creole (Carribean)	Russian
Creole (Haitian)	Sanskrit
Czech	Scottish Doric
Dutch	Scottish Gaelic
Estonian	Serbian
Farsi (Persian)	Slovak
Finnish	Sorbian
Galician	Spanish
German	Twi
Greek	Uzbek
Gypsy	Welsh
Hungarian	Zapotec (Isthmus)
Icelandic	

Hippocrene Concise Dictionary

Nahuatl-English
English-Nahuatl
(Aztec)

FERMIN HERRERA

HIPPOCRENE BOOKS, INC.
New York

© 2004 Fermin Herrera

ISBN 0-7818-1011-6

For information, address:
    Hippocrene Books, Inc.
    171 Madison Avenue
    New York, NY 10016
    www.hippocrenebooks.com

*Cataloging-in-Publication data available from the
Library of Congress.*

Printed in the United States of America.

Contents

The Nahuatl Language

Nahuatl, also known as Aztec or Mexican, is the most widely spoken indigenous language of North America. It was spoken by the Aztecs centuries ago and continues to be spoken by millions in Mexico and Central America today. It belongs to the Uto-Aztecan family of languages, a linguistic complex that is very widely diffused throughout central and northeastern Mexico as well as the American Southwest. It is related to the Huichol language of Nayarit, the Yaqui and Rarámuri (Tarahumara) of Chihuahua, the Hopi of Arizona, the Shoshone of Wyoming, the Comanche of Texas, the Luiseño of California, and the Paiute of Oklahoma.

The golden age of the language coincided with the period of Aztec dominance from the early fifteenth to the early sixteenth century. During this period the language spread from central to western Mexico, to the Gulf Coast, and into Central America. Nahuatl enjoyed its greatest flowering in the Valley of Mexico, where the great cities of the empire were located: Tetzcohco, Mexihco-Tenochtitlan, and Tlacopan, the capitals of the Nahuatl Empire.

Before the period of Spanish contact, Nahuatl was written in an indigenous pictographic script, which continued to be used well into the seventeenth century.

Spanish priests and Nahuatl scribes began to record the
Nahuatl language in the Spanish alphabet during the
1520s. A rich body of literature was collected and is found
in hundreds of manuscripts that preserve the form of
the language as it was used several hundred years ago.
In addition, sixteenth-century Spanish priests in Mexico
compiled word lists and wrote grammatical treatises that
described the language of the time. The Nahuatl variety
reflected in these early works is called classical Nahuatl.
It is the formal, literary style of the language.

In the modern era, Nahuatl continues to be spoken by
several million people in various parts of Mexico and Central America. Regional varieties of Nahuatl (some of which
are known as Nahuat and Nahual) are found in southern
Mexico City, the region of Puebla and Cholula, Tlaxcala,
the Huasteca area of San Luis Potosí, Querétaro, Hidalgo,
and Veracruz; Jalisco and Michoacán, the Isthmus of
Tehuantepec, and in El Salvador.

The last twenty-five years has seen a resurgence of interest
in the cultivation of the Nahuatl language and Nahuatl
literature both in Mexico and in the United States. The
model, especially in Central Mexico, has been for the
most part the classical variety of Nahuatl. This dictionary
reflects usage largely based on classical norms.

Nahuatl Pronunciation Guide

Letter	Sound
a	as in father
au	as in out
c	before /e/ and /i/ as in set; elsewhere, as in cap
ch	as in chew
cu	as in queen
e	as in bet
h	as in happy
hu	as in wet
i	as in machine
l	as in lamb (except in final –tl)
m	as in more
n	as in no
o	as in or
p	as in spoke
qu	as in kept
t	as in ton
tl (word ending)	no equivalent in English. Pronounce by touching the back of the teeth with the tip of the tongue and releasing the air laterally (side of the tongue). Do **not** pronounce as kettle, sprinkle, or metal.

tz	as in pizza; also, as in see
u	as in fool
uh	as in when
x	as in shoe
y	as in you
z	as in sun

Key to Pronunciation Scheme

Symbol	Sound
ä	as in father
ou	as in out
ĕ	as in pet
ee	as in machine
o	as in or
oo	as in fool
k	as in cat
kw	as in queen
λ	Pronounce by touching the back of the teeth with the tip of the tongue and releasing the air laterally (side of the tongue). **Do not** pronounce as kettle, sprinkle, or metal.

Accent

The accent in Nahuatl falls on the second from last syllable, as illustrated in the examples below. Bold type indicates the accented syllable.

nican (*here*)
nee-kän

coyotl (*coyote*)
ko-yoλ

The exception to this pattern occurs in direct address. When a person is being addressed, an accented /e/ is suffixed, as in the examples below. Bold type indicates the accented syllable.

Simple Form	Direct Address
nonantzin	nonantzin**e**
(*mother*)	(*oh, mother*)
no-**nän**-seen	no-nän-seen-**ĕ**
nopilhuan	nopilhuan**e**
(*my children*)	(*oh, my children*)
no-**peel**-wän	no-peel-wän-**ĕ**

Terminal /–ia/ is pronounced as two separate sounds:
ee-ä, with the accent on /i/, as in the examples below.
Bold type indicates accented syllable.

Word	Pronunciation Scheme
machtia (to teach)	*mäch-**tee**-ä*
ahuia (to be happy)	*ä-**wee**-ä*
pia (to have)	*pee-ä*

Pronunciation Examples

Word	Pronunciation Scheme
ce (*one*)	sĕ
cihuatl (*woman*)	**see**-wätλ
calli (*house*)	**cäl**-lee
icxitl (*foot*)	**eek**-sheetλ
michin (*fish*)	**mee**-cheen
cualli (*good*)	**kwäl**-lee
ozomahtli (*monkey*)	o-so-**mäh**-tlee
cuahuitl (*tree*)	**kwä**-weetλ
quemah (*yes*)	**kĕ**-mäh
tepuztli (*metal*)	tĕ-**poos**-tlee
xamitl (*adobe*)	**xä**-meeλ

Abbreviations

adj.	adjective
adv.	adverb
art.	article
aux.	auxiliary
conj.	conjunction
dir.	direct
exclam.	exclamation
impers. v.	impersonal verb
interj.	interjection
interr. pron.	interrogative pronoun
irreg.	irregular
iv.	intransitive verb
loc.	locative
n.	noun
neg.	negative
num.	number
part.	particle
poss.	possessive
prep.	preposition
pron.	pronoun
reflex. v.	reflexive verb
sing.	singular
suff.	suffix
tv.	transitive verb
v.	verb

Basic Grammar

Nouns

Singular Nouns

Nahuatl nouns take singular and plural suffixes. They do not have gender. Singular nouns take the suffixes **–tl, –tli, –li, –in**; plural nouns take the suffixes **–h, –meh, –tin**. Nouns consist of a stem and a suffix (singular or plural).

Noun stems that end in a vowel take the singular suffix **–tl**.

EXAMPLES:

Stem	+	*Suffix*	*Complete Noun*
a	+	tl	atl (*water*)
te	+	tl	tetl (*stone*)
zoqui	+	tl	zoquitl (*mud*)

Noun stems that end in a consonant (except –l–) take the singular suffix –**tli**.

EXAMPLES:

Stem	+	Suffix	Complete Noun
nan	+	tli	nantli (*mother*)
tah	+	tli	tahtli (*father*)
miz	+	tli	miztli (*puma*)

Noun stems that end in –**l**– take the singular suffix –**li**.

EXAMPLES:

Stem	+	Suffix	Complete Noun
xal	+	li	xalli (*sand*)
chil	+	li	chilli (*hot pepper*)
pil	+	li	pilli (*child*)

A few noun stems that end in a consonant take the singular suffix –**in**.

EXAMPLES:

Stem	+	Suffix	Complete Noun
zol	+	in	zolin (*quail*)
chapul	+	in	chapulin (*grasshopper*)
mich	+	in	michin (*fish*)

Plural Nouns

Nouns ending in –**tl** that refer to people change the singular suffix to –**h** when plural. Those that refer to animals change it to –**meh**.

EXAMPLES:

Singular	Plural
tlaca**tl** (*person*)	tlaca**h** (*persons*)
cihua**tl** (*woman*)	cihua**h** (*women*)
ichca**tl** (*lamb*)	ichca**meh** (*lambs*)
pitzo**tl** (*pig*)	pitzo**meh** (*pigs*)

Nouns ending in –**tl** and –**li** change these to –**tin** when plural.

EXAMPLES:

Singular	Plural
nan**tli** (*mother*)	nan**tin** (*mothers*)
tah**tli** (*father*)	tah**tin** (*fathers*)

Nouns ending in **–in** usually change to **–meh** when plural.

EXAMPLES:

Singular	Plural
pipiolin (*bee*)	pipiol**meh** (*bees*)
ocuilin (*worm*)	ocuil**meh** (*worms*)

The following nouns have a special plural form. They take the above plural suffixes and reduplication of the first syllable.

Singular	Plural
conetl (*child*)	**coconeh** (*children*)
pilli (*child*)	**pipiltin** (*children*)
teotl (*god*)	**teteoh** (*gods*)
ticitl (*phisician*)	**titicih** (*physicians*)
teuctli/tecuhtli (*lord*)	**teteuctin/tetecuhtin** (*lords*)

The nouns *ichpochtli* (girl) and *telpochtli* (boy) repeat the /**–po–**/ instead of the first syllable:

Singular	Plural
ichpochtli (*girl*)	ich**po**poch**tin** (*girls*)
telpochtli (*boy*)	telo**po**poch**tin** (*boys*)

Compound Nouns

When two nouns are combined, the first of these drops
the singular suffix (**–tl**, **–tli**, **–li**, or **–in**); the second retains
it. The first noun describes the second, as in English.

EXAMPLES:

ahuacatl	+	molli	>	**ahuaca**molli
(*avocado*)		(*sauce*)		(*avocado sauce, guacamole*)
ixtli	+	tetl	>	**ix**tetl
(*eye*)		(*ball*)		(*eyeball*)
molli	+	caxitl	>	**mol**caxitl
(*sauce*)		(*bowl*)		(*sauce bowl*)
michin	+	omitl	>	**mich**omitl
(*fish*)		(*bone*)		(*fish bone*)

Noun stems ending in **–i** usually drop it when com-
pounded.

EXAMPLES:

quilitl	+	milli	>	**quil**milli
(*vegetable*)		(*field*)		(*vegetable patch, field*)
maitl	+	tepuztli	>	**ma**tepuztli
(*hand*)		(*axe*)		(*hand axe*)

Nouns stems ending in **–hui** change to –uh when com-
pounded.

EXAMPLES:

cuahuitl	+	tlactli	>	**cuauh**tlactli
(*tree*)		(*trunk*)		(*tree trunk*)
xihuitl	+	nelhuatl	>	**xiuh**nelhuatl
(*herb*)		(*root*)		(*herb root*)

Chichi (dog) does not take a singular marker. *Tenamitl*
(wall) has *tenan–*as its stem.

Possessives

The possessive prefixes are attached to the noun stem.
The singular suffix is dropped but is sometimes replaced
by **–uh**. Possesseive plural nouns take the suffix **–huan.**
The possessive prefixes are:

Singular	Plural	Nonspecific
no *my*	**to** *our*	**te** *someone's, people's*
mo your	**amo** *your*	
i *his*	**im/in** *their*	

EXAMPLES:

Noun	Noun with Possessive
calli (*house*)	**no**cal (*my house*)
nantli (*mother*)	**to**nan (*our mother*)
teotl (*god*)	**in**teo**uh** (*their god*)
atl (*water*)	**n**auh (*my water*)
conetl (*chilled*)	**te**cone**huan** (*someone's children*)
tototl (*bird*)	itoto**huan** (*his birds*)

Adjectives

Adjectives are placed before the noun, as in English. They do not have gender. They agree in number with the noun that they modify. Adjectives that end in **–li** change this suffix to **–tin** in the plural. Those that end in **–c** and **–qui** change to **–queh** and those that end in **–h** add **–queh**.

EXAMPLES:

Singular	Plural
cua**lli** tlacatl (*good person*)	cua**ltin** tlacah (*good persons*)
tilti**c** tototl (*black bird*)	tlilti**queh** totomeh (*black birds*)
tlatziuh**qui** oquichtli (*lazy man*)	tlatziuh**queh** oquichtin (*lazy men*)
yollo**h** cihautl (*intelligent woman*)	yolloh**queh** cihuah (*intelligent women*)

There are several ways to form the comparative and superlative of adjectives. The easiest is to place the adverb *ocachi* before the adjective for the comparative and either *huel* or *cenca* for the superlative, as illustrated in the examples below.

Positive	Comparative	Superlative
yectli *(beautiful)*	**ocachi** yectli *(more beautiful)*	**huel** yectli/**cenca** yectli *(most beautiful)*
piltic *(thin)*	**ocachi** piltic *(thinner)*	**huel** piltic/**cenca** piltic *(thinnest)*

Pronouns

Subject Pronouns

Singular	Plural
ni– *I*	**ti**– *we*
ti– *you*	**am/an**– *you*
Ø: *he*	**Ø:** *they*

These prefixes are attached to verbs to indicate the doer of the action, as in these examples: ***ni**choca* (I cry), ***ti**choca* (you cry), *choca* (he cries). The absence of a prefix indicates third person. The plural prefix *am*– is used before vowels and the letters /m/ and /p/; *an*– is used elsewhere, as in the following examples: **amahuiah** (you are happy), **ammayanah** (you are hungry), **ampinotlah-toah** (you speak a foreign language); **antlahcuiloah** (you write), **anquizah** (you leave).

The subject pronouns are also attached to nouns and adjectives to indicate identity, as in the following examples:

Nimexihcatl.	*I am Mexican.*
Tipipiltin.	*We are children*
Ticualli.	*You are kind.*

Object Pronouns

Singular	*Plural*
nech– *me*	**tech**– *us*
mitz– *you*	**amech**– *you*
c– (next to a vowel, except /i/) *him*	**quim**– (before vowels, /m/, and /p/) *them*
qu– (before /i/) *him*	**quin**– (elsewhere) *them*
qui– (elsewhere) *him*	

Nonspecific Object Pronouns

te– *someone, people*
tla– *something*

These pronouns indicate both direct and indirect object.
They are always attached to a verb and are placed after the
subject pronoun. *Te–* and *tla–* are used to indicate objects
that are nonspecific.

EXAMPLES:

Direct Object

Ti**nech**tlazohtla.	*You love me.*
Ni**mitz**tlazohtla.	*I love you.*
Ni**c**tlazohtla.	*I love him.*
Ni**te**machtia.	*I teach someone.*
Ni**tla**namaca.	*I sell something.*

Indirect Object

Ti**nech**maca atl.	*You give me water.*
Ni**mitz**maca amoxtli.	*I give you a book.*
Ni**c**namaquiltia petlatl.	*I sell him a mat.*
Ni**te**machtia nahuatlahtolli.	*I teach people Nahuatl.*

EXAMPLES OF *c–*, *qu–*, *qui–*, *quim–*, *quin–*:

Ni**c**tlazohtla.	*I love him.*
Ni**qui**tta.	*I see him.*
An**qui**tlazohtlah.	*You (plural) love him.*
Ni**quim**itta.	*I see them.*
Ni**quin**tlazohtla.	*I love them.*

Reflexive Pronouns

Singular	Plural
nino– *myself*	**tito**– *ourselves*
timo– *yourself*	**ammo**– *yourselves*
mo– *himself*	**mo**– *themselves*

Reflexive pronouns are used to indicate that the subject acts upon itself. Many Nahuatl verbs require the use of the reflexive pronouns even though they're is no reflexive action indicated. These are called reflexive verbs and are labeled as such in this dictionary.

EXAMPLES:

Reflexive Action

Ninopahtia.	*I cure myself.*
Timopahtia.	*You cure yourself.*

Reflexive Verb (non-reflexive action)

Ninotlaloa.	*I run*
Timozahua.	*You abstain from food.*

Personal Pronouns

Singular	Plural
nehhuatl/nehhua/neh *I*	tehhuantin *we*
tehhuatl/tehhua/teh *you*	amehhuantin *you*
yehhuatl/yehhua/yeh *he*	yehhuantin *they*

These pronouns can be used alone. They are not attached to verbs. They are often used to reinforce the subject of a verb, as in these examples:

Nehhuatl nichoca.   *I cry.*
Tehhuatl ticualli.   *You are kind.*

Demonstrative Pronouns

Singular	*Plural*
inin *this*	**inintin** or **inihqueh** *these*
inon *that*	**inontin** or **inihqueh on** *those*

Indefinite Pronouns

aquin	*Who?*	someone
ac	*Who?*	Used in compounds. EXAMPLES: *Ac te?* (Who are you) and *Tac te?* (Who are you?)
aca	*someone*	

Relative Pronouns

The particle *in* is used as a relative pronoun. It is used as a subject and object, and may be translated as who, whom, which, that. It does not take gender or number.

EXAMPLES:

Tehhuatl **in** ticuica.	*You are the one who sings.*
Tehhuatl **in** onimitzihtac yalhua.	*You are the one whom I saw yesterday.*
Xiccua tamalli **in** oquichiuh nonantzin.	*Eat the tamale that my mother made.*

Verbs

Nahuatl verbs indicate tense (present, future, past), voice (active or passive), and mood (indicative or optative). The following outline shows the subject prefixes, tense suffixes, and number suffixes for the active and passive indicative.

Subject Prefixes		Tense Suffixes		Number Suffixes	
Singular	*Plural*			*Singular*	*Plural*
ni– *I*	ti– *we*	Present:	Ø	Ø	–h
ti– *you*	am/an– *you*	Imperfect: –*ya*	Ø	Ø	-h
Ø: *he*	Ø: *they*	Future: –*z*	Ø	Ø	–queh
		Habitual: –*ni*	Ø	Ø	–h
		Preterit: Ø	–*c*/–*qui*	Ø	–queh
		Pluperfect: –*ca*	Ø	Ø	–h

Present Tense

The present tense does not take a tense marker. The plural suffix is **–h**. For example:

Model Conjugation

Singular	Plural
Nichoca	**Ti**choca**h**
(*I cry*)	(*We cry*)
Tichoca	**An**choca**h**
(*You* cry)	(*You* cry)
Choca	Choca**h**
(*He cries*)	(*They cry*)

Note: The second and third person (singular and plural) also have a reverential form, as indicated after each tense.

Reverential

Singular	Plural
Timochoquilia	Ammochoquilia**h**
(*You cry*)	(*You cry*)
Mochoquilia	Mochoquilia**h**
(*He cries*)	(*They cry*)

Imperfect Tense

The imperfect takes the tense marker **–ya** and the plural suffix **–h**.

Model Conjugation

Singular	Plural
Nichoca**ya**	Tichoca**yah**
(I was crying)	*(We were crying)*
Tichoca**ya**	Anchoca**yah**
(You were crying)	*(You were crying)*
Choca**ya**	Choca**yah**
(He was crying)	*(They were crying)*

Reverential

Singular	Plural
Timochoquilia**ya**	Ammochoquilia**yah**
(You were crying)	*(You were crying)*
Mochoquilia**ya**	Mochoquilia**yah**
(He was crying)	*(They were crying)*

Future Tense

The future takes the tense marker **–z** and the plural suffix **–queh**.

Model Conjugation

Singular	Plural
Nichoca**z**	Tichoca**zqueh**
(*I will cry*)	(*We will cry*)
Tichoca**z**	Anchoca**zqueh**
(*You will cry*)	(*You will cry*)
Choca**z**	Choca**zqueh**
(*He will cry*)	(*They will cry*)

Reverential

Singular	Plural
Timochoquili**z**	Ammochoquili**zqueh**
(*You will cry*)	(*You will cry*)
Mochoquili**z**	Mochoquili**zqueh**
(*He will cry*)	(*They will cry*)

Habitual Present

The habitual present takes the tense marker **–ni** and the plural suffix **–h**.

Model Conjugation

Singular	Plural
Nichoca**ni**	Tichoca**nih**
(*I usually cry;*	(*We usually cry;*
I am a crier)	*we are criers*)
Tichoca**ni**	Anchoca**nih**
(*You usually cry;*	(*You usually cry;*
you are a crier)	*you are criers*)
Choca**ni**	Choca**nih**
(*He usually cries;*	(*They usually cry;*
he is a crier)	*they are criers*)

Reverential

Singular	Plural
Timochoquilia**ni**	Ammochoquilia**nih**
(*You usually cry*)	(*You usually cry*)
Mochoquilia**ni**	Mochoquilia**nih**
(*He usually cries*)	(*They usually cry*)

Preterit Tense

The preterit tense is based on the preterit stem, which must be learned. This dictionary provides preterit stems for all verb entries. The preterit tense is characterized by the use of the preterit stem and the following features: 1) prefix **/o/** 2) singular suffix **–c/–qui** 3) plural suffix **–queh**.

The preterit stem is formed as follows:

a) Some verbs drop the final vowel to form the preterit stem:

Present Stem	Preterit Stem
ana (*take*)	an
cochi (*sleep*)	coch
iloti (*return*)	ilot
nequi (*want*)	nec
notza (*call*)	notz
patlani (*fly*)	patlan

Model Conjugation

Singular	Plural
Onipatlan	**O**tipatlan**queh**
(*I flew*)	(*We flew*)
Otipatlan	**O**ampatlan**queh**
(*You flew*)	(*You flew*)
Opatlan	**O**patlan**queh**
(*He flew*)	(*They flew*)

Reverential

Singular	Plural
Otimopatlaniti**h** (*You flew*)	**O**ammopatlanitih**queh** (*You flew*)
Omopatlaniti**h** (*He flew*)	**O**mopatlanitih**queh** (*They flew*)

b) Some verbs (those that end in **–ia/–oa**) delete the final vowel and replace it with **–h**.

Present Stem	Preterit Stem
ilhu**ia** (*say*)	ilhui**h**
mach**tia** (*teach*)	machti**h**
tlahcuil**oa** (*write*)	tlahcuilo**h**
tlaht**oa** (*speak*)	tlahto**h**
tlaxcal**oa** (*make tortillas*)	tlaxacalo**h**

Model Conjugation

Singular	Plural
Onitlahto**h** (*I spoke*)	**O**titlahto**hqueh** (*We spoke*)
Otitlahto**h** (*You spoke*)	**O**antlahto**hqueh** (*You spoke*)
Otlahto**h** (*He spoke*)	**O**tlahto**hqueh** (*They spoke*)

Reverential

Singular	Plural
Otimotlahtolti**h**	**O**ammotlahtolti**hqueh**
(*You spoke*)	(*You spoke*)
Omotlahtolti**h**	**O**motlahtolit**hqueh**
(*He spoke*)	(*They spoke*)

c) Some verbs do not change stems but use singular suffix **–c**.

Present Stem	Present Stem + Singular suffix **–c** (Preterit form)
choca (*cry*)	choca**c**
cuica (*sing*)	cuica**c**
huetzca (*laugh*)	huetzca**c**
temo (*descend*)	temo**c**

Model Conjugation

Singular	Plural
Onichoca**c**	**O**tichoca**queh**
(*I cried*)	(*We cried*)
Otichoca**c**	**O**anchoca**queh**
(*You cried*)	(*You cried*)
Ochoca**c**	**O**choca**queh**
(*He cried*)	(*They cried*)

Reverential

Singular	Plural
Otimochoquili**h**	**O**ammochoquili**hqueh**
(*You cried*)	(*You cried*)
Omochoquili**h**	**O**mochoquili**hqueh**
(*He cried*)	(*They cried*)

d) A few verbs add a final **–h**.

Present Stem	Preterit Stem
cua (*eat*)	cua**h**
mama (*carry*)	mama**h**
mozoma (*be angry*)	mozoma**h**
pa (*paint*)	pa**h**

Model Conjugation

Singular	Plural
Onitlacua**h**	**O**titlacua**hqueh**
(*I ate*)	(*We ate*)
Otitlacua**h**	**O**antlacua**hqueh**
(*You ate*)	(*You ate*)
Otlacua**h**	**O**tlacua**hqueh**
(*He ate*)	(*They ate*)

Reverential

Singular	Plural
Otimotlacualti**h**	**O**ammotlacualti**hqueh**
(*You ate*)	(*You ate*)
Omotlacualti**h**	**O**motlacualti**hqueh**
(*He ate*)	(*They ate*)

e) Some verbs have special preterit stems that have to be memorized.

Present Stem	Preterit Stem
ahuia (*be content*)	ahuix
chihua (*make*)	chiuh
pehua (*begin*)	peuh
polihui (*perish*)	poliuh
pohua (*count*)	pouh
pia (*guard*)	pix
cocoya (*be sick*)	cocox
yocoya (*invent*)	yocox

Model Conjugation

Singular	Plural
Onicocox (*I became sick*)	**O**ticocox**queh** (*We became sick*)
Oticocox (*You became sick*)	**O**ancocox**queh** (*You became sick*)
Ococox (*He became sick*)	**O**cocox**queh** (*They became sick*)

Pluperfect Tense

The pluperfect tense is based on the preterit stem. It takes the prefix **/o/**, tense marker **–ca,** and plural suffix **–h**

Model Conjugations

Singular	Plural
Onipatlan**ca** (*I had flown*)	**O**tipatlan**cah** (*We had flown*)
Otipatlan**ca** (*You had flown*)	**O**ampatlan**cah** (*You had flown*)
Opatlan**ca** (*He had flown*)	**O**patlan**cah** (*They had flown*)

Singular	*Plural*
Onitlahtoh**ca** (*I had spoken*)	**O**titlahtoh**cah** (*We had spoken*)
Otitlahtoh**ca** (*You had spoken*)	**O**antlahtoh**cah** (*You had spoken*)
Otlahtoh**ca** (*He had spoken*)	**O**tlahtoh**cah** (*They had spoken*)

Singular	*Plural*
Onichoca**ca** (*I had cried*)	**O**tichoca**cah** (*We had cried*)
Otichoca**ca** (*You had cried*)	**O**ancho**cah** (*You had cried*)
Ochoca**ca** (*He had cried*)	**O**choca**cah** (*They had cried*)

Singular	*Plural*
Onitlacuah**ca** (*I had eaten*)	**O**titlacuah**cah** (*We had eaten*)
Otitlacuah**ca** (*You had eaten*)	**O**antlacuah**cah** (*You had eaten*)
Otlacuah**ca** (*He had eaten*)	**O**tlacuah**cah** (*They had eaten*)

Singular	Plural
Onicocox**ca**	**O**ticocox**cah**
(*I had become sick*)	(*We had become sick*)
Oticocox**ca**	**O**ancocox**cah**
(*You had become sick*)	(*You had become sick*)
Ococox**ca**	**O**cocox**cah**
(*He had become sick*)	(*They had become sick*)

Optative

The optative is used to indicate wishes and commands. It is formed by placing *ma* before the verb, as in these examples: *ma nicuica* (May I sing), *ma ticuica* (May you sing). The second person (singular and plural) replaces the subject pronouns *ti–* and *am–* with *xi–*. For example, *ma **xi**cuica* (Sing!) and *ma **xi**cuicacan* (Sing!) The plural marker for this for is *–can*. Verbs that end in *–ia* and *–oa,* drop the final vowel.

Model Conjugation

Singular	Plural
ma nicuica	**ma** ticuica**can**
(*May I sing*)	(*May we sing*)
ma xicuica	**ma xi**cuica**can**
(*Sing!*)	(*Sing!*)
ma cuica	**ma** cuica**can**
(*May he sing*)	(*May they sing*)

A more direct command is expressed by dropping *ma*: *xiccaqui* (Listen!), *xihuallauh* (Come here!), etc.

The negative form of the optative uses *macahmo* instead of *ma*.

Model Conjugation

Singular	Plural
macahmo nicuica *(May I not sing)*	**macahmo** ticuica**can** *(May we not sing)*
macahmo **xi**cuica *(Do not sing)*	**macahmo** **xi**cuica**can** *(Do not sing)*
macahmo cuica *(May he not sing)*	**macahmo** cuica**can** *(May they not sing)*

Reverential

Singular	Plural
Macahmo **xi**mocuicati *(Do not sing)*	**Macahmo** ximocuicati**can** *(Do not sing)*
Macahmo mocuicati *(May he not sing)*	**Macahmo** mocuicati**can** *(May they not sing)*

Passive Voice

The passive voice is formed by attaching the subject prefixes and corresponding tense and number markers to the passive stem. The passive stem is usually derived by adding the suffix *–lo* to the present stem. *Tlazohtla* (to love) becomes *tlazohtlalo* (to be loved), *pohua* (to count) becomes *pohualo* (to be counted), etc. Stems that end in *–ia* and *–oa* drop the final /a/ before adding *–lo*. *Machtia* (to teach) becomes *machtilo* (to be taught), *ihcuiloa* (to write) becomes *ihcuilolo* (to be written), etc.

Verb stems that end in *–ca* or *–qui* usually replace these endings with *–co*. *Maca* (to give) becomes *maco* (to be given), *caqui* (to hear) becomes *caco* (*to be heard*), etc.

There are passive stems that must be learned through observation. For example, *ahci* (to reach) has passive stem *ahxihua* (to be reached), *i* (to drink) has *ihua* (to be drunk), *imacaci* (to fear) has *imacaxo* (to be feared), etc.

Present Tense

Model Conjugation

Singular	Plural
Nimachti**lo**	Timachti**loh**
(*I am taught*)	(*We are taught*)
Timachti**lo**	Ammachti**loh**
(*You are taught*)	(*You are taught*)
Machti**lo**	Machti**loh**
(*He is taught*)	(*They are taught*)

Imperfect Tense

Model Conjugation

Singular	Plural
Nimachtiloya *(I was being taught)*	Timachtiloyah *(We were being taught)*
Timachtiloya *(You were being taught)*	Ammachtiloyah *(You were being taught)*
Machtiloya *(He was being taught)*	Machtiloyah *(They were being taught)*

Future Tense

Model Conjugation

Singular	Plural
Nimachtiloz *(I will be taught)*	Timachtilozqueh *(We will be taught)*
Timachtiloz *(You will be taught)*	Ammachtilozqueh *(You will be taught)*
Machtiloz *(He will be taught)*	Machtilozqueh *(They will be taught)*

Preterit Tense

Model Conjugation

Singular	Plural
Onimachtiloc (*I was taught*)	Otimachtiloqueh (*We were taught*)
Otimachtiloc (*You were taught*)	Oammachtiloqueh (*You were taught*)
Omachtiloc (*He was taught*)	Omachtiloqueh (*They were taught*)

Pluperfect Tense

Model Conjugation

Singular	Plural
Onimachtiloca (*I had been taught*)	Otimachtilocah (*We had been taught*)
Otimachtiloca (*You had been taught*)	Oammachtilocah (*You had been taught*)
Omachtiloca (*He had been taught*)	Omachtilocah (*They had been taught*)

The Impersonal

The impersonal voice is used when the subject of the verb is not identified. That is, no person is specified as being the performer of the action. The emphasis is strictly on the action itself, not on the person executing it. The subject can be translated as "one" or "people." For example, *cuico* (people sing, one sings), *tlacualo* (people eat, one eats).

The impersonal is formed like the passive stem stem. If the verb is transitive, it takes an object marker in the impersonal as well.

EXAMPLES:

Intransitive Verbs

Active Voice	*Impersonal Voice*
cuica (*to sing*)	cuic**o** (*one sings*)
choloa (*to flee*)	cholol**o** (*one flees*)
yoli (*to live*)	yoli**hua** (*one lives*)

Transitive Verbs

Active Voice	*Intransitive Voice*
temachtia	temachti**lo**
(*to teach*)	(*one teaches*)
tlahcuiloa	tlahcuilo**lo**
(*to write*)	(*one writes*)
tlaxcalchihua	tlaxaclachihua**lo**
(*to make tortillas*)	(*one makes tortillas*)

The impersonal has only one form (3rd person singular) for every tense. It does not take subject prefixes or number markers.

EXAMPLES:

Present:	temachtilo (*one teaches*)
Imperfect:	temachtiloya (*one was teaching*)
Future:	temachtiloz (*one will teach*)
Preterit:	otemachtiloc (*one taught*)
Pluperfect:	otemachtiloca (*one had taught*)

Verbal Nouns

Preterit Stems

The preterit stem is used as a verbal noun. It may be translated into English as a present participle.

EXAMPLES:

Singular	Plural
temachtih (*teacher*)	temachtihqueh (*teachers*)
tlahcuiloh (*writer*)	tlahcuilohqueh (*writers*)
cacchiuhqui (*shoemaker*)	cacchiuhqueh (*shoemakers*)
amoxnamacac (*bookseller*)	amoxnamacaqueh (*booksellers*)

Instrumental Nouns

When the suffix **–ni** is attached to the impersonal of transitive or intransitive verbs, the result is a noun that indicates the means or instrument by which the action of the verb is performed.

EXAMPLES:

Impersonal Form	Instrumental Noun
tepahtilo (*one cures people*)	tepahtilo**ni** (*a cure, instrument for curing people*)
cochihua (*one sleeps*)	cochihua**ni** (*sleep aid*)

Passive Verbal Nouns

When the suffix **–ni** is attached to the passive form, the resulting noun conveys the sense that it is worthy or capable of receiving the action of the verb.

EXAMPLES:

Passive Form	Passive Verbal Noun
macho (*it is known*)	macho**ni** (*knowable*)
maco (*it is given*)	maco**ni** (*it can or should be given*)

This form of the passive can take the various subject prefixes.

EXAMPLES:

Niihtalo**ni** (*I am visible*)	Tihtalo**nih** (*We are visible*)
Tiihtalo**ni** (*You are visible*)	Amihtalo**nih** (*You are visible*)
Ihtalo**ni** (*He is visible*)	Ihtalo**nih** (*They are visible*)

Place Names

Place names in Nahuatl are formed by attaching suffixes that indicate location (–c, –co, –pan, –titlan, –tlan) to noun stems.

EXAMPLES:

Stem of mazatl (*deer*) + –tlan (*land of*)
> Maza**tlan** (*land of deer*)

Stem of tenochtli (*cactus*) + –titlan (*place next to*)
> Tenoch**titlan** (*place next to the cactus*)

The locative suffixes –can and –yan are also used in place names. –*Can* is attached to preterit stems and –*yan* is attached to impersonal stems.

EXAMPLES:

michhuah (*fish owner*) + –can
> Michhuah**can** (*place of the fish owners*)

tlacualo (*people eat*) + –yan
> tlacualo**yan** (*dining room*)

Nahuatl-English Dictionary

A

aaquia *tv.* use (*Preterit: ontlaaquih*)
aaquilli *adj.* useful
aaquilloh *adj.* usable
aaquillotl *n.* usefulness
aaquiloni *adj.* usable
ac *pron.* Who?
aca *pron.* someone
acacalotl *n.* grebe, diving bird
acahuelteconi *n.* helm, rudder
acalaquia *reflex. v.* dive (*Preterit: oninacalquih*); *tv.* submerge (*Preterit: onitlaacalaquih*)
acalcuahpamitl *n.* sail
acallapanaliztli *n.* shipwreck
acalli *n.* boat
acaltecoyan *n.* dock, pier, wharf
acaltetepon *n.* scorpion
acaltic *adj.* having grooves
acalyacatl *n.* bow (*boat*)
acanozomo *adv.* perhaps not
acapetlatl *n.* reed mat
acatepuzotl *n.* hook
acatl *n.* reed
acaxitl *n.* pool
acayotl *n.* urethra; penis
acectli *n.* icicle

acelin *n.* nit
ach *adv.* perhaps, possibly
achahuitl *n.* marsh, swamp
achca *adv.* frequently
achi *adv.* a little
achica *adv.* often
achitlahtolli *n.* morpheme
achiton *adv.* a little bit
achitzin *adv.* a little
achiuhqui *adv.* almost
achiuhtequixtiloni *n.* camera
achtli *n.* seed
achto *adv.* first
achtontli *n.* great grandfather
achtopa *adv.* before
achtopa *adv.* first
achtopahualla *n.* predecessor
achtopaneitalli *adj.* foreseen
achtopaneittaliztli *n.* foresight
achtopanyauh *adj.* previous
achtopapaneitalli *adj.* previous
achtotipa *adv.* before
acochcayotl *n.* coffee
acocilin *n.* tiny freshwater shrimp
acocollapaliuhqui *adj.* finicky
acpatl *n.* algae
actihuetzi *iv.* sink (*Preterit: onactihuetz*)
acuecueyachin *n.* leech
acuenyoh *adj.* wavy
acueyotl *n.* wave; tide
acuxa *n.* needle
acxohua *iv.* sneeze (*Preterit: oniacxouh*)
ahachichi *adv.* little by little

ahahuatilpializtli *n.* irregularity
ahahuatilpiani *adj.* irregular
ahahulia *tv.* pamper (*Preterit: oniteahahuilih*)
ahcan *adv.* nowhere
ahcazomo *adv.* maybe not
ahci *iv.* arrive (*Preterit: oniahcic*)
ahcializcopa *adv.* involuntarily
ahciani *adj.* involuntary
ahcic *adj.* completed
ahcihcamati *tv.* understand well; know well
    (*Preterit: onitlaahcihcamat*)
ahcihcamatiliztli *n.* understanding
ahcitiliztli *n.* goal, objective
ahco *adv.* up
ahcohuic *adv.* upward
ahcolchimalli *n.* shoulder blade
ahcolli *n.* shoulder
ahcolnacayotl *n.* biceps
ahcoltetl *n.* muscle
ahcoltzontli *n.* hair on back of shoulders, back hair
ahcopa *adv.* upward
ahcoquetza *tv.* bid (*Preterit: onitlaahcoquetz*)
ahcoquiliztli *n.* ascent
ahcoquiza *iv.* ascend (*Preterit: onahcoquiz*)
ahcuallahtolli *n.* profanity
ahcualli *adj.* bad
ahcualnenqui *adj.* immoral
ahcualtiliztli *n.* injustice
ahhuachtli *n.* dew
ahhuelcahualloh *adj.* essential, indispensable
ahhuelchihualloh *adj.* impractical
ahhuelitalloh *adj.* imperceptible
ahhuelitilli *adj.* handicapped

ahhuelittoc *adj.* invisible
ahhuelli *adj.* impossible
ahhuelneltococ *adj.* incredible
ahhueltlaaquic *adj.* impenetrable
ahihuianyoh *adj.* indefinite
ahihuianyotica *adv.* indefinitely
ahitechnecahualiztli *n.* infidelity
ahitztic *adj.* insipid; simple
ahixtlamatqui *adj.* indiscreet
ahmelactic *adj.* indirect
ahmelahuaca *adv.* indirectly
ahmelahualiztica *adv.* unjustly
ahmimatcanemiliztli *n.* indecency
ahmimatcanenqui *adj.* indecent
ahmimati *adj.* insane
ahmitla *pron.* nothing
ahmo *adv.* no
ahmo cualli *adj.* bad; unjust
ahmo cualneci *adj.* ugly
ahmo melahuac *adj.* sinister; indirect; incorrect; unjust
ahmo monequi *adj.* illicit
ahmo nacayoh *adj.* lean
ahmo tlacanexiliztli *n.* ugliness
ahmo zan miecpa *adv.* not often
ahmomachiliztli *n.* ignorance
ahmomelahualiztli *n.* injustice
ahmoneneuhcayotl *n.* difference
ahmoneneuhqui *adj.* different
ahmotlein *pron.* nothing
ahnamiqueh *n.* bachelor; spinster; *adj.* unmarried; *n.* single,
   not married
ahneconi *adj.* illicit
ahnecuitiliztli *n.* negation

ahneltocac *adj.* skeptical
ahnempehualiztica *adv.* with impunity
ahnempehualtiliztli *n* exemption; impunity
ahnempehualtilloh *adj.* exempt
ahnenamictiliztli *n.* celibacy
ahnepanolli *n.* swamp
ahnoce *conj.* or
ahnozo *conj.* or
ahoc *adv.* no longer
ahocmo *adv.* no longer
ahpahtihuani *adj.* unhealthful; unsanitary
ahpinahualiztli *n.* immodesty
ahpinahuani *adj.* immodest, shameless
ahpohualiztli *n.* infinite
ahquimati *n.* idiot; Who knows?
ahteixaxiliztli *n.* mystery
ahtepahtic *adj.* incurable
ahtetechmonecoc *adj.* inconvenient
ahtetechmonequiliztli *n.* inconvenience
ahtetlatqui *adj.* improper
ahtlacaquini *adj.* deaf; disobedient
ahtlacatl *n.* rascal
ahtlacatlahtoani *adj.* vulgar
ahtlacayotl *n.* cruelty
ahtlahtlacoleh *adj.* innocent
ahtlahuilcitlalin *n.* planet
ahtlamiliztica *adj.* infinite
ahtlapololloh *adj.* indelible
ahtlapopolhuilloh *adj.* unforgivable
ahtlatlacoliztli *n.* innocence
ahtlatecpanalli *adj.* illegal
ahtlatzonquixtilloh *adj.* inexhaustible

ahtle *pron.* nothing
ahtle quimati *adj.* ignorant
ahtlein *pron.* nothing
ahtlematini *adj.* ignorant
ahtleyecyotl *n.* melancholy
ahtzopelic *adj.* insipid
ahuacamolli *n.* guacamole
ahuacatl *n.* avocado
ahuatl *n.* oak; thorn
ahuatomatl *n.* acorn
ahuatza *iv.* drain, wring (*Preterit: onahuatz*)
ahuauhtli *n.* caviar
ahuecatlan *n.* high sea
ahuehuetl *n.* cedar; cypress
ahuelic *adj.* insipid
ahuelli *n.* game
ahuia *iv.* be happy (*Preterit: onahuix*)
ahuiancalli *n.* brothel, whorehouse
ahuiani *n.* prostitute, courtesan, whore
ahuiillahtoani *n.* braggart; jokester; *adj.* vain
ahuilaca *adj.* playful
ahuilhuehue *n.* dirty old man
ahuiliztli *n.* happiness
ahuilli *n.* pleasure; toy
ahuilnemi *iv.* fornicate; live a dissolute life
    (*Preterit: onahuilnen*); waste time
ahuilnemiliztli *n.* fornication; lechery, lust
ahuilnenqui *n.* fornicator
ahuilquizaliztli *n.* vice, corruption
ahuitl *n.* aunt
ahyecolic *adj.* intolerable
ahyecoliztli *n.* intolerance
ahyecoltoc *adj.* intolerant

ahzo *adv.* perhaps
aic *adv.* never
aic miquiliztli *n.* immortality
aictlanqui *adj.* unending
aililiztli *n.* action, activity
aitectli *n.* gulf
aitiliztlahtolli *n.* verb
aitztetl *n.* gizzard
alactic *adj.* slippery
alahua *iv.* slide, slip (*Preterit: onialahuac*), *reflex. v.* slide, slip
    (*Preterit: oninalahuac*)
alahuac *adj.* slippery
alalox *n.* orange
Alamanecatl *n.* German
Alamanian *n.* Germany
alaztic *adj.* slippery
alo *n.* guacamaya
aloyotl *n.* scrotum
altepanayotl *n.* capital
altepecuaxochtli *n.* border, boundary
altepehuah *n.* town resident
altepemaitl *n.* outskirts, suburb; peasant; village
altepenechicoltin *n.* community
altepenechiconyotl *n.* community
altepetepuzocuilquixohuayan *n.* subway station
altepetequipanoliztli *n.* public service, work
altepetl *n.* town, city
altepetlacatl *n.* citizen
altepetlazotlalli *adj.* popular
altepeyollohtli *n.* civic center, downtown
altia *reflex. v.* bathe (*Preterit: oninaltih*)
amacalli *n.* bookstore, stationery store
amacayetl *n.* cigarette

amacuahuitl *n.* fig tree
amaihcuiloliztli *n.* letterhead
amaitl *n.* lake
amaizhuatl *n.* page
amalacachtli *n.* wheel
amanamacoyan *n.* bookstore, stationery store
amaniliztli *n.* storm
amantecatl *n.* artisan
amantli *n.* pool, lake
amapatoa *iv.* play cards (*Preterit: onamapatoh*)
amapatoliztli *n.* card game
amapohualiztli *n.* reading
amatequitl *n.* agenda, work plan; program
amatitlaniloyan *n.* post office
amatl *n.* paper, document
amatlahcuiloh *n.* scribe; secretary
amatlahcuilolli *n.* letter
amatlahcuilolnextiloni *n.* pamphlet
amatlahcuilolqxiquipilli *n.* mailbox
amatlahcuilotontli *n.* ticket
amatlahtolli *n.* reading
amatlaixpanhuiani *n.* journalist
amatlaixpanhuiloni *n.* newspaper
amatlazontli *n.* registry
amatocaihcuilolli *n.* business card; identification card
ameyalcaxitl *n.* basin
ameyalli *n.* fountain, spring
amictlan *n.* abyss, high sea
amilotl *n.* white fish
amimilli *n.* wave
aminitzcuintli *n.* greyhound
amintli *n.* diarrhea
amiqui *iv.* be thirsty (*Preterit: onamic*)

amiquiliztli *adj.* thirst
amiquini *adj.* thirsty
amiquiztli *adj.* thirst
amiztli *n.* sea lion
amo *poss. pron.* your (*Plural*)
amochitl *n.* tin
amohuan *adv.* with you (*Plural*)
amolcaxitl *n.* soap dish
amolli *n.* root used as soap
amono *adv.* neither, nor
amoxcalli *n.* library
amoxmachiotl *n.* book title; index
amoxmiccacuiloni *n.* obituary
amoxnamacac *n.* book vendor
amoxnamacoyan *n.* bookstore
amoxneihcuiloni *n.* notebook, memo book
amoxpialoyan *n.* library
amoxpohua *iv.* read a book (*Preterit: onamoxpouh*)
amoxpohuani *n.* one who reads books; learned
amoxpouhqui *n.* one who reads books; learned
amoxquiliuhcayotl *n.* book cover
amoxtentli *n.* book margin
amoxtlahcuiloh *n.* author, writer
amoxtlatiloyan *n.* bookcase
amoxtli *n.* book
amoxtocaitl *n.* book title
amoxxexeloliztli *n.* chapter
ampahtihuani *adj.* unhealthful, unsanitary
amumuxtli *n.* mold, moss
ana *tv.* capture, take (*Preterit: onitean*)
analco *adv.* on the other side of the river or ocean
analli *n.* bank (*river*)

anca *conj.* therefore
Anglitlallahtolli *n.* English language
Anglitlalli *n.* England
Anglitlaltecatl *n.* Briton or Englishman
anquichichi *n.* greyhound; hunting dog
aocmo *adv.* not anymore
aocmo huehcauh *adv.* shortly, in a minute
aompayotl *n.* misfortune
aoquic ad*v.* never again
aoztoc *n.* high sea
apantli *n.* bridge; canal; ditch
apazyahualli *n.* tub
apilolli *n.* cup
apipiloyac *n.* waterfall
apiztli *n.* hunger
apitza *iv.* have diarrhea (*Preterit: onapitz*)
apitzalli *n.* diarrhea
apoctli *n.* water vapor, vapor
aqui in tonatiuh *n.* sunset
aquimamachiliztli *n.* foolishness; stubbornness
aquin *pron.* someone; *interr. pron.* Who?
atecochtli *n.* cistern
atecocolli *n.* large shell used as musical instrument
atecui *tv.* castrate (*Preterit: oniteatecuic*)
ateimachitica *adv.* suddenly
atemaliztli *n.* dropsy
atemia flood; *tv.* (*Preterit: onitlaatemih*); *reflex. v.* be flooded
    (*Preterit omatemih*)
atemillotl *n.* flood
atemoliztli *n.* indigestion
atempach *adj.* infested with lice
atenemachpan *adv.* suddenly
atenemachtih *adj.* sudden

atenqui *adj.* flooded
atenxochitl *n.* water flower
atepocatl *n.* tadpole
atequixtia *tv.* castrate (*Preterit: oniteatequixtih*)
atetl *n.* testicle
atexicolli *n.* scrotum
atezcaihtaloni *n.* water level
atezcatl *n.* puddle
atezquilitl *n.* watercress
atl *n.* water; liquid
atl quinoquia *reflex. v.* urinate (*Preterit: atl onicnoquih*)
atlacatl *n.* sailor
atlacoani *n.* water bucket
atlacomolli *n.* well
atlacoyoctli *n.* sewer
atlacui *tv.* carry water (*Preterit: oniatlacuic*)
atlacuihuayan *n.* well, deep pool
atlahuitl *n.* canyon, valley
atlanchanehqueh *n.* shellfish
atlantema *tv.* submerge (*Preterit: onitlaatlanten*)
atlapachoni *n.* umbrella
atlapalli *n.* feather; population; town
atlatl *n.* spear thrower
atlatlacamahmaniliztli *n.* storm
atlatlalacatl *n.* goose, gander
atlatzacuhtli *n.* dam
atlauhtli *n.* canyon, valley, ravine
atlauhxomolli *n.* valley
atliatl *n.* mustache
atoco *iv.* drown (*Preterit: onatococ*)
atococ *adj.* drowned
atocoliztli *n.* drowning
atoctli *n.* fertile land

atolli *n.* corn gruel, corn beverage, porridge
atolocatl *n.* tadpole
atoltic *adj.* ripe, soft
atolticayotl *n.* ripeness
atonahui *iv.* have fever and chills (*Preterit: onatonauh*)
atonahuiztamchihualoni *n.* thermometer
atonahuiztli *n.* fever and chills
atotonilli *n.* hot water
atoyapitzactli *n.* brook, small stream
atoyatetl *n.* river pebble
atoyatl *n.* river
atzanalquilitl *n.* watercress
atzcalli *n.* shell
auh *conj.* and
auh yequene *adv.* finally
auhtzin *adv.* yes
axa/axan *adj.* current, modern
axca *adj.* current, modern; *adv.* now
axcahuah *adj.* wealthy
axcaitl *n.* property (*Stem: axca–*)
axcan *adv.* now; today
axcan cahuitl *n.* present tense
axcancayotl *n.* the present
axictli *n.* whirlpool
axihuayan *n.* hotel
axilia *tv.* achieve, reach a goal (*Preterit: onitlaaxilih*)
axiliztli *n.* success
axiltia *tv.* accompany (*Preterit: oniteaxiltih*);
     complete (*Preterit: onitlaaxiltih*); *tv.* supplement
     (*Preterit: onitlaaxiltih*)
axin *n.* type of facial paint, makeup
axitia *reflex. v.* approach (*Preterit: oninaxitih*)
axitontli *n.* bomb; water bubble

axixa *reflex. v.* urinate; defecate (*Preterit: oninaxix*)
axixcalli *n.* bathroom
axixcomitl *n.* urinal
axixpiztli *n.* urethra
axixtli *n.* urine; feces
axno *n.* donkey
axolotl *n.* salamander
ayac *pron.* no one
ayacachoa *iv.* play a rattle (*Preterit: niayacachoh*)
ayacachtli *n.* rattle
ayactlatlacatl *n.* solitude
ayahui *impers. v.* there is fog (*Preterit: oayauh*)
ayahuitl *n.* fog; mist; smoke
ayahmo *adv.* not yet
ayahmo huehcauh *adv.* not long ago, recently
ayahmo huicci *adj.* raw, uncooked
ayahmo icuhci *adj.* raw, uncooked
ayatl *n.* cloth made from maguey fiber
ayauhcalli *n.* chapel, place of prayer
ayauhcozamalotl *n.* rainbow
ayauhcuahuitl *n.* pine
ayauhcuauhtla *n.* pine grove
ayauhtic *adj.* misty
ayauhyotl *n.* darkness
ayaxcan *adv.* barely, with difficulty
ayaxcanyotica *adv.* slowly; barely, with difficulty
ayaxcanyotl *n.* slowness
ayoa *iv.* be filled with water (*Preterit: oayoh*)
ayoh *adj.* juicy, watery
ayohachtli *n.* pumpkin seed
ayohhuachtli *n.* pumpkin seed
ayohtli *n.* pumpkin, squash
ayohxochitl *n.* squash flower

ayohxochquilitl *n.* squash flower
ayohyolli *n.* pumpkin seed
ayotectli *n.* sea turtle
ayotia *tv.* water down (*Preterit: onitlayotih*)
ayotl *n.* juice; stew; tear; turtle
ayotochcacahuatl *n.* armadillo shell
ayotochtli *n.* armadillo
ayuhmomatini *adj.* suspicious
azcalli *n.* alabaster
azcapotzalli *n.* anthill
azcatl *n.* ant
azcaxalli *n.* anthill
azcayoh *adj.* full of ants
aztacoyotl *n.* anteater
aztatl *n.* stork, heron
aztecatl *n.* Aztec
aztli *n.* wing

C

–c *suff.* in, on, place of
ca *iv.* be (*Plural: cateh*)
–ca *suff.* with, by means of
ca ye *adv.* certainly
caca *n.* frog, toad
cacahuatetl *n.* cacao bean
cacahuatl *n.* cacao; peanut
cacalaca *iv.* make noise with a rattle (*Preterit: onicacalacac*)
cacalachin *n.* cockroach
cacalachtli *n.* clay rattle; skinny person
cacallan *n.* hamlet
cacalotl *n.* crow; raven

cacamatl *n.* small ear of corn that grows by larger ones
cacapaca *n.* clapping
caccencaye *adv.* especially
cacchihualoyan *n.* shoe factory
cacchiuhqui *n.* shoemaker
caccohcopinqui *adj.* barefooted
caccopina *reflex. v.* take off one's shoes
    (*Preterit: oninocacopin*)
caccopinqui *adj.* barefooted
caccualtilia *tv.* tune (*Preterit: onitlacaccualtilih*)
cacemi *adv.* once and for all
cachi cualli *adv.* better
cacmecatl *n.* shoelace
cacnamacoyan *n.* shoe store
cacpehuallotl *n.* shoe heel
cactia *reflex. v.* put on one's shoes (*Preterit: oninocactih*)
cacticac *adj.* vacant, empty, unoccupied
cacticacayotl *n.* empty space, free time
cactimaniliztli *n.* loneliness, solitude
cactli *n.* sandal; shoe
cactlilli *n.* black shoe shine
cacxopetlatl *n.* sole (*shoe*)
cafetzin *n.* coffee
cahcallahtli *n.* hamlet
cahtli *interr. pron.* Which one?
cahua *tv.* abandon, leave behind (*Preterit: onitlacauh*)
cahuactic *adj.* hot
cahuahcalli *n.* stable
cahuahtlacualoyan *n.* manger, trough
cahuahyo *n.* horse
cahuahyocalli *n.* stable
cahuahyo itzapiniloca *n.* spur
cahualli *n.* spider web; abandoned; widow, widower

cahuitamachihuani *n.* timekeeper
cahuitepuztamachihualoni *n.* clock
cahuitl *n.* time; hour; schedule
caizca *impers. v.* here is
calachin *n.* cockroach
calacohuayan *n.* door
calaqui *iv.* enter (*Preterit: onicalac*)
calaqui in tonatiuh *n.* sunset
calaquia *tv.* insert (*Preterit: onitlacalaquih*)
calaquiliztli *n.* entrance (*act*)
calatl *n.* frog
calcahua *iv.* move from one house to another
    (*Preterit: onicalcauh*)
calcatl *n.* resident
calchialoyan *n.* living room
calchiuhcamatiliztli *n.* architecture
calchiuhcamatini *n.* architect
calchiuhqui *n.* mason
calcuahuitl *n.* beam (*of a house*)
calcuechtli *n.* soot
calehcapohtli *n.* neighbor
calhueyohtli *n.* street
calixco *n.* façade
calixtli *n.* foyer, lobby
callampa *n.* corridor; *adv.* outside
callan *adv.* outside
callanquixtia *tv.* take outside (*Preterit: onitlacallanquixtih*)
callapanhuetzian *n.* spire
callatotoniloni *n.* heater
calli *n.* house
calmachtiloyan *n.* school
calmana *iv.* build a house, construct a building
    (*Preterit: onicalman*)

calmanani *n.* architect
calmecac *n.* school, college, university
calmelactli *n.* hallway
calnepaniuhqui *n.* two-story house
calocuilin *n.* cocoon
calohtli *n.* street
calpixcayotl *n.* stewardship
calpixqui *n.* majordomo, steward
calpulli *n.* neighborhood
calquetza *iv.* build a house, construct a building
    (*Preterit: onicalquetz*)
calqui *n.* resident, homeowner
caltenco *n.* patio
caltencuahuitl *n.* door, gate
caltentli *n.* door, entrance; walkway on side of house
calteputzco *adv.* behind the house
caltequitl *n.* homework
caltzalantli *n.* causeway; street
calxomilin *n.* bedbug
camacahua *iv.* make a slip of the tongue
    (*Preterit: oniccamacauh*)
camachalcuauhyotl *n.* jawbone
camachalli *n.* jaw
camachaloa *iv.* open one's mouth (*Preterit: onicamachaloh*)
camachalomitl *n.* jawbone
camacoyactli *n.* glutton
camaixquemitl *n.* bedspread
camaixquemmitl *n.* bedspread
camanalli *n.* joke, prank
camapantli *n.* cheek
camapinauhqui *adj.* shy (*eating or speaking*)
camapotoniliztli *n.* bad breath
camatapalli *n.* palate

camatl *n.* mouth
camatzontli *n.* facial hair; beard
camohpalli *adj.* dark purple
camohtli *n.* yam
campa *adv.* Where?
can *adv.* Where?
–can *suff.* in, on; place where
cana *adv.* somewhere
canah *adv.* somewhere
canahuac *adj.* thin, fine light
canahuacantli *n.* temple (*head*)
canahuacayotl *n.* finesse
canauhquilitl *n.* purslane, *verdolagas*
canauhtli *n.* duck
canel *adv.* so it is
cantetetic *adj.* having big cheeks; stupid
cantli *n.* cheek
capizcayotl *n.* fox
capolin *n.* small, dark berry; cherry
capulin *n.* small, dark berry; cherry
caqui *tv.* hear (*Preterit: onitlacac*)
caquilizcaxitl *n.* disc (*recording*)
caquilizcopinaloni *n.* cassette recorder
caquilizcopinaloni in tonameyotica *n.* compact disc
caquilizmimilli *n.* sound wave
caquiztepanitlazaloni *n.* radio station
caquiztli *n.* phoneme
caquiztli *n.* sound
caticac *adj.* empty
catleh *interr. pron.* Which one?
catlehhuatl *interr. pron.* Which one?
catzactiliztli *n.* uncleanliness, lack of hygiene
catzahua *tv.* soil, dirty (*Preterit: onitlacatzahuac*)

caxahua *iv.* become thin; decrease (*Preterit: onicaxahuac*)
caxani *iv.* become loose (*Preterit: onicaxan*)
caxania *tv.* loosen, untie (*Preterit: onitlacaxanih*); *reflex. v.*
   have a relapse, become ill again (*Preterit: oninocaxanih*)
caxanqui *adj.* loose
caxapo *n.* wild grape
caxitl *n.* bowl, plate
caxmanaloyan *n.* cupboard
caxmanaloyan *n.* pantry
caxpializtli *n.* funnel, spout
Caxtillalpan *n.* Spain
Caxtillan *adj.* Spanish
Caxtillan ajo *n.* garlic
Caxtillan camohtli *n.* carrot
Caxtillan chilli *n.* black pepper; clove; ginger
Caxtillan epazotl *n.* spearmint
Caxtillan xonacatl *n.* garlic
Caxtillancopa *adv.* in Spanish
Caxtillantlacatl *n.* Spaniard
Caxtillantlahtolli *n.* Spanish language
Caxtillantlaxcalli *n.* bread
Caxtillanxochitl *n.* rose
Caxtiltecatl *n.* Spaniard
caxtolli *num.* fifteen
cayaniya *tv.* break money (*Preterit: onitlacayanix*)
cayo *n.* rooster
cayotl *adj.* originating from
ce *num.* one
cea *iv.* agree (*Preterit: onicez*)
cealiztica *adv.* voluntarily
cealiztli *n.* will
cealtia *tv.* convince, persuade (*Preterit: onitecealtih*)
ceani *n.* consenting person
cecancahuitl *n.* interval

cecec *adj.* cold

cececni *adv.* in different places, here and there

cecelicayotl *n.* cartilage

cecenca *adv.* a lot

cecencahua *tv.* prepare (*Preterit: onitlacecencauh*)

cecepatic *adj.* terrifying

cecepoctli *n.* knuckle

cecmiqui *iv.* be cold (*Preterit: onicecmic*)

cecni *adv.* in another place

cecnimani *adj.* independent

cecnitlacah *n.* nation

cecnitlacapohui *n.* fellow countryman

cecnitlacatiliztli *n.* nationality

cecnitlacayoh *adj.* national

cecuappitzahui *iv.* cramp (*Preterit: onicecuappitzauh*)

cecuizpan *n.* winter

cehcemilhuitica *adv.* every day

cehcemmetztli *adj.* monthly

cehcenmetztica *adv.* monthly

cehcentlamantli iyeliz *n.* kind

cehcenxomahtli *n.* spoonful

cehcenyohuac *adv.* every night

cehcepa *adv.* sometimes

cehpayahui *impers. v.* snow (*Preterit: ocehpayauh*)

cehpayahuitl *n.* snow; ice cream

cehpayahuitl huetzi *impers. v.* snow
    (*Preterit: cepayahuitl ohuetz*)

cehpayauhnamacoyan *n.* ice-cream parlor

cehua *impers. v.* it is cold (*Preterit: ocehuac*)

cehualli *n.* shadow

cehuayan *adv.* in the shadow

cehui *iv.* cool down, rest (*Preterit: oniceuh*)

cehuia *tv.* allay, calm (*Preterit: onitecehuih*)

cehuiliztli *n.* calm; rest
cehuilli *n.* rest
celia *iv.* receive, accept (*Preterit: onitlacelih*)
celic *adj.* fresh, new, tender
celiloyan *n.* living room
celticayotl *n.* freshness; tenderness
cemacuahuitl *n.* spoonful
cemahcic *adj.* complete, perfect
cemanahuac *n.* world
cemanahuactlalmachiotl *n.* map (*world*)
cemanahuatl *n.* world, universe
cemanallahtoa *iv.* joke, jest (*Preterit: onicemanallahtoh*)
cemanca *adv.* simply
cemani *adj.* simple
cemaniliztli *n.* simplicity
cemantoctlalli *n.* mainland
cemaxacatl *n.* communal property
cemaxcanehmatiliztli *n.* commonsense
cemelli *n.* joy
cemi *adv.* once and for all
cemihcac *n.* always
cemihcac yoliliztli *n.* immortality
cemihcayotl *n.* eternity
cemihtoa *tv.* promise (*Preterit: ontlacemihtoh*)
cemilhuitequitl *n.* chore
cemilhuitl ceyohual *adv.* day and night
cemmahpilli *n.* inch
cemmanca *n.* eternally
cemmancayeni *adj.* stable, long lasting
cemmanyan *adv.* forever
cempohua *tv.* add (*Preterit: oniccempouh*)
cempohualli *num.* twenty
cempohualpa *adv.* twenty times

cempohualxochitl *n.* marigold
cenca *adv.* much, very, a lot
cenca ahcualli *adj.* worse
cenca cualli *adv.* very well
cenca cualtic *adj.* important
cencahua *tv.* perfect (*Preterit: onitlacencauh*); *tv.* conclude
  (*Preterit: onitlacencauh*)
cencahueyac *adj.* immense
cencalli *n.* family; household
cencamatl *n.* snack
cencapatiyoh *adj.* expensive
cencatlacatl *adj.* gentle
cencatlacayotl *n.* gentleness
cencatlahuelli *adj.* terrible, very bad; worst
cencuauhticcalli *n.* skyscraper
cenhuelitini *adj.* all powerful
cenitlacaxellotl *n.* independence
cenneloa *tv.* mix (*Preterit: onitlacenneloh*)
cennetlaloliztli *n.* race
cennohuian *adv.* in all places
cenquizca *adv.* entirely, perfectly
cenquizca mahuiztic *adj.* majestic
cenquizca mahuizzotl *n.* majesty
centetica *adv.* completely
centetl *adj.* whole
centlaantli *n.* bunch, cluster
centlacxitl *n.* foot (*verse meter*)
centlahco *n.* half
centlaixca *adv.* simply
centlaixtli *adj.* simple
centlaixxotl *n.* simplicity
centlalia *tv.* join; gather (*Preterit: onitlacentlalih*);
  reflex. v. convene, get together (*Preterit: oninocentlalih*)

centlalilli *n.* heap, pile
centlamantin *n.* herd
centlamantinyolqueh *n.* flock, herd
centlamapictli *n.* handful
centlamatilizamoxtli *n* encyclopedia
centlamohtzolli *n.* handful
centlapactli tlaxcalli *n.* a piece of tortilla
centlapal *adv.* from one side, from one side to another
centlapitzaliztli *n.* symphony
centlatzayantli *n.* piece, portion
centlazotl *n.* stitch
centli *n.* corn; ear of dried corn
centzontli *num.* four hundred
centzummayeh *n.* centipede
cenxumahtli *n.* spoonful
cenyeliztli *n.* family
cenyohuac *adv.* all night
Cepanca Tlahtohcayotl *n.* United States
Cepanca Tlahtohcayotl chaneh *n.* American
cepantin *adj.* together
cepohualiztli *n.* numbness
cepohui *iv.* become numb (*Preterit: onicepouh*)
cetiliztli *n.* union, unity
cetl *n.* ice
cetlacayotl *n.* close relative
ceyotl *n.* fat, grease
chacalin *n.* large shrimp
chacayolli *n.* callus
chachalaca *iv.* talk a lot; chirp (*Preterit: onichachalacac*)
chachalacaliztli *n.* murmur, uproar
chachalaquiztli *n.* murmur, uproar
chachalotl *n.* squirrel
chachamahua *tv.* flatter (*Preterit: onitechachamauh*)

chachamahualiztli *n.* vanity
chahualiztli *n.* envy, jealousy
chahuanantli *n.* stepmother
chahuapapalotl *n.* moth
chahuapilli *n.* woman's stepchild
chahuati *iv.* be jealous (*Preterit: onichahuatic*)
chahuiztli *n.* plague; plant disease; bad luck
chalaniliztli *n.* confusion, uproar
chalchihuitl *n.* jade
chalia *tv.* use or wear something for first time
    (*Preterit: ontlachalih*)
chamahua *iv.* grow, get fat (*Preterit: onichamahuac or
    onichamauh*)
chamahuac *adj.* fat, chubby; thick, dense
chamatl *n.* kid, child
chaneh *n.* homeowner, resident (*Plural: chanehqueh*)
chantia *reflex. v.* reside (*Preterit: oninochantih*)
chantlatquitl *n.* furniture
chantli *n.* home
chapopohtli *n.* asphalt, tar
chapulin *n.* grasshopper
chayahua *tv.* sprinkle, scatter (*Preterit: onitlachayauh*)
chayelahuiltiloni *n.* toy
chayothli *n.* the chayote fruit
chechelotl *n.* squirrel
Checotlahtocayotl *n.* Czech Republic
chia *iv.* wait (*Preterit: onitechix*)
chiahuacayotl *n.* oil
chiahuitl *n.* plant louse
chiahuiztli *n.* bodily fluid; oil; plant disease
chiahuizzoh *adj.* oily
chian *n.* chia seed
chicactic *adj.* firm, solid; powerful; advanced in age

chicahua *iv.* be or become strong (*Preterit: onichicahuac*)
chicahuac *adj.* strong; solid, firm
chicahualiztli *n.* strength; solidity; soundness
chicha *n.* alcoholic beverage made from corn
chichi *n.* dog (*Plural: chichimeh*); *iv.* suck, suckle
    (*Preterit: onichichic*)
chichializtli *n.* bitterness
chichic *adj.* bitter
chichicatl *n.* bile; bitterness
chichico *adv.* from side to side
chichictli *n.* stain
chichihualayonamacoyan *n.* dairy
chichihualayotetzauhtli *n.* cheese
chichihualayotl *n.* milk
chichihualixmexcayotl *n.* serum
chichihualli *n.* breast
chichihualtecomatl *n.* udder
chichihualyacatl *n.* nipple
chichiltic *adj.* red
chichinaca *iv.* feel pain (*Preterit: onichichinacac*)
chichtli *n.* whistle; owl; sorcerer
chicnahui *num.* nine
chicolli *n.* hook
chicome *num.* seven
chicotlamati *iv.* suspect (*Preterit: onichicotlamat*)
chicotlamatini *adj.* suspicious
chicoyotl *n.* suspicion; *adj.* sinister
chictlapanqui *adj.* metallic
chicuace *num.* six
chicuahtli *n.* owl
chicuei *num.* eight
chicueyilhuitl *n.* week
chihcha *iv.* spit (*Preterit: onichihchac*)

chihchitl *n.* saliva
chihua *tv.* make (*Preterit: onitlachiuh*)
chihualiztli *n.* possibility; ease
chilachtli *n.* hot pepper seed
Chillaltohcayotl *n.* Chile
chilli *n.* hot pepper, chili
cillotia *tv.* add chili (*Preterit: onitlachillotih*)
chilmolli *n.* hot sauce
chiltic *adj.* red
chiltototl *n.* cardinal (*bird*)
chimalli *n.* shield
chinamitl *n.* enclosure; hedge; neighborhood; town
chinoa *tv.* scorch, singe (*Preterit: onitlachinoh*)
chipahua *tv.* clean, purify (*Preterit: onitlachipahuac*);
    iv. be clean (*Preterit: onichipahuac*)
chipahuac *adj.* clean
chipahuaca *n.* purity, cleanliness
chipahuacatlahtoani *n.* good conversationalist
chipahuacayotl *n.* purity; beauty
chipahualiztli *n.* hygiene
chipahyayaliztli *n.* underarm odor
chipilotl *n.* crystal
chiqui *tv.* scrape (*Preterit: onitlachic*)
chiquihuitl *n.* basket
chiquilichtli *n.* cicada
chitahtli *n.* hammock
chiuhqui *n.* person having authority or power
chiyahuac *adj.* greasy, grimy
chiyahuacayotl *n.* lard
choca *iv.* cry (*Preterit: onichocac*)
chocolatic *adj.* dark brown
chocolatl *n.* chocolate
choctia *tv.* cause to cry (*Preterit: onitechoctih*)

choloa *iv.* run away, flee (*Preterit: onicholoh*)
choloani *n.* fugitive
chontalli *n.* stranger
chopilin *n.* cricket
choquiliztli *n.* crying
choquiliztzahtzi *iv.* cry loudly, sob
    (*Preterit: onichoquiliztzahtzic*)
ciacatl *n.* armpit; tobacco
ciahualcaxitl *n.* soup tureen
ciahui *iv.* be tired, fatigued (*Preterit: oniciauh*)
ciahuiztli *n.* fatigue
cialtic *adj.* comfortable
ciammiqui *iv.* be tired (*Preterit: oniciammic*)
ciciammicqui *adj.* tired
ciciammiquiliztli *n.* fatigue
cicitlalmatiliztli *n.* astronomy
cicitlaltepuzacalli *n.* spaceship
cihtli *n.* grandmother; hare
cihuaayotl *n.* female secretion
cihuacahuayo *n.* mare
cihuacocolli *n.* menstruation
cihuaconetl *n.* daughter
cihuacuacuahueh *n.* cow
cihuacuecuech *n.* prostitute, whore
cihuahtla *n.* bride, fiancée
cihuahuah *adj.* married (*masc.*)
cihuahuanyolcayotl *n.* kinship
cihuaixhuiuhtli *n.* granddaughter
cihuamicqui *n.* widower
cihuamiqui *iv.* become a widower (*Preterit: onicihuamic*)
cihuamiztli *n.* lioness
cihuamontli *n.* daughter-in-law
cihuanacayotl *n.* vagina

cihuanelpiloni *n.* belt for women
cihuapillahtocatzintli *n.* queen
cihuapilli *n.* daughter; lady
cihuatenyoh *n.* heroine
cihuateopixcacalli *n.* convent
cihuateopixqui *n.* nun
cihuatepiltzintilli *n.* adopted daughter
cihuatic *adj.* effeminate
cihuatl *n.* woman
cihuatl iacayo *n.* vagina
cihuatlacamichin *n.* mermaid
cihuatlahueliloc *n.* womanizer; evil woman
cihuatlahyelli *n.* placenta
cihuatlampa *n.* west
cihuatlatlatquitl *n.* dress; female wardrobe
cihuayolloh *adj.* effeminate
cilin *n.* small snail
cinocuilin *n.* corn worm
cintli *n.* corn; ear of dried corn
cipactli *n.* crocodile
citlalin *n.* star
citlalloh *adj.* full of stars
ciyacatl *n.* underarm
ciyahua *tv.* soak (*Preterit: onitlaciyauh*)
ciyahuac *adj.* soaked
–co *suff.* in, on, place of
coachihua *tv.* invite (*Preterit: onitecoachiuh*)
coacihui *iv.* suffer from gout; be paralyzed
    (*Preterit: onicoaciuh*)
coacihuiztli *n.* gout; paralysis; rheumatism
coacuechtli *n.* snake rattle
coaiztlactli *n.* snake venom
coamichin *n.* eel

coanotza *tv.* invite someone to eat (*Preterit: onitecoanotz*)

coatequitl *n.* communal work

coatetl *n.* snake egg

coatl *n.* snake; twin

coatlacah *n.* confederation, alliance

coatlantli *n.* canine, incisor, fang

cochcahua *tv.* allow someone to sleep
    (*Preterit: onitecochcauh*)

cochcamachaliztli *n.* yawn

cochcamachaloa *iv.* yawn (*Preterit: onicochcamachaloh*)

cochcayotia *reflex. v.* have dinner (*Preterit: oninocohcayotih*)

cochcayotilli *n.* dinner

cochcayotl *n.* dinner, nighttime meal

cochehua *tv.* wake someone (*Preterit: onitecochehuac*);
    reflex. v. wake up (*Preterit: oninococheuh*)

cochi *iv.* sleep (*Preterit: onicoch*)

cochiantli *n.* bedroom, dormitory

cochihualoyan *n.* bedroom, dormitory

cochihuayan *n.* bedroom; dormitory, sleeping quarters; inn

cochini *n.* sleeper

cochipilotl *n.* cocoon

cochitta *iv.* dream (*Preterit: onitlacochittac*)

cochmiqui *iv.* be sleepy (*Preterit: onicochmic*)

cochmiquini *adj.* drowsy, very sleepy

cochnenqui *n.* sleepwalker

cochotl *n.* parrot

cochqui *adj.* asleep

cochtemictli *n.* dream

cochtemiqui *iv.* dream (*Preterit: onicochtemic*)

cochtlahtoa *iv.* speak while asleep (*Preterit: onicochtlahtoh*)

cochtlapiazohua *iv.* wet one's bed (*Preterit: onicochtlapiazouh*)

cochtotolca *iv.* snore (*Preterit: onicochtotolcac*)

coco *n.* servant
cocoa *reflex. v.* be sick (*Preterit: oninococoh*)
cococ *adj.* spicy
cococoyactli *n.* glutton
cocohtli *n.* turtledove; throat, windpipe
cocoleh *adj.* impatient, irritable
cocolia *tv.* hate (*Preterit: onitecocolih*)
cocoliznexiloni *n.* symptom
cocolli *n.* anger; illness, pain; quarrel
cocolochtic *adj.* curly, rolled up
cocoltzin *n.* cross
coconeh impahticauh *n.* pediatrician
coconeh intepahticauh *n.* pediatrician
coconeti *iv.* behave like a child (*Preterit: oniconetic*)
coconeyotl *n.* childishness
cocoti *iv.* have acne, pimples (*Preterit: onicocotic*)
cocotl *n.* pimple, sore; esophagus, windpipe
cocoxcacalli *n.* hospital
cocoxqui *adj.* sick
cocoya *iv.* be sick (*Preterit: onicocox*)
cocoyotl *n.* vein
cohua *tv.* buy (*Preterit: onitlacouh*)
cohuacihuiliztli *n.* palsy
colihui *iv.* curve (*Preterit: onicoliuh*)
colli *n.* grandfather; grandparent; ancestor
coloix *n.* cabbage
colotl *n.* scorpion
coloz *n.* cross
coltic *adj.* curved, twisted
comalli *n.* griddle
comic atolli *n.* gruel, porridge
comitl *n.* pot, jug; barrel
comonqui *adj.* hot

compaletzin *n.* compadre
concanauhtli *n.* goose
conchiuhqui *n.* pot maker
coneatl *n.* newborn infant
conechichilli *n.* newborn infant
conequimiliuhcayotl *n.* diaper
conetl *n.* baby, child (*Plural: coconeh*)
conetzotzomahtli *n.* diaper
coneyoh *adj.* childlike
–copa *suff.* in the manner of; toward
copactli *n.* palate
copalli *n.* incense
Copan *n.* Cuba
copina *tv.* copy (*Preterit: onitlacopin*); extract
copini *iv.* slip away (*Preterit: onicopin*)
copitl *n.* firefly
copitztic *adj.* narrow
cotoctli *n.* crumb, morsel; fragment, piece
cotona *tv.* cut (*Preterit: onitlacoton*); pinch
    (*Preterit: onitecoton*)
cotoncayotl *n.* fraction, fragment, piece, portion
cotonqui *adj.* broken
cototzahui *iv.* shrink (*Preterit: ocototzauh*)
cototzic *adj.* indecisive, undecided
cototzyotl *n.* indecision
cotziliztli *n.* cramp
cotzilli *n.* cramp
cotztetl *n.* calf muscle; calf (*leg*)
cotztlapachoni *n.* legging
cotztli *n.* calf (*leg*)
coxolihtli *n.* pheasant
coxtal *n.* sack
coyahuac *adj.* broad, wide

coyahualiztli *n.* breadth, wideness
coyahualli *adj.* broad, wide
coyamenacahuatzalli *n.* bacon
coyametl *n.* boar, pig-like hoofed animal, peccary
coyauhqui *adj.* torn, full of holes
coyoctic *adj.* pierced
coyoctli *n.* hole
coyolacatl *n.* fishing pole
coyolli *n.* bell; rattle; hook
coyolomitl *n.* awl
coyonca *n.* opening
coyonehnemi *iv.* walk on all fours (*Preterit: onicoyonehnen*)
coyonia *tv.* dig, make a hole, pierce, perforate
    (*Preterit: onitlacoyonih*)
coyonqui *adj.* perforated, pierced
coyotl *n.* coyote; *n.* non-indigenous person;
    acculturated indigenous person
coyotzin *n.* parakeet, parrot
cozahtli *n.* weasel
cozamalotl *n.* rainbow
cozantli *n.* lynx
cozauhqui *adj.* yellow
cozcacuauhtli *n.* eagle vulture
cozcatl *n.* jewel, necklace
coznochtli *n.* yellow prickly pear
cozolcuicatl *n.* lullaby
cozolli *n.* crib
coztic *adj.* yellow
coztictlacatl *n.* Asian
Coztictlacatlalpan *n.* Asia
coztictototl *n.* oriole
coztli *n.* necklace
cua *tv.* eat (*Preterit: onitlacuah*)

cuaatequia *tv.* baptize; pour water on the head
  (*Preterit: onitecuaatequih*)
cuaatequiliztli *n.* baptism
cuacehualoni *n.* hat
cuachcalli *n.* canopy
cuachicpalli *n.* cushion
cuachipahua *tv.* brush someone's hair (*onitecuachipauh*)
cuachocuilin *n.* worm that eats cloth; clothes moth
cuachpamitl *n.* banner, flag
cuachpantli *n.* banner, flag
cuachtli *n.* cloth, fabric; blanket; cape; cover
cuacuachiahuizzotl *n.* butter
cuacuahitl *n.* grove
cuacuahnacatl *n.* beef
cuacuahtentzoneh *n.* goat
cuacuahueh *n.* bull, cow, ox; *adj.* horned
cuacuahuehconetl *n.* calf (*cow*)
cuacuahuitl *n.* antler, horn
cuacualtzin *adj.* pretty
cuacuamminalolli *n.* bullfight
cuacuappixqui *n.* cowboy, shepherd
cuacuauhchoca *iv.* bellow (*Preterit: onicuacuauhchocac*)
cuacuauhconetl *n.* calf (*cow*)
cuacuauhnacatl *n.* beef
cuacuauhpixqui *n.* cowhand
cuaehuayotl *n.* scalp; dandruff
cuahcuahtic *adj.* adult, grown-up; tall, high
cuahuetztic *adj.* pointed
cuahuihuica *reflex. v.* nod, move one's head
  (*Preterit: oninocuahuihuic*)
cuahuitl *n.* tree; wood, lumber, firewood; stick, club
cuahximaloyotl *n.* carpentry
cuaihuintic *adj.* lightheaded

cuaitl *n.* head
cuaiztalli *n.* gray hair
cualancayotl *n.* anger; impatience
cualani *iv.* be angry (*Preterit: onicualan*)
cualaniliztli *n.* anger; indignation
cualanini *adj.* impatient
cualantli *n.* anger
cualcan *n.* a good place; good or appropriate time; *adv.* early
cualcancayotl *n.* opportunity
cualle *n.* power
cualli *adj.* good
cualli ic *adv.* well, fine
cualli iyollo *adj.* virtuous
cuallinemoani *n.* ethics
cuallotl *n.* goodness
cualneci *iv.* look beautiful (*Preterit: onicualnez*)
cualnemiliceh *adj.* virtuous
cualnexiliztli *n.* beauty, elegance
cualnezca *adj.* beautiful (*used in compounds*)
cualnezcatlahtoani *n.* one who speaks well
cualnezcayotl *n.* beauty
cualnezquentic *adj.* handsome
cualnezqui *adj.* beautiful
cualoni *adj.* edible
cualtic *adj.* interesting
cualtilia *tv.* repair (*Preterit: onitlacualtilih*)
cualtiliztli *n.* virtue
cualtzin *adj.* pretty
cuamatlatl *n.* cap; hairnet
cuammitl *n.* lever
cuanaca *n.* chicken; rooster
cuanacayotl *n.* scalp
cuanextli *n.* dandruff

cuapetlanqui *adj.* bald
cuapintic *adj.* pointed
cuappantli *n.* hip
cuatepehui *iv.* go bald (*Preterit: onicuatepeuh*)
cuatepoltic *adj.* not tapered, having no point or top; wearing no hat; a tree without foliage
cuatequixquitl *n.* dandruff
cuatextli *n.* brain
cuatezonoa *tv.* shear (*Preterit: onitecuatezonoh*)
cuatilanmicalini *n.* bullfighter
cuatlaltatzicoltiloni *n.* pitchfork
cuatlapechtli *n.* pillow
cuatlapoliliztli *n.* madness, confusion
cuatlapololtia *iv.* be confused (*Preterit: onicuatlapololtih*)
cuatlecoz *adj.* blond
cuatohuitztic *adj.* pointed
cuauhacatl *n.* pole; post
cuauhayacachtli *n.* mahogany tree
cuauhcactli *n.* clog
cuauhcalli *n.* crate, cage; jail
cuauhcalpixqui *n.* jailer
cuauhcamac *n.* forest
cuauhcamohtli *n.* yucca
cuauhchohchopihtli *n.* woodpecker
cuauhcuechtli *n.* sawdust
cuauhecahuaztli *n.* ladder
cuauhhuiztic *n.* chip, splinter
cuauhicxitl *n.* leg (*table*)
cuauhmahmazohualticoni *n.* cross
cuauhmahmazouhticatzin *n.* crucifix
cuauhmaitl *n.* branch
cuauhmecaexotl *n.* vanilla plant
cuauhmochitl *n.* tamarind

cuauhnacayotl *n.* tree wood
cuauhnamacoyan *n.* lumberyard
cuauhnecomitl *n.* beehive
cuauhnecuhtli *n.* honey
cuauhpantli *n.* stretcher
cuauhpilli *n.* sapling, small tree
cuauhpitztic *adj.* thin; stiff, paralyzed
cuauhquequex *n.* woodpecker
cuauhtentli *n.* trunk; edge of forest
cuauhtextli *n.* sawdust
cuauhtic *n.* tall
cuauhtlacatl *n.* woodsman, resident of a forest
cuauhtlacentemaliztli *n.* woodwork
cuauhtlachihchiuhqui *n.* carpenter
cuauhtlactli *n.* tree trunk
cuauhtlacuilolchichiquiloni *n.* pencil sharpener
cuauhtlah *n.* forest, wilderness
cuauhtlahcuilolcalli *n.* pencil holder
cuauhtlahcuiloloni *n.* pencil
cuauhtlalilli *n.* fagot
cuauhtlanchaneh *n.* savage
cuauhtlapechnamaconi *n.* counter
cuauhtlapechtli *n.* table
cuauhtlapitzalli *n.* wooden flute
cuauhtlatquitamachihualli *n.* mannequin
cuauhtlaxillotl *n.* post (*wood*)
cuauhtli *n.* eagle
cuauhtzontetl *n.* tree trunk
cuauhxeloloni *n.* axe
cuauhximaliztli *n.* carpentry
cuauhximalli *n.* splinter
cuauhximaloyan *n.* carpenter shop
cuauhxinqui *n.* carpenter

cuauhyahualoni *n.* frame
cuauhzonectli *n.* cork
cuaxicalli *n.* skull
cuaxicalmonamicyan *n.* fontanel
cuaxilhuaztli *n.* hairbrush
cuayacapitztic *adj.* pointed
cuayohuinti *iv.* be stunned (*Preterit: onicuayohuintic*)
cuayolcueptoc *adj.* confused
cuayollohtli *n.* crown of the head
cuayollotl *n.* brain
cuechahuac *adj.* humid
cuechahualiztli *n.* humidity, moisture, dampness
cuechahuallotl *n.* humidity, moisture, dampness
cuechahuia *tv.* dampen (*Preterit: onitlacuechahuih*)
cuechohua *tv.* grind (*Preterit: onitlacuechouh*)
cuechtic *adj.* ground, powdered
cuectli *n.* fox
cuecuel *adv.* quickly
cuecuepa *tv.* size up (*Preterit; oniccuecuep*); turn over
    (*Preterit: ontlacuecuep*)
cuecuetzoca *iv.* itch (*Preterit: onicuecuetzocac*)
cuecuetzocaliztli *n.* itch
cuecueyoca *iv.* be ticklish (*Preterit: onicuecueyocac*)
cuecueyoctli *n.* ticklishness
cuehcuelihui *iv.* cramp (*Preterit: onicuehcueliuh*)
cuehcuelihuiztli *n.* cramp
cueitl *n.* skirt
cuel *adv.* already
cueloa *tv.* bend, fold (*Preterit: onitlacuechoh*)
cuemitl *n.* furrow, trench; cultivated land, plowed land
cuemochitl *n.* tamarind
cuepa *reflex. v.* return (*Preterit: oninocuep*)
cuepcayotl *n.* turn

cueponi *iv.* bud, blossom, sprout (*Preterit: onicuepon*)

cueptli *n.* sod

cuetlachtli *n.* wolf

cuetlahuia *iv.* wither (*Preterit: onicuetlahuiac &
     onicuetlahuix*)

cuetlahuic *adj.* withered

cuetlani *iv.* subside, calm down, diminish; move, tremble;
     have a high fever (*Preterit: onicuetlan*)

cuetlauhqui *adj.* withered

cuetlaxcactli *n.* leather shoe

cuetlaxcolli *n.* earthworm

cuetlaxmaxtlatl *n.* chaps

cuetlaxmecatl *n.* leather strap

cuetlaxtic *adj.* leathery

cuetlaxtli *n.* hide

cuetzpal *n.* glutton

cuetzpalin *n.* lizard

cuexantli *n.* apron; lap

cuexcochtetl *n.* nape

cuexcochtli *n.* nape

cueyatl *n.* frog

cuezcomatl *n.* granary

cuezolli *n.* sadness

cui *tv.* take, grasp (*Preterit: oniccuic*)

cuica *iv.* sing (*Preterit: onicuicac*)

cuicaamatl *n.* songbook

cuicani *n.* singer

cuicanitl *n.* poet

cuicapiquiliztli *n.* composition

cuicapiquini *n.* song composer

cuicapixqui *n.* poet

cuicatia *iv.* play music (*Preterit: onicuicatih*)

cuicayocuya *iv.* compose a song (*Preterit: onicuicayocux*)

cuichtli *n.* soot
cuicuiltic *adj.* many colored; spotted
cuicuitzcatl *n.* swallow
cuilolnezqui *n.* picturesque
cuiloni *n.* passive homosexual partner
cuiquiztli *n.* singing
cuitlacaxiuhyantli *n.* kidney
cuitlachichiquilli *n.* backbone
cuitalcoatl *n.* tapeworm
cuitlacochin *n.* corn fungus
cuitlacochtli *n.* corn fungus
cuitlacomitl *n.* urinal
cuitlacuepa *iv.* retreat (*Preterit: onicuitalcuep*)
cuitlalpicayotl *n.* belt
cuitlananacatic *adj.* obese
cuitlananacatzcayotl *n.* obesity
cuitlapanomitl *n.* backbone
cuitlapanteputzchichiquilli *n.* spine
cuitlapantli *n.* back
cuitlapilhueyac *n.* rat
cuitlapilli *n.* tail
cuitlapilyo citlalin *n.* shooting star
cuitlatl *n.* excrement, residue; abscess, tumor, growth
cuitlaxayacatl *n.* hip, buttock
cuitlaxcolli *n.* intestine
cuitlaxcolpitzactli *n.* small intestine
cuitlaxcoltomactli *n.* large intestine
cuitlaxochitl *n.* poinsettia
cuix *adv.* perhaps
cuixantli *n.* apron; lap
cuixin *n.* hawk
cuiyantlanacatentli *n.* sausage
culanto *n.* cilantro

E

ecacahuatl *n.* bean pod

ecahuilli *n.* shade, shadow

ecapahtli *n.* laurel

ecapotzitl *n.* black bean

ecayotl *n.* vein

ecoztli *n.* yellow bean

ecue *exclam.* oh!

ecuxoa *iv.* sneeze (*Preterit: onecuxoh*)

ecuxoliztli *n.* act of sneezing

ehcauhtic *adj.* light, not heavy

ehecacehuaztli *n.* fan

ehecamalacotl *n.* typhoon; waterspout

ehecaquiahuitl *n.* rainstorm

ehecatia *tv.* ventilate (*Preterit: onitlaehecatih*)

ehecatl *n.* wind

ehua *reflex. v.* get up (*Preterit: oninehuac*)

ehuaamatl *n.* parchment

ehuacoyoctli *n.* pore

ehuahuehuetl *n.* tambourine

ehuamecatl *n.* leather strap

ehuatl *n.* skin, hide, rind; scale (*fish*)

ehuatlapitzalhuehuetl *n.* organ

ehuatlapitzaltzotzonqui *n.* organist

ehuaxiquipilli *n.* bag made of leather

elchiquihuitl *n.* breast

elcomalli *n.* spleen

electzontlanexpeuhcayotl *n.* light bulb

elehuetzca *iv.* snicker (*Preterit: onelhuehuetzcac*)

elehuia *tv.* desire, want (*Preterit: onitlaelehuih*)

ellelquiza enjoy oneself; be afflicted (*Preterit: onellelquiz*)
elleltia *tv.* hinder, prevent (*Preterit: oniteelleltih*);
    repent *reflex. v.* (*Preterit: oninoelleltih*)
elli *n.* liver
elmimicqui *n.* stutterer
elmimiqui *iv.* stammer, stutter (*Preterit: onelmimic*)
elotl *n.* corn, ear of fresh corn
elotzontli *n.* corn tassel
elpannacatl *n.* pectoral
elpantli *n.* chest
eltapachtli *n.* liver
eltemiliztli *n.* stomachache
eltzaccatl *n.* entrails
eltzatzacui *iv.* stammer, stutter (*Preterit: oneltzatzacuic*)
epatl *n.* skunk
epatzactli *n.* lentil
epazohtli *n.* wormseed, epazote, green plant
epazotl *n.* wormseed, green plant
epitzahuac *n.* string bean
eptli *n.* oyster; pearl; shell
etextli *n.* bean paste
etic *n.* heavy
etiliztli *n.* heaviness, weight
etl *n.* bean
etlacualli *n.* fried beans
etlah *n.* bean field
Eutlocpa *n.* Europe
exotl *n.* green bean
ezcocoliztli *n.* dysentery
ezquiza *iv.* bleed (*Preterit: oniezquiz*)
eztic *adj.* red
eztli *n.* blood
ezzoh *adj.* bloody

G

Galian *n.* France
Galian chaneh *n.* French person
Galiantlahtolli *n.* language
Galitlaltecatl *n.* French person

H

Helenoyan *n.* Greece
Helenoyan chaneh *n.* Greek
Helenoyantlahtolli *n.* Greek language
heuhueyotl *n.* old age (*male*)
hicox *n.* fig
Hollalpan *n.* Holland
huacalli *n.* crate
huacax *n.* cow
huacaxayotl *n.* beef stew
huaccatlatlaxiztli *n.* tuberculosis
huaccayotl *n.* drought, dryness
huachtli *n.* seed
huactli *n.* falcon
huahualoa *tv.* bark (*Preterit: onitlahuahualoh*)
huahuatl *n.* caterpillar
hualhuica *tv.* bring (*Preterit: onitlahualhuic*)
huallaaquia *tv.* bid (*Preterit: onihuallaaquih*)
huallaaquiani *n.* bidder
huallaliztli *n.* arrival
huallaquiliztli *n.* bid
huallauh *iv.* come (*Preterit: onihualla*)
hualpatiuhtli *n.* fare, tariff
huan *conj.* and, with, in the company of

huanyolqui *n.* relative
huapahua *iv.* cramp (*Preterit: onihuapahuac*); be or become strong (*Preterit: onihuapahuac*)
huapahualizlti *n.* cramp; education; effort
huapallahcuilolhuaztli *n.* blackboard, chalkboard
huapalli *n.* board, beam
huapallotl *n.* mold
huapalnamacoyan *n.* lumberyard
huaqui *iv.* dry (*Preterit: ohuac*)
huaquiliztli *n.* drought, dryness
huaquiztli *n.* drought, dryness
huatzintica *n.* morning
huauhtli *n.* amaranth
huaxin *n.* gourd; vetch
huayolcayotl *n.* kinship
huehcahua *tv.* delay, pause, stop(*Preterit: onitecauh*)
huehcahuitia *tv.* age (*onitlahuehcahuitih*); detain for an extended period (*Preterit: onitehuehcahutih*)
huecapantic *adj.* high, tall
huecauhtica *adv.* for a while
huehca *adv.* far, far away
huehca chaneh *n.* foreigner, stranger
huehca tlacatl *n.* foreigner, stranger
huehcahualiztli *n.* tardiness
huehcapa *adv.* from afar
huehcapan *adv.* from afar; *n.* something high
huehcapancayotl *n.* height
huehcapaniuhqui *n.* esteemed, revered person
huehcatlachiani *adj.* farsighted
huehcatlan *n.* abyss, something deep
huehcatlanyotl *n.* depth
huehcauh *adv.* long time
huehcauhcayotl *n.* antiquity

huehcauhpa *adv.* later; a while ago
huehhuetlatquitl *n.* patrimony
huehueh *adj.* old (*Plural: huehuetqueh*)
huehuehcauhtica *adv.* rarely
huehuehcayomatiliztli *n.* archeology
huehuehcayomatini *n.* archeologist
huehuehti *iv.* age (*Preterit: onihuehuetic*)
huehuehyotl *n.* old age
huehuelatzin *n.* cripple
huehueliztli *n.* old age
huehuequiza *iv.* become old, advanced in years
    (*Preterit: onihuehuequiz*)
huehuetcayotl *n.* old age
huehuetilizlti *n.* old age (*male*)
huehuetl *n.* large vertical drum
huehuetzca *iv.* laugh (*Preterit: onihuehuetzcac*)
huehuetzcaliztli *n.* loud laughter
huehuetzpalin *n.* iguana
huehuetzquilia *tv.* ridicule (*Preterit: onitlahuehuetzquilih*)
huehxolotl *n.* turkey
huei *adj.* large
huei cuauhcomitl *n.* pipe
hueicalli *n.* building
hueicayotl *n.* greatness, solemnity
hueiteopixcatlahtoani *n.* pope
hueitlahtocatitlantli *n.* diplomat
hueitlahtohcayotl *n.* realm
huel *adv.* well, very, exceedingly; to be able (*with future tense*)
huelatzin *n.* cripple
huelcaquiztilloh *adj.* loud, resounding
huelcen *adv.* entirely
huelic *adj.* tasty, delicious
huelicamati *tv.* taste (*Preterit: onic-huelicanat*)

huelicayotl *n.* taste, flavor
huelichpochotl *n.* virginity
huelihcuac in huilohua *n.* point of departure
hueliliztli *n.* taste, flavor; power, ability
hueliotl *n.* power
hueliti *adj.* competent
huelitiliztli *n.* ability, competency; authority; faculty; possibility
hueliyoh *adj.* powerful
hueliz *adv.* perhaps
huelizyeztica *adv.* probably
huellamati *iv.* be happy (*Preterit: onihuellamat*)
huellayacanaliztli *n.* primacy
huelmati *tv.* taste good (*Preterit: onic-huelmat*);
    reflex. v. feel well (*Preterit: oninohuelmat*)
huelnexiliztli *n.* grace
hueltetlahtol *n.* language
hueltic *adj.* tasty
hueltiliztli *n.* ability; possibility
hueltiuhtli *n.* sister
huentia *tv.* present as a gift (*Preterit: onitlahuentih*);
    reflex. v. also (*Preterit: oninohuentih*)
huentli *n.* gift
huepulli *n.* man's sister-in-law; woman's brother-in-law
huetzca *iv.* laugh (*Preterit: onihuetzcac*)
huetzi *iv.* fall (*Preterit: onihuetz*)
huetzitia *reflex. v.* sit (*Preterit: omohuetzitih*)
huetzpalin *n.* iguana
huetzquiztli *n.* laughter
huetztoc *adj.* lying down
huexolotl *n.* turkey
huexotl *n.* willow
huey altepetl *n.* city; province
huey atezcatl *n.* lake

huey atl *n.* ocean, sea
huey citlalin *n.* morning star
huey cualocatl *n.* cancer
huey ehecatl *n.* whirlwind
huey mahuiztic *adj.* solemn
huey mapilli *n.* thumb
huey mecatl *n.* towrope
huey tlahtoani *n.* president
huey yehyecatl *n.* whirlwind
hueyac *adj.* long
hueyacayotl *n.* length
hueyaltepecalaconi *n.* city gate
hueyapancatlalli *n.* island
hueyapaztli *n.* tub
hueyaxcahuah *adj.* wealthy
hueyohtli *n.* avenue, highway
huezhuaztli *n.* woman's sister-in-law
–huic *dir. suff.* against, toward
huica *tv.* carry, take (*Preterit: onitlahuicac*)
huichtli *n.* dew
huictli *n.* stick for digging, shovel, spade
huihuilteccantli *n.* joint
huihuitoca *iv.* shiver (*Preterit: onihuihuitocac*)
huilantli *n.* cripple
huiloconetl *n.* pigeon
huilotl *n.* dove
huipana *tv.* organize (*Preterit: onitlahuipan*)
huipantli n. row, file, line
huipilli *n.* blouse
huiptla *adv.* day after tomorrow
huiteconi *n.* chisel
huitequi *tv.* flog, beat (*Preterit: onitlahuitec*)
huiteyolihtlacoani *adj.* sarcastic

huiteyolihtlacoliztli *n.* sarcasm
huitz *iv.* come (*Preterit: onihuitza*)
huitzilin *n.* hummingbird
huitzoctli *n.* hoe
huitziloxitl *n.* balm
huitzitzilin *n.* hummingbird
huitzitziltetl *n.* opal
huitzquiltzontecomatl *n.* artichoke
huitztlacuatl *n.* porcupine
huitztlampa *n.* south
huitztli *n.* maguey point; thorn

I

i– *poss.* his/her/its
i *tv.* drink (*Preterit: onitlaic*)
ic *prep.* with; *interr. adv.* When?
ica *prep.* with, by means of; for
ica paquiliztli *adv.* with pleasure
icacaquiztli *n.* consonant
icah *adv.* sometime
icali *reflex. v.* fight (*Preterit: oninical*)
icampa *suff.* behind
iccemmaniyan *adv.* forever
iccen *adv.* finally
icel *adj.* alone
icelticaquiztli *n.* vowel
iceltlaquempapaconi *n.* washing machine
ichantzinco *adv.* in his home
ichcacuahuitl *n.* ceiba tree
ichcatl *n.* cotton, lamb
ichcatlazuptli *n.* canvas
ichiaya in chichihualayotl *n.* cream

ichpana *tv.* sweep (*Preterit: onitlachpan*)
ichpocaconetl *n.* little girl
ichpocatl *n.* maiden
ichpochcahualli *n.* spinster
ichpochtli *n.* girl (*Plural: ichpopochtin*)
ichtaca *adv.* secretly
ichtacacalac *n.* intruder
ichtacaconetl *n.* illegitimate child
ichtacanonotza *reflex. v.* whisper (*Preterit: oninichtacanonotz*)
ichtacapitzani *n.* snitch, tattletale
ichtacateilhuini *n.* snitch, tattletale
ichtacatlachixqui *n.* spy
ichtacayoh *adj.* secret
ichtacayotl *n.* secret
ichteca *adv.* secretly
ichtecqui *n.* thief
ichtequi *tv.* steal (*Preterit: onitlaichtec*)
ichtequiliztli *n.* theft
ichtli n. maguey thread
ici *adv.* here
icniuhtli *n.* friend; brother
icniuhyotl *n.* friendship
icnocihuatl *n.* widow; spinster
icnohuah *adj.* compassionate
icnohuahcayotl *n.* compassion; gentleness
icnoitta *iv.* be compassionate (*Preterit: oniteicnoittac*)
icnooquichtli *n.* widower; bachelor
icnopillotl *n.* orphanhood
icnopilloyan *n.* orphanage
icnotl *n.* orphan; poor
icnotlacatl *n.* orphan
icnotlacayotl *n.* orphanhood; poverty
icnoyocan *n.* orphanage

icnoyoh *adj.* compassionate; gentle
icnoyohualiztli *n.* mercy
icnoyotl *n.* orphanhood; poverty, misery
icoltia *reflex. v.* desire (*Preterit: oninotlacoltih*)
-cpac *suff.* on top of, over
icpalalli *n.* furniture
icpalli *n.* chair
icpatl *n.* string, thread
icpatlahuiloni *n.* wick
icpitl *n.* firefly
icuh *n.* younger sibling
icuhtontli *n.* great grandchild; younger sibling
icuitlapan *prep.* behind
icximachiyotl *n.* footprint
icxinequentiloni *n.* sock
icxipehpechli *n.* sole
icxipetlalli *n.* footprint
icxitl *n.* foot
-icxitlan *loc. suff.* at the foot of
icxopalli *n.* sole of the foot
iczan *adv.* once upon a time
iczotl *n.* yucca
ihcac *adj.* erect, standing
ihcatoc *adj.* standing
ihcica *iv.* breathe rapidly, pant (*Preterit: onihcicac*)
ihcihui *iv.* hurry (*Preterit: onihciuh*)
ihcihuiliztli *n.* hurry
ihciuhca *adv.* promptly, quickly, soon
ihciuhca tepuztototl *n.* jet
ihciuhca tlachihua *tv.* improvise (*Preterit: iciuhca onitlachiuh*)
ihciuhca tlachihualiztli *n.* improvisation
ihciuhcapan *adv.* early in the morning
ihciuhcatitlancalli *n.* post office
ihciuhcatitlanmachiyotl *n.* stamp (*postal*)

ihciuhcayoh *adj.* prompt, speedy

ihciuhcayotl *n.* hurry; promptness, speed

ihcuac *adv.* when

ihcuaquinon *adv.* then, at that moment

ihcuiloa *tv.* write (*Preterit: onitlahcuiloh*)

ihhuitl *n.* feather

ihnecui *tv.* smell (*Preterit: onitlahnecuh or onitlahnecu*)

ihpotoctli *n.* vapor

ihqui *adv.* so (*in this manner*), thus, like, as

ihquiti *iv.* knit (*Preterit: onihquit*)

ihquitihualoni *n.* loom

ihquitiloni *n.* loom

ihta *tv.* see (*Preterit: onitlaihtac*)

ihtacatl *n.* food ration, morsel

ihtic *prep.* inside, within

ihtitl *n.* stomach, belly; interior

ihtlacoa *tv.* harm, damage; sin (*Preterit: onitlaihtlacoh, onitlahtlacoh*)

ihtoloca *n.* history (*oral*)

ihtoni *adj.* visible

ihtotia *reflex. v.* dance (*Preterit: oninihtotih*)

ihtotiani *n.* dancer

ihuamontli *n.* daughter-in-law

ihuan *conj.* and, with, in the company of

ihuianyotl *n.* modesty

ihuinti *iv.* be drunk (*Preterit: onihuintic*)

ihuintia *tv.* intoxicate, make drunk (*Preterit: oniteihuintih*)

ihuintic *adj.* drunk

ihuintiliztli *n.* drunkenness

ihyohuiliztli *n.* fast

ihyomiqui *iv.* suffocate (*Preterit: onihyomic*)

ihyomiquiztli *n.* asphyxia

ihyotia *reflex. v.* breathe (*Preterit: oninihyotih*)

ihyotl *n.* breath
ihyotzecoliztli *n.* glottal stop
ihza *iv.* wake up (*Preterit: onihzac*)
ihzac *adj.* awake
ihzotla *reflex. v.* vomit (*Preterit: oninihzotlac*)
iihta *tv.* size up (*Preterit: oniquiihtac*)
iihyo motzahtzacuani *n.* asthmatic
iihyoh *adj.* spiritual
iihyomiqui *iv.* suffocate (*Preterit: oniihyomic*)
iihyotia *reflex. v.* breathe (*Preterit: oniniihyotih*)
iihyotl *n.* breath; spirit
iihyotzacua *reflex. v.* suffocate (*Preterit: oniniihyotzauc*)
iixpan *loc.* in front of him or her, in his or her presence
ilama *n.* old woman (*Plural: ilamatqueh*)
ilamatiliztli *n.* old age (*female*)
ilamatzapotl *n.* chirimoya (*fruit*)
ilamayotl *n.* old age (*female*)
ilcahua *tv.* forget (*Preterit: onitlailcauh*)
ilcahualiztli *n.* oblivion, forgetfulness
ilhuia *tv.* say, tell (*Preterit: oniquilhuih*)
ilhuicaatentli *n.* shore, beach
ilhuicacpatlani *n.* angel
ilhuicacpatlanpixqui *n.* guardian angel
ilhuicacpatlanqui *n.* angel
ilhuicamatiliztli *n.* astronomy
ilhuicatl *n.* sky; heaven
ilhuiceh *adv.* especially
ilhuilli *n.* favor; payment
ilhuipixqui *n.* steward of a town festival
ilhuitl *n.* day; feast day, holiday, birthday
ilhuitl pieloni *n.* holiday
ilhuitlapohualamoxtli *n.* ritual calendar
ilihuiz *adv.* thoughtlessly, without consideration

ilihuizqui *adj.* indifferent
ilihuiztli *n.* indifference
ilnamiqui *tv.* remember (*Preterit: onitlalnamic*)
ilnamiquilizyotl *n.* mind
iloti *iv.* return, turn back (*Preterit: onilot*)
ilotiliztli *n.* return
ilpia *tv.* tie (*Preterit: onitlalpix*)
ilteconi *adj.* absorbable
imacaci *tv.* fear, respect, revere (*Preterit: onitlamacaz*)
imacaxoni *adj.* fearsome; formidable
imman *n.* hour; *adv.* it is time
immani *adv.* it is time
imiquiztica tlaneltiliani *n.* martyr
imixpan *loc.* in front of them, in their presence
immanel *adv.* though, however
immanin *adv.* at this hour, now
immanon *adv.* at that hour
immanyotl *n.* opportunity
imonequiyan *adv.* at the right time
imoztlayoc *adv.* the next day
in *art.* the
in–/im– *poss.* their
in ahtle *prep.* without (*anything*)
in ahzo *adv.* probably
in ayac *prep.* without anyone present
in oquic *adv.* meanwhile
in oquic *conj.* while
in yez *n.* future
in yuh *adv.* as soon as
inantzicatl *n.* coral snake
inayacpatiyoh *adj.* null and void
inic *conj.* so that; by means of, with
inic centetl *adj.* first

inicatohueimapil *n.* inch
inici *adv.* recently
inihcuac *adv.* then
inin *pron.* this
iniuh *adv.* like
iniuhqui *adv.* like
inon *pron.* that one
intla *conj.* if
intlanel *conj.* although; however
ipampa *conj.* because
ipan *prep.* in, on; during the time of
ipanyotl *n.* opportunity
ipatiuh *n.* cost
iquin *inter. adv.* when?
itauhcayotl *n.* fame
–itech *prep.* concerning
itech chicotlamachoni *n.* suspect
itech necahualotiuh *n.* executor
itechpa *prep.* about, concerning
ithualli *n.* patio
ithui *impers. v.* it is day
ititlapohui *iv.* burst (*Preterit: onititlapouh*)
itixihuiliztli *n.* dropsy
itla *pron.* something
itlacauhnelonqui *adj.* mestizo
itlah *pron.* something
itonia/itoni *iv.* perspire (*Preterit: niiton, niitonih*)
itonilli *n.* perspiration
itqui *tv.* carry; govern (*Preterit: onitlatquic*)
itquin *adv.* when?
itta *tv.* see (*Preterit: onitlaittac*)
ittitia *reflex. v.* appear, reveal one's self (*Preterit: oninoteittitih*)
ittoni *adj.* visible

itzcalli *n.* flank, side
itzcuinconetl *n.* puppy
itzcuintli *n.* dog
itzmina *tv.* cut someone; make someone bleed
    (*Preterit: oniteitzmin*)
itzomia *reflex. v.* blow one's nose (*Preterit: oninitzomih*)
itztic *adj.* cold
itztimotlalia *tv.* premeditate (*Preterit: onitlaitztimotlalih*)
itztli *n.* obsidian; knife
itztoc *adj.* visible
iuhqui *adv.* so (*in this manner*), thus, like, as
ixaca *adv.* face down
ixacanehnemi *iv.* crawl (*Preterit: onixacanehnen*)
ixachi *adj.* much, many (*Plural: ixachtin, ixachintin*)
ixayotl *n.* tear
ixca *tv.* heat on a griddle; broil (*Preterit: onitlaxcac*)
ixcahua *tv.* neglect (*Preterit: onitlaixcauh*)
ixcapitztic *adj.* one eyed
ixcauhtli *n.* tick
ixchicotic *adj.* cross-eyed
ixchihchiqui *tv.* erase (*Preterit: onitlaixchichic*)
–ixco *suff.* in front of
ixcochcoyoctic *adj.* having sunken eyes
ixcocochi *iv.* nap (*Preterit: onixcoch*)
ixcocoliztli *n.* eye disease
ixconexiliztli *n.* countenance, facial features
ixcopina *tv.* photograph, take a picture (*Preterit: onitlaixcopin*)
ixcopitzotic *adj.* having a dirty face
ixcuacualtzin *adj.* pretty
ixcuahmolli *n.* eyebrow
ixcuahmolquehquetza *reflex. v.* frown
    (*Preterit: oninixcuahmolquehquetz*)
ixcuaitl *n.* forehead

ixcuamulli *n.* eyebrow
ixcuamulquehquetza *reflex. v.* frown
   (*Preterit: oninixcuamulquehquetz*)
ixcuatetl *n.* forehead
ixcuatl *n.* forehead
ixcuatzontli *n.* bangs (*hair*); mane
ixcueloa *iv.* nod in agreement (*Preterit: onixcueloh*)
ixcuepa *tv.* deceive (*Preterit: oniteixcuep*)
ixcuepoctic *adj.* cross-eyed
ixcueponqui *adj.* cross-eyed
ixcuilchilli *n.* lachrymal
ixcuitlatl *n.* eye rheum
ixeh nacaceh *adj.* having good judgment
ixehuaniliztli *n.* theater
ixehuatl *n.* eyelid; facial skin
ixhuetzca *iv.* smile (*Preterit: oniixuetzcac*)
ixhuetzqui *adj.* goood natured, smiling
ixhui *iv.* gorge (*Preterit: onixhuic*)
ixhuic *adj.* stuffed
ixhuintic *adj.* dizzy
ixhuitia *tv.* stuff (*Preterit: oniteixhuitih*)
ixhuiuhmontli *n.* great-son-in-law
ixhuiuhtli *n.* grandchild, granddaughter, grandson
ixili *tv.* lynch (*Preterit: oniteixil*)
iximachiyotl *n.* clue
iximachoni *adj.* evident, known
ixiptla *n.* image, picture
ixiptlatl *n.* representative
ixiptlayolin *n.* cinema; movie theater
ixiptlayollan *n.* movie theater
ixiptlayotl *n.* image, picture
ixiuhqui *adj.* resembling, similar
ixmahuiztic *adj.* pleasant

ixmana *tv.* make level (*Preterit: onitlaixman*)
ixmaniliztli *n.* surface
ixmanqui *adj.* level, plane
ixmati *tv.* recognize (*Preterit: oniteixmat*)
ixmelactic *adj.* upright, erect
ixnacatl *n.* flesh of the face
ixneliuhqui *adj.* intricate
ixnenetl *n.* pupil of the eye
ixnotza *tv.* gesture to someone (*Preterit: oniteixnotz*)
ixocuilin *n.* pimple, boil, acne
ixpahpaltic *adj.* blind
ixpancaitta *tv.* witness (*Preterit: onitlaixpancaittac*)
ixpantilia *tv.* divulge (*Preterit: onicteixpantilih*)
ixpehpena *tv.* recognize (*Preterit: oniteixpehpen*)
ixpehualtia *tv.* invade (*Preterit: oniteixpehualtih*)
ixpetlanqui *adj.* polished, shiny
ixpetzoa *iv.* analyze, examine (*Preterit: oninixpetzoh*)
ixpia *tv.* guard someone (*Preterit: oniteixpix*)
ixpilli *n.* eyelash
ixpiqui *reflex. v.* close the eyes (*Preterit: oninixpic*);
    tv. roll a tortilla (*Preterit: onitlaixpic*)
ixpopoyoti *iv.* be blind (*Preterit: oniixpopoyotic*)
ixpopoyotiliztli *n.* blindness
ixpopoyotzin/ixpopoyotl *adj.* blind
ixpoxcauhqui *adj.* rancid
ixquich *adv.* all; so much
ixquichca *adv.* until
ixquichcauh *adv.* as long as
ixquichic *adj.* voluminous
ixquichin *n.* volume, size
ixquichihueli *adj.* almighty
ixquimilli *adj.* negligent

ixtecuecuech *adj.* stupid
ixteliuhtzontli *n.* sideburn
ixtelolohtli *n.* eye, eyeball
ixtentli *n.* eyelid
ixtetl *n.* eyeball
ixtetziltic *adj.* cross-eyed
ixtezcaticoni *n.* eyeglasses
ixtezcatl *n.* eyeglasses; lens
ixtlacchichi *n.* coyote
ixtlacmiztli *n.* wildcat
ixtlahpach *adv.* upside down
ixtlahua *tv.* pay (*Preterit: onitetlaxtlauh*)
ixtlahuacan *n.* battlefield
ixtlahuatl *n.* desert; field; plain
ixtlamatqui *adj.* skillful
ixtlapa *adv.* crosswise, sideways
ixtlapal *adv.* crosswise, sideways
ixtlapohuiliztli *n.* discovery
ixtli *n.* face; eye; surface
ixtohmitl *n.* eyebrow
ixtolohtli *n.* eye
ixtomoniliztli *n.* sty
ixtopehua *tv.* push, shove (*Preterit: onixtopeuh*)
ixtotolicihuiliztli *n.* cataract
ixtozotl *n.* insomnia
ixtzontli *n.* facial hair
ixxolochahui *iv.* develop facial wrinkles (*Preterit: nixxolochauh*)
ixyehyecoa *tv.* examine, scrutinize; test
    (*Preterit: onitlaixyehyecoh*)
ixzahuatl *n.* pimple
iyelli *n.* flatulence
iyolic *adv.* slowly, little by little

iz *adv.* here, behold
izca *adv.* here, behold
izcah *adv.* here, behold
izcalia *tv.* encourage, educate (*Preterit: oniteizcalih*);
    reflex. v. revive (*Preterit: oninozcalih*)
izcatqui *adv.* here, behold
izhuatl *n.* leaf
izquitl *n.* popcorn, toasted corn
izquiztepiton *n.* hand-brush, small broom
izquiztli *n.* broom
iztac *n.* white
iztacaxitl *n.* saltshaker
iztachichic *adj.* very salty
iztacquilitl *n.* purslane, edible weed
iztacteocuitlaoztotl *n.* silver mine
iztacteocuitlatl *n.* silver
iztactic *adj.* white
iztalectic *adj.* pale
iztaquetl *n.* white bean
iztatl *n.* salt
iztayo *adj.* salty
iztecocoliztli *n.* ingrown nail
iztetl *n.* fingernail; toenail
iztetzintli *n.* hangnail
iztlacati *iv.* lie (*Preterit: oniniztlacat*)
iztlacatiliztli *n.* lie
iztlacatlahtolli *n.* lie
iztlacatqui *n.* liar
iztlacmeya *iv.* drool (*Preterit: oniztlacmex*)
iztlactli *n.* saliva; poison, venom; lie
iztlacyoh *adj.* poisonous
iztlaectiliztli *n.* paleness
iztlaqui *tv.* salivate; savor (*Preterit: onitlaiztlac*)

M

ma *tv.* capture, hunt (*Preterit: onitlamah*); *aux. part.* may (*positive commands*)

maca *tv.* give (*Preterit: onitlamacac or onitlamac*); *adv.* no (*negative command*)

macahmo, macamo, mahcamo *aux. part.* do not (*negative commands*)

macahua *tv.* let go of (*Preterit onitlamacauh*)

macehualcopa *adv.* in Nahuatl

macehuallahtolli *n.* native language; common speech

Macehuallalpan *n.* North America

macehualli *n.* indigenous person; peasant

macehualti *iv.* be happy; fulfill one's wishes (*Irreg. Preterit: onomacehualtic*)

macehualtiliztli *n.* reward; happiness

macehualtin *n.* people

macehuia *reflex. v.* deserve; reach one's goal (*Preterit: oninotlamacehuih*)

macel *adv.* at least

mach *adv.* possibly, perhaps

machihua *tv.* maneuver (*Preterit: onitlamachiuh*)

machiliztli *n.* knowledge

machiltia *tv.* inform (*Preterit: onitemachiltih*)

machiotl *n.* example; image; model; sign

machiotlahtolli *n.* comparison; metaphor

machiuhcayotl *n.* maneuver

machiyohcuillotl *n.* glyph, hieroglyph

machiyohcuiloa *tv.* write in hieroglyphs (*Preterit: onitlamachiyohcuiloh*)

machiyohcuiloliztli *n.* glyphic writing

machiyohcuilollotl *n.* glyph, hieroglyph

machiyotia *tv.* mark (*Preterit: onitlamachiyoh*)

machiyotl *n.* mark

machizeh *adj.* informed, knowledgeable
machiztia *tv.* divulge (*Preterit: onictemachiztih*)
machontequixtinenelli *n.* hodgepodge
machotoc *adj.* maimed
machtia *tv.* teach (*Preterit: onitemachtih*)
machtli *n.* nephew
macihui *conj.* although
maciuhqui *conj.* nevertheless
macochoa *reflex. v.* embrace (*Preterit: oninomacochoh*)
macpalli *n.* palm of the hand
macpatopilli *n.* cane
macueleh *interj.* hopefully
macuextli *n.* bracelet, bracelet of precious stones
macuilcampa *n.* pentagon
macuilli *num.* five
macuilpoalxiuhcayotl *n.* century
maehuatl *n.* glove
mahcic *adj.* solid, firm
mahciconi *n.* solidity; soundness
mahciticayotl *n.* maturity
mahmatca *adv.* skillfully, carefully
mahmatcatzin *adv.* very skillfully, very carefully
mahmauhqui *adj.* cunning
mahpilli *n.* finger
mahtlactli *num.* ten
mahui *iv.* fear, be afraid (*Preterit: onimauh*)
mahuichichiuhcalli *n.* gallery
mahuiltiliztli *n.* game
mahuiznotza *iv.* speak with respect (*Preterit: onitemahuiznotz*)
mahuiztic *adj.* admirable
mahuiztilia *tv.* honor (*Preterit: onitemahuiztilih*)
mahuiztli *n.* respect, honor

mahuizzotl *n.* dignity, honor; solemnity

mailpia *tv.* fetter, handcuff, manacle (*Preterit: onitemailpix*)

maitl *n.* hand; arm; branch

malacachoa *tv.* roll up (*Preterit: onitlamalacachoh*)

malacatl *n.* spindle

malcochoa *reflex. v.* embrace (*Preteri: oninomalcochoh*)

malina *tv.* twist (*Preterit: onitlamalin*)

malina *tv.* twist something on one's leg
   (*Preterit: onitlamalin*)

malinqui *adj.* twisted, crooked

malli *n.* captive, prisoner

mama *tv.* carry on one's back (*Preterit: onitlamamah &
   onitlamamac*)

mamalhuaztli *n.* shoulder bag

mamali *tv.* drill, perforate (*Preterit: onitlamamalihuac*)

mametlatl *n.* stone used for grinding corn

man *loc. suff.* place of, in, on

mana *tv.* offer, present (*Preterit: onitlaman*)

manel *conj.* although

mani *iv.* exist (*Preterit: oniman*)

manilia *tv.* offer; place in front of (*Preterit: onitetlamanilih*)

maololli *n.* fist

mapachin *n.* racoon

mapachtli *n.* racoon

mapiccatl *n.* glove

mapicthli *n.* fist

mapihpichoa *iv.* whistle (*Preterit: onimapihpichoh*)

mapihpichtli *n.* whistle

mapilhueyacatl *n.* middle finger

mapilli *n.* finger

mapiltontli *n.* small finger

mapilxocoyotl *n.* pinkie finger

maquechtli *n.* wrist

maquixtia *tv.* free; preserve; save (*Preterit: onitemaquixtih*)
maquizlti *n.* bracelet
matca *adv.* peacefully, calmly
matepuztli *n.* hand axe; sword; ring
matequia *reflex. v.* wash one's hands (*Preterit: oninomatequih*)
matequipanoa *tv.* maneuver (*Preterit: otlamatequipanoh*)
matetexoni *n.* stone pestle, grinder
matlahcuilolli *n.* manuscript
matlalhuayo itetecuicaca *n.* pulse
matlalin *adj.* blue, blue-green
matlapechtli *n.* glove
matlatl *n.* net
matlequiquiztli *n.* rifle; shotgun
matoca *reflex. v.* masturbate (*Preterit: oninomatocac*)
matopehua *tv.* push with the hands (*Preterit: onitematopeuh*)
matzahtli *n.* pineapple
matzitzquiloni *n.* crank; handle
matzolli *n.* fist
matzotzopaztli *n.* forearm, arm
mauhcamiqui *iv.* be terribly afraid (*Preterit: onimauhcamic*)
mauhcatlacayotl *n.* cowardice
mauhcatlayecoani *n.* coward
mauhqui *adj.* fearful
mauhtia *tv.* scare, frighten (*Preterit: onitemauhtih*)
maxactli *n.* crotch; thigh; vulva
maxalli *n.* earwig
maxatl *n.* crotch; thigh
maxotlaztli *n.* ring
maxtlatl *n.* loincloth; swaddling clothes, diaper
maxtli *n.* loincloth
mayana *iv.* be hungry (*Preterit: onimayan*)
mayanaliztli *n.* hunger, famine
mayantli *n.* hunger

mayatl *n.* dark green beetle
mayeccantli *n.* right hand
mayectli *n.* right hand
mayecuele *adv.* hopefully
mayotzincuepani *n.* acrobat
mazaatemitl *n.* tick
mazacoatl *n.* large snake
mazaconetl *n.* fawn
mazaehuatl *n.* animal hide, deer skin
mazamailpia *iv.* handle animals (*Preterit: onimazamailpih*)
mazamolli *n.* dish made from game
mazanacatl *n.* venison
mazannel *conj.* although, even if
mazaohtli *n.* deer trail; evil path
mazatenilpicatl *n.* bridle
mazatl *n.* deer; animal
mazatlacualli *n.* fodder, hay
mazatlacualoyan *n.* manger
mazatlacualtiloyan *n.* manger
mazo *conj.* although
mecahuehuetl *n.* guitar; harp
mecahuehuetzotzona *iv.* pluck a guitar or harp
   (*Preterit: onimecahuehuetzotzon*)
mecahuehuetzotzonani *n.* guitarist
mecahuehuetzotzonqui *n.* guitarist; harpist
mecahuiteconi *n.* whip
mecapalli *n.* trumpline, device for carrying loads
mecatl *n.* string, rope; lover
mecatlapohua *iv.* foretell the future (*Preterit: onimecatlapouh*)
mecatlapouhqui *n.* fortune-teller
mecayotl *n.* lineage
mehputza *iv.* belch (*Preterit: onimehputz*)
mehua *reflex. v.* get up (*Preterit: onineuh*)

melac *adj.* correct

melactic *adj.* straight, long

melahua *tv.* straighten, correct; unroll, unwind; proceed
directly (*Preterit: onitlamelahuac*)

melahuac *adj.* correct; honest, true, positive; straight

melahuaca *adv.* correctly; simply

melahuacacaqui *tv.* understand correctly
(*Preterit: onitlamelahuacac*)

melahuacaihtoa *tv.* explain (*Preterit: onicmelahuacaihtoh*)

melahuacaihtoa *tv.* explain clearly
(*Preterit: onitlamelahuacaihtoh*)

melahuacaihtotiztli *n.* explanation

melahualiztli *n.* simplicity

melauhcaitta *tv.* aim (*Preterit: onitlamelauhcaitta*)

melauhcaittaloni *n.* level

melaztic *adj.* straight

meocuilin *n.* maguey worm

meolli *n.* maguey sap

metl *n.* maguey

metlamaitl *n.* stone tool used for grinding corn

metlapilli *n.* stone tool used for grinding corn

metlatl *n.* stone grinder

metzcocoxqui *adj.* lame

metzilpicayotl *n.* garter

metznequentiloni *n.* stocking

metzontli *n.* grass root

metztlalhuatl *n.* nerve of the leg

metztlaquemitl *n.* pants

metztli *n.* month; moon; thigh

metztli cualo *n.* eclipse of the moon

metztona *impers. v.* the moon shines (*Preterit: ometztonac*)

metztonalli *n.* moonlight

metztzontli *n.* leg hair

mexcalatl *n.* unfermented maguey juice
mexcalli *n.* cooked maguey, mescal
mexihcacopa *adv.* in Nahuatl
mexihcatl *n.* Mexican
mexihcatlacatl *n.* Mexican
mexihcatlaholcopa *adv.* in Nahuatl
mexihcatlahtolli *n.* Nahuatl language
mexihcayotl *n.* Mexicanness, everything associated with Mexico
meya *iv.* flow (*Preterit: omex*)
meyalli *n.* fountain, spring, source
meyollohtli *n.* maguey heart, shoot
meyotl *n.* ray
mezotl *n.* dried maguey leaf
miac *adv.* much, a lot
miahuatl *n.* corn stalk; corn stalk flower
micampa *adv.* excuse me (*when passing behind someone*)
micampatzinco *adv.* (*reverential*) excuse me (*when passing behind someone*)
miccacoyoctli *n.* grave
miccacuahuitl *n.* skeleton
miccahuah *n.* someone in mourning
miccahuahcayotl *n.* mourning
miccailhuitl *n.* day of the dead
miccapetlacalli *n.* tomb
miccatechan *n.* mortuary
miccatequimilolli *n.* shroud
miccatilmahhuah *n.* someone in mourning
michehuatl *n.* fish scale or skin
michin *n.* fish
michinix *n.* wart
michmolli *n.* dish made from fish
michnamacac *n.* fish vendor
michnamacoyan *n.* fish market

michomitetl *n.* fish bone
michomitl *n.* fish bone
michpahtli *n.* walnut tree
michpilli *n.* fish egg
michpihpiloa *tv.* fish (*Preterit: onimichpihpiloh*)
michpihpiloani *n.* fisherman
michtetl *n.* fish egg
micquetl *n.* cadaver, corpse
micqui *adj.* dead, deceased
micquitlahuatztli *n.* mummy
mictia *tv.* kill (*Preterit: onitemictih*)
mictlampa *n.* north
mictlanchaneh *n.* devil
miec *adj.* much, many
miec xiuhtia *iv.* be advanced in years (*Preterit: onimiecxiuhtih*)
mieccan *adv.* in many places
miecpa *adv.* many times
miectincihuapixcayotl *n.* polygamy
miectincihuapixqui *adj.* polygamous
miectlacatl *n.* crowd, throng
mihcacoyoctli *n.* grave
mihcacuahuitl *n.* skeleton
mihcahuah *n.* someone in mourning
mihcahuahcayotl *n.* mourning
mihcailhuitl *n.* day of the dead
mihcapetlacalli *n.* tomb
mihcatechan *n.* mortuary
mihcatequimilolli *n.* shroud
mihcatilmahhuah *n.* someone in mourning
mihcatlacoyoctli *n.* grave
mihmatca *adv.* skillfully
mihtoa *impers. v.* it is said (*Preterit: omihtoh*)
mihtotiani *n.* dancer

millacatl *n.* peasant, farmer
millatlatquitl *n.* farming tool
millatquitl *n.* farming tool
milli *n.* field
milpanecatl *n.* peasant, farmer
milpazolli *n.* thicket, underbrush
miltequitcatlatquitl *n.* farm workers tool
miltequitini *n.* farm worker
miltequitqui *n.* farm worker
mimatqui *adj.* honest
mimilihui *iv.* bud, grow; become round (*Preterit: omimiliuh*)
mimiliuhcayotl *n.* roundness
mimiliuhqui *adj.* round
mimiloa *reflex. v.* revolve, roll (*Preterit: oninomimiloh*)
mimiltic *adj.* round
mimiqui *iv.* have an epileptic attack (*Preterit: onimimic*)
mimiquiliztli *n.* epilepsy
mina *tv.* cut; shoot an arrow (*Preterit: onitlamin*)
miqui *iv.* die (*Preterit: onimic*)
miquiliztli *n.* death
miquini *adj.* mortal
miquiztli *n.* death
misah tenanquililpiltontli *n.* altar boy
misahtlapalehuiani *n.* altar boy
mitl *n.* arrow; penis
mixatl *n.* drizzle
mixcoatl *n.* tornado
mixihuiliztli *n.* childbirth
mixihuitia *tv.* assist in childbirth (*Preterit: onitemixihuitih*)
mixincayotl *n.* fish scale
mixpan *adv.* please; excuse me; cheers
mixpantzinco *adv.* (*reverential*) please; excuse me; cheers
mixpetzoani *adj.* analytical

nixtemi *adj.* cloudy
mixtentimani *adj.* cloudy
mixtentoc *adj.* cloudy
mixtlapaloani *adj.* reckless
mixtli *n.* cloud
mizotlani *n.* one who vomits
mizquitl *n.* mesquite
miztli *n.* mountain lion
mizton *n.* cat
mo *reflex. pron.* 2nd and 3rd person (*Sing. and Plural*);
    poss. your (*Sing. and Plural*)
moacalaquia *reflex. v.* board (*Preterit: oninoacalquih*)
mocahua *reflex. v.* be quiet (*Preterit: oninocauh*)
mocahuani *adj.* quiet, silent
mocecac *adv.* excuse me (*when passing to the side of someone*)
mocecactzinco *adv.* (*reverential*) excuse me (*when passing to
    the side of someone*)
mochantia *reflex. v.* reside (*Preterit: oninochantih*)
mochantilia *reflex. v.* reside (*Preterit: ininochantilih*)
mochihua *reflex. v.* happen, occur; become (*Preterit: omochiuh*)
mochihualiztli *n.* consequence, result
mochipa *adv.* always
mocnomatini *adj.* humble
mocochcayotia *reflex. v.* have dinner
    (*Preterit: oninocochcayotih*)
mococoa *reflex. v.* be sick (*Preterit: oninococoh*)
mocuallapiquiani *n.* hypocrite
mocuani *adj.* edible
mocuecueptinemi *reflex. v.* toss and turn
    (*Preterit: oninocuecueptinen*)
mocuehcueptinemi *reflex. v.* come and go
    (*Preterit: oninocuehcueptinen*)
mocuitlahuiani *n.* inspector

mohuan *adv.* with you (*Sing.*)
mohuelmati *reflex. v.* feel well (*Preterit: oninohuelmat*)
moitzputza *iv.* belch (*Preterit: onimoitzputz*)
molcaxitl *n.* sauce bowl
molicpitl *n.* elbow
moliniani *adj.* portable
molli *n.* sauce; dish; soup
molochtic *adj.* curly
moloni *iv.* flow; spread out; overrun (*Preterit: omolon*)
molotl *n.* sparrow
momaimatini *adj.* dexterous
momaiztlacoani *n.* wrestler
momanahuia *reflex. v.* defecate (*Preterit: oninomanahuih*)
momanepanohqui *adj.* married
momaquitzquia *reflex. v* shake hands
  (*Preterit: oninomaquitzquih*)
momatequia *reflex. v.* wash one's hands
  (*Preterit: oninomatequih*)
momatini *adj.* affable
momatotopehuiani *n.* ball player
momauhtiani *adj.* frightened, scared
momolocatl *n.* bubble
momoztla *adv.* daily
momoztli *n.* altar
monamiccan *n.* last year
monamictia *reflex. v.* get married (*Preterit: oninonamictih*)
monamicyan *n.* summit, top
moneconi *n.* importance
monecqui *adj.* arrogant
monemachtih *adj.* ready
monemilizcuepqui *n.* convert
monequi *impers. v.* it is necessary (*Preterit: omonec*)
monequiliztli *n.* necessity

monnantli *n.* mother-in-law
monomateixpahuih *n.* litigant
mononotzaliztli *n.* meeting, conference
montahtli *n.* father-in-law
montli *n.* son-in-law
mopohuani *adj.* arrogant, haughty
mopouhcatlahtoani *n.* charlatan, quack
mopouhqui *adj.* proud; vain
moquetza *reflex. v.* stand up (*Preterit: oninoquetz*)
moquexquitzahuiani *n.* thinker
motemaquixtih *adj.* exonerated
motenehua *impers. v.* it is said
motenehuani *adj.* arrogant
motepachihuih *n.* spy
moteputztiani *n.* deserter
motetzincohuani *adj.* whoring
motlacuia *reflex. v.* be indebted (*Preterit: oninotlacuih*)
motlacuih *adj.* indebted
motlacuitlahui *adj.* diligent, industrious, careful
motlahtlayehuiani *n.* beggar
motlahtlayehuih *n.* beggar
motlahtolneltiani *adj.* exact
motlahtolneltiliztli *n.* exactness
motlaliani *adj.* sitting; tranquil
motlalih *adj.* sitting; tranquil
motlaloani *n.* fugitive, runner
motlancuaquetza *reflex. v.* kneel (*Preterit: oninotlancuaquetz*)
motlanehuiani *n.* tenant
motlazohcamatini *adj.* grateful
motlazohmatini *adj.* grateful
motohtli *n.* squirrel; chipmunk
motolinia *adj.* poor
motquihtaliztli *n.* integrity, purity

motquitini *adj.* whole
motzicoani *adj.* slow, sluggish
motzinnamacani *n.* prostitute, whore
motzotzonaliztli *n.* suspense
moxicoani *adj.* envious
moyectocani *n.* hypocrite
moyehyecoa *reflex. v.* practice (*Preterit: oninoyeyecoh*)
moyetztica *iv.* be
moyococotl *n.* insect bite
moyoleuhqui *adj.* in love
moyollopanqui *adj.* in love
moyollotepitztiliani *adj.* long-suffering, patient; intolerant
moyoni *iv.* swarm (*Preterit: onimoyon*)
moyotl *n.* mosquito
moztla *n.* tomorrow
moztla teotlac *adv.* tomorrow afternoon
moztlacayotl *n.* future
moztlati *iv.* arrive the next day (*Preterit: onimoztlat*)
moztlatia *iv.* arrive the next day (*Preterit: onimoztlatih*)
muchi *adj.* all; a lot, much

N

nacaayotl *n.* meat stew
nacacahua *iv.* abstain from eating meat (*Preterit: oninacacacauh*)
nacacahualiztli *n.* fasting, abstaining from eating meat
nacamulli *n.* meat dish
nacanamacani *n.* butcher
nacanamacoyan *n.* butcher shop
nacaocuilin *n.* maggot
nacaquixtiloni *n.* a utensil for extracting meat from a pot
nacatamalli *n.* meat tamale
nacatetl *adj.* naked

nacatl *n.* meat
nacatlaoyotl *n.* meat pie
nacatlapalollotl *n.* juice from meat
nacatlapatzcaayotl *n.* juice from meat
nacayocantli *n.* hip
nacayoh *adj.* fleshy, fat
nacayomihmiquiliztli *n.* palsy
nacayotia *reflex. v.* grow fat, gain weight
    (*Preterit: oninonacayotih*)
nacayotl *n.* flesh
nacazcocoliztli *n.* earache
nacazcuitlatl *n.* earwax
nacazeh *n.* listener
nacazhueyac *adj.* big-eared
nacazihta *tv.* look at someone with affection; look sideways
    (*Preterit: onitenacazihtac*)
nacazitta *tv.* look at someone with affection; look sideways
    (*Preterit: onitenacazittac*)
nacaztapal *adj.* deaf
nacaztli *n.* ear
nacaztzatza *adj.* deaf
nacaztzatzayotl *n.* deafness
nachcapanquetza *tv.* prefer (*Preterit: onitenachcapanquetz*)
nacicic *adv.* on the side, from the side
nacochtli *n.* earring
nactia *reflex. v.* stop; stay (*Preterit: oninonactih*)
nahnacatl *n.* mushroom
nahnahuati *iv.* have a venereal disease (*Preterit: oninahnahuatic*)
nahpa *adv.* four times
–nahuac *suff.* next to
nahuacopa *adv.* in Nahuatl
nahuahtequi *tv.* hug (*Preterit: onitenahuahtec*)
nahualcalaqui *iv.* enter secretly (*Preterit: oninahuacalacac*)

nahualcalaquiliztli *n.* act of entering secretly
nahualcaqui *tv.* guess someone's thoughts
  (*Preterit: onitenahualcac*)
nahualcui *tv.* steal (*Preterit: onitlanahualcuic*)
nahualhuia *tv.* cast a spell (*Preterit: onitenahualhuih*)
nahualiztli *n.* sorcery
nahuallazohtla *tv.* pretend to love someone
  (*Preterit: onitenahuallazohtlac*)
nahualli *n.* sorcerer, witch
nahuallotl *n.* sorcery
nahuatia *tv.* order, command; send word, inform
  (*Preterit: onitlanahuatih*)
nahuatillaliani *n.* lawmaker
nahuatillaliliztli *n.* constitution
nahuatillapaltiliztli *n.* validity
nahuatillapaltli *adj.* valid
nahuatilli *n.* duty; law
nahuatl *n.* good sounding; Nahuatl
nahuatlahtoa *iv.* speak Nahuatl (*Preterit: oninahuatlahtoh*)
nahuatlahtoani *n.* Nahuatl speaker
nahuatlahtoh *n.* interpreter; Nahuatl speaker
nahuatlahtolcalli *n.* Nahuatl language school
nahuatlahtolcopa *adv.* in Nahuatl
nahuatlahtolcuepa *iv.* translate (*Preterit: oninahualtlahtolcuep*)
nahuatlahtoliztli *n.* translation
nahuatlahtolli *n.* Nahuatl language
nahuatlahtoltlamachtilcalli *n.* Nahuatl language school
nahuatlamatiliztli *n.* Nahuatl culture
nahui *num.* four
–nal *loc. suff.* on the other side
–nalco *loc. suff.* on the other side
nalquixti *iv.* have diarrhea (*Preterit: oninalquixtic*)
nalquixtilli *n.* diarrhea

nalquizcacaqui *tv.* understand well (*Preterit: onitlanalquizcacac*)

nalquizcaitta *tv.* know or understand well
   (*Preterit: onitlaquizcaittac*)

nalquizcamati *tv.* know well (*Preterit: onitlanalquizcamat*)

naltic *adj.* fluorescent

naltoctic *adj.* clear, transparent

naltona *iv.* be clear, transparent; daytime (*Preterit: onaltonac*)

naltonac *adj.* clear, transparent

naltonahtimani *iv.* shine (*Preterit: onaltonatimanca*)

namaca *tv.* sell (*Preterit: onitlanamacac*)

namictia *tv.* adjust; equalize (*Preterit: onitlanamictih*)

namictli *n.* husband

nanacatl *n.* mushroom

nanahtli *n.* mother

nanahuatl *n.* leprosy; venereal disease; pustule; lump, swelling

nanatzca *iv.* creak (*Preterit: oninanatzcac*)

nanauhtli *n.* merchandise

nanquilia *tv.* answer (*Preterit: onitenanquilih*)

nantli *n.* mother

nanyotl *n.* motherhood; womb

napaloa *tv.* support; carry a child (*Preterit: onitlanapaloh*)

naranja xocotl *n.* orange

nauhcampa *n.* square

nauhcampa nacaceh *adj.* squared

nauhcuicanimeh *n.* quartet

naxca *n.* my property; it is mine

neahuiltiliztli *n.* entertainment, hobby, recreation, game

neahuiltiloni *n.* game, toy, anything that entertains

nealahualoyan *n.* slide, slippery spot

nealtilatl *n.* water for bathing; pool for public bath

nealtilcalli *n.* public bath

nealtiliztli *n.* act of bathing

nealtiloyan *n.* place where one bathes
neaxixaloyan *n.* urinal
necahualiztica *adv.* silently
necahualiztli *n.* silence
necaliliztli *n.* battle
necaliztli *n.* battle
necallotiloyan *n.* territory
necauhcayotl *n.* memento, memory, souvenir, remembrance; remains, trace
necauhtli *adj.* silent
necehuiliztli *n.* rest
necetiliztli *n.* unity
nechca *adv.* there
nechcacopa *adv.* thither, in that direction
nechcapa *adv.* there, there below
nechihchihualiztli *n.* manufacture, act o filmmaking; adornment
nechichitiloni *n.* nipple
nechicoliztli *n.* association
nechihualiztli *n.* event, occurrence; fact
nechipahualoyan *n.* Purgatory
neci *iv.* appear, seem (*Preterit: oninez*); *adj.* evident
necnimatic *adj.* humiliating
necnotecaliztli *n.* humility
necoc *adv.* on both sides
necoc yaotl *n.* traitor
necocmomaimati *adj.* ambidextrous
necoctetencatl *n.* kidney
neconi *adj.* desirable; beneficial; necessary; lovable
necuacehualpatlahuac *n.* hat
necuahuihuintil *n.* giddiness
necuanaliztli *n.* transfer

necuatl *n.* honey water, unfermented maguey juice
necuhpathli *n.* syrup
necuhtamallli *n.* tamale sweetened with honey
necuhtic *adj.* sweet
necuhtiliztli *n.* sweetness
necuhtlachihchihualpitzac *n.* gelatin
necuhtlachihchihualtic *n.* jam, jelly
necuhtlatzoyonilli *n.* molasses
necuhtli *n.* honey; unfermented maguey juice; pulque
necuilacatztli *n.* molasses
Necuiltonolacalquixohuayan *n.* Puerto Rico
neelehuiliztli *n.* selfishness
neellelquixtiliztli *n.* pastime
neh *pron.* I
nehcaliliztli *n.* battle
nehcaliztli *n.* battle
nehhua *pron.* I
nehhuatl *pron.* I
nehnemi *iv.* walk, go about (*Preterit: oninehnen*)
nehnemiliztepozcalli *n.* car
nehnemiliztepuzcalnemachilia *tv.* drive
    (*Preterit: oninehnemiliztepuzcalnemachilih*)
nehnemiliztepuzcalnemachiliani *n.* driver
nehnemiliztli *n.* trip, journey; pilgrimage
nehnemini *n.* traveler
nehnencachialoyan *n.* hotel, inn
nehnencachixqui *n.* innkeeper
nehnencatzintli *n.* pilgrim
nehnenqui *n.* traveler; nomad, vagabond
nehneuca *adv.* likewise, equally
nehneuhcayotl *n.* sameness, uniformity, equality
nehneuhqui *adj.* equal, same
nehtolli *n.* promise, vow

nehtoltiliztli *n.* vow
nehtotiliztli *n.* ballet; dance
nehtotiloyan *n.* dance hall; discotheque
nehuan *adv.* together
nehuecauiliztli *n.* delay
nehuehcatlachialoni *n.* compass
nehueililiztli *n.* arrogance, pride
nehuelyollotiloni *adj.* faithful, loyal
nehuentiliztli *n.* religious pilgrimage
nehuimatiloni *n.* conceit
neicaliliztli *n.* skirmish
neihuintiliztli *n.* drunkenness
neiihyotzacualiztli *n.* asthma
neixcuamotzompihuani *n.* tweezers (*eyebrow*)
neixcuitilamatl *n.* copy; libretto
neixcuitilli *n.* example, model
neixihtlacoliztli *n.* freckle
neixiptlatiliztli *n.* substitution; theatrical performance
neixnamiquiliztli *n.* contest
neixtlapaloliztica *adv.* recklessly
neizahuiliztli *n.* surprise
nel *adv.* truly
nelhuatl *n.* root
nelhuayotl *n.* root, base, foundation
nelhuicac *n.* sky, heaven
nelhuicactli *n.* sky, heaven
nelhuiliztli *n.* project; purpose; resolution
nelleltiliztli *n.* repentance
nelli *adj.* positive; true
nellimachiyotl *n.* vestige
neloa *tv.* mix, stir; rock (*Preterit: onitlaneloh*)
nelpiloni *n.* girdle, belt; sash
neltic *adj.* true

neltihtica *adv.* positively

neltilia *tv.* prove; testify; verify (*Preterit: onitlaneltilih*)

neltililoni *adj.* probable; verifiable

neltiliztemachtiani *n.* preacher

neltiliztenonotzani *n.* preacher

neltiliztli *n.* certainty; truth; verification

neltiloni *n.* verification

neltoca *tv.* believe (*Preterit: onitlaneltocac*)

neltoquiliztli *n.* belief, faith

nemacahualtiliztli *n.* divorce, separation

nemachilia *tv.* polish (*Preterit: onitlanemachilih*)

nemachiliani *n.* pilot

nemachiyohtiloni *n.* track

nemachtilizcehuillotl *n.* vacation (*school*)

nemachtiliztli *n.* lesson; study; teaching, instruction, training; prudence

nemachtilli *n.* study, learning

nemachtiloyan *n.* school

nemachtli *n.* trick

nemactilia *reflex. v.* grant (*Preterit: oninonemactilih*)

nemactiliztli *n.* marriage

nemactli *n.* gift

nemahmauhtiliztli *n.* fear (*felt by oneself*)

nemailpiloni *n.* handcuff, manacle

nemalhuiliztli *n.* decency; honesty; seriousness

nemalhuilli *adj.* serious

nemanepanoliztli *n.* wedding

nemapopohualoni *n.* towel

nemaquixtiliztli *n.* salvation

nemaquixtiloyan *n.* asylum, refuge

nematcatlahuanaliztli *n.* continence

nematcayotl *n.* civility, courtesy, manners

nematequilcaxitl *n.* washbowl

nematequiloni *n.* washbowl
nematihuani *n.* feeling, sensation
nematihuannextia *tv.* express condolences
 (*Preterit: onitenematihuannextih*)
nematihuannextiloni *n.* condolence
nematihuantlanextilli *n.* condolence
nematiliztli *n.* care, caution; honesty; skill
nematotopehuiliztli *n.* basketball
nemauhtiliztli *n.* cowardice
nemeyalnamacoyan *n.* dairy
nemi *iv.* live (*Preterit: oninen*)
nemian *n.* durational, lifespan
nemilia *tv.* think; premeditate (*Preterit: onitlanemilih*)
nemiliceh *n.* being
nemilizamatl *n.* biography; written history, chronicle
nemiliztlacualli *n.* provisions
nemiliztlahcuiloani *n.* chronicler, historian
nemiliztlahcuilolli *n.* written chronicle, history
nemiliztlahtollotl *n.* legend; oral history
nemiliztli *n.* life, existence; character
nemiliztoca *v.* follow or imitate someone's life
 (*Preterit: onitenemiliztocac*)
nemilizzotl *n.* experience
nemini *n.* inhabitant
nemocihuiliztli *n.* agony
nemohuayan *n.* dwelling, residence
nemomotzoloni *n.* rake
nemontemi *n.* five extra days of the indigenous calendar
nempanca *adv.* in vain
nen *adv.* in vain
nenacaztahtaconi *n.* q-tip
nenactiliztli *n.* stop; stay
nenahuatiliztli *n.* agreement, pact, treaty

nenamictiliztli *n.* marriage
nencayotl *n.* subsistence
nenechicoliztli *n.* assembly
nenecuilhuaztli *n.* seal
nenehuia *iv.* symbolize (*Preterit: oninenehuih*)
nenehuilia *tv.* weigh (*Preterit: onitlanenehuilih*)
nenehuiloni *n.* symbol
neneloa *tv.* mix (*Preterit: onitlaneneloh*)
nenemmictiliztli *n.* gesture, grimace, smirk
nenepanoliztli *n.* sex
nenepilli *n.* tongue
nenepilmaxaltic *n.* rumor monger
nenetl *n.* doll
neneuhca *adv.* likewise, equally
neneuhcayotl *n.* sameness, uniformity, equality
neneuhqui *adj.* same
neneuhtia *tv.* identify (*Preterit: onitlaneneuhtih*)
nennenqui *n.* loafer, good-for-nothing
nenomahuiliztli *n.* free will
nenonotzalizlti *n.* reconciliation
nenonotzaloyan *n.* auditorium, hall (*meeting*)
nenotzalli *n.* agreement
nenotzaltiliztli *n.* reconciliation
nenotztli *n.* decision, resolution
nenquixtia *tv.* waste (*Preterit: onitlanenquixtih*)
nenquiza *iv.* fail; work in vain; be unhappy (*Preterit: oninenquiz*)
nenquizaliztica *adv.* unfortunately
nenquizaliztli *n.* failure; misfortune
nenquizani *adj.* unfortunate
nenquizcatlamatiliztli *n.* useless knowledge
nenquizqui *adj.* unfortunate
nentahyotl *n.* paternal irresponsibility
nenti *iv.* fail (*Preterit: oninentic*)

nentlacatl *n.* worthless person
nentlamati *iv.* be concerned, worried (*Preterit: oninentlamat*)
nentlamatiliztli *n.* anguish, grief
nentoc *adj.* alive
nenya *adv.* in vain, uselessly
neocuiliztli *n.* hangover
neohtlamachtiloni *n.* itinerary
neohtlatocaliztli *n.* march
nepa *adv.* from there
nepahyacahuitzminallotl *n.* injection
nepanoa *tv.* investigate (*Preterit: onitlanepanoh*)
nepanotl *adj.* double; *adv.* mutually
nepantla tonalli *adv.* midday
nepantla tonatiuh *adv.* midday
–nepantlah *suff.* in the middle of
nepantlahtli *n.* middle
nepantlahyotl *n.* lunch
nepantlaquitl *n.* communal property
nepantlazohtla *reflex. v.* love one another
  (*Preterit: otitonepantlazohtlac*)
nepapan *adj.* various, diverse
nepapan tlacah *n.* different nations, ethnic group
nepechtequiliztli *n.* humility
nepiloloni *n.* handle
nequetzaliztli *n.* perplexity
nequetzalli *adj.* perplexed
nequi *tv.* want; desire sexually (*Preterit: onitlanec*)
nequittallo *n.* discovery
nequiztli *n.* something desirable
netatiliztli *n.* honesty
neteelehuiltilliztli *n.* longing, yearning
Netellalli *n.* Netherlands
netelohchiquiliztli *n.* friction

netemachiliztli *n.* hope
netemalaciahualiztli *n.* shower
netempohpoloani *n.* napkin
netencuepaliztli *n.* retraction
netennonotzaliztli *n.* contract
neteomatiliztli *n.* superstition
neteomatini *adj.* superstitious
neteomatqui *adj.* superstitious
neteotiliztli *n.* worship
netepiltzintiliztli *n.* adoption
netepiltzintilli *n.* adopted son
netequipacholiztli *n.* anguish
neteyaotiliztli *n.* debate
netimalquizaliztli *n.* oozing
netititlaniliztli *n.* message
netlacamatiliztli *n.* satisfaction
netlacatpapaquiliz *n.* birthday
netlacualizcahualtiliztli *n.* diet
netlacuilli *n.* debt; loan
netlahahualmicqui *n.* victim
netlahtolchicahualiztli *n.* affirmation
netlahtolmachtiloni *n.* grammar
netlahtolmelahualo *n.* notice
netlahtolneltiliztica *adj.* exactly
netlahtolpehpechtiliztli *n.* topic
netlahtoltemachtiloni *n.* grammar
netlahtoltequipacholiz *n.* innuendo
netlahuililoni *n.* lamp
netlamachtilli *n.* wealth, good fortune
netlampopoaloni *n.* toothbrush
netlancuihcuihuani *n.* toothpick
netlanehuiliztli *n.* excuse; loan
netlaneuhtilizcalli *n.* brothel, whorehouse

netlaneuhtilizlti *n.* prostitution
netlanyectiloni *n.* toothpick
netlapaloliztli *n.* boldness, audacity
netlatlaloloyan *n.* racetrack
netlatlaxililiztli *n.* abortion
netlazohcamatiliztli *n.* gratitude
netlazohtlaliztli *n.* self-esteem
netle *interj.* hey!
netloc *adv.* jointly, together
netocaihcuiloliztli *n.* signature
netoliniliztli *n.* lack; poverty
netoliniztli *n.* mercy
netzicoliztica *adv.* slowly
netzicoliztli *n.* slowness, sluggishness
netzinnamacoyan *n.* brothel, whorehouse
netzoncuiliztli *n.* revenge
netzotzonaliztli *n.* suspense
neuhcayotl *n.* breakfast
nexatl *n.* lye
nexayacapohpoaloni *n.* handkerchief
nexayotl *n.* water with limestone
nexcomitl *n.* pot for boiling corn
nexhuacayotl *n.* scab
nexicoliliztli *n.* envy
nexicoliztli *n.* envy
nexicolli *n.* envy; selfishness
nexiliztli *n.* appearance, manifestation
neximalcalli *n.* barber shop
neximaliztli *n.* shave
neximaloni *n.* razor; razor blade
nexitlapaloliztli *n.* recklessness
nexpaca *tv.* wash with lye (*Preterit: ontilanexpac*)
nextamalli *n.* corn dough

nextia *tv.* reveal, clarify; discover; invent (*Preterit: onitlanextih*)
nextic *adj.* ash colored, grey; blue
nextilia *tv.* manifest (*Preterit: onictenextilih*)
nextiloyan *n.* observatory
nextli *n.* ash
nexxoh *adj.* ashen
neyacapohpohualoni *n.* handkerchief
neyaocehuiliztli *n.* truce
neyaotlaliztli *n.* skirmish
neyectiloyan *n.* Purgatory
neyehyecoliztli *n.* exercise
neyexiliztli *n.* flatus, fart
neyocoyaliztli *n.* free will
neyolaliliztli *n.* solace
neyolcantlazohtlaliztli *n.* patriotism
neyolcantlazohtlani *n.* patriot
neyolcocoliztli *n.* repentance
neyolcocoltiliztli *n.* passion
neyolcuepaliztli *n.* change of heart, change of mind; repentance
neyolcuitiliztli *n.* confession
neyolehualoni *n.* enthusiasm, excitement; motive
neyoliximachiliztli *n.* conscience
neyolmiquiliztli *n.* horror
neyolnonotzaliztli *n.* meditation; imagination
neyolpololiztli *n.* doubt
nezahualiztli *n.* fast
nezcaliliztli *n.* ability; prudence, discreetness; resurgence
nezcayotia *tv.* mean, signify; express (*Preterit: onitlanezcayotih*)
nezcayotl *n.* sign
nezotlaliztli *n.* nausea
nezqui *adj.* evident
ni iuhqui *adv.* also
nican *adv.* here

nicancopa *adv.* hither
niltze *interj.* hello
niman *adv.* then, immediately
nimanic *adv.* immediately
nino *pron.* myself
nipa *adv.* through here; there; from there
Niponian *n.* Japan
Niponian chaneh *n.* Japanese person
Niponiantlahtolli *n.* Japanese language
nitlapahtia *tv.* repair (*Preterit: onitlapahtih*)
nixtamalli *n.* corn dough
no *conj.* also; *poss.* my
noca *adv.* while
nocalehcapo *n.* neighbor
nocalnahuac tlacatl *n.* neighbor
nochi *adj.* all
nochipa *adv.* always
nochtli *n.* cactus fruit, prickly pear
nocomatzin *interj.* general greeting: good morning, afternoon, evening
nocuel *adv.* again
nohhuian *adv.* everywhere
nohhuian macho *adj.* public, well-known
nohhuianyoh *adj.* universal
nohhuianyotica *adv.* generally
nohhuiyan *adv.* everywhere
nohmah *adv.* still, yet; spontaneously
nohmatca *adv.* still, yet
nohnotza *tv.* admonish, reprimand, counsel (*Preterit: onitenohnotz*)
nohpalli *n.* cactus
nohuan *adv.* with me
nohuanyolqui *n.* relative

noihqui *conj.* also
noihuan *conj.* also
Nolpopocayan *n.* Central America
nonca *adv.* while
noncuah *adv.* separately
nonochiliztli *n.* conversation
nonohtli *adj.* dumb (*mute*)
nonotza *tv.* talk with (*Preterit: onitenonotz*)
nontli *adj.* dumb (*mute*)
noquia *tv.* pour or spill liquid (*Preterit: onitlanoquih*);
    have diarrhea (*Preterit: onicnoquih*)
noquiliztli *n.* diarrhea
noquiloni *n.* laxative
notehuanyolqui *n.* relative
notzalli *n.* surname
noyuhqui *adj.* also
nozo *conj.* or

O

oc *adv.* still; not yet
ocachi *adv.* a little more; more
occalli *n.* cellar
occampa *adv.* from two places
occampa olinia *reflex. v.* stagger, totter
    (*Preterit: occampa ninolinih*)
occan *adv.* in two places
occe *adj.* another
occe tlamantli *pron.* something else
occenca ahmo *adv.* less
occepa *adv.* again
occequi *adj.* another
ocelotl *n.* jaguar; ocelot

ochpahuaztli *n.* broom
ochpantli *n.* road
oc hualca inic ahcualli *adj.* worse
oc ihuahtzinco *adv.* very early
ocnamacoyan *n.* pulque bar, bar
ocnemi *adj.* still living
ococentli *n.* pine cone; pineapple
ococenyollohtli *n.* pine nut
ococuauhcecenton *n.* pine cone; pineapple
ococuauhtlah *n.* pine grove
ococuizalli *n.* parrot
ocoicpalli *n.* chair made of pine
ocopetlatl *n.* fern
ocopilli *n.* torch made of pine branches
ocotl *n.* pine log; torch
ocotlah *n.* pine grove
ocotochin *n.* bobcat
ocotzotl *n.* liquidambar
octacatl *n.* measure of length, measuring stick;
    standard, model; role model
octacayotl *n.* height
octlahuanqui *adj.* drunk
octli *n.* fermented maguey juice, pulque
ocuia *reflex. v.* have a hangover (*Preterit: oninocuih*)
ocuilicpatl *n.* silk
ocuilin *n.* worm
oc ye cualli *adv.* better
oc yohuahtzinco *adv.* very early
ohcalnehnenqui *n.* gadabout, gossip-monger
ohcaltontli *n.* alley
ohmaxac *n.* at the crossroads, crossroads
ohmaxalco *n.* at the crossroads, crossroads
ohmaxalli *n.* crossroads, intersection

ohmiquilitl *n.* plant used for seasoning, *yerba santa*
ohpitzactli *n.* trail, path
ohtlamachiliztli *n.* method
ohtlamaxac *n.* at the crossroads, crossroads
ohtlamaxalli *n.* crossroads, intersection
ohtlatl *n.* type of plant, *otate*, bamboo
ohtlatoca *iv.* march (*Preterit: onohtlatocac*)
ohtlatocaliztli *n.* trip, journey, travel, pilgrimage
ohtlatocani *n.* traveler, one who makes a trip or journey,
    pilgrim
ohtli *n.* road, path, street
ohtlica *adv.* in the road
ohtlipan *adv.* in the road
ohtoca *iv.* travel, follow a road, march (*Preterit: oniohtocac*)
ohuanecuhtli *n.* cane or corn syrup
ohuaatl *n.* sugar cane juice
ohuatl *n.* sugar cane; corn stalk
ohui tepanchihualiztli *n.* disaster
ohui tepan yaliztli *n.* disaster
ohuihcaiihyotini *adj.* breathless
ohuihcan *n.* dungeon
ohuih *adj.* difficult; dangerous
ohuihcayotl *n.* difficulty; danger
ohxitl *n.* resin
olin *n.* movement, quake, stirring
olini *iv.* move, quake (*Preterit: oolin and oolinqui*)
olinia *tv.* move (*Preterit: onitlaolinih*)
olintli *n.* movement
ollama *iv.* play the indigenous rubber-ball game
    (*Preterit: onollan*)
ollamaliztli *n.* indigenous rubber-ball game
ollamani *n.* ball player
ollamia *reflex. v.* play ball (*Preterit: oninollamih*)

ollanqui *n.* ball player

olli *n.* rubber

ollotl *n.* center, middle

Olmecatl *n.* Olmec

ololiuhcyotl *n.* roundness

ololiuhqui *adj.* round

ololli *n.* ball, something round; heap, pile

ololohua *tv.* gather (*Preterit: onitlaololohuh*)

ololtic *adj.* round

olotl *n.* corn cob

oltemalacatl *n.* tire

omahcic *n.* mature

omahcic metztli *n.* full moon

ome *num.* two

ometlahtoleh *adj.* bilingual

ometlahtolloh *adj.* bilingual

ometlahtollotl *n.* bilingualism

omeyolloh *adj.* devious, two-faced

omeyollohua *reflex. v.* hesitate, waiver; doubt
    (*Preterit: oninomeyollohuac*)

omeyollohualiztli *n.* hesitation

omiceceyotl *n.* marrow

omicicuilli *n.* rib

omipatolli *n.* dice (*game*)

omitetl *n.* bone; needle

omitiliztli *n.* osteoporosis

omitl *n.* bone; needle

omixochitl *n.* lily

omochiuh *n.* event, occurrence

ompa *adv.* there, over there

ompehualiztli *n.* beginning; departure

onca *iv.* there is (*Preterit: oncatca*)

oncan *adv.* there
onoc *iv.* be lying down; be ill (*Preterit: ononoya and ononoca*)
onohuayan *n.* site
onoliztli *n.* bed; illness
onoyan *n.* bed
onteittaliztli *n.* visit
onteittani *n.* visitor
ontetocaitl *n.* nickname; surname
ontetoquiliani *n.* successor
ontetoquiliztli *n.* succession
ontocaitl *n.* surname
onyez *iv.* there will be
opahuac *adj.* hard
opanoc cahuitl *n.* past tense
opochmaitl *n.* left hand
opochmayeh *adj.* left-handed
opochtli *n.* left side; left hand; *adj.* left
oquichayutl *n.* sperm, semen
oquichconetl *n.* son
oquichehua *tv.* attack (*Preterit: onoquicheuh*)
oquichehualiztli *n.* attack
oquichehuani *n.* attacker; *adj.* aggressive
oquichhuah *adj.* married (*fem.*)
oquichhuia *tv.* tolerate (*Preterit: onitlaoquichhuih*)
oquichixhuiuhtli *n.* grandson
oquichmicqui *n.* widow; sperm, semen
oquichmihqui *n.* widow
oquichnacayoh *n.* strong, virile
oquichnacayotl *n.* male genitalia
oquichotl *n.* sperm, semen
oquichpilli *n.* son; child
oquichtli *n.* man; *adj.* male
oquichyollohtli *n.* virility, energy, courage

otahtli *n.* type of reed
otlatl *n.* bamboo
Otomitl *n.* person from Otompan, Otomí
otztia *iv.* become pregnant (*Preterit: onotztih*);
    tv. impregnate (*Preterit: oniteotztih*)
otztiliztli *n.* pregnancy
otztli *adj.* pregnant
otzyotl *n.* pregnancy
oxitl tlanechicolpahtli *n.* ointment
oyametl *n.* cedar
oza *tv.* anoint, rub on (*Preterit: oniteoz*)
ozomahtli *n.* monkey
Oztalian chaneh *n.* Australian
Oztlalian *n.* Australia
Oztlian *n.* Austria
Oztlian chaneh *n.* Austrian
oztocayotl *n.* mineral
oztomecacalli *n.* inn, hotel
oztomecatl *n.* merchant
oztotl *n.* cave
oztoyoh *adj.* full of caves

P

pa *tv.* color, dye, paint (*Preterit: onitlapah*)
paatla *tv.* dissolve (*Preterit: onitlapaatlac*)
paca *tv.* wash (*Preterit: onitlapac and onitlapacac*)
pacca *adv.* happily, joyfully
paccaahuiltia *iv.* play, frolic (*Preterit: onipacahuiltih*)
paccaahuiltini *adj.* playful
paccanemiliztli *n.* peace
paccatzatzilia *tv.* acclaim, cheer (*Preterit: onitepaccatzatzilih*)

paccayeliztli *n.* health

pachihuia *reflex. v.* spy (*Preterit: onicnopachihuih*)

pachoa *tv.* govern, manage; hug, squeeze someone
(*Preterit: onitepachoh*); cover (*Preterit: onitlapachoh*);
reflex. v. approach, draw near (*Preterit: oninopachoh*)

pachtic *adj.* warped; sunken

pacqui *adj.* happy, joyful

pactia *iv.* enjoy something (*Preterit: onicpactih*);
tv. please (*Preterit: onitepactih*)

pactinemi *iv.* be in good health (*Preterit: onipactinen*);
adj. exuberant; healthy

pactinemiliztli *n.* health; exuberance

pacyotl *n.* joy, happiness

pahatliliztli *n.* act of taking medication; dose, potion

pahca *adv.* happily

pahcaahuiltia *iv.* play, frolic (*Preterit: oniphacahuiltih*)

pahcaahuiltini *adj.* playful

pahcalli *n.* pharmacy

pahcanemiliztli *n.* peace; good health

pahcatzahtzilia *tv.* acclaim, cheer (*Preterit: onitepaccatzahtzilih*)

pahcayeliztli *n.* health

pahchihchihua *tv.* prepare a remedy (*Preterit: onipahchihchiuh*)

pahchihchiuhqui *n.* pharmacist

pahchihua *tv.* prepare a remedy (*Preterit: onpahchiuh*)

pahixmatqui *n.* herbalist

pahmatzopinia *tv.* vaccinate (*Preterit: onitepahmatzopinih*)

pahyo *n.* scarf, shawl; handkerchief

pahpaltic *adj.* wet

pahpatla *n.* banana leaf

pahpiani *n.* pharmacist

pahqui *adj.* happy, joyful

pahtelolohtontli *n.* pill

pahti *iv.* get well (*Preterit: onipahtic*)

pahtia *tv.* cure (*Preterit: onitepahtih*)
pahtic *adj.* cured
pahtiloni *adj.* curable
pahtli *n.* medicine, remedy, cure
pahyacahuitzmina *tv.* inject (*Preterit: onitepahyacahuitzmin*)
pahyo *n.* napkin
pahzoltic *adj.* entangled
paina *iv.* run fast (*Preterit: onipain*)
painaliztli *n.* speed
painalli *adj.* fast, prompt, quick
painaltlecopatl *n.* post office
painani *n.* messenger
–pal *suff.* by means of
palancapozahualiztli *n.* abscess, tumor
palancatotoltetl *n.* rotten egg
palani *v.* trot, spoil (*Preterit: onipalan*)
palaniliztli *n.* pus
palanqui *adj.* rotten, spoiled
palaxtli *n.* infection, sore, ulcer
palehuia *tv.* help (*Preterit: onitepalehuih*)
paltic *adj.* wet
pamitl *n.* flag, banner
–pampa *suff.* on account of
–pan *suff.* in, place where
panahuia *tv.* subjugate; surpass (*Preterit: onitepanahuih*)
panahuiltia *tv.* postpone (*Preterit: onitlapanahuiltih*);
    prefer (*Preterit: onicpanahuiltih*)
panatl *n.* honeycomb
pancholoa *iv.* jump (*Preterit: onipancholoh*)
panchololiztli *n.* jump
panhuetzi *iv.* ascend (*Petereit: onipanhuetz*)
pani *adv.* up
paninezqui *adj.* obvious

pano *iv.* pass (*Preterit: onipanoc*)
panoliztli *n.* crossing
panolti *interj.* hello
panoltihtzino *interj.* hello (*reverential*)
panoni *n.* passenger (*on a ship*)
pantlaxilia *tv.* reveal a secret (*Preterit: onictepantlaxilih*)
pantlaza *tv.* reveal a secret (*Preterit: onicpantlaz*)
pantli *n.* flag, banner
pantzin *n.* bread
papahtli *n.* long hair
papal *adj.* gossipy, talkative
papalchihua *iv.* gossip, chatter, exaggerate, lie
     (*Preterit: onipapalchiuh*)
papallotl *n.* chatter
papaloa *tv.* lick (*Preterit: onitlapapaloh*)
papalohua *tv.* lick (*Preterit: onitlapahpalouh*)
papalotl *n.* butterfly; kite
papalotontli *n.* small butterfly, moth
papas *n.* potato
papatla *tv.* change, change continuously
     (*Preterit: onitlapapatlac*)
papatlaca *iv.* shiver; vibrate (*Preterit: onipapatlacac*)
papatlatza *reflex. v.* flutter, flap the arms like wings
     (*Preterit: oninopapatlaz*)
papatztic *adj.* spongy
paqui *iv.* be happy (*Preterit: onipac*)
paquiliztica *adv.* with pleasure
paquiliztli *n.* happiness, joy
paquini *adj.* happy
pati *iv.* melt (*Preterit: opat*)
patitl *n.* price
patiuhtli *n.* price; wage
patiyoh *n.* expensive

patiyotl *n.* price, value; wage
patiyotlalia *tv.* appraise (*Preterit: onitlapatiyotlalih*)
patla *tv.* change (*Preterit: onitlapatlac*)
patlac *adj.* wide
patlachohua *tv.* crush (*Preterit: onitlapatlachouh*)
patlachtic *adj.* crushed
patlactic *adj.* very wide
patlahuac *adj.* wide
patlani *iv.* fly (*Preterit: onipatlan*)
patlaniliztli *n.* flight
patlanilli *n.* flight
patlanilizcaxitl *n.* flying saucer
patlanizcaxitl *n.* flying saucer
patlaniztepozcalli *n.* airplane
patlantiquiza *iv.* leave with haste; jump, leap
  (*Preterit: onipatlantiquiz*)
patoani *n.* gambler
patolli *n.* a type of dice game
patox *n.* duck
patzca *tv.* wring, squeeze (*Preterit: onitlapatzcac*)
patzcalli *n.* traditional meal for Dia de Muertos (*Day of
  the Dead*)
patzcatl *n.* juice
patzmicqui *adj.* irritable; fatigued
patzmictli *n.* anger; bad mood
patzmiqui *iv.* be angry; be sad (*Preterit: onipatzmic*)
paxalolli *n.* stroll, outing
payatl *n.* caterpillar; worm
pazaloa *tv.* tangle (*Preterit: onitlapazaloh*)
pehpechtli *n.* mattress; cover, saddle blanket, saddle
pehpena *n.* select, pick
pehua *iv.* begin (*Preterit: onipeuh*); *tv.* defeat
  (*Preterit: onitepeuh*)

pehualiztli *n.* beginning, source, origin; cause
pehuani *adj.* initial
peltic *adj.* spacious
pepechtli *n.* mattress; cover
pepetla *tv.* comb (*Preterit: onitepepetlac*)
pepetotl *n.* top, toy
pepeyoctli *n.* pendant; tick
pepeyolcuahuitl *n.* poplar
petlacalli *n.* basket, container; urn
petlani *iv.* shine (*Preterit: onipetlan*)
petzoa *tv.* shine, polish (*Preterit: onitlapetzoh*)
petztic *adj.* shiny, polished
petztli *n.* pyrite; shiny stone used for making mirrors
peuhcayotl *n.* origin
pexohuia *tv.* weigh (*Preterit: onitlapexohuih*)
peyotl *n.* peyote
pezohtli *n.* badger
pia *tv.* have; guard (*Preterit: onitlapix*)
piaztic *adj.* slender, svelte
piccatl *n.* covering, wrapping
picietl *n.* tobacco
picihyatl *n.* tobacco leaf
pilahuiltia *iv.* play with children (*Preterit: onipilahuiltih*)
pilcac *adj.* hanging
pilhuah *n.* parent; *adj.* pregnant
pilli *n.* child; noble (*Plural: pipiltin*)
pilloh *adj.* childlike
pillotl *n.* nobility; things associated with children
pilmamah *n.* babysitter
piloa *tv.* hang (*Preterit: onitlapiloh*)
pilpohtli *n.* wife (*first*)
pilpotl *n.* wife (*first*)
piltia *iv.* be born (*Preterit: onipiltih and onipiltiac*)

piltian *adv.* at an early age, during childhood

piltic *n.* gentleman; *adj.* elegant, noble; fine, thin; tender

pilticayotl *n.* nobility, dignity, elegance

piltzintia *reflex. v.* adopt (*Preterit: oninotepiltzintih*)

pinacatl *n.* black beetle

pinahua *iv.* be ashamed, embarrassed (*Preterit: onipinahuac and onipinauh*)

pinahuac *adj.* ashamed

pinahuaca *adv.* with shame

pinahualiztli *n.* shame, embarrassment

pinauhtic *adj.* humiliating

pinauhtica *adv.* with shame

pinauhtlahtolli *n.* obscenity, profanity

pinolli *n.* sweetened flour made from ground toasted corn; ground corn

pinotl *n.* stranger, foreigner

pinotlahtoa *iv.* speak a foreign language (*Preterit: onipinotlahtoh*)

piocalli *n.* chicken coop

pioxcalli *n.* chicken coop

pipica *iv.* drip (*Preterit: opipicac*)

pipicaliztli *n.* dripping

pipillotl *n.* childishness; foolishness

pipilnequi *reflex. v.* claim to be younger (*Preterit: oninopipilnec*)

pipilolli *n.* earring

pipinqui *adj.* coppery

pipiolin *n.* wild bee

piptontli *n.* great grandmother

piquia *tv.* wrap (*Preterit: onitlapiquih*)

pitza *tv.* blow (*Preterit: nitlapitz*)

pitzahua *iv.* be or become thin, narrow (*Preterit: onipitzahuac*)

pitzahuac *adj.* skinny, thin, slender, narrow

pitzahuac etl *n.* lentil

pitzini *iv.* open, crack, split (*Preterit: opitzin*)

pitzoa *tv.* kiss (*Preterit: onitepitzoh*)

pitzocalli *n.* pigpen

pitzometzhuatzalli *n.* ham, bacon

pitzonacatl *n.* pork

pitzotl *n.* pig

pitzotlahtolli *n.* foul language

pitztli *n.* bone; seed; pepita

pixahuiliztli *n.* snowfall

pixca *iv.* pick, harvest (*Preteri: onipixcac*)

pixoa *tv.* plant seeds, sow (*Preterit: onitlapixoh*)

pixquitl *n.* harvest

pochmaitl *n.* left hand

pochotl *n.* ceiba tree

pochtecati *iv.* sell merchandise, be involved in commerce
(*Preterit: onipochtecatic*)

pochtecatl *n.* merchant

pochtli *n.* left hand

poctic *adj.* smoked; brownish

poctli *n.* smoke

pocyotl *n.* smoke, vapor

pohpolhuia *tv.* forgive (*Preterit: onitetlapohpolhuih*)

pohpoztequi *tv.* break; fold (*Preterit: onitlapohpoztec*)

pohtli *n.* companion, friend

pohua *tv.* count; tell; read (*Preterit: onitlapouh*)

pohualiztli *n.* count; reading; telling

pohualiztli itlanonotzaloni *n.* telephone number

pohui *iv.* be respected, esteemed, valued (*Preterit: onipouh*);
tetech ~ belong to (*Preterit: tetech onipouh*)

polantototl *n.* canary

polihui *iv.* perish, die (*Preterit: onipoliuh*)

polihuini *adj.* perishable, mortal
poliuhqui *adj.* lost
polo *n.* donkey
poloa *tv.* conquer (*Preterit: onitepoloh*); *iv.* lose, be defeated
poloni *iv.* stammer, stutter (*Preterit: onipolon*)
Polonian *n.* Poland
Polonian chaneh *n.* Pole
Poloniantlahtolli *n.* language
polozacatl *n.* hay
popoca *iv.* smoke (*Preterit: onipopocac*)
popocacitlalin *n.* comet
popochcomitl *n.* incense vessel
popochtli *n.* incense; perfume
popolhuia *tv.* forgive (*Preterit; onitetlapopolhuih*)
popoloc *adj.* talkative
popoloca *iv.* speak unintelligibly; speak a foreign language
    (*Preterit: onipopolocac*)
popolocatl *adj.* barbaric
popolocayotl *n.* barbarism
popolochtli *n.* bubble
popoquihtli *n.* firefly
popotl *n.* straw
popoyacpil *adj.* dark
popoyecatl *n.* firefly
popoyotl *adj.* blind
popozoca *iv.* foam (*Preterit: opopozocac*)
popozoctli *n.* foam, froth
potoni *iv.* smell bad, stink (*Preterit: onipoton*)
potoniliztli *n.* foul smell
potonqui *adj.* having a foul odor, rotten
potzalli *n.* mound
poxacuatl *n.* roadrunner
poxcahui *iv.* become moldy; rusty (*Preterit: opoxcauh*)

poxcauhqui *adj.* moldy; rusty (*metals*)
poyec *adj.* salty
poyelia *tv.* add salt to food; (*Preterit: onitlapoyelih*)
poyelpahtic *adj.* very salty
poyotl *n.* something evil
poyoxcalli *n.* chicken coop
pozactic *adj.* swollen
pozahua *tv.* inflate something (*Preterit: onitlapozahuac*);
    iv. swell (*Preterit: onipozahuac*)
pozahuac *adj.* swollen
pozahui *impers. v.* swell (*Preterit: opozauh*)
pozahuiliztli n. swelling, inflamation
pozolli *n.* stew; foam rubber
pozonalloh *adj.* foamy
pozoncayotl *n.* foam
pozoni *iv.* boil (*Preterit: opozon*)
pozonia *tv.* cook; boil (*Preterit: onitlapozonih*)
pozonqui *adj.* boiled; upset
poztecqui *adj.* broken
poztehqui *adj.* broken
poztequi *iv.* break something (*Preterit: onitlapoztec*)
putzalli *n.* mound

Q

quechcochtetl *n.* nape
quechcochtli *n.* nape
quechcuahyotl *n.* collarbone
quecholli *n.* flamingo, spoonbill
quechpalli *n.* lock of hair on the back of the neck
quechquemitl/quechquemmitl *n.* a type of blouse
quechtepolli *n.* nape
quechtetl *n.* neck, collar

quechtli *n.* neck, collar
quechtzontli *n.* mane
quehqueleh *adj.* ticklish
quehquelli *n.* ticklishness
quehqueloa *tv.* tickle; mock (*onitequehqueloh*);
    reflex. v. make a mistake (*oninoquehqueloh*)
quehqueloliztli *n.* joke, mockery
quehtolli *n.* gums
quemah *adv.* yes
quemi *tv.* dress (*Preterit: onicquen*)
quemitl/quemmitl *n.* clothing; blanket
quemmach *interr. adv.* How is it possible?
quemman *adv.* sometimes; *interr. adv.* At what time? When?
quemmaniyan *adv.* sometimes; some day
quenamih *interr. adv.* In what condition?
quenin *adv.* how
quentecemitquiani *n.* politician
quentecemitquiliztli *n.* politics
quentia *tv.* dress (*Preterit: onitequentih*)
quequelli *n.* ticklishness
quequetzolli *n.* heel
quequeyolli *n.* ankle
quequeza *tv.* trample (*Preterit: onitlaquequez*);
    reflex. v. mate (*birds*), pair (*Preterit: omoquequez*)
quetza *tv.* raise, erect (*Preterit: onitlaquetz*)
quetzalcacehuaztli *n.* elaborate fan used in ceremonies
quetzalchalchihuitl *n.* blue or green precious stone
quetzalhuitztli *n.* feather of the quetzal bird
quetzalichtli *n.* a type of maguey
quetzalitztli *n.* nephrite; emerald
quetzaliztli *n.* act of leaving
quetzalli *n.* quetzal feather; *adj.* beautiful
quetzaltic *adj.* beautiful

quetzaltototl *n.* peacock; quetzal bird
quetzalyollotl *n.* generous, good-hearted
quexquich *interr. pron.* How much?
quexquichcauh *adv.* Until when?
quexquitzahuia *reflex. v.* reflect (*Preterit: oninoquexquitzahuih*)
quezqui *interr. pron.* How many? How much?
quezquican *adv.* In how many places? In how many parts?
quezquipa *adv.* How many times?
queztli *n.* crotch
quiahuatl *n.* door; rainwater
quiahuatlah *n.* rainy season
quiahui *iv.* rain (*Preterit: oquiauh*)
quiahuitl *n.* rain
quicempaccayotl *n.* happiness; prosperity
quicempahcayotl *n.* happiness; prosperity
quihtoznequi *iv.* it means
quilatl *n.* water with herbs, vegetable soup
quilitl *n.* weed; vegetable; *adj.* green
quilmach *adv.* perhaps, possibly
quilmaitl *n.* leaf
quilmilli *n.* garden, vegetable patch, orchard
quiltic *adj.* green
quiltototl *n.* parrot, parakeet
quiltonilli *n.* vegetable
quimatini *adj.* crafty
quimichin *n.* mouse
quimichpatlan *n.* bat
quimilli *n.* package, wrapping
quimiloa *tv.* cover; wrap (*Preterit: onitlaquimiloh*)
quimiloloni *n.* case
quimmach *adv.* perhaps, possibly
quin *adv.* then, afterwards

quin axcan *adv.* barely; a short while ago
quin izqui *adv.* a short time ago
quin onez *adj.* modern
quin tlacatiliztli *n.* posterity, future generation
quinachic *adv.* a brief while ago; previously
quinametl *n.* giant
quinaxcatica *adv.* currently
quinez *adj.* modern
quinopiltia *tv.* congratulate (*Preterit: onicnopiltih*)
quintepan *adv.* later
quiotl *n.* maguey stalk
quiquiztli *n.* conch shell (*used as a musical instrument*)
quiquiztozcapanahuia *iv.* make a telephone call, phone (*Preterit: oniquiquiztozcapanahuih*)
quiquiztozcapanahuilli *n.* telephone call
quiquiztozcapanahuiloyan *n.* telephone office
quiquiztozcapanauhqui *n.* telephone operator
quitzquia *tv.* support (*Preterit: onitlaquitzquih*)
quixohuayan *n.* exit
quixtia *tv.* copy; extract (*Preterit: onitlaquixtih*); imitate (*Preterit: onitequixtih*)
quiyahuac *adv.* outside
quiza *iv.* leave (*Preterit: oniquiz*)
quizaliztli *n.* migration, act of leaving
quizayan *n.* origin, beginning

R
Romatlahtolli *n.* Romance language
Rusian *n.* Russia
Rusian chaneh/chane *n.* Russian
Rusiantlahtolli *n.* Russian language

T

tacatli *n.* sandal

tacatl *n.* bush, shrub; basil

tahtia *iv.* become a father (*Preterit: ontahtih*)

tahtli *n.* father

talhuellotl *n.* impatience

talyohualloh *adj.* gloomy

tamachihua *tv.* measure; weigh (*Preterit: onitlatamachiuh*)

tamalchihua *tv.* make tamales (*Preterit: onitamalchiuh*)

tamalli *n.* tamale

tamaloa *iv.* make tamales (*Preterit: onitamaloh*)

tamazolin/tamazollin *n.* toad

tanahtli *n.* a basket with two handles

tancaxtic *adj.* slow

tapachtli *n.* sea shell

tapahzolli *n.* nest

tapalcatl *n.* piece of broken pottery, sherd

tapalcatlapantli *n.* tile roof

tapalcaxpichtli *n.* roofing tile

tapayaxin *n.* chameleon

tapayolli *n.* ball

tapayoltic *adj.* round

tatapahtli *n.* cloth, rag

tatapalihuiztli *n.* welt

tauhca *n.* fame

te– *poss.* someone's, people's; *pron.* someone; people

teaahuilia *tv.* have fun (*Preterit: oniteaahulih*)

teaahuililiztli *n.* fun

teachcauh *n.* older brother

teahcualihtoliztli *n.* curse

teamanaliztli *n.* restlessness, uneasiness

teaxcapantlazohtlaliztli *n.* patriotism

teaxcapantlazohtlani *n.* patriot
teca *reflex. v.* lie down (*Preterit: oninotecac*); *tv.* spread, smear (*Preterit: onitlatecac*); *prep.* regarding someone, about someone (*disparagingly*)
tecactli *n.* sandal, shoe
tecalli *n.* alabaster
tecaltzacualoyan *n.* dungeon
tecaltzacuilli *n.* convict, prisoner
tecanetopehualiztli *n.* hoax, joke
tecapactli *n.* slap
tecapani *tv.* slap (*Preterit: onitetecapan*)
tecciztli *n.* seashell; trumpet
tecciztozcapanahuiloyan *n.* telephone office
teceliliztli *n.* reception
tecelilli *n.* guest
tecelilloh *adj.* hospitable
tecelillotl *n.* hospitality
teceliloyan *n.* hospice
tecemicniuh *adj.* kind, affable
tecemicniuhyotl *n.* kindness
tecemitqui *n.* government
–tech *suff.* regarding, next to
techachamahualiztli *n.* flattery
techalotl *n.* squirrel
techiahuacatlatlatiloni *n.* gasoline
techializtli *n.* hope; illusion
techichi *n.* a type of dog
teci *tv.* grind (*Preterit: onitlatez*)
tecihuauh *n.* wife
tecihui *impers. v.* hail falls (*Preterit: oticihuic*)
tecihuitl *n.* hail
tecihuitl huetzi *impers. v.* it is hailing (*Preterit: tecihuitl ohuetz*)
tecilli *n.* cocoon

teciyotl *n.* honor
tecoanotzaliztli *n.* invitation
tecoanotzqui *n.* host
tecochitiani *n.* innkeeper
tecochtlayecchiuhtli *n.* mausoleum
tecochtlazalli *adj.* drugged
tecochtlazantli *n.* drug; narcotic
tecochtli *n.* guest; pit, grave
tecohtli *n.* owner
tecolli *n.* charcoal
tecolotl *n.* owl
tecomatl *n.* container, jug, clay pot
teconalchichiquiloni *n.* pencil sharpener
teconalli *n.* pencil
tecotonaliztli *n.* pinch
tecpan *n.* palace
tecpancalli *n.* palace
tecpantlacah *n.* those in the service of the palace
tecpantlapiquini *n.* politician
tecpatl *n.* flint
tecpillahtolli *n.* formal speech
tecpiltic *adj.* courteous, well-mannered
tecpin *n.* flea
tecpoa *iv.* announce, proclaim (*Preterit: ontecpoh*)
tecpoyotl *n.* town crier
tecpoyotlahtolli *n.* announcement, proclamation
tectli *n.* rattlesnake
tecuacan *n.* capital city
tecuacuilli *n.* idol
tecualiztli *n.* bite
tecuancoatl *n.* rattlesnake
tecuancocoyaliztli *n.* hydrophobia, rabies
tecuani *n.* beast, dangerous animal

tecuanyotl *n.* ferociousness
tecuhtlahcuiloh *n.* notary public
tecuhtlahcuiloloyan *n.* notary's office
tecuhtlahtoh *n.* judge, magistrate; senator
tecuhtlahtoliztli *n.* senate
tecuhtlahtoloyan *n.* forum
tecuhtli *n.* lord (*Plural: tetecuhtin*)
tecuhyotl *n.* lordship
tecuicanamiquiliztli *n.* concert (*song*)
tecuicihtli *n.* crab
tecuilontiani *n.* active homosexual partner; bisexual
tecuitlatl *n.* algae, spirulina
tecuixin *n.* alligator
teelleltilizlti *n.* hindrance, obstacle
teextli *n.* man's brother–in-law
teh *pron.* you (*Sing.*)
tehhua *pron.* you (*Sing.*)
tehhuantin *pron.* we
tehhuatl *pron.* you (*Sing.*)
tehpochtli *n.* dull person
tehuanyolcayotl *n.* blood relationship
tehuanyollatlacolli/tehuanyotlatlacolli *n.* incest
tehuanyolqui *n.* blood relative
tehuapahualiztli *n.* education
tehuehuetzquitiani *n.* clown, comedian, comic; *adj.* witty
tehuellamachtih *adj.* pleasurable
tehuetzquitiani *n.* clown, comedian
tehuiconi *n.* bus
tehuicpanehualli *n.* riot, uprising
tehuilotl *n.* crystal; glass
tehuiltic *adj.* glossy
tehuitequi *tv.* wound (*Preterit: onitehuitec*)
teiccauh *n.* younger brother

teicneliliztli *n.* kindness, charity
teicneliloni *n.* privilege
teicniuhnechicoliztli *n.* party, social gathering
teicnoihtaliztli *n.* mercy
teicnoihtani *adj.* merciful
teicnoittaliztli *n.* mercy
teicnotecaliztli *n.* humiliation
teicnottani *adj.* merciful
teihcihuitiliztli *n.* hurry
teihcuiloani *n.* lithographer
teihtaliztli *n.* visit
teihuintih *adj.* intoxicating
teiihyotzacuani *adj.* suffocating
teilhuia *tv.* accuse (*Preterit: oniteteilhuih*)
teilnamiqui *tv.* mention (*Preterit: oniteilnamic*)
teilnamiquiliztli *n.* mention
teilpiloyan *n.* jail, prison
teittaliztli *n.* visit
teitztli *n.* glass
teixcotzinco *interj.* excuse me
teixcuepa *tv.* deceive, swindle, trick (*Preterit: oniteixcuep*)
teixiliztli *n.* lynching
teixiptlaamatl *n.* photograph
teixmachtia *tv.* present (*Preterit: oniteixmachtih*)
teixneloliztli *n.* chaos, disorder
teixnotza *tv.* wink (*Preterit: oniteixnotz*)
teixpahtiani *n.* ophthalmologist
teixpahtih *n.* ophthalmologist
teixpan *adv.* publicly, in front of people
teixpantlaliliztli *n.* presentation
teixpantlanamaquiliztli *n.* auction
teixpanyotl *n.* public
teixpehualiztli *n.* invasion

teixpehualtiani *n.* invader
teixquetzaliztli *n.* election
teixtlahtoa *tv.* wink (*Preterit: oniteixtlahtoh*)
teixhui *n.* grandchild
teixhuiuh *n.* grandchild
teizahuiliztl *n.* admiration
teiztlacahuiani *n.* impostor
tel *conj.* but
telchihua *tv.* hate, despise (*Preterit: onitetelchiuh*)
telchitl *n.* joy at someone else's misfortune
telolohpahtli *n.* pill
teloloktopehualiztlapechtli *n.* billiard table
telpocatl *n.* young man
telpochcalli *n.* school, college, university
telpochcayotl *n.* youth
telpochtli *n.* young man (*Plural: telpopochtin*)
tema *reflex. v.* take a steam bath (*Preterit: oninoten*);
    tv. place, put (*Preterit: onitlaten*)
temacahuiliztli *n.* license
temacehual *n.* vassal
temachiltiliztli *n.* information
temachtiani *n.* teacher
temachtihqui *n.* teacher
temachtilcalli *n.* school
temachtilli *n.* lesson
temachtiloyan *n.* school
temachtli *n.* trust
temachyotl *n.* trust
temahmauhtih *adj.* terrifying, horrible
temahmauhtiliztli *n.* threat; fear (*felt by others*)
temahmazohualtia *tv.* crucify (*Preterit: onitemahmazohualtih*)
temahmazohualtiliztli *n.* crucifixion
temahuac *adj.* infectious

temahualiztli *n.* infection; pollution, contamination
temahualli *adj.* infected
temalacatl *n.* stone wheel, wheel
temalacatlatlehcahuiloni *n.* pulley
temalli *n.* pus; infection
temalloa *iv.* get filled with pus (*Preterit: otemalloac*)
temalloh *adj.* having pus
temamatiliztli *n.* intestinal obstruction (*empacho*); indigestion
temamatlatl *n.* stone stairway
temanahuiliztli *n.* protection
temaquixtiani *n.* savior, liberator
temaquixtihqui *n.* savior, liberator
temaquixtiliztli *n.* liberty; salvation, liberation; preservation
temaquixtiloni *n.* preservative
tematlatl *n.* sling, slingshot
temauhcaittani *adj.* shy, unsociable
temauhtih *adj.* scary, frightful
temazcalli *n.* steam bath
temecahuiteconi *n.* whip
temecatl *n.* vine
temetztepilolli *n.* plumb
temetztli *n.* clay pot; lead
temictih *adj.* fatal
temictli *n.* dream
temimilo *iv.* roll (*Preterit: onitemimiloc*)
temiqui *iv.* dream (*Preterit: onitemic*)
temitia *tv.* fill, stuff (*Preterit: onitlatemitih*)
temmina *tv.* peck at; sting (*Preterit: onitetemmin*)
temo *iv.* descend (*Preterit: onitemoc*)
temoa *tv.* look for (*Preterit: ontlatemoh*)
temohuia *tv.* lower; digest (*Preterit: onitlatemohuih*)
temolin *n.* gadfly, horsefly
temoliztli *n.* descent

temolotl *n.* stone for grinding chile pepper

temoxtli ehecatl *n.* sickness, pestilence

tempilli *n.* beak

tempiqui *reflex. v.* close one's mouth (*Preterit: oninotempic*)

tempitzoa *tv.* kiss (*Preterit: onitetempitzoh*)

tempohpoaloni *n.* napkin

tempohua *tv.* spell; recite or say something from memory (*Preterit: onitlatempouh*)

tena *iv.* groan, moan (*Preterit: oniten*)

tenacayotetequiliztli *n.* autopsy

tenacazpahtiani *n.* ear doctor

tenacazpahtih *n.* ear doctor

tenahuatilli *n.* law, order

tenaliztli *n.* groan

tenamaztli *n.* three stones used to support a pot; triplets

tenamic *n.* spouse

tenamicqui *n.* adversary, rival

tenamihqui *n.* adversary, rival

tenamiquiliztli *n.* meeting, encounter

tenamiquini *n.* opponent

tenamitl *n.* wall

tenanquiahuatl *n.* outskirts

tenanyoh *n.* having walls; *adj.* maternal

tenayotl *n.* saliva

tencahualli *n.* leftovers (*from a meal*)

tencapania *reflex. v.* chomp (*Preterit: ninotencapanih*)

tenchalli *n.* chin

tenchichinalpocyo *n.* cigar

tencuacua *adj.* biting

tencualaconi *n.* bib

teneh *adj.* sharp

teneh tlahtoleh *adj.* talkative

tenehua *tv.* promise; say (*Preterit: onitlateneuh*)

tenehualiztli *n.* rumor
tenemactli *n.* gift
tenemauhyotl *n.* terror
tenemilizmachiliztli *n.* anthropology
tenemilizmatiliztli *n.* anthropology
tenemilizmatini *n.* anthropologist
tenemmacatica *adv.* freely
tenemmaco *adj.* complimentary, free
tenenepilcuappachoa *tv.* gag (*Preterit: onitenenepilcuappachoh*)
tenenepilpacholoni *n.* gag
tenexpololli *n.* mortar
tenextetl *n.* limestone
tenextlazaloloni *n.* planer, trowel
tenextli *n.* limestone
tenexzoquitl *n.* mortar
teneyeyecoltiliztli *n.* temptation
tenhuitztli *n.* beak
tenihtoa *tv.* spell (*Preterit: ontilatenihtoh*)
teniza *iv.* have breakfast (*Preterit: oniteniz*)
tenizaloni *n.* lunch
tennamiqui *tv.* kiss (*Preterit: onitetennamic*)
Tenochcatl *n.* Aztec from Tenochtitlan
tenonotzaloni *n.* telephone
tenpopocalotl *n.* cigar
tenqui *adj.* full, stuffed
tentlacihuiztli *n.* craving; snack
tentlahueliloc *adj.* using crude language
tentli *n.* edge; lip; margin; lid
tentzacua *n.* plug, cork, cover
tentzitzipitlahtoa *iv.* lisp (*Preterit: onitentzitzipitlahtoh*),
    nenempochtlahtoa (*Preterit:*
tentzoniztalli *n.* grey hair on beard
tentzontli *n.* mustache

tentzoyoh *adj.* bearded, mustachioed
tenxipalli *n.* lip
tenyoh *adj.* famous; *n.* hero
tenyotl *n.* fame
teoamoxtli *n.* sacred book, scripture
teoatl *n.* ocean, deep water
teocallapanhuetzian *n.* spire
teocalli *n.* temple, church
teocaltontli *n.* hermitage
teocaltototl *n.* sparrow
teocihui *iv.* be hungry (*Preterit: oniteochiuh*);
   tv. (*Preterit: onicteociuh*)
teocihuiliztli *n.* hunger
teocihuini *adj.* hungry
teociuhqui *adj.* hungry
teoconetl *n.* godchild
teocuicatl *n.* religious song, hymn
teocuitlaamatl *n.* tinsel
teocuitlacayotl *n.* treasure
teocuitlacozcanamacoyan *n.* jewelry store
teocuitlamecatl *n.* gold chain
teocuitlaoztotl *n.* gold mine
teocuitlapixcalli *n.* treasury
teocuitlapixcoyan *n.* treasury
teocuitlatl *n.* gold
teohuah *n.* priest
teoixpan nelihtoa *iv.* swear (*Preterit: teoixpan onelihtoh*)
teomahuizmelahualoni *n.* liturgy
teonantli *n.* godmother
teopantli *n.* temple, church
teopixcacalli *n.* monastery, rectory
teopixcalli *n.* church
teopixcatlahtoani *n.* prelate

teopixcatlahtocapillotl *n.* hierarchy
teopixcatlaquitl *n.* cassock, clerical garb, vestment
teopixcayotl *n.* clergy, priesthood
teopixqui *n.* priest
teopouhqui *adj.* causing sadness
teoquichhui *n.* husband
teotahtli *n.* godfather
teotemachtilli *n.* sermon
teotetl *n.* jet, coal
teotia *reflex. v.* worship (*Preterit: oninotlateotih*)
teoticanantli *n.* godmother
teoticatahtli *n.* godfather
teotl *n.* god (*Plural: teteoh*)
teotlac *n.* afternoon
teotlactzin *interj.* good afternoon
teotlahtolli *n.* bible
teotlaitlania *reflex. v.* pray (*Preterit: oninoteotlaitlanih*)
teotlaquiltih *interj.* good evening; good afternoon (*late*)
teotoca *tv.* idolize (*Preterit: onitlateotocac*)
teoxihuitl *n.* fine turquoise
teoyoh *adj.* spiritual
teoyoticatlahtoani *n.* bishop
teoyotl *n.* divinity
teoyotlamanalli *n.* host, wafer (*Eucharist*)
tepach *n.* fermented drink
tepahnamaconi *n.* enema; laxative
tetlahpaloliztli *n.* greeting
tetlahpalolli *n.* greeting
tepahtiani *n.* doctor, physician
tepahtih *n.* doctor, physician
tepahtiliztli *n.* act of curing
tepalcatl *n.* earthenware, potsherd
tepalconetl *n.* illegitimate child

tepalehuiliztli *n.* favor
tepallahtoliztli *n.* law (*profession*)
tepaltequitqui *n.* day laborer
tepaltzinco *adv.* on someone else's property
tepamitl *n.* stone wall
tepan hualahcic *n.* incident
tepan yani *n.* adulterer
tepan yauhqui *n.* adulterer
tepancalli *n.* corral, pen (*enclosure*)
tepanchiuhqui *n.* bricklayer, mason
tepancochqui *n.* guest
tepanihcaliztli *n.* presidency
tepantemoni *n.* escalator
tepantlahtoa *tv.* influence (*Preterit: onitepantlahtoh*)
tepantlahtoani *n.* lawyer
tepantlahtollotl *n.* influence
tepantlayecohuaca *adv.* temporarily
tepantlayecohuani *adj.* temporary
tepantleconi *n.* escalator
tepantli *n.* wall
tepanyaliztli *n.* adultery, marital infidelity
tepatlactli *n.* slab of stone
tepatlahcuiloni *n.* blackboard
tepehpenaliztli *n.* election
tepehpenani *n.* one who chooses or elects, elector
tepehpetlaliztli *n.* compliment, flattery
tepehpetlani *n.* flatterer; *adj.* flattering
tepehuah *n.* conqueror
tepehualiztli *n.* conquest
tepehuani *n.* conqueror
tepehui *iv.* fall; be scattered (*Preterit: onitepeuh*)
tepeihtic *n.* valley
tepeitzcuintli *n.* wild dog-like animal

tepeixco *n.* slop, ridge
tepeticpac *n.* mountain peak; on top of the hill
tepetl *n.* hill, mountain
tepetla *n.* mountain range, hilly area
tepetlacalli *n.* grave, tomb
tepetlalli *n.* slope
tepetlatl *n.* slate (*stone*), porous rock
tepetztli *n.* smooth rock
tepexitl *n.* cliff; large rock
tepicilli *n.* debris; gravel
tepilli *n.* vulva, female genitalia
tepilolli *n.* string
tepinia *tv.* punch (*Preterit: onitetepinih*)
tepipiani *n.* spy, stalker
tepitoyotl *n.* smallness
tepitztic *adj.* hard, solid
tepixqui *n.* guardian
tepochcoyotl *adj.* dimwitted
tepoliuhtitlzaliliztli *n.* confusion
tepolli *n.* penis
teponazoa *iv.* play a small horizontal drum called teponaztli
    (*Preterit: oniteponazoh*)
teponazoani *n.* one who plays teponaztli
teponazoh *n.* one who plays teponaztli
teponaztli *n.* a slotted horizontal drum played with rubber
    tipped mallets
tepotztli *n.* back
teulli *n.* penis
tepuntic cuahuitl *n.* stump
teputzeh *adj.* strong, powerful
teputzmama *tv.* carry on one's back
    (*Preterit: onitlateputzmamah*)
teputzoh *adj.* humpbacked

teputzohtic *adj.* humpbacked
teputzotl *n.* hump
teputztli *n.* back; shoulder
tepuzcacalachtli *n.* doorbell
tepuztli *n.* copper; metal; axe
tepuzapaztli *n.* kettle
tepuzcactli *n.* horseshoe
tepuzcaxitl *n.* copper vessel
tepuzchichiconi *n.* file
tepuzchicolli *n.* link; metal staff, cane
tepuzcoliuhqui *n.* corkscrew
tepuzcomitl *n.* pan
tepuzcuacalalahtli *n.* helmet
tepuzcuacualoni *n.* pliers, tweezers
tepuzhuictli *n.* hoe
tepuzhuitztli *n.* spur
tepuzichiconi *n.* file
tepuzicpamacuecuetzoloni *n.* telegraph
tepuzicpamacuecuetzoloyan *n.* telegraph office
tepuzicpateiximachtiloni *n.* telegram
tepuzicpatemachiltiliztli *n.* telegram
tepuzicpatl *n.* wire
tepuzmachiyopilcac *n.* medal
tepuzmachiyotiloni *n.* branding iron
tepuzmactli *n.* machete
tepuzmacuahuitl *n.* sword
tepuzmecatlahtoa *iv.* speak on the telephone
    (*Preterit: onitepuzmecatlahtoh*)
tepuzmetztli *n.* satellite
tepuzmolcaxitl *n.* blender
tepuzmoyotl *n.* helicopter
tepuzneahuiltiloni *n.* carnival rides
tepuzocuilquixohuayan *n.* train station

tepuzohpitzactli *n.* railroad
tepuzohtli *n.* railroad track
tepuzomitl *n.* metal awl
tepuzpetlahuia *tv.* file (*Preterit: onitepuzpetlahuih*)
tepuzpitzcoyan *n.* blacksmith shop
tepuzpitzqui *n.* blacksmith
tepuzpoxcauhcayotl *n.* rust
tepuztenmecayotl *n.* bridle
tepuzteyolehuallahtoloni *n.* phonograph, record player
tepuzteyolehualoni *n.* machine
tepuztlaanoni *n.* pincers; tongs
tepuztlacaconi *n.* radio
tepuztlacualcehuiloni *n.* refrigerator
tepuztlacualitztiloni *n.* refrigerator
tepuztlacuihcuiloni *n.* chisel
tepuztlahcuiloh *n.* typist
tepuztlahcuiloloni *n.* typewriter
tepuztlahcuiloloyan *n.* print shop
tepuztlahtzomaloni *n.* sewing machine
tepuztlahuilanalli *n.* subway train
tepuztlahuilmachiyotl *n.* signal light (*traffic*)
tepuztlahuiteconi *n.* lightning rod
tepuztlaitztiloni *n.* refrigerator
tepuztlalli *n.* rust; metal filings
tepuztlalloh *n.* rusted
tepuztlaloa *iv.* rust (*Preterit: otepuztlaloh*)
tepuztlamatzomaloni *n.* sewing machine
tepuztlaoliniloni *n.* motor
tepuztlateconi *n.* scissors
tepuztlatexoni *n.* blender
tepuztlatlatquitl *n.* tool
tepuztlatzacualoni *n.* bolt; key; lock
tepuztlatzoaloni *n.* blender

tepuztlahtzomaloni *n.* sewing machine
tepuztlazohua *iv.* iron, press (*Preterit: ontepuztlazouh*)
tepuztlazohualoni *n.* iron (*clothes*)
tepuztototl *n.* airplane
tepuzyahualli *n.* ring
tepuzyollomatiliztli *n.* engineering (*mechanical*)
tepuzyollomatini *n.* engineer (*mechanical*)
tepuzyollotl *n.* motor
tepuzyollotlatexoni *n.* blender
tequechcotonani *n.* executioner
tequelonmaltiliztli *n.* fraud
tequi *tv.* cut (*Preterit: onitelatec*)
tequiahuatl *n.* arch
tequihuah *n.* person in authority
tequihuahyotl *n.* authority
tequini *n.* worker
tequipachoa *iv.* worry; be busy (*Preterit: onitequipachoh*)
tequipan *n.* work season; work place; office
tequipanoani *n.* worker, laborer
tequiti *iv.* work (*Preterit: onitequit*)
tequitiloyan *n.* workshop
tequitl *n.* job, occupation; work; load; tax, tribute
tequitlahcuiloa *iv.* work as a secretary
    (*Preterit: onitequitlahcuiloh*)
tequitlahcuiloh *n.* secretary
tequitlalli *n.* land owned communally
tequitqui *n.* worker, laborer
tequixquitl *n.* bicarbonate of soda
tequixtiloyan *n.* quarry
tequiyoh *adj.* difficult, requiring hard work
tequiyotl *n.* business; servitude
tetahyoh *adj.* paternal
tetech monequiliztli *n.* need

tetech tlaahcoliztli *n.* debt
tetech tlapoliuhtaliztli *n.* debt
tetechnematiliztli *n.* habit
tetechnetemachiliztli *n.* confidence, trust
teteihcuilolizltli *n.* lithography
tetelchihua *tv.* offend, outrage (*Preterit: onitetelchiuh*)
tetellan *n.* rocky terrain
tetemminaliztli *n.* peck, sting
teteochihualizltli *n.* blessing
teteononotzalizltli *n.* sermon
teteononotzaloni *n.* sermon
tetepetlacoyoniani *n.* engineer (*civil*)
tetepetlacoyoniliztli *n.* engineering (*civil*)
tetepontli *n.* knee; shin; tree trunk
tetequilli *n.* scar
tetetla *n.* rocky terrain
teteyoh *adj.* rocky
tetic *adj.* hard, stonelike
teticayotl *n.* hardness
tetl *n.* stone; grain; egg; ball; anything smooth and round
tetl cuahuitl *n.* punishment
tetlacacahuililli *n.* heritage; inheritance
tetlacahualtiliztli *n.* hindrance, obstacle; interruption
tetlacamatiliztli *n.* obedience
tetlacaquitiliztli *n.* indication; punishment
tetlachihualtiliztli *n.* violence
tetlacualtiani *n.* waiter
tetlacualtiliztli *n.* feeding
tetlacuicuiliani *n.* thief
tetlacuicuilli *n.* engraving
tetlahcuiloa *tv.* engrave (*Preterit: onitetlahcuiloh*)
tetlahcuilolizltli *n.* inscription on stone
tetlahcuilolli *adj.* etched in stone

tetlahcuilolli *n.* engraving
tetlahtlaniliztli *n.* question
tetlahtli *n.* rocky terrain
tetlahtolanaliztli *n.* interrogation; interview
tetlahtolanani *n.* interrogator; interviewer
tetlahtolilochtiliztli *n.* contradiction
tetlahtolmachiotl *n.* quotation mark
tetlahtolpinahuiliztli *n.* insult
tetlahtolpinauhtiliztli *n.* insult
tetlahuehuetzquitih *n.* clown, comedian
tetlahuetzquitiani *n.* clown, comedian
tetlalhuiliztli *n.* invitation
tetlampahtiani *n.* dentist
tetlampahtih *n.* dentist
tetlancopinqui *n.* dentist
tetlanextiliztli *n.* publication
tetlanoquililoni *n.* laxative
tetlanquechiliztli *n.* bite
tetlantzontopileh *n.* mayor
tetlaocoliani *adj.* merciful
tetlaocoliliztli *n.* pity, compassion
tetlaocoliztli *n.* alms
tetlaocoltih *adj.* causing pity
tetlapanaloyan *n.* quarry
tetlapanani *n.* stonecutter
tetlapanqui *n.* stonecutter
tetlapohpolhuilli *n.* forgiven
tetlapohpolhuiliztli *n.* forgiveness, pardon
tetlatlacuiltiani *n.* lender
tetlatlamaniloni *n.* lottery
tetlatlaneuhtiani *n.* lender
tetlatlaneuhtiloni *n.* loan
tetlatlanuehtiliztli *n.* loan

tetlatlauhtilli *n.* favor
tetlatlauhtiloni *n.* request
tetlatzacuilcalli *n.* penitentiary, prison
tetlatzacuiliztli *n.* punishment
tetlatzacuilli *n.* convict, prisoner
tetlatzacuiloyan *n.* penitentiary, prison
tetlatzohuililiztli *n.* thesis
tetlatzontequilia *tv.* sentence (*Preterit: onitetlatzonquilih*)
tetlatzontequiliztli *n.* sentence, judgment (*law*)
tetlatzotzonaliztli *n.* concert (*music*)
tetlaxtlahuilli *n.* reward
tetlayehyecalhuiani *n.* imitator
tetlayehyecalhuiliztli *n.* imitation
tetlayehyecalhuiloni *adj.* imitable
tetlazohtlaliztli *n.* love
tetlazohuiliztli *n.* argument
tetlilquixtia *tv.* photograph (*Preterit: onitetlilquixtih*)
tetlilquixtiani *n.* photographer
tetlocolia *tv.* give away (*Preterit: onitetlocolih*)
tetocaihcuiloa *tv.* register (*Preterit: onitetocaihcuiloh*)
tetocaihcuiloliztli *n.* registration
tetocani *n.* wasp (*yellow*); one who buries people
tetocapatlachihualnepanoliztli *n.* conjugation
tetocapatlahquetl *n.* pronoun
tetocoyan *n.* burial place, cemetery
tetoquiliztica *adv.* successively
tetoquiliztli *n.* burial, act of burying
tetotoncaimachiyoca *n.* temperature
tetzahtzililiztli *n.* shouting (*at someone*)
tetzahuac *adj.* sticky
tetzahuiliztli *n.* omen
tetzahuitl *n.* omen
tetzauhtlacololli *n.* ribbon

tetzauhtlahtlacoani *n.* criminal
tetzauhtlahtlacolli *n.* crime
Tetzcocatl *n.* person from Tetzcoco
tetzimpahnamaconi *n.* enema; laxative
tetzolihui *iv.* heal (*Preterit: otetzoliuh*)
tetzonyotl *n.* beginning
tetzotzonqui *n.* stonecutter
teuctli *n.* lord (*Plural: teteuctin*)
–teuh *suff.* like, in the manner of
teuhtia *tv.* pulverize (*Preterit: onitlateuhtih*)
teuhtic *adj.* dusty
teuhtli *n.* dust
teuhtli tlahzolli *n.* vice
teuhyotl *n.* dust cloud
texalli *n.* stone used for grinding
texamicalquetzallotl *n.* construction materials
texcalcuichtli *n.* soot from the oven
texcalli *n.* oven
texcan *n.* bedbug
texiliztli *n.* grinding
texima *iv.* cut stone (*Preterit: onitexin*)
teximani *n.* barber
texinqui *n.* stonecutter; barber
texipinehuayotequiliztli *n.* circumcision
texochhuiani *n.* laughing stock
texochtiani *adj.* witty
texochtiliztli *n.* wit, wittiness
texochtilizzotl *n.* wittiness
texocotl *n.* a type of fruit
texolotl *n.* small stone for grinding sauce ingredients
texotic *adj.* blue
textlaoyo *n.* tortilla filled with bean paste
textli *n.* brother-in-law; flour; dough

teyacanaliztli *n.* government, administration, act of governing
teyacanani *n.* director, leader
teyacanqui *n.* director, leader, boss, chief, head
teyacantihqui *n.* precursor
teyaochihualiztli *n.* hostility
teyaouh *n.* enemy; *adj.* hostile
teyeliztli *n.* nature
teyocoyani *n.* god, the one who creates people
teyolahcocuiliztli *n.* stimulation
teyolehua *tv.* court, woo (*Preterit: oniteyoleuh*)
teyolia *n.* soul
teyolihtectiliztli *n.* inspiration
teyolitia *n.* soul
teyollaliztli *n.* mortgage
teyollocuani *n.* vampire
teyolmachiyotiliztli *n.* sacrament
teyolnonotzaliztli *n.* advice
teyolnotzaloni *n.* vocation
tezcapetzticoni *n.* curtain
tezcatl *n.* mirror; glass
tezoaloni *n.* knife
tezontli *n.* volcanic rock
tezontzapotl *n.* mamey
tezqui *n.* person who grinds corn
teztlatic *n.* glutton
tiacauh *n.* chief, boss; *adj.* brave
tiachcatl *n.* older; higher in rank
tianquiztli *n.* marketplace; plaza
–tica *suff.* with, by means of
ticitl *n.* physician (*Plural: titicih*)
ticiyotl *n.* medicine, art of healing
tilamatlazaloa *tv.* upholster (*Preterit: onitilamatlazaloh*)
tilamatlazaloani *n.* upholsterer
tilana *tv.* pull, haul (*Preterit: onitlatilan*)

tilictic *adj.* taut, tense, tight

tilini *iv.* become tight, tense; stretch (*Preterit: onitilin*)

tilinia *tv.* stretch, tighten; compress (*Preterit: onitlatilinih*)

tilinqui *adj.* taut, tense, tight

tilintoc *adj.* taut, tense, tight

tilmahicxipehpechtli *n.* carpet

tilmahocuilin *n.* clothes moth

tilmahtlahcuilolli *n.* painting

tilmahtlazaloa *tv.* upholster (*Preterit: onitilmahtlazaloh*)

tilmahtlazaloani *n.* upholsterer

tilmahtlazalolli *n.* upholstery

tilmahtli *n.* cape; cloth; sarape; curtain

timalquiza *tv.* ooze (*Preterit: onitimalquiz*)

–titlan *suff.* by, near, next to

tititza *reflex. v.* stretch and yawn (*Preterit: oninotititz*)

titlani *tv.* send (*Preterit: ontetitlan*)

titlantli *n.* messenger, envoy, representative

tiyacauhqui *adj.* fearless

tiyahcauh *n.* soldier

tizatl *n.* chalk;*adj.* gray

tla *pron.* something; *conj.* if

tlaacanoni *n.* shovel

tlaahcocuini tetl *n.* magnet

tlaahcoquetza *iv.* bid (*Preterit: onitlaahcoquetz*)

tlaahcoquetzani *n.* bidder

tlaahuilcahualiztli *n.* negligence

tlaantli *n.* captive

tlaaquia *tv.* introduce (*Preterit: onitlaaquih*)

tlaaquiliztli *n.* introduction

tlaaquiltetl *n.* planer, trowel

tlaaxiltiliztli *n.* supplement

tlaaxitihquetl *n.* appendix

tlacacahuililotiuh *n.* heir

tlacaccualtiliani *n.* tuner (*person*)

tlacaccualtililoni *n.* tuning device, tuner

tlacaccualtiliztli *n.* tuning

tlacace *interj.* oh!

tlacacemele *n.* monster

tlacachihua *iv.* conceive children; bear children
(*Preterit: onitlacachiuh*)

tlacaciuhcayotl *n.* meekness

tlacaciuhqui *adj.* meek

tlacaconemiliztli *n.* peace, tranquility

tlacacoyan *n.* auditorium; tribunal, hearing

tlacacoyeliztli *n.* security

tlacacqueh *n.* audience

tlacacqui *adj.* alert, diligent

tlacactli *adj.* heard; understood

tlacah *n.* people; *conj.* that is

tlacahzo *interj.* Oh, my God!

tlacahua *tv.* omit (*Preterit: onitlacauh*)

tlacahuah *n.* one who has servants

tlacahualtia *tv.* hinder; interrupt; prevent
(*Preterit: onitetlacahualtih*)

tlacahueyac *n.* giant

tlacahuilli *n.* remains

tlacaicniuhtli *adj.* sociable

tlacaicniuhyoh *adj.* social

tlacaicniuhyotl *n.* society

tlacaihtaliztli *n.* hypocrisy

tlacaipotoctli *n.* perspiration

tlacaittaliztli *n.* hypocrisy

tlacalaquia *iv.* pay tax, tribute (*Preterit: onitlacalaquih*)

tlacalaquilli *n.* tax, tribute

tlacamacuecuetzoa *tv.* manipulate

(*Preterit: onitlacamacuecuetzoh*)

tlacamacuecuetzoani *n.* manipulator

tlacamati *tv.* obey (*Preterit: onitetlacamat*)

tlacamazatl *n.* violent or brutal person

tlacamazayotl *n.* cruelty, brutality

tlacamecayotl *n.* lineage

tlacamiccati *iv.* become perverted (*Preterit: onitlacamiccatic*)

tlacamichin *n.* bass (*fish*)

tlacamixpoloc *n.* bully

tlacanahuatilli *n.* natural law

tlacanechicoltiloyan *n.* community

tlacanechicoltin *n.* community

tlacaquiliztli *n.* ability; judgment, opinion

tlacaquitia *tv.* indicate; punish (*Preterit: onitlacaquitih*)

tlacatecatl *n.* commander of a *xiquipilli* (*battalion of 8,000 men*); general

tlacatecolotl *n.* devil

tlacati *iv.* be born (*Preterit: onitlacati and onitlacat*)

tlacatilia *tv.* produce offspring (*Preterit: onitetlacatilih*)

tlacatilizilhuitl *n.* birthday

tlacatiliztli *n.* birth

tlacatiyan *n.* place of birth

tlacatl *n.* person, human

tlacauhtli *n.* omission, space

tlacaxinachtli *n.* semen

tlacaxoxouhcayotl *n.* freedom, liberty, independence

tlacaxoxouhqui *n.* free, independent

tlacayeliztli *n.* human nature

tlacayomatiliztli *n.* anthropology

tlacayomatini *n.* anthropologist

tlacayotl *n.* body; humanity, human nature; compassion, benevolence; personality

tlacazcaltia *iv.* educate (*Preterit: onitlacazcaltih*)

tlacazcaltiani *n.* educator, tutor

tlacazo *adv.* certainly

tlacahzolli *n.* glutton

tlacahzolnanahuatl *n.* venereal disease

tlacaztalli *n.* native person of fair skin

tlacecencahualiztli *n.* preparation

tlacehuilizpan *n.* rest, vacation

tlaceliloyan *n.* lodging

tlacemihtoliztli *n.* definition

tlacempahcayotl *n.* happiness; prosperity

tlacempohualiztli *n.* total

tlacencahua *tv.* finish, conclude; repair (*Preterit: onitlacencauh*)

tlacencahualiztli *n.* perfection

tlacencahualtia *tv.* deprive (*Preterit: onitetlacencahualtih*)

tlacencahuani *n.* repairperson

tlacentlalilamatl *n.* inventory

tlachcuitl *n.* sod

tlachia *tv.* see, look (*Preterit: onitlachix*)

tlachializtli *n.* ingenuity, talent; vision, view, observation

tlachialoni *n.* view

tlachialoyan *n.* window; observatory

tlachicahualtiliztli *n.* support

tlachicauhtli *adj.* husky, robust

tlachichiconi *n.* brush

tlachichina *iv.* smoke cigarettes (*Preterit: onitlachichin*)

tlachichinalli *n.* tobacco

tlachichinolli *n.* cigarette

tlachichitia *iv.* nurse (*Preterit: onitlachichitih*)

tlachichiuhcan *n.* workshop

tlachicoyan *n.* hidden place

tlachihchiuhcayotl *n.* occupation

tlachihualeh *n.* creator, maker; author

tlachihualiztlahtolli *n.* verb

tlachihualiztli *n.* act of doing something, performance of an act; verb

tlachihualli *n.* creation, work; *adj.* made

tlachihualoyan *n.* factory

tlachihualtepetl *n.* pyramid

tlachiuhcan *n.* factory

tlachipahualiztli *n.* purification

tlachipahuani *n.* purifier

tlachipintli *n.* drop

tlachiquilli *n.* hill

tlachixqui *n.* sentinel, guard

tlachpahuaztli *n.* broom

tlachpana *iv.* sweep (*Preterit: onitlachpan*)

tlachtli *n.* ball court; rubber-ball game

tlacihuiztli *n.* mole (*skin*)

tlaciuhcayotl *n.* fate

tlacnelilli *adj.* privileged

tlacnopilhuiliztli *n.* gain

tlacnopilhuilloh *adj.* profitable

tlacochtli *n.* spear

tlacohcouhqui *n.* buyer

tlacohti *iv.* work as a slave, servant (*Preterit: onitlacohtic*)

tlacohtli *n.* serf, servant, slave

tlacohualiztli *n.* shopping, buying

tlacohualli *n.* purchase

tlacohualoni *n.* coin, money

tlacohuani *n.* buyer

tlacohyotl *n.* servitude, slavery, serfdom

tlacomolli *n.* hole, pit; ravine, gorge

tlaconextli *n.* ashes

tlacopinalli *n.* type

tlacopintli *n.* copy, reproduction; type, mold
tlacotl *n.* stalk, stem; stick, rod
tlacouhqui *n.* buyer
tlacoyoctli *n.* hole; cupboard
tlacpac *adv.* up
tlacpaccayotl *n.* top, summit; roof
tlacpaconetl *n.* stepchild
tlacpahuitectli *n.* man's stepchild
tlacpaicniuhtli *n.* a parent's brother
tlacpanantli *n.* stepmother
tlacpatahtli *n.* stepfather
tlacticpaccayotl *n.* worldliness; *adj.* mundane, worldly
tlactli *n.* torso; chest
tlacuahcua *tv.* chew; bite (*Preterit: onitlacuahcuah*)
tlacuahuactecpatl *n.* diamond
tlacuahuitequi *iv.* knock (*on door*) (*Preterit: onitlacuahuitec*)
tlacualchihualoyan *n.* kitchen
tlacualchiuhcan *n.* kitchen
tlacualchiuhqui *n.* cook
tlacualhuapalitl *n.* dining table
tlacualillotia *tv.* nourish (*Preterit: onitlacualillotih*)
tlacualillotiliztli *n.* nutrition
tlacualillotqui *adj.* nutritious
tlacualitztiloni *n.* refrigerator
tlacualizpan *n.* mealtime
tlacualiztli *n.* act of eating
tlacualli *n.* food
tlacualmihmiqui *iv.* choke on food (*Preterit: onitlacualmihmic*)
tlacualnextia *tv.* decorate, adorn; find something to eat
 (*Preterit: onitlacualnextih*)
tlacualontlapechtli *n.* dining table
tlacualoyan *n.* dining room, restaurant
tlacualtia *tv.* feed (*Preterit: onitetlacualtih*)

tlacualtiliani *n.* one who repairs, restores, mends
tlacualtiliztli *n.* remedy, solution; repair
tlacualtlapechtli *n.* dining table
tlacualtzohtzomahtli *n.* napkin
tlacuapololiztli *n.* error, mistake
tlacuatequilli *adj.* baptized
tlacuatzin *n.* opossum
tlacuauh *adv.* strongly
tlacuauhtilia *iv.* have an erection (*Preterit: onitlacuauhtilih*)
tlacuauhtlamatiliztli *n.* confidence, hope, faith
tlacuepcayotilia *tv.* avenge (*Preterit: onitetlacuepcayotilih*)
tlacuihcui *tv.* sculpt (*Preterit: onitlacuihcuic*)
tlacuihcuic *n.* sculptor
tlacuihcuiliztli *n.* sculpture
tlacuihcuilotl *n.* opossum
tlacuihcuini *n.* sculptor
tlacuiltia *tv.* light (*Preterit: onitlacuiltih*);
    lend (*Preterit onitetlacuiltih*)
tlacuitlahuiloliztli *n.* inspection
tlacxitamachihualoni *n.* foot (*measure*)
tlacxitla *adv.* below; lying below (*small area*)
tlaehecahuiloni *n.* ventilator
tlaehecatiliztli *n.* ventilation
tlaehecatiloni *n.* ventilator
tlaelehuiliztli *n.* appetite; greed
tlaelpaquiliztli *n.* sensuality
tlaelpaquini *adj.* sensual
tlaeltiloni *n.* magnet
tlahcahtli *n.* daytime
tlahcatzin *interj.* good morning
tlahchiquini *n.* maguey juice collector
tlahco *n.* half

tlahcoihualli *n.* midnight
tlahcoquetzaliztli *n.* bid
tlahcotepiton *adj.* inferior
tlahcotompohualoni *n.* number
tlahcotonalli *n.* midday
tlahcotonatiuh *n.* midday
tlahcotonatiuh cochi *iv.* take a siesta (*Preterit: tlahcotonatiuh onicoch*)
tlahcotonatiuh cochiztli *n.* siesta
tlahcotontli *n.* piece
tlahcoyan *n.* waist
tlahcoyohualli *n.* midnight
tlahcoyohuan *n.* midnight
tlahcuiloh *n.* writer, scribe
tlahcuilolhuahuanilli *n.* drawing
tlahcuilolhuapalitl *n.* blackboard
tlahcuilolhuaztli *n.* blackboard
tlahcuilolli *n.* writing; written; letter
tlahcuiloloni *n.* pen (*writing*)
tlahcuilolpamitl *n.* alphabet
tlahmah *n.* surgeon; physician who is a specialist
tlahmatqui *n.* surgeon; physician who is a specialist
tlahmolotl *n.* large paddle for mixing
tlahpalli *n.* courage, strength; effort
tlahpaloa *tv.* greet (*Preterit: ontetlahpaloh*)
tlahtlacoa *tv.* harm, offend, do evil, sin (*Preterit: onitlahtlacoh*)
tlahtlacoani *n.* sinner
tlahtlacoleh *n.* sinner
tlahtlacolli *n.* offense; sin; fault
tlahtlacoloh *adj.* offensive; sinful
tlahtlani *iv.* ask (*Preterit: onitlahtlan*)
tlahtlania *tv.* ask, interrogate, question; interview (*Preterit: onitetlahtlanih*)

tlahtlaniliztli *n.* inquiry
tlahtlanilmachiotl *n.* question mark
tlahtlaoyotl *n.* bean taco, tortilla stuffed with beans
tlahtlapoaloni *n.* key
tlahtli *n.* uncle
tlahtoa *iv.* speak (*Preterit: onitlahtoh*)
tlahtohcacihuapilli *n.* princess
tlahtohcaicpalli *n.* throne
tlahtohcamecayotl *n.* dynasty
tlahtohcapilli *n.* prince
tlahtohcateixiptla *n.* mayor
tlahtohcatetitlaniliztli *n.* embassy
tlahtohcatitlantli *n.* ambassador
tlahtohcayeyantli *n.* throne
tlahtohcayotl *n.* rule, realm, lordship, dominion
Tlahtohcayotl in Cepanca *n.* United States
Tlahtohcayotl in Cepanca chaneh *n.* American (*U.S.*)
tlahtolana *tv.* interrogate; interview (*Preterit: onitetlahtolan*)
tlahtolaxiltia *iv.* research (*Preterit: onitlahtolaxiltih*)
tlahtolaxiltiani *n.* researcher
tlahtolaxiltillotl *n.* research
tlahtolcentlalilli *n.* unanimity
tlahtolcentlaliztica *adv.* unanimously
tlahtolchichiuhqui *n.* poet
tlahtolchihualiztli *n.* poetry, poem
tlahtolcuepa *tv.* translate (*Preterit: onitlatlahtolcuep*)
tlahtoliochtia *tv.* contradict (*Preterit: onitetlahtoliochtih*)
tlahtolitqui *n.* ambassador
tlahtollamiliztli *n.* suffix
tlahtolli *n.* language, speech; saying; word
tlahtollotl *n.* history; tradition
tlahtolmaca *tv.* advise (*Preterit: onitetlahtolmacac*)
tlahtolmatiliztli *n.* linguistics

tlahtolmatini *n.* linguist
tlahtolmelahua *tv.* explain; inform
    (*Preterit: onitlahtolmelahuac*)
tlahtolmelahualiztli *n.* explanation; information
tlahtolnamic *adj.* unanimous
tlahtolnamiquiliztica *adv.* unanimously
tlahtolnamiquiliztli *n.* unanimity
tlahtolnezcayoamoxtli *n.* dictionary
tlahtolnezcayotl *n.* meaning
tlahtolpalehuia *tv.* recommend (*Preterit: onitetlahtolpalehuih*)
tlahtolpalehuiztli *n.* recommendation
tlahtolpehualiztli *n.* prefix
tlahtoltecpanaliztli *n.* vocabulary
tlahtoltecpantli *n.* vocabulary
tlahtoltlapohualmachiyutl *n.* telephone number
tlahtzin *n.* uncle
tlahtzoma *tv.* sew (*Preterit: onitlahtzon*)
tlahtzomaliztepuztli *n.* sewing machine
tlahtzomaloni *n.* needle
tlahtzomani *n.* seamstress, tailor
tlahtzonqui *n.* seamstress, tailor
tlahtzontli *adj.* sewn
tlahuacqui *n.* drought
tlahuahualoa *iv.* bark; howl (*Preterit: onitlahuahualoh*)
tlahuahuanilli *n.* drawing
tlahuahuatzaliztli *n.* barking
tlahuana *iv.* get drunk (*Preterit: onitlahuan*); scratch with
    the nails
tlahuanoni *n.* cup, goblet
tlahuanqui *adj.* drunk
tlahuapahualiztli *n.* guidance, instruction, direction
tlahuapahualli *adj.* bred, brought up
tlahuazancoliuhqui *n.* comma
tlahuehca *adj.* spacious

tlahuehuetzconi *adj.* ridiculous (*thing*)
tlahuehuetzqui *adj.* ridiculous (*person*)
tlahuelcuepilia *tv.* reject (*Preterit: onitlahuelcuepilih*)
tlahueleh *adj.* impatient; angry; fierce
tlahuelihtolli *n.* obscenity, profanity
tlahueliloc *adj.* evil
tlahuelitta *tv.* hate (*Preterit: onitetlahuelittac*)
tlahuellahtolli *n.* obscenity, profanity
tlahuelli *n.* anger, rage, fury, indignation
tlahuentiliztli *n.* invitation
tlahuilcalli *n.* lantern
tlahuilchicahualizmecatl *n.* cable
tlahuilixiptla *n.* camera
tlahuilli *n.* light, lamp
tlahuilmeyallotl *n.* electric current
tlahuilzayulin *n.* firefly
tlahuipanaliztli *n.* organization
tlahuitectli *n.* wound; *adj.* wounded, struck
tlahuitequiliztletl *n.* electricity
tlahuitolli *n.* bow
tlahuizcalli *n.* dawn
tlahxillacalli *n.* neighborhood
tlahzolchihua *tv.* waste (*Preterit: onitlatlahzolchiuh*)
tlahzollalli *n.* trash
tlahzolli *n.* trash, filth
tlahzomaloyan *n.* tailor shop
tlaicxitoca *tv.* frequent (*Preterit: onitlaicxitocac*)
tlaicxitocac *adj.* frequent
tlaicxitocatica *adv.* frequently
tlaihiyoanani tetl *n.* magnet
tlaihtlaniani *n.* beggar
tlailli *n.* drink; alcoholic beverage
tlailotlac *n.* judge

tlaipantililiztli *n.* prosperity
tlaitia *iv.* drink chocolate or atole; have breakfast
 (*Preterit: onitlaitih*); *tv.* give breakfast to someone
 (*Preterit: onitetlaitih*)
tlaixaxiliztli *n.* understanding
tlaixcopinalli *n.* copy
tlaixcopinaloni *n.* camera; copy machine; picture, photograph
tlaixcuahuitl *n.* threshold
tlaixcuepalli *n.* lie
tlaixcuepani *n.* hypocrite
tlaiximachiliztli *n.* knowledge; science; study
tlaixmachiliztli *n.* knowledge; science; study
tlaixmatini *n.* scientist
tlaixmatiliztli *n.* wisdom
tlaixnextiliztli *n.* interest; profit
tlaixnextoc *adj.* interesting
tlaixpancaittani *n.* witness
tlaixpantlaliliztli *n.* presentation
tlaixpechotl *n.* sheet
tlaixpetzoni *n.* lacquer
tlaixtemoliztli *n.* scrutiny
tlaixtepinilli *n.* punch
tlaixtomahuac *adj.* foolish, silly; thoughtless, insensitive
tlaixtomahualiztli *n.* foolishness, silliness; thoughtlessness,
 insensitivity
tlalancalli *n.* basement
tlalayohtli *n.* wild squash
tlalcacahuatl *n.* peanut
tlalcahualiztli *n.* oblivion, forgetfulness
tlalchi *adv.* on the ground
tlalchiuhqui *n.* farmer
tlalconetl *n.* potato bug
tlaletzalli *n.* wasp (*brown*)

tlaletzatl *n.* wasp (*brown*)

tlalhuactli *n.* island

tlalhuaquiliztli *n.* drought

tlalhuatic *adj.* nervous

tlalhuatl *n.* nerve

tlalhuatl itetecuica *n.* pulse

tlalhuatl itetecuicaca *n.* pulse

tlalhuayoh *adj.* nervous

tlalhuayotl *n.* nervousness

tlalhuipixqui *n.* steward of a town festival

tlalia *tv.* put, place (*Preterit: onitlatlalih*); *reflex. v.* sit down (*Preterit: oninotlalih*)

tlalia in tomin *tv.* save money (*Preterit: onictlatlalih in tomin*)

tlallancalli *n.* cellar

tlallantepuztlahuilanalli *n.* subway train

tlalli *n.* earth, land

tlalli ipocyoh *n.* vapor

tlalmaitl *n.* field hand

tlalmantli *n.* plain; platform, quay

tlamatca *adv.* patiently

tlalmiqui *iv.* die on land (*Preterit: onitlalmic*)

tlalmomoztli *n.* altar made of earth

tlalnamico *adj.* imaginary

tlalnamiconi *n.* memorandum; memo notebook

tlalnamictli *n.* something remembered or agreed upon; *adj.* memorable

tlalnamiquiliztli *n.* memory; mind; thought

tlalnamiquilli *adj.* mental

tlalnamiquiloni *n.* mind

tlalnantli *n.* country, nation

tlaloa *reflex. v.* run (*Preterit: oninotlaloh*)

tlalocan *n.* heaven

tlalocuilin *n.* earthworm

tlalolin *n.* earthquake

tlalolini *impers. v.* the earth quakes (*Preterit: otlalolin*)

tlaloliniliztli *n.* earthquake

tlaloztotl *n.* mine

tlalpan *adv.* on the ground

tlalpantli *n.* floor

tlaltamachihuani *n.* engineer

tlaltepuztli *n.* hoe

tlaltequi *tv.* sip; absorb (*Preterit: onitlaltec*)

tlaltequiztli *n.* sip; absorption

tlalteyoh *adj.* cloddy

tlalticpac *n.* earth; *adv.* on earth

tlalticpaccayotl *n.* worldliness, earthly things; licentiousness;
    adj. mundane, worldly

tlaltzontli *n.* border, limit

tlalxayotl *n.* mud, mire, silt, slime

tlalxocotl *n.* alum, salt like substance used for dying and washing

tlalzacuhtli *n.* clay; plaster

tlama *n.* surgeon

tlamacahuiliztli *n.* license

tlamacazqui *n.* priest; one who makes an offering

tlamaceuhqui *n.* hermit

tlamach *adv.* slowly

tlamachia *tv.* handle (*Preterit: onitlatlamchih*)

tlamachiliztli *n.* science; knowledge

tlamachiyotl *n.* mark

tlamachtilli *n.* pupil; one who is taught

tlamachtilyehyecoliztli *n.* exam

tlamah *n.* surgeon; physician who is a specialist

tlamahtzin *adj.* smooth, soft

tlamahuizolli *n.* marvel; miracle; deed; amusement

tlamahuizoltic *adj.* marvelous, miraculous, wonderful

tlamahuizoltica *adv.* miraculously

tlamamah *n.* carrier
tlamamalli *n.* load, something carried
tlamamalxiquipilli *n.* sack
tlamamatlatl *n.* degree, grade, rung, stairs, step; ladder
tlamanalli *n.* gift, offering
tlamaneloa *iv.* swim (*Preterit: onitlamaneloh*)
tlamaneloani *n.* swimmer
tlamaneloloyan *n.* swimming pool
tlamanenel *adj.* miscellaneous
tlamani *n.* hunter
tlamanitiliztli *n.* characteristic, feature; custom, tradition
tlamannenellotl *n.* ingredient
tlamantlahtolmachtiloni *n.* formula
tlamantlaneltiloyan *n.* laboratory
tlamantli *n.* object, thing
tlamatcanemiliztli *n.* peace
tlamatelhuia *tv.* rub on (*Preterit: onitetlamatelhuih*)
tlamatequipanoni *n.* maneuver
tlamati *tv.* know, grasp (*Preterit: onitlamach*)
tlamatiliztlazohtlaliztli *n.* philosophy
tlamatiliztlazohtlani *n.* philosopher
tlamatiliztli *n.* science; knowledge; culture
tlamatini *n.* one who knows, a wise person, scholar, sage; scientist
tlamatiniyotl *n.* experience
tlamatqui *n.* physician who is a specialist
tlamelahuacachihualiztli *n.* justice
tlamelauhcachihuani *adj.* appropriate, suitable
tlamelauhcaittaloni *n.* aim; marksmanship
tlameme *n.* carrier
tlami *iv.* end (*Preterit: onitlan*)
tlamiliztli *n.* end
tlamimilolli *adj.* turned around, inverted; knoll

tlaminqui *n.* hunter
tlamixtemi *adj.* cloudy
tlampalanaliztli *n.* tooth decay
–tlan *loc. suff.* land of
tlanacazantli *n.* square
tlanacaztli *n.* frame; corner of a building
tlanachcapanquetzaliztli *n.* preference
tlanachcapanquetzalli *adj.* preferable
tlanahnamic *n.* spice
tlanahuaihtoa *tv.* say in or translate into Nahuatl
 (*Preterit: onitlanahuaihtoh*)
tlanahuatia *tv.* order, command; inform
 (*Preterit: onitlanahuatih*)
tlanamacac *n.* vendor
tlanamaquiliztli *n.* meeting, encounter; sale, commercial
 transaction; commerce
tlananquiliztli *n.* answer, response
tlanapaloliztli *n.* support
tlancochtli *n.* molar
tlancuaitl *n.* knee
tlancualoliztli *n.* tooth decay
tlancuitlatl *n.* plaque (*of teeth*)
tlanechicoltiquetl *n.* conjunction
tlanelhuayotl *n.* root
tlaneloa *iv.* row (*Preterit: onitlaneloh*)
tlanelolli *adj.* mixed
tlaneltiliani *n.* witness
tlaneltilih *n.* witness
tlaneltililiztica *adv.* probably
tlaneltililiztli *n.* affirmation; proof
tlaneltiliztli *n.* testimony
tlaneltocani *n.* believer
tlaneltoquiliztli *n.* belief, conviction, faith

tlanemachililoni *n.* polishing machine
tlanemachiliztli *n.* polish
tlanematcachihualiztli *n.* curiosity
tlanemililiztli *n.* idea
tlanenehuiliztli *n.* hypothesis
tlanenelolli *n.* mixture
tlanenequiliztli *n.* urge
tlaneneuhtililiztli *n.* identity
tlanenpoloa *tv.* waste (*Preterit: onitlanenpoloh*)
tlanepanoliztli *n.* investigation
tlanequiliztli *n.* wish, desire, will; sexual desire, urge
tlanexillotl *n.* window
tlanextia *tv.* illuminate (*Preterit: onitlanextih*)
tlanextilia *tv.* teach, show (*Preterit: onitetlanextilih*)
tlanextiliztli *n.* light, brilliance, clarity; teaching
tlanextilli *n.* revelation, discovery; window; *adj.* discovered
tlanextli *n.* light, brilliance, clarity
tlani *adv.* below, down; *tv.* win (*Preterit: onitlatlan*)
tlanihuic *adv.* downward
tlanipa *adv.* downward
tlanitlaza *tv.* humiliate (*Preterit: onitetlanitlaz*)
tlanitztli *n.* shin, tibia
tlanixcuatl *n.* front teeth
tlanomitl *n.* ivory
tlanoncuaquixtilli *n.* exception
tlanontozaloni *n.* telephone
tlanonotzalontlapohualli *n.* telephone number
tlanoquilli *n.* diarrhea
tlanoquiloni *n.* laxative
tlanquechiliztli *n.* bite
tlantlacentlaliloni *n.* dentures
tlantli *n.* teeth
tlaocolli *n.* sorrow, sadness

tlaocoya *iv.* be sad (*Preterit: onitlaocox*)

tlaocoyaliztli *n.* sadness

tlaolli *n.* corn; dried corn kernel

tlaoltextli *n.* corn dough; ground corn, cornstarch

tlaoltzontli *n.* corn silk

tlaoxtli *n.* kernel of corn

tlaoyotl *n.* pie, turnover

tlapa *tv.* paint (*Preterit: onitlapah*)

tlapacaihiyohuiliztli *n.* patience

tlapacani *n.* one who washes

tlapacholiztli *n.* pressure

tlapaconi *n.* sink, wash bowl; soap

tlapacoyan *n.* laundromat

tlapacqui *n.* one who washes

tlapactecalli *n.* curse

tlapactli *n.* crumb; crust

tlapahmatzopiniliztli *n.* vaccination

tlapalanalolli *n.* brush stroke

tlapalanaloni *n.* paint brush

tlapalaquia *tv.* paint; engrave (*Preterit: onitlatlapalaquih*)

tlapalaquilli *n.* painting (*work*)

tlapalehuiani *n.* helper

tlapalihuiztli *n.* strength; effort

tlapaliliztli *n.* trade

tlapaliztli *n.* process of dying or painting

tlapalli *n.* color; paint; *adj.* red

tlapalnamictiliztli *n.* hue

tlapaloa *reflex. v.* dare (*Preterit: oninotlapaloh*)

tlapalolizlti *n.* taste

tlapaloni *n.* dye

tlapalteoxihuitl *n.* ruby

tlapaltic *adj.* strong

tlapaltzintli *n.* young man

tlapanahuiliztli *n.* advantage
tlapanahuiltiliztli *n.* preference
tlapanahuiltilli *adj.* preferable; postponed
tlapanco *n.* terrace
tlapanhuehuetl *n.* bass drum
tlapanhuetzconi *n.* piñata
tlapani *iv.* break (*Preterit: otlapan*)
tlapanohua *iv.* suffer (*Preterit: onitlapanouh*)
tlapanoliztli *n.* suffering
tlapanqui *adj.* broken
tlapantli *n.* roof
tlapatiyotlaliani *n.* appraiser
tlapatiyotlaliliztli *n.* appraisal
tlapatl *n.* thistle, jimsonweed
tlapatla *tv.* trade (*Preterit: onitlapatlac*)
tlapatzquitl *n.* juice
tlapazolotl *n.* tangle
tlapechneittaloni *n.* theater box
tlapechtlahcuiloni *n.* desk
tlapechtli *n.* bed; platform, scaffold
tlapehualli *n.* trap
tlapetantli *n.* lightning
tlapetlani *iv.* flash with lightning (*Preterit: otlapetlan*);
   n. one who pours, spills
tlapetlaniliztli *n.* lightning; spilling, pouring
tlapializtli *n.* vigil, watch
tlapialoyan *n.* warehouse
tlapiazcomitl *n.* bladder
tlapiazohua *iv.* urinate (*Preterit: onitlapiazouh*)
tlapiaztecomatl *n.* bladder
tlapiaztli *n.* urine
tlapic *adv.* falsely; in vain
tlapicqui *n.* liar

tlapictennamiqui *iv.* swear in vain (*Preterit: onitlapoctennamic*)

tlapictlahtoa *iv.* lie, speak falsely or without purpose
(*Preterit: onitlapictlahtoh*)

tlapictlahtoani *n.* liar

tlapihqui *n.* liar

tlapihuia *iv.* grow, increase, multiply (*Preterit: onitlaphihuih*);
tv. increase, multiply (*Preterit: onitlatlapihih*)

tlapihuilia *tv.* sell cheaply, increase the size or weight
(*Preterit: onictetlapehuilih*)

tlapilchihuani *n.* sinner

tlapilolcanahuac *n.* curtain

tlapiqui *tv.* pretend (*Preterit: onitlapic*)

tlapiquia *tv.* slander (*Preterit: onitetlapiquih*)

tlapiquiliztli *n.* fiction

tlapitzalli *n.* flute

tlapitzaloyan *n.* concert hall

tlapitzoto *n.* cockroach

tlapitzqui *n.* one who plays a wind instrument

tlapixcacalli *n.* cabin

tlapixqui *n.* guard, guardian

tlapoa *tv.* open, uncover (*Preterit: onitlahtlapoh*)

tlapohpohualoni *n.* scrubber; sink

tlapohpolhuaztli *n.* eraser

tlapohua *tv.* open, uncover (*Preterit: onitlahtlapouh*)

tlapohualiztli *n.* accountancy, bookkeeping; reading

tlapohuallotl *n.* arithmetic

tlapohualmachiyutl *n.* number

tlapohualmatiliztli *n.* mathematics

tlapohualmatini *n.* mathematician

tlapohui *iv.* open (*Preterit: onitlapouh*)

tlapotonilli *adj.* feathered

tlapouhcayomatini *n.* accountant

tlapouhcayotl *n.* accounting

tlapouhqui *n.* counter; narrator; accountant; *adj.* open
tlapoztectli *n.* crease, fold
tlaqueh *n.* having a big body
tlaquehtzomaliztli *n.* bite
tlaquehua *tv.* rent (*Preterit: onitlatlaqueuh*)
tlaquehualli *n.* unskilled laborer; farmhand
tlaquehuia *reflex. v.* hire (*Preterit: oninotetlaquehuih*)
tlaquemitl *n.* clothing
tlaquemmitl *n.* clothing
tlaquentia *reflex. v.* dress (*Preterit: onintlaoquentih*)
tlaquixtiani *n.* imitator
tlaquixtiliztli *n.* imitation
tlaquixtilli *n.* copy
tlaquixtiloni *adj.* imitable
tlatamachihua *tv.* measure (*Preterit: onitlatamachiuh*)
tlatecpana *tv.* put in order (*Preterit: onitlatecpan*)
tlatecpanalpixqui *n.* police officer
tlatecpanaltecuitlahuiani *n.* police officer
tlatectli *n.* cut, wound; something cut
tlatecuintli *n.* thunder
tlateiniloni *n.* piñata
tlatelchihualoni *adj.* despicable
tlatemohuiliztli *n.* digestion
tlatemolia *tv.* question (*Preterit: onitetlatemolih*)
tlatenehua *iv.* promise; express, say; criticize, gossip about
    someone (*Preterit: onitlateneuh*)
tlatenehualoni *n.* gossip about someone
tlatenquixtia *tv.* pronounce (*Preterit: onitlatenquixtih*)
tlatenquixtiliztli *n.* pronunciation
tlatentia *tv.* sharpen (*Preterit: onitlatentih*)
tlatentilli *adj.* sharp
tlatentli *n.* strip
tlatenyotiliztli *n.* esteem

tlateomatiliztli *n.* ceremony

tlateotocani *n.* pagan

tlatepotzco *adv.* behind

tlatepuztoca *tv.* nail (*Preterit: onitlatepuztocac*)

tlatepuztoconi *n.* nail

tlatequiloni *n.* cutting tool; sissors; saw

tlatequipanoh *n.* laborer, worker

tlatequipanoliztli *n.* act of working

tlatetzahua *iv.* thicken (*Preterit: onitlatetzahuac*)

tlatetzauhtli chichihualayotl *n.* cheese

tlatexoni *n.* blender

tlathui *impers. v.* dawn (*Preterit: otlathuic*)

tlatia *tv.* hide; burn (*Preterit: onitlatlatih*)

tlatla *iv.* be burning (*Preterit: onitlatlac*)

tlatlacalhuia *tv.* offend (*Preterit: onitetlatlacalhuih*)

tlatlacatililiztli *n.* generation

tlatlacatililli *n.* offspring; creation

tlatlacatl *adj.* benign

tlatlaci *iv.* cough, have a cold (*Preterit: onitlatlaz*)

tlatlaciztli *n.* cough

tlatlacuiltia *tv.* lend (*Preterit: onitetlatlacuiltih*)

tlatlahtoa *iv.* talk a lot; chatter (*Preterit: onitlatlahtoh*)

tlatlahtolantli *n.* interviewee

tlatlahuanallotl *n.* orgy

tlatlaliani *n.* composer

tlatlaliliztli *n.* idea

tlatlalilli *n.* invention

tlatlama *tv.* fish with a net (*Preterit: onitlatlan*)

tlatlamachiani *adj.* crafty

tlatlaneuhtia *tv.* lend (*Preterit: onitetlaneuhtih*)

tlatlanextilli *adj.* illuminated

tlatlanilzitli *n.* victory

tlatlapalaquiliztli *n.* painting (*act*)

tlatlapoloni *n.* key
tlatlatilcuahuitl *n.* firewood
tlatlatiloni *n.* fuel
tlatlauhqui *adj.* red
tlatlauhtia *tv.* beg (*Preterit: onitetlatlauhtih*)
tlatlilanaliztli *n.* sketch
tlatlilanqui *n.* illustrator
tlatlilquixtiloni *n.* photograph, picture
tlatliltzicuiniliztli *n.* accent mark; tilde
tlatocayotl *n.* title
tlatoctli *n.* sown field; something planted or buried
tlatoltecahuialoyan *n.* factory
tlatoltecahuiltitletl *n.* fireworks
tlatotoniloni *n.* heater
tlatquihuah *adj.* wealthy, rich
tlatquihuiconi *n.* baggage
tlatquipialoyan *n.* closet
tlatquitl *n.* patrimony, possessions
tlatzacuillotl *n.* door
tlatzacuillotzotzona *iv.* knock (*on door*)
  (*Preterit: onitlatzacuillotzotzon*)
tlatzacuiltia *tv.* punish (*Preterit: onitlatzacualtih*)
tlatzacuiltiloni *adj.* punishable
tlatzcan *n.* cypress
tlatzetzeloloni *n.* sieve
tlatzihui *iv.* be or feel lazy (*Preterit: onitlatziuh*)
tlatzihuiliztli *n.* laziness
tlatzilinia *iv.* ring a bell (*Preterit: onitlatzilinih*)
tlatziliniani *n.* bell-ringer
tlatzintiani *n.* founder, initiator; precursor; *adj.* initial
tlatzintiloni *n.* initiative
tlatzintla *adv.* below; lying below (*large area*)
tlatzintlan *adv.* below; lying below (*large area*)

tlatzitzilitza *iv.* ring a bell (*Preterit: tlatzitzilitz*)
tlatzitzilitzani *n.* bell-ringer
tlatzitzquiliztli *n.* support *tv.* support
tlatziuhcayotl *n.* laziness
tlatziuhqui *adj.* lazy
tlatzomia *tv.* meow (*Preterit: onitlatlatzomih*)
tlatzonquizcanequiliztli *n.* will
tlatzopiniliztli *n.* injection, shot, vaccination
tlatzopintli *n.* period (*punctuation*)
tlatzotzona *iv.* play a musical instrument
      (*Preterit: onitlatzotzon*)
tlatzotzonqui *n.* musician
tlatzoyonilli *adj.* fried
tlauhcampa *n.* east
tlauhquechol *n.* duck like bird
tlauhtli *n.* gift
tlaxacualoa *tv.* rub (*Preterit: onitlaxacualoh*)
tlaxapochtli *n.* hole, pit
tlaxcalcentetl *n.* loaf
tlaxcalchihua *tv.* make tortillas (*Preterit: onitlaxcalchiuh*)
tlaxcalhuentli *n.* host
tlaxcalixca *tv.* bake (*Preterit: onitlaxcalixcac*)
tlaxcalixcac *n.* baker
tlaxcalli *n.* tortilla
tlaxcalmana *tv.* make tortillas (*Preterit: onitlaxcalman*)
tlaxcalnamacoyan *n.* tortilla shop
tlaxcaloa *tv.* make tortillas (*Preterit: onitlaxcaloh*)
tlaxexelaquilli *adj.* useful
tlaxexelaquillotl *n.* usefulness
tlaxexeloliztli *n.* division
tlaxichtli *n.* arrow
tlaxilacalli *n.* neighborhood
tlaxillotl *n.* prop

tlaxintli *n.* cuckold
tlaxiuhzaloloni *n.* tile
tlaxochpitzactli *n.* braid
tlaxomolli *n.* corner
tlaxopehualli *n.* kick
tlaxopeuhtli *n.* kick
tlaxotla *iv.* plow (*Preterit: onitlaxotlac*)
tlaxotlaliztli *n.* act of plowing
tlaxotlalli *n.* ploughed land
tlaxquitl *n.* something roasted
tlaxtlahualiztli *n.* pay
tlaxtlahuia *tv.* reward (*Preterit: onitetlaxtlahuih*)
tlaxtlahuilia *tv.* pay (*Preterit: onitetlaxtlahuilih*)
tlaxtlahuilli *n.* pay, salary
tlayacanqui *n.* chief, boss, director, head
tlayamanilli *adj.* mild
tlayancuilia *tv.* use something for the first time
    (*Preterit: onitlayancuilih*)
tlayancuililiztli *n.* renovation
tlayaoyahualoni *n.* siege
tlayecanquetl *n.* chief, boss, head
tlayecchihchiuhtli *adj.* elegant
tlayehualtia *tv.* reproach (*Preterit: onitetlayehualtih*)
tlayehyecatiliztli *n.* ventilation
tlayocoxtli *n.* invention
tlayohua *iv.* get dark, overcast (*Preterit: otlayohuac*)
tlayohualli *n.* darkness
tlayolapanallapictli *n.* plan
tlayollotepitzhuiliztli *n.* patience, suffering, tolerance
tlayolmalacacholli *adj.* corrupt
tlayolmelahualiztli *n.* information
tlaza *tv.* throw (*Preterit: onitlatlaz*)
tlazacani *n.* carrier

tlazalolli *n.* building

tlazazacani *n.* carrier

tlazohcamati *adv.* thank you; *tv.* thank
  (*Preterit: onictlazohcamat, onictlazohcamah*)

tlazohneci *impers. v.* it is rare (*Preterit: otlazohnez*)

tlazohpilli *n.* lord

tlazohtetl *n.* precious stone

tlazohti *iv.* be expensive (*Preterit: otlazohtic*)

tlazohticatlahtolli *n.* kind, affectionate words

tlazohtiliztli *n.* affection, love

tlazohtla *tv.* love (*Preterit: onitetlazohtlac*)

tlazohtlahtolli *n.* kind, affectionate words

tlazohtlaloni *adj.* affable, amiable, lovable

tlazohtli *adj.* precious, dear, valuable

tlazohualoyan *n.* clothesline

tlaztalehualli *adj.* rose-colored, flesh-colored

tle *pron.* What?

tle inic ahmo *adv.* Why not?

tle ipampa *adv.* Why?

tleamanalli *n.* stove

tleca *adv.* Why?

tlecalli *n.* chimney

tlecaxitl *n.* incense burner

tlecoacihuiztli *n.* diarrhea

tlecopatl *n.* office

tlecuahuitl *n.* wooden device for staring a fire

tlecuazco *n.* brazier

tlecueponi *iv.* explode (*Preterit: onitlecuepon*)

tlecuezallotl *n.* flame; spark, ember

tlecuilli *n.* fireplace

tlehcahuia *tv.* lift, raise (*Preterit: onitlatlehcahuih*)

tlehco *iv.* ascend (*Preterit: onitlehcoc*)

tlehcoliztli *n.* ascent

tlehcoltia *tv.* lift, raise (*Preterit: onitlatlecoltih*)
tlehuacqui *adj.* cooked
tlehuatza *tv.* broil, cook, grill (*Preterit: onitlatlehuatz*)
tleica *adv.* Why?
tleica ahmo *adv.* Why not?
tlein *pron.* What? **~ omochiuh?** What is happened?
tlemaco *n.* fire shovel
tlemaitl *n.* incense ladle; scoop for carrying fire
tlemiahuatl *n.* flame
tlemiyahuatl *n.* flame
tlemiqui *iv.* be very hot (*Preterit: onitlemic*)
tlemolli *n.* food; meal; stew; mole
tlemoyotl *n.* spark
tlenamactli *n.* a type of incense
tlenenepilli *n.* flame
tlenenequiliztli *n.* whim
tlenequiliztli *n.* desire
tlenotzin *interj.* at your service
tlepapalotl *n.* fire moth; flame
tlepiaztli *n.* candleholder
tlepitza *iv.* blow on a fire (*Preterit: onitlepitz*)
tlepopocaliztli *n.* fever
tlequihquiztelolohtli *n.* bullet
tlequihquiztelolotl *n.* bullet
tlequihquiztlalli *n.* gunpowder; brimstone, sulfur
tlequihquiztli *n.* firearm; gun
tlequihquiztontli *n.* pistol
tlequiza *iv.* be very hot (*Preterit: onitlequiz*)
tletema *tv.* roast (*Preterit: onitlaten*)
tletl *n.* fire
tletlalia *iv.* start a fire (*Preterit: onitletlalih*)
tlexictetl *n.* hot stone used to heat the steam bath
tlexictli *n.* hearth; heating area of steam bath (*temazcalli*)

tlexochtli *n.* hot coal
tlexocuahuitl *n.* ashes from wood
tlexotlaltiloni *n.* tinder
tleyoh *adj.* fiery
tlilana *tv.* draw, sketch (*Preterit: onitlatlilan*)
tlilazcatl *n.* poisonous black ant
tlilehui *iv.* blacken, become black (*Preterit: onitlileuh*)
tlilehuiliztli *n.* blackness; blackening
tliletl *n.* black bean
tlilhuia *tv.* dye black, darken, make something dark
    (*Preterit: onitlatlilhuih*)
tlilihui *iv.* blacken, become black (*Preterit: onitliliuh*)
tlilihuiliztli *n.* blackness; blackening
Tliliuhqueh inchan *n.* Africa
tlilli *n.* black ink; *adj.* black
tlilli tlapalli *n.* writing; knowledge; wisdom
tlillotia *tv.* dye black, darken, make something dark
    (*Preterit: onitlatlilloh*)
tliltetl *n.* dot, period (*punctuation*)
tliltic *adj.* black
tliltic tepuztli *n.* iron (*mineral*)
tlilxochitl *n.* vanilla
tlitlilectic *adj.* freckly
–tloc *suff.* next to, near
tlohtli *n.* hawk, falcon
to– *poss.* our
toca *tv.* bury; plant (*Preterit: onitlatocac*);
    follow (*Preterit: onitetocac*)
tocaamatl *n.* roster
tocahcencahquetl *n.* adjective
tocahtli *n.* name
tocaihcuiloa *tv.* enroll (*Preterit: onitetocaihcuiloh*)
tocaihcuilolamatl *n.* business card, identification card

tocaitl *n.* name; noun

tocapeyotl *n.* gauze

tocatl *n.* spider

tocatlalia *tv.* enroll, register (*Preterit: onitetocatlalih*)

tocatzahualli *n.* spider web

tocayoh *n.* namesake; signed document

tocayotia *tv.* name (*Preterit: onitetocayotih*)

tocayotl *n.* name

tocazahualli *n.* spiderweb

tochin *n.* rabbit

tochohmitl *n.* rabbit fur

tochohtli *n.* rabbit trail; evil path

tochtli *n.* rabbit

tocochia *n.* eyebrow

tocolhuan *n.* ancestors

tocoyonya *n.* loin

toctli *n.* plant; corn plant; maguey plant

toehuayo *n.* skin

tohmitl *n.* fine hair, fuzz, down, fur, fleece, wool

tohmiyoh *adj.* hairy, furry

tohpolli *n.* terrace

tohtoma *tv.* untie (*Preterit: onitlatohton*)

tohuan *adv.* with us

tohueixopil *n.* big toe

tolcalli *n.* arch

tolichtli *adj.* anemic

tolin *n.* grassy reed, sedge, bulrush

tolina *iv.* be hungry, crave food (*Preterit: onitolinac*);
   be anemic (*Preterit: onitolin*)

tolinia *reflex. v.* be poor (*Preterit: oninotolinih*)

tolixtli *adj.* anemic

toloa *iv.* bow, lower the head (*Preterit: onitoloh*);
   tv. swallow (*Preterit: onitlatoloh*)

toloatzin *n.* type of medicinal plant

tololiztli *n.* bowing

tolontic *adj.* round, spherical

tolontli *n.* sphere

tolotica *adv.* with bowed head

Tolquian *n.* Turkey

Tolquian chaneh *n.* Turk

Tolquiantlahtolli *n.* Turkish language

Toltecatl *n.* Toltec; urban; artist

toltecayotl *n.* art; civilization

toma *tv.* release; unroll, unwind (*Preterit: onitlaton*)

tomahua *iv.* become fat; grow (*Preterit: onitomahuac*); *reflex. v.* (*Preterit: oninotomahuac*)

tomahuac *adj.* fat

tomatl *n.* tomato

tomin *n.* money

tomiyahuayocan *n.* loin

tompiahtli *n.* large basket made of palm

tona *impers. v.* be sunny, shine, be hot (*Preterit: otonac*)

tonacayo *n.* the human body, flesh

tonacayocan *n.* buttock

tonacayotl *n.* nourishment; fruits of the earth

tonahuiztli *n.* malaria

tonalamatl *n.* almanac, calendar

tonalco *adv.* during the summer

tonalcochqui *n.* one who takes a nap or siesta; *adj.* sleepy

tonalhuacqui *adj.* sun-dried

tonalhuaqui *iv.* die or wither because of lack of water (*Preterit: otonalhuac*)

tonalhuatza *tv.* dry in the sun (*Preterit: onitlatonalhuatz*)

tonallan *n.* summer, hot season; *adv.* during the summer

tonallapohualoni *n.* calendar

tonalli *n.* day; heat of the sun; luck

tonalmicqui *adj.* sunburned or dried

tonalmihqui *adj.* sunburned or dried

tonalmiqui *iv.* be very hot (*Preterit: onitonalmic*)

tonalmiquiliztli *n.* extreme heat (*weather*)

tonalmitl *n.* ray of the sun

tonameyoh *adj.* radiant

tonameyotl *n.* ray of the sun

tonatiuh *n.* sun

tonatiuh icalaquiyan *n.* west

tonatiuh icalaquiyancayotl *adj.* western

tonatiuh iquizayan *n.* east

tonatiuh iquizayantlacatl *n.* person from the east; Asian

tonatiuh quizayancayotl *n.* eastern

tonayampa *adv.* toward the east

tonayan *adv.* toward the east; during the day

tonayan cochi *iv.* take a siesta (*Preterit: tonayan onicoch*)

tonayan cochiztli *n.* siesta

tonehua *iv.* suffer, feel pain, hurt (*Preterit: onitonehuac and onitoneuh*)

topanehuayo *n.* skin

topileh *n.* sheriff, constable

topilli *n.* errand boy; messenger; rod, staff, cane

topitzahuayan *n.* waist

toptli *n.* coffer, chest, box

totecuacan *n.* city

totoca *tv.* dismiss, drive away (*Preterit: onitetotocac*)

totolacatecomatl *n.* inkwell

totolacatl *n.* quill, feather for writing

totolcalli *n.* henhouse

totolcozcatl *n.* type of mushroom

totolhuauhtli *n.* bird amaranth

totolin *n.* hen turkey

totollaapozonilli *n.* turkey stew

totollaehuatzalli *n.* roast turkey hen
totoltecacalli *n.* egg shell
totolteehuatl *n.* membrane of an egg
totoltemolli *n.* porridge made from eggs
totoltepalan *n.* rotten egg
totoltetl *n.* egg
totoltetl icuztica *n.* egg yolk
totoltetl iiztaca *n.* egg white
totomicqui *adj.* impotent
totomitl *adj.* feathered arrow
totomiyoh *adj.* hairy, furry
totomochtli *n.* dried corn husk
totomoliuhca *n.* set of buttons
totomoliuhqui *n.* button
totomonaliztli *n.* plague
totomoniliztli *n.* blister
totonca atolli *n.* gruel, porridge
totoncapahtli *n.* medicine for fever
totonia *iv.* become hot; *tv.* heat (*Preterit: onitlatotonih and onitlatotonix*)
totoniliztamachihualoni *n.* thermometer
totoniliztli *n.* heat; fever
totonilizzotl *n.* feverishness
totonillotl *n.* fever; heat
totoniyalotl *n.* fever
totonqui *adj.* hot
totopochtic *adj.* toasted
totopochtli *n.* toasted corn chip
tototenhuitztli *n.* beak of a bird
tototentli *n.* beak of a bird
tozan *n.* gopher
tozcacualactli *n.* phlegm

tozcacuitlatl *n.* phlegm
tozcananalca *adj.* hoarse
tozcapanoloni *n.* larynx
tozcapapaca *iv.* gargle (*Preterit: onitozcapapacac*)
tozcapapaconi *n.* gargling
tozcatl *n.* voice; throat
tozcayacacuitlatl *n.* phlegm
tozoa *iv.* spend the night without sleeping (*Preterit: onitozoh*)
tozozcuicatl *n.* vigil song
tozquinamiquiliztli *n.* concert (*choral*)
tozquitl *n.* throat; voice
toztli *n.* yellow-headed parrot
tzaccayotl *n.* lid, cover
tzacua *tv.* close; enclose (*Preterit: onitlatzauc*)
tzacualli *n.* enclosure; mound; platform; pyramid
tzacuhtli *n.* glue, paste
tzahtzani *n.* town crier
tzahtzi *iv.* yell (*Preterit: onitzahtzic*)
tzahtzilia *tv.* yell at someone (*Preterit: onitetzahtzilih*)
tzahtziliztli *n.* shouting; singing of birds
tzahtzini *adj.* loudmouthed
tzahua *iv.* knit, spin yarn, weave (*Preterit: onitzauh*)
tzahualli *n.* spider web
–tzalan *loc. suff.* in the middle of, among
tzanatl *n.* blackbird
tzapalotl *n.* banana
tzapatl *n.* dwarf
tzapinia *tv.* prick (*Preterit: onitetzapinih*)
tzapotl *n.* zapote fruit
tzauctli *n.* glue, paste
tzetzeloa *tv.* shake (*Preterit: onitzetzeloh*)
tzicahuaztli *n.* comb

tzicapotzalli *n.* anthill
tzicaputzalli *n.* anthill
tzicatepetl *n.* anthill
tzicatl *n.* a large poisonous ant
tzictli *n.* chewing gum
tzicuinoliztli *n.* sigh; sobbing; hiccup
tzicunoa *iv.* sigh; sob; have hiccups (*Preterit: onitzicunoh*)
tzilacayohtli *n.* a bluish-green squash
tzilictic *adj.* having a clear sound like a bell
tzilin *n.* small bell
tzilini *iv.* ring (*Preterit: otzilin*)
tzilinia *tv.* ring a bell (*Preterit: onitlatzilinih*)
tzilli *n.* small bell
tzimmicqui *adj.* impotent
tzimmiquiliztli *n.* impotence
tzinacantli *n.* bat
tzinacaztli *n.* bat
tzinicpalli *n.* seat
tzinitzcan *n.* black bird
tzinpitzahuac *adj.* thin at the base
tzinquiza *iv.* turn back, retreat, regress (*Preterit: onitzinquiz*)
tzintamalli *n.* buttock, hip
tzintetl *n.* base of a wall
tzinti *iv.* begin (*Preterit: onitzintic*)
tzintia *tv.* begin something, initiate (*Preterit: onitlatzintih*)
tzintiliztli *n.* foundation; beginning
tzintlantli *n.* behind, rump, buttock
tzintli *n.* anus; buttock; lower body; behind; bottom;
    base, foundation
tzintomahuac *adj.* thick at the base
tzipitl *n.* sickly child
tzitzicuincocoyaliztli *n.* stabbing pain
tzitzitl *n.* a type of turquoise used in mosaics

tzitzquia *tv.* support (*Preterit: onitlatiztizquih*)

tzoalli *n.* amaranth seed dough

tzocatl *n.* wart

tzocohuaztli *n.* comb

tzocotontli *adj.* lowest

tzocuil *n.* goldfinch

tzocuitlatl *n.* perspiration

tzohpilotl *n.* vulture

tzohuia *tv.* rope (*Preterit: onotlatzohuih*)

tzoltic *adj.* narrow

tzompatic *adj.* perfect

tzompilahui *iv.* have a cold (*Preterit: onitzompilauh*)

tzompilihui *iv.* have a cold (*Preterit: onitzompiliuh*)

tzompilli *n.* cold (*illness*)

tzoncalli *n.* headdress; wig

tzoncuaitl *n.* hair ends

tzoncui *reflex. v.* take revenge, avenge (*Preterit: oninotzoncuic*)

tzonhuaztli *n.* hairbrush

tzonicpalli *n.* headrest, pillow

tzoniztac *adj.* having gray or white hair

tzoniztalli *n.* gray or white hair

tzonocuilcualiztli *n.* splitting of the hair

tzonquixtia *tv.* finish (*Preterit: onitlatzonquixtih*)

tzonquiza *iv.* grow hair; end (*Preterit: onitzonquiz*)

tzonquizcayotl *n.* end

tzonquizqui *adj.* finished

tzontecomatl *n.* head

tzonteconcocoliztli *n.* headache

tzonteconcocolli *n.* headache

tzonteconehua *tv.* give a headache; tire (*Preterit: onitetzonconeuh*)

tzonteti *iv.* be stubborn, rebellious (*Preterit: onitzontet*)

tzontetia *iv.* be disobedient, rebellious (*Preterit: onitzontetix*)

tzontetl *n.* rebellious, stubborn
tzonteyotl *n.* disobedience, rebellion; opposition
tzontic *adj.* perfect
tzontlacalolli *n.* ribbon (*hair*)
tzontli *n.* 400; hair
tzopelic *adj.* sweet, tasty
tzopelicayotl *n.* sweetness
tzopiloan *n.* scavenger
tzopinia *tv.* prick, inject (*Preterit: onitetzopinih*)
tzotl *n.* filth; sweat; pine turpentine
tzotzocatl *n.* stingy
tzotzocayotl *n.* avarice
tzotzona *tv.* strike; play an instrument
    (*Preterit: onitlatzotzon*)
tzotzotl *n.* pimple, boil, skin eruption
tzoyoh *adj.* dirty
tzoyonia *tv.* fry (*Preterit: onitlatzoyonih*)
tzoyonqui *adj.* fried
tzoyotl *n.* perspiration; anus

U
ulli *n.* rubber
uncan *adv.* there

V
vino xococ *n.* vinegar

X
xachtli *n.* sediment
xacualoa *tv.* knead (*Preterit: onitlaxacualoh*)

xahcalcuauhitztli *n.* top of a hut

xahcalli *n.* hut

xahcaltzuma *tv.* cover a hut with thatch
 (*Preterit: onixahcaltzun*)

xahualli *n.* makeup

xalipicilli *n.* very fine sand

xalla *n.* sandy ground

xalli *n.* sand

xalo *n.* pitcher, jug

xalpan *n.* sandy ground

xaltetl *n.* gravel, pebble

xalxocotl *n.* guava

xamactic *adj.* cracked

xamani *iv.* break, shatter (*Preterit: onixaman*)

xamania *tv.* break something (*Preterit: onitlaxamanih*)

xamanqui *adj.* cracked

xamitl *n.* adobe

xayacatl *n.* face, mask

xayacatlachihchihualli *n.* mask

xayacayotia *tv.* disguise, conceal (*Preterit: onitexayacayotih*)

xayotl *n.* feces

xelhuaztli *n.* brush (*for cleaning*), hair brush

xelihui *iv.* split in half (*Preterit: oxeliuh*)

xelihuini *adj.* divisible

xeliuhqui *adj.* divided, split in half

xeloa *tv.* split something (*Preterit: onitlaxeloh*)

xeltic *n.* change (*money*)

xexelaquia *tv.* use (*Peterit: onitlaxexelaquih*)

xexeloliztli *n.* division

xeyotl *n.* rash

xicalli *n.* gourd

xicaltecomatl *n.* gourd

xicamatl *n.* jicama

xicmecayotl *n.* umbilical cord

xicoa *reflex. v.* envy, desire without hope; support (*weight*);
(*Preterit: oninoxicoh*); *tv.* deceive (*Preterit: onitexicoh*)

xicohcuitlaocotl *n.* candle

xicohcuitlatl *n.* wax

xicohtli *n.* bumblebee

xicolli *n.* vest

xictli *n.* navel

xihuitl *n.* turquoise, year, comet, herb (*Stem: xiuh–*)

xihxitini *iv.* fall apart, crumble (*Preterit: oxihxitin*)

xillanhuia *tv.* protect (*Preterit: onitexillanhuih*)

xillantli *n.* stomach, womb

xilotl *n.* ear of tender corn

xima *tv.* shave; give a haircut (*Preterit: onitexin*);
cut (*Preterit: onitlaxin*); commit adultery (*Preterit:
onitetlaxin*); *reflex. v.* shave (*Preterit: oninoxin*)

xinachtli *n.* seed

xinachyotl *n.* semen, sperm

xincayotl *n.* scab

xiomichin *n.* trout

xipalli *n.* lip

xipehua *tv.* skin, prune, trim, peel, remove the crust
(*Preterit: onitlaxipeuh*)

xipincuayotequi *tv.* circumcise

xipintli *n.* prepuce, foreskin

xippalli *adj.* blue; turquoise

xippopoa *tv.* pull weeds (*Preterit: onitlaxippopoh*)

xiquipilacoquizaloni *n.* globe

xiquipilli *n.* bag, pouch; battalion of 8,000 soldiers

xiquipiltontli *n.* bag

xiquitic *adj.* potbellied

xitic *adj.* not working, broken

xitini *iv.* tumble, fall, perish (*Preterit: onixitin*)

xitinia *tv.* overthrow, bring down, destroy; disperse
  (*Preterit: onitexitinih*)
xitiniliztli *n.* fall
xitinqui *adj.* broken; fallen
xitlahuac *n.* straight
xitomatl *n.* red tomato
xittomoniliztli *n.* blister
xiuhcahuitl *n.* season
xiuhcamohtli *n.* sweet potato
xiuhizhuatl *n.* plant leaf
xiuhnelhuatl *n.* herb root
xiuhpahnamacac *n.* herbalist
xiuhpopoa *tv.* pull weeds (*Preterit: onitlaxiuhpopoh*)
xiuhtlacualli *n.* vegetable; vegetable salad
xiuhtlah *n.* place full of weeds
xiuhtlahcuiloh *n.* historian, chronicler
xiuhtlahtli *n.* place full of weeds
xiuhtlalia *tv.* bother (*Preterit: onitexiuhtlalih*)
xiuhtlamatiliztli *n.* botany
xiuhtomolli *n.* turquoise
xiuhtototl *n.* blue cotinga (*bird*)
xiuhuitzolli *n.* crown adorned with precious stones
xiuhzaloliztli *n.* mosaic work
xixicuin *n.* glutton
xixicuinoa *tv.* eat too much (*Preterit: onitlaxixicuinoh*)
xixicuiyotl *n.* gluttony
xiyotia *reflex. v.* follow an example (*Preterit: oninoxiyotih*)
xiyotl *n.* example; itch
xochhuia *tv.* tell jokes, make people laugh
  (*Preterit: onitexochhuih*)
xochichinancalli *n.* garden
xochicihuiztli *n.* hemorrhoids
xochicomitl *n.* flower pot; flower vase

xochicualcotona *tv.* pick fruit (*Preterit: onixochicualcoton*)
xochicualcuahuitl *n.* fruit tree
xochicualli *n.* fruit; banana
xochihcualcuahuitl *n.* fruit tree
xochihcualli *n.* fruit; banana
xochihuah *n.* magician; sorcerer
xochihuia *tv.* charm; pay flirtatious compliment; seduce; caress (*Preterit: onitexochihuih*)
xochinamacac *n.* florist, flower vendor
xochinamacoyan *n.* flower shop
xochipalli *adj.* orange
xochipixqui *n.* gardener
xochipoloa *reflex. v.* eat sweets (*Preterit: oninoxochipoloh*)
xochitapachtli *n.* finest jade
xochitepancalli *n.* garden; park
xochitic *adj.* beautiful
xochitl *n.* flower; plant
xochitl cuicatl *n.* poetry, the arts
xochitla *n.* garden
xochitlahtoani *n.* poet
xochitlahtolli *n.* poetry, poem
xochitlenamactli *n.* perfume
xochitototl *n.* oriole
xochiyoh *adj.* flowery
xochiyotl *n.* oil
xochizhuatl *n.* rose petal
xochtia *tv.* tell jokes, make people laugh (*Preterit: onitexochtih*); *iv.* vomit (*Preterit: onixochtih*)
xochtic *adj.* very young, not speaking yet
xochtlalpictli *n.* bouquet
xochtoconi *n.* flowerpot
xoco *n.* last daughter
xocoa *tv.* reject (*Preterit: onitexocoh*)

xococ *adj.* sour
xocoliztli *n.* sourness
xocomecamilli *n.* vineyard
xocomecatl *n.* grapevine, vine
xocomecayollotl *n.* grape
xocomicqui *n.* drunk
xocomihqui *n.* drunk
xocomiquini *adj.* drunk
xoconochtli *n.* bitter prickly pear
xocotextli *n.* leaven, yeast
xocotl *n.* bittersweet fruit; fruit; plum
xocotl lima *n.* lime
xocotl limón *n.* lemon
xocoyaliztli *n.* heartburn; sourness
xocoyoh *n.* tree with fruit
xocoyollohtli *n.* fruit pit
xocoyomati *tv.* pamper (*Preterit: onitexocoyomat*)
xocoyotl *n.* youngest or last son or daughter
xocpalixtli *n.* sole of the foot
xocpalli *n.* sole of the foot
xoctli *n.* clay pot
xocue *n.* lame, cripple
xohueyac *adj.* having a long stem, long legs
xohuiac *adj.* having a long stem, long legs
xoletl *n.* mushroom
xolhuaztli *n.* brush (*for cleaning*), hairbrush
xoloca *iv.* sit on one's heels (*Preterit: onixolocatca*)
xolochahui *iv.* wrinkle with age, wither (*Peterit: onixolochauh*)
xolochoa *tv.* wrinkle something; fold (*Preterit: onitlaxolochoh*)
xolochtic *adj.* wrinkled
xolochticayotl *n.* wrinkle
xolochtli *n.* wrinkle
xoloitzcuintli *n.* hairless dog

xololohtli *n.* small flute, hornpipe
xolonqui *adj.* steamed (*cooked*)
xolopihayotl *n.* liquor, intoxicating beverage
xolopihnemiliztli *n.* foolishness
xolopihtica *adv.* foolishly
xolopihtli *n.* fool; bum; insane; devil
xolopihyotl *n.* foolishness; insanity, madness
xolotl *n.* creature; monster; servant
xomahtli *n.* wooden spoon
xomalli *n.* wooden spoon
xomilin *n.* an edible insect
xomolli *n.* corner
xomotl *n.* duck
xomulco caltech nemini *adj.* homeless
xonacatl *n.* onion
xonexca *iv.* warn (*Preterit: onixonexcac*)
xopan *n.* spring (*season*); summer
xopaniztempan *n.* summer, spring (*season*)
xopaniztli *n.* spring (*season*)
xopantlacayotl *n.* that which grows in spring
xopantlah *n.* spring (*season*); rainy season
xopechtli *n.* foundation of a building
xopehua *tv.* kick someone (*Preterit: onitexopeuh*)
xopetlatl *n.* foundation of a building
xopiliztitl *n.* toenail
xopilli *n.* toe
xopilonquizac *n.* bunion
xopiltecuhtli *n.* big toe
xopilxocoyotl *n.* small toe
xotamachihualoni *n.* foot (*measure*)
Xotiyo *adj.* Jewish
xotl *n.* leg; foot (*in compound constructions: ninixopaca, I wash my feet*)

xotla *iv.* be hot, be on fire, catch fire; have a fever; blossom
  (*Preterit: onixotlac*)
xotlac *adj.* hot; open; in blossom
xotlapalli *n.* hoof
xoxalli *n.* cyst; *n.* tumor
xoxocotl *n.* guava
xoxoctic *adj.* green; blue
xoxotla *tv.* cut, make an incision; make bleed
  (*Preterit: onitexoxotlac*)
xoxotlani *n.* firefly; one who makes an incision, cuts
xoxouhqui *adj.* green; raw
xupanhuia *tv.* work the fields in the rainy season
  (*Preterit: onitlaxupanhuih*)
xupantla *n.* rainy season

Y

ya *iv.* go (*Preterit: oniya*); *adv.* already
yacacuitlatl *n.* mucus
yacaezquiza *iv.* bleed from the nose (*Preterit: oniyacaezquiz*)
yacahtzolli *n.* nose
yacahuitzoa *tv.* taper, sharpen (*Preterit: onitlayacahuitzoh*)
yacahuitztic *adj.* tapered
yacana *tv.* manage (*Preterit: oniteyacan*); *tv.* lead
  (*Preterit: oniteyacan*)
yacapani *adj.* nasal
yacapantli *n.* firstborn
yacapitzactic *adj.* tapered
yacapitzahua *tv.* taper (*Preterit: onitlayacapitzahuac*)
yacapitzahuac *adj.* tapered
yacatl *n.* nose, tip
yacatolli *n.* mucus

yacatticatlalia *tv.* prefer (*Preterit: oniteyacatticatlalih*)

yacatzolcoyoc *n.* nostril

yacatzolli *n.* nose

yacatzompilihuiztli *n.* flu, cold

yacatzontli *n.* nose hair

yalhua *n.* yesterday

yalhua ihualli *n.* night before last

yalhua yohuac *n.* night before last

yalhua yohualli *n.* night before last

yahualli *n.* circle, wheel

yahualmachiotl *n.* parenthesis

yahualmachiotlahcuilolli *n.* parenthesis

yahualoa *tv.* encircle (*Preterit: onitlayahualoh*)

yahualtic *adj.* round

yahuitl *adj.* navy blue

yaliztli *n.* departure

yamactic *adj.* soft

yamanqui *adj.* mild; soft, delicate; sweet; pleasant

–yan *suff.* place where

yancuic *adj.* new

yancuican *adv.* recently

yancuilia *tv.* renovate; use for first time
(*Preterit: onitlayancuilih*)

yancuiliztli *n.* novelty, something new

yani *n.* pilgrim

yaochichua *tv.* make war (*Preterit: oniteyaochiuh*)

yaochiuhqui *n.* soldier

yaocuicatl *n.* war song

yaomiqui *iv.* die in battle (*Preterit: oniyaomic*)

yaoquizcateyacanqui *n.* commander

yaoquizcatlahtoani *n.* general

yaoquizcayacanqui *n.* commander

yaoquizcayotl *n.* army

yaoquizcayutl *n.* army
yaoquizqueh *n.* army
yaoquizqui *n.* soldier, warrior
yaotl *n.* enemy
yaotlachixqui *n.* spy
yaotlalli *n.* battlefield
yaotlatquitl *n.* weapons of war
yaoyahualoa *tv.* siege (*Preterit: onitlayaoyahualoh*)
yaoyotl *n.* war
yapalli *adj.* black
yapalteopixcanequentiloni *n.* cassock
yapaltic *adj.* black
yatepa *adv.* later, afterward
yauh *iv.* go (*Preterit: oniyauh*)
yauhtli *n.* fog, mist
yayapalectic freckly *adj.*
yayauhqui *adj.* darkish, black
ye *adv.* certainly; already
ye huehcauh *adv.* a long time ago
ye ixquich *adv.* enough
ye nechca *adv.* a few days ago
ye nepa *adv.* in the past
ye ohuiptla *adv.* day before yesterday
ye tlahca *adv.* it is late
ye tlayohuac *adv.* nighttime
ye yehce *adv.* a short while ago
yec *adv.* well, fine
yecacehuaztli *n.* flyswatter
yecatl *n.* fresh, sweet water
yeccantli *adj.* right
yeccaqui *tv.* understand (*Preterit: onitlayeccac*)
yeceh *conj.* but, nevertheless
yecmaitl *n.* right hand

yecnacayoh *adj.* good looking
yecnemi *adj.* moral
yecnemiliztli *n.* morality
yecnequi *reflex. v.* pretend to be good (*Preterit: oninoyecnec*)
yecoa *tv.* test (*Preterit: onitlayecoh*)
yecolli *n.* test
yecomitl *n.* pot for boiling beans
yecquetza *reflex. v.* dress well (*Preterit: oninoyecquetz*)
yectel *adv.* a few days ago
yectema *tv.* tune an instrument (*Preterit: onitlayecten*)
yectenehua *tv.* praise, venerate, bless (*Preterit: onitlayecteneuh*)
yectiliztli *n.* goodness,virtue
yectlahtoleh *adj.* having a good voice
yectli *adj.* correct; good; beautiful; innocent
yectli iyollo *adj.* virtuous
yecuel *adv.* already
yecyotl *n.* goodness; beauty; correctness
yeh *pron.* he, she, it
yeh ica *adv.* for that reason
yeh imman *adv.* it is time
yeh oncan *adv.* it is time
yehcamalacotl *n.* typhoon, waterspout
yehhuantin *pron.* they
yehhuatl *pron.* he, she, it
yehica *conj.* since
yehuantin *pron.* they
yehuatl *pron.* he, she, it
yehyecaquiahuitl *n.* rainstorm
yehyecatiliztli *n.* ventilation
yei *num.* three
yeliztli *n.* being
yelizyotl *n.* character, nature; being
yelli *n.* liver

yenepa *adj.* ancient; *adv.* formerly, in ancient times
yepatl *n.* skunk
yepazohtli *n.* wormseed, green plant
yequeneh *adv.* finally
yetic *adj.* heavy
yexcampa *n.* triangle
yexi *reflex. v.* fart (*Preterit: oninyex*)
yexochitl *n.* flower of the tobacco plant
yeyantli *n.* place, seat
yez *iv.* there will be
yeztli *n.* blood
yocoxca *adv.* meekly; gently
yocoxcatlacatl *n.* a peaceful person
yocoxcayotl *n.* peace; contentment; modesty
yocoya *tv.* invent, conceive, make, create
    (*Preterit: onitlayocox*)
yohhuicuitl *n.* rectum
yohque *adv.* so (*in this manner*), thus, like, as
yohuac *adv.* at night
yohuahtzinco *adv.* early in the morning
yohualcuicatl *n.* serenade
yohualcuicatlacaconi *n.* serenade
yohualli *n.* night
yohualnepantla *n.* midnight
yohualpapalotl *n.* moth
yohualtica *adv.* at night
yohuaquiltihtzino *interj.* good night
yolahcocui *reflex. v.* fall in love (*Preterit: oninoyolahcocuic*)
yolcan *n.* birthplace
yolcapahmatiliztli *n.* veterinary medicine
yolcapahmatini *n.* veterinarian
yolcapahtiani *n.* veterinarian
yolcatl *n.* animal

yolcatontli *n.* small insect
yolcatzacualli *n.* zoo
yolcayotl *n.* nourishment
yolceuhcayotl *n.* mildness, gentleness, docility
yolceuhqui *adj.* mild, gentle, docile
yolchicahuac *adj.* brave
yolchicahualiztli *n.* effort
yolcocoa *reflex. v.* be sad; repent (*Preterit: oninoyolcocoh*)
yolcuepa *iv.* change one's mind (*Preterit: oniyolcuep*)
yolhueiliztli *n.* generosity
yoli *iv.* live; be born (*Preterit: oniyol*)
yolic *adj.* slow
yolicniuh *adj.* intimate
yolicniuhtli *n.* dear friend
yolihtlacoa *iv.* offend (*Preterit: oniyolihtlacoh*)
yolilizoh *adj.* spiritual
yoliliztli *n.* spirit
yolitl *n.* mule
yoliuhtlalia *tv.* satisfy (*Preterit: oniteyoliuhtlalih*)
yoliuhyaliztli *n.* free will
yolixmachiliztli *n.* psychology
yolixmatini *n.* psychologist
yolizma *adj.* perceptive
yolizmatiliztli *n.* biology
yolizmatini *n.* biologist
yolizmatqui *adj.* discreet
yoliztli *n.* life
yollalia *tv.* console (*Preterit: oniteyollalih*)
yollamicqui *adj.* cowardly
yollamictia *tv.* horrify (*Preterit: oniteyollamictih*)
yollamiquilzitli *n.* cowardice
yolli *n.* heart
yollocayotl *n.* ability

yollochamahuac *adj.* having a thick center
yollococihuatl *n.* middle-aged woman
yollocococ *adj.* cruel
yollococoxqui *adj.* insane
yollocuecuepqui *adj.* fickle; variable
yollocuepcayotl *n.* fickleness
yollohco *n.* center
yollohtli *n.* heart
yollohuapahuac *adj.* brave, courageous
yollohxochitl *n.* magnolia
yolloixtli *n.* esophagus
yollolohtli *n.* heart
yollomachtilli *adj.* docile
yollopiltic *adj.* generous
yollotepahtiani *n.* cardiologist
yollotepitztilia *reflex. v.* be patient, tolerant; strive
(*Preterit: oninoyollotepitztilih*)
yollotetic *adj.* incorrigible
yollotetl *n.* resolute
yollotiliztli *n.* bravery, courage
yollotl *n.* heart
yollotlahueliloc *adj.* crazy
yollotlahuelilocatiliztli *n.* insanity
yollotonehualiztli *n.* bereavement, sadness
yollotoneuhqui *adj.* bereaved, distressed, sad
yolloxochitl *n.* magnolia
yolloxocotl *n.* pit
yolloyamancayotl *n.* tolerance
yolmaca *tv.* stimulate, give life (*Preterit: oniteyolmacac*)
yolmaxiltia *reflex. v.* think, reflect (*Preterit: oninoyolmaxiltih*)
yolmelahuac *adj.* honest, just, fair
yolmiqui *iv.* be afraid; faint (*Preterit: oniyolmic*)
yolmotquitializtli *n.* sincerity

yolmotquitiani *adj.* sincere
yolnentoc *adj.* unreliable, inconsistent, unstable
yolpaqui *iv.* be happy (*Preterit: oniyolpac*)
yolpaquiliztli *n.* joy, enjoyment
yolpoliuhqui *n.* a madman
yolqui *n.* animal; *adj.* alive
yolquimil *adj.* stupid
yolteohuia *tv.* foretell (*Preterit: onitlayoltohuih*)
yoltequipacholli *n.* doubt
yoltexpahuacentetl *n.* loaf
yoltextlaoyotl *n.* cake
yoltextlaxcalli *n.* wafer
yoltextli *n.* pinole
yoltitlan *n.* stomach
yoltzotzona *reflex. v.* doubt (*Preterit: oninoyoltzotzon*)
yolyamanqui *adj.* gentle of heart
yomotlantli *n.* side
yoyolin *n.* animal, small animal; insect; *adj.* alive
yoyoliton *n.* mosquito
yoyomiquiliztli *n.* itching
yoyomoca *iv.* itch (*Preterit: oniyoyomocac*)
yoyomoctli *n.* testicle; kidney
yuh nematiliztli *n.* opinion, judgment
yuh quiz *adj.* natural
yuh quizaliztli *n.* condition
yuh quiznacayoh *adj.* sexual
yuh quiztli *n.* idiosyncrasy, peculiarity
yuhcateyollo *n.* intention
yuhcateyolqui *adj.* intentional
yuhcatiliztli *n.* culture; form; figure; aspect
yuhcatlatiliztli *n.* lack
yuhcatlayotl *n.* emptiness
yuhcayotl *n.* manner

yuhqui *adv.* so (*in this manner*), thus, like, as
yuhqui ihuintic *adj.* happy, euphoric
yuhqui yeliztli *n.* instinct
yuhquimma *adv.* seemingly
yuhquin *adv.* so (*in this manner*), thus, like, as
yuhyotica *adv.* naturally

Z

za ica in *adv.* shortly
za nelli *adv.* absolutely
zaca *tv.* transport (*Preterit: onitlazacac*)
zacahuitztli *n.* weed
zacaixtlahuatl *n.* uncultivated land
zacamecatl *n.* rope made of grass
zacamilli *n.* grassland
zacaocuilin *n.* grass worm
zacaomitl *n.* grass
zacapehpechtli *n.* bed made of grass
zacapetlatanahtli *n.* reed basket
zacapilli *n.* clitoris
zacatanahtli *n.* reed basket
zacatextli *n.* hay
zacatl *n.* grass
zacatlah *n.* savannah
zacatzontetl *n.* sod, clod
zacaxahcalli *n.* grass hut
zaciquin *adv.* whenever
zacotl *n.* ferret
zahua *reflex. v.* abstain from food, fast (*Preterit: oninozauh*)
zahuac *n.* throat infection
zahualli *n.* spider web
zahuatl *n.* smallpox; pimple; scab

zahuayoh *adj.* having pimples
zahzaliuhyantli *n.* joint
zalihui *iv.* be pasted, glued (*Preterit: onizaliuh*)
zaliuhyantli *n.* joint
zaloa *tv.* glue, paste, learn (*Preterit: onitlazaloh*)
zan *adv.* only
zan achic *adj.* momentary
zan achiltica *adv.* momentarily
zan achitonca *n.* moment, brief moment
zan ahmo yuhqui *adv.* backwards
zan cualcan *adv.* in a short while, shortly
zan cuel *adv.* in a short while, shortly
zan cuelachic *n.* instant
zan icuepca *adv.* backwards
zan ixquichcacahuitl *n.* moment
zan nenca *adv.* in vain
zan niman *adv.* right away
zan queh *adv.* of course
zan quezquipa *adv.* a few times
zan tepitzin *adv.* just a little
zan tequi *adv.* frequently, often
zan tlahco *n.* average, medium
zanilli *n.* fable, story; conversation
zaniztlachiani *adj.* nearsighted
zannen nenemi *adj.* homeless
zanoquiztic *adj.* fortuitous
zanoquiztica *adv.* by chance, fortuitously
zanoquiztiliztli *n.* chance
zanyeyuhqui *adj.* natural
zapalotl *n.* banana
zatepan *adv.* later, afterward
zatlatzonco *adv.* finally
zayolin *n.* fly

zayolloa *iv.* be infested with flies (*Preterit: ozayolloac*)
zazaca *tv.* carry, transport (*Preterit: onitlazazacac*)
zazaltic *adj.* sticky
zazan *adv.* without reason; in vain; too much, excessively
zazan campa *adv.* anywhere
zazanca *adv.* hypothetically, supposing that
zazanactli *n.* lung
zazanilli *n.* narration; dialogue; joke
zazo *adv.* it doesn't matter
zazo aquin *pron.* anyone
zazo canin *adv.* anywhere
zazo quemman *adv.* anytime
zazo tlein *pron.* anything
zazocampa *adv.* anywhere
zecactli *n.* armpit
zoa *tv.* draw blood from someone (*Preterit: onitezoh*)
zohuatl *n.* woman
zolcanauhtli *n.* wild duck
zoletl *n.* pinto bean
zolin *n.* quail
zollahtoa *iv.* sing like a quail (*Preterit: onizollahtoh*)
zoloa *tv.* use; make old; ruin (*Preterit: onitlazoloh*)
zoloni *iv.* snore (*Preterit: onizolon*)
zolotia *tv.* dirty; smear (*Preterit: onitlazolotih*)
zoma *reflex. v.* be angry (*Preterit: oninozomah*)
zomaleh *adj.* angry, furious
zomalia *reflex. v.* become angry (*Preterit: oninozomalih*)
zomalli *n.* anger
zonectic *adj.* porous
zonecticulli *n.* sponge
zoquiacqui *adj.* mired
zoquiahuiltia *reflex. v.* be idle (*Preterit: oninozoquialhuiltih*)
zoquialtia *tv.* soil, smear with mud (*Preterit: onitlazoquialtih*)

zoquiaqui *iv.* fall in the mud (*Preterit: onizoquiac*)

zoquiatl *n.* silt, mire, marsh, swamp

zoquicanauhtli *n.* goose

zoquihciuhqui *n.* potter

zoquinacochtli *n.* clay ear plug

zoquipachoa *tv.* spread manure in the field
      (*Preterit: onitlazoquipachoh*)

zoquitecomatl *n.* clay jug

zoquiteixiptla *n.* clay statue

zoquitelolohtli *n.* clump of earth

zoquiti *iv.* get muddy (*Preterit: onizoquitic*)

zoquitic *adj.* muddy; soft; wet

zoquitl *n.* mud; clay

zoquitlatquitl *n.* earthenware, something thing made of clay

zoquixayacatl *n.* clay mask

zoquixicohcuitlatl *n.* impure beeswax

zoquiyoh *adj.* muddy

zoquiyotl *n.* residue

zotl *n.* piece of cloth

zotlahua *tv.* discourage, take strength away from
      (*Preterit: onitezotlahuac*); *iv.* faint, swoon
      (*Preterit: onizotlahuac*)

zotlahuac *adj.* weak

zotlahualiztli *n.* fainting; weakness

zotlauhqui *adj.* faint; downcast; discouraged

zotolcactli *n.* sandal made of palm leaf

zotolin *n.* palm (*tree*)

zotolla *n.* palm grove

zotolpetlatl *n.* mat made of palm leaves

zotzona *iv.* knock (*Preterit: onictzotzon*)

zoyacapolin *n.* palm date

zoyachiquihuitl *n.* basket of palm leaves

zoyapetlatl *n.* mat made of palm leaves

zoyatanahtli *n.* basket made of palm leaves
zoyatl *n.* palm (*tree*)
zozolca *iv.* snore (*Preterit: onizozolcac*)
zozoloca *iv.* buzz (*Preterit: onizozolocac*)
zozolocaliztli *n.* buzzing, noise
zozolocpitzqui *n.* flutist
zozoloctli *n.* flute
zozoloquiztli *n.* drone; hissing
zozoltic *adj.* old

English-Nahuatl Dictionary

A

a few days ago *adv.* yectel, yenechca
a few times *adv.* zan quezquipa
a little *adv.* achica
a little more *adv.* ocachi
a lot *adv.* cecenca
a short time ago *adv.* quin axcan, quin izqui
abandon *tv.* cahua (*Preterit: onitlacauh*)
abate *iv.* cuetlani (*Preterit: onicuetlan*)
ability *n.* huelitiliztli, huelitiliztli, nezcaliliztli, yollocayotl, tlacaquiliztli
able *adj.* huel (*with future tense*)
abortion *n.* netlatlaxililiztli
abscess *n.* palancapozahualiztli, cuitlatl
absolutely *adv.* huel en, za nelli
absorb *tv.* tlaltequi (*Preterit: onitlaltec*)
absorbable *adj.* ilteconi
absorption *n.* tlaltequiztli
abstain from food *reflex. v.* zahua (*Preterit: oninozauh*)
abyss *n.* amictlan, huehcatlan
accent mark *n.* tlatliltzicuiniliztli
accept *tv.* celia (*Preterit: onitlacelih*)
acclaim *tv.* paccatzatzilia (*Preterit: onitepaccatzatzilih*), pahcatzatzilia (*Preterit: onitepahcatzatzilih*)
accompany *tv.* axiltia (*Preterit: oniteaxiltih*)
accordion *n.* petlacalmecahuehuetl

accountancy *n.* tlapohualiztli

accountant *n.* tlapouhcayomatini, tlapouhqui

accounting *n.* tlapouhcayotl

achieve *tv.* axilia (*Preterit: onitlaaxilih*)

acne *n.* ixocuilin

acorn *n.* ahuatomatl

acrobat *n.* mayotzincuepani

action *n.* aililiztli

active *adj.* aini

activity *n.* aililiztli

add *tv.* cempohua (*Preterit: oniccempouh*)

adjective *n.* tocahcencahquetl

adjust *tv.* namictia (*Preterit: onitlanamictih*)

administration *n.* teyacanaliztli

admirable *adj.* mahuiztic

admiration *n.* teizahuiliztli

admonish *tv.* nohnotza (*Preterit: onitenohnotz*)

adobe *n.* xamitl

adopt *reflex. v.* piltzintia (*Preterit: oninotepiltzintih*)

adopted daughter *n.* cihuatepiltzintilli

adopted son *n.* netepiltzintilli

adoption *n.* netepiltzintiliztli

adorn *tv.* tlacualnextia (*Preterit: onitlacualnextih*), tlamahuichihchihua (*Preterit: onitlamahuichihchiuh*)

adorned *adj.* tlayecchihchiuhtli

adult *n.* grown-up

adulterer *n.* tetlaximani, tetlaxinqui, tepan yani

adultery *n.* tetlaximaliztli; **commit ~** *tv.* tetlaxima (*Preterit: onitetlaxin*)

advantage *n.* tlapanahuiliztli

adverb *n.* tlachihualcencahquetl

adversary *n.* tenamicqui, tenamihqui

advice *n.* teyolnonotzaliztli

advise *tv.* tlahtolmaca (*Preterit: onitetlahtolmacac*)
advocate *n.* tepantlahtoani
affable *adj.* momatini, tlazohtlaloni
affection *n.* tlazohtlaliztli, tlazohtiliztli
affirmation *n.* tlaneltililiztli
affliction *n.* netequipacholiztli
afraid *adj.* ixmauhqui, mauhcamicqui;
    be ~ *iv.* mahui (*Preterit: onimauh*),
    mauhcamiqui (*Preterit: onimauhcamic*)
Africa *n.* Tliliuhqueh inchan
afternoon *n.* teotlac
afterward *adv.* zatepan, yatepa
again *adv.* occepa, nocuel
against *suff.* –huic
age *iv.* huehueti (*Preterit: onihuehuetic*); *tv.* huehcahuitia
    (*onitlahuehcahuitih*)
agenda *n.* amatequitl
aggressive *adj.* oquichehuani
agony *n.* nemocihuiliztli
agree *iv.* cea (*Preterit: onicez*)
agreement *n.* nenahualiztli, nenotzalli
agriculture *n.* millacayotl
aim *n.* tlamelauhcaittaloni; *tv.* melauhcaitta
    (*Preterit: onitlamelauhcaitta*)
air *n.* ehecatl
airplane *n.* patlaniztepozcalli, tepozpapalotl, tepoztototl
alabaster *n.* azcalli, tecalli
alert *adj.* tlacacqui
algae *n.* acpatl
alive *adj.* nentoc, yolqui, yoyolin
all *adj.* ixquich, nochi, muchi
all night *adv.* cenyohuac

all-powerful *adj.* cenhuelitini
allay *tv.* cehuia (*Preterit: onitecehuih*)
alley *n.* ohcaltontli
alliance *n.* coatlacah
alligator *n.* tecuixin
almanac *n.* tonalamatl
almighty *adj.* ixquichihueli
almost *adv.* achiuhqui
alms *n.* tetlaocoliztli
alone *adj.* icel
alphabet *n.* tlahcuilolpamitl
already *adv.* ya, ye, cuel, ye cuel
also *conj.* no, no ihuan, noihqui, ni iuhqui
altar *n.* momoztli, tlalmomoztli
altar boy *n.* misahpalehuiani, misah tenanquililpiltontli
although *conj.* macihui, manel, mazannel, mazo
alum *n.* tlalxocotl
always *adv.* cemihcac, mochipa, nochipa
amaranth *n.* huauhtli
ambassador *n.* tlahtohcatitlantli, tlahtolitqui
ambidextrous *adj.* necocmomaimati
America *n.* Macehuallalpan (*continent*)
American *n.* Tlahtohcayotl in Cepanca chaneh (*U.S.*);
    Cenca Tlahtohcayotl chaneh
amiable *adj.* tlazohtlaloni
among *suff.* –tzalan
analytical *adj.* mixpetzoani
analyze *iv.* ixpetzoa (*Preterit: oninixpetzoh*)
ancestor *n.* colli
ancient *adj.* yenepa
and *conj.* auh, ihuan (*in the company of*)
anemic *adj.* tolichtli, tolixtlil; **be ~** *iv.* tolina
    (*Preterit: onitolin*)

angel *n.* ilhuicacpatlanqui, ilhuicacpatlani;
   guardian ~ ilhuicacpatlanpixqui
anger *n.* cocolli, cualaniliztli, cualantli, cualancayotl,
   patzmictli, tlahuelli, zomalli
angry *adj.* cualanqui, cocoleh, zomaleh; **be** ~ *iv.* cualani
   (*Preterit: onicualan*), patzmiqui (*Preterit: onipatzmic*);
   reflex. v. zoma (*Preterit: oninozomah*)
anguish *n.* nentlamatiliztli
animal *n.* yolcatl, mazatl, yolqui, yoyolin (*small*)
ankle *n.* quequeyolli
announce *iv.* tecpoa (*Preterit: ontecpoh*)
announcement *n.* tecpoyotlahtolli
anoint *tv.* oza (*Preterit: oniteoz*)
another *adj.* occe, occequi
answer *n.* tenanquiliztli; *tv.* nanquilia (*Preterit: onitenanquilih*)
ant *n.* azcatl; **full of ants** *adj.* azcayoh
anteater *n.* aztacoyotl
anthill *n.* azcapotzalli, azcaputzalli, azcaxalli, tzicatepetl,
   tzicapotzalli, tzicaputzalli
anthropologist *n.* tlacayomatini, tenemilizmatini
anthropology *n.* tlacayomatiliztli, tenemilizmachiliztli,
   tenemilizmatiliztli
antiquity *n.* huehcauhcayotl
antler *n.* cuacuahuitl
anus *n.* tzintli, tzoyotl
anyone *pron.* zazo aquin, zazo tlein
anytime *adv.* zazo quemman
anywhere *adv.* zazo canin, zazocampa
apart *adv.* noncuah
appear *iv.* neci (*Preterit: oninez*); *reflex. v.* ittitia
   (*Preterit: oninoteittitih*)
appearance *n.* nexiliztli

appendix *n.* tlaaxitihquetl
appetite *n.* tlaelehuiliztli
apple *n.* xocotl
appraisal *n.* tlapatiyotlaliliztli
appraise *tv.* patiyotlalia (*Preterit: onitlapatiyotlalih*)
appraiser *n.* tlapatiyotlaliani
approach *reflex. v.* axitia (*Preterit: oninaxitih*)
appropriate *adj.* tlamelauhcachihuani
appropriateness *n.* tlamelauhcachihualiztli
apron *n.* cuexantli, ihtipampilcatl
arch *n.* tequiahuatl, tolcalli
archeologist *n.* huehuehcayomatini
archeology *n.* huehuehcayomatiliztli
architect *n.* calmanani, calchiuhcamatini
architecture *n.* calchiuhcamatiliztli
argue *tv.* tlatzohuilia (*Preterit: onitetlatzohuilih*)
argument *n.* tetlazohuiliztli, tetlatzohuililiztli
arithmetic *n.* tlapohuallotl
arm *n.* maitl, matzotzopaztli (*forearm*)
armadillo *n.* ayotochin, ayotochtli
armpit *n.* ciyacatl, ciacatl, zecactli
army *n.* yaoquizcayotl; yaoquizqueh
arrival *n.* huallaliztli
arrive *iv.* ahci (*Preterit: oniahcic*)
arrive the next day *iv.* moztlati (*Preterit: onimoztatic*)
arrogance *n.* nehueililiztli
arrogant *adj.* mopohuani, moneconi, motenehuani
arrow *n.* mitl, tlaxichtli, totomitl (*feathered*
art *n.* toltecayotl
artichoke *n.* huitzquiltzontecomatl
artisan *n.* amantecatl
artist *n.* toltecatl, tlamatilizmatini

as *adv.* yuh, yuhqui, yuhquin, yohque, ihqui, iuhqui
as long as *adv.* quexquichcauh, ixquichcauh
as soon as *adv.* in oyuh
ascend *iv.* tlehco (*Preterit: onitlhecoc*);
   ahcoquiza (*Preterit: onahcoquiz*),
   panhuetzi (*Petereit: onipanhuetz*)
ascent *n.* tlehcoliztli, ahcoquiliztli
ash *n.* nextli; *adj.* nextic, nexxoh
ashamed *adj.* pinahuac; *iv.* pinahua (*Preterit: onipinahuac
   and onipinauh*)
ashes from wood *n.* tlexocuahuitl, tlaconextli
Asia *n.* Coztictlacatlalpan
Asian *n.* coztictlacatl; tonatiuh iquizayantlacatl
ask *tv.* tlahtlani (*Pretrit: onitetlahtlan*)
asleep *adj.* cochqui
aspect *n.* yuhcatiliztli
asphalt *n.* chapopohtli
asphyxia *n.* ihyomiquiztli
assembly *n.* nenechicoliztli
association *n.* nechicoliztli
asthma *n.* neiihyotzacualiztli
asthmatic *n.* iihyo motzahtzacuani
astronomer *n.* ilhuicamatini
astronomy *n.* cicitlalmatiliztli, ilhuicamatiliztli
asylum *n.* nemaquixtiloyan
at an early age *adv.* piltian
at night *adv.* yohuac, yohualtica
At what time? *adv.* quemman
at your service *interj.* tlenontzin
attack *n.* oquichehualiztli; *tv.* oquichehua
   (*Preterit: onoquicheuh*)
attacker *n.* oquichehuani

attentive *adj.* tlatta
auction *n.* teixpantlanamaquiliztli
audacity *n.* netlapaloliztli
audience *n.* tlacacqueh
auditorium *n.* nenonotzaloyan, tlacacoyan
aunt *n.* ahuitl
Australia *n.* Oztlalian
Australian *n.* Oztalian chaneh
Austria *n.* Oztlian
Austrian *n.* Oztlian chaneh
author *n.* tlachihualeh
authority *n.* tequihuahyotl, huelitiliztli;
    person in ~ *n.* tequihuah
automobile *n.* in icel moliniani, molinini
autopsy *n.* tenacayotetequiliztli
autumn *n.* tonalco
avarice *n.* tzotzocayotl
avenge *tv.* tlacuepcayotilia (*Preterit: onitetlacuepcayotilih*),
    tzoncui (*Preterit: oninotzoncuic*)
avenue *n.* hueyohtli
average *n.* zan tlahco
avocado *n.* ahuacatl
awake *n.* ihzac
awesome *adj.* tlamahuizoltic
awl *n.* coyolomitl, tepuzomitl
ax *n.* cuauhxeloloni, tepoztli
Aztec *n.* Aztecatl

B

baby *n.* conetl (*Plural: coconeh*)
babysitter *n.* pilmamah
bachelor *n.* ahnamiqueh, icnooquichtli

back *n.* cuitlapantli, teputztli, tepotztli; ~ **hair** *n.* ahcoltzontli
backbone *n.* cuitlachichiquilli, cutilapanomitl
backpack *n.* quimilli
backwards *adv.* zan ahmo yuhqui, zan icuepca
bacon *n.* coyamenacahuatzalli, pitzonacahutazalli
bad *adj.* ahcualli, ahmo cualli
bad breath *n.* camapotoniliztli
bad mood *n.* patzmictli
badger *n.* pezohtli
bag *n.* ehuaxiquipilli (*leather*), xiquipilli, xiquipiltontli
baggage *n.* tlatquihuiconi
bake *tv.* tlaxcalixca (*Preterit: onitlaxcalixcac*)
baker *n.* tlaxcalixcac
bald *adj.* ahtomiyoh, cuapetlanqui; **go** ~ *iv.* cuatepehui
    (*Preterit: onicuatepeuh & onicuatepehuac*)
ball *n.* matopehtli, ololli, tapayolli
ball court *n.* tlachtli
ball game *n.* tlachtli
ball player *n.* momatotopehuiani, ollamani, ollanqui,
    tlamatopehuani
ballet *n.* nehtotiliztli
balm *n.* huitziloxitl
bamboo *n.* ohtlatl, otlatl
banana *n.* polatanox, xochihcualli, xochicualli, tzapalotl,
    zapalotl; ~ **leaf** *n.* pahpatla
bangs *n.* ixcuatzontli (*hair*)
bank *n.* analli (*river*); tominpialcalli (*financial*),
    tomincalpialoyan
banner *n.* cuachpantli, pamitl, pantli
baptism *n.* tecuaatequiliztli
baptize *tv.* cuaatequia (*Preterit: onitecuaatequih*)
baptized *adj.* tlacuatequilli
bar *n.* neihuintiloyan, netlahuanaloyan, ocnamacoyan

barbaric *adj.* popolocatl
barbarism *n.* popolocayotl
barbeque grill *n.* tepuztlapechtlatlahuatzaloni
barber *n.* teximani, texinqui
barber shop *n.* neximalcalli
barefooted *adj.* caccopinqui, caccohcopinqui
barely *adv.* quin axcan, ayaxcan, ayaxcanyotica
bark *tv.* huahualoa (*Preterit: onitlahuahualoh*)
barking *n.* tlahuahuatzaliztli
barrel *n.* comitl
base *n.* tzintli, tzintetl (*wall*), nelhuayotl;
    at the ~ of *loc. suff* -icxitlan
basement *n.* tlalancalli
basil *n.* tacatl
basin *n.* ameyalcaxitl
basket *n.* chiquihuitl , petlacalli, tanahtli (*with two handles*),
    tompiahtli (*large palm*)
basketball *n.* nematotopehuiliztli
bass *n.* tlacamichin (*fish*)
bat *n.* quimichpatlan, tzinacantli, tzinacaztli
bath *n.* nealtilatl, nealtiliztli, nealtiloyan (*place*)
bathe *reflex. v.* altia (*Preterit: oninaltih*)
bathroom *n.* axixcalli
battalion *n.* xiquipilli
battle *n.* mitl chimalli, necaliliztli, necaliztli, nehcaliliztli,
    nehcaliztli
battlefield *n.* ixtlahuacan, yaotlalli
be *iv.* ca (*Plural: cateh*), moyetztica; **there is** onca;
    there will ~ onyez
beach *n.* ilhuicaatentli
beak *n.* tototenhuitztli (*bird*), tototentli (*bird*), tenhuitztli,
    huitztli
beam *n.* calcuahuitl, huapalli (*house*)

bean *n.* etl, yetl, ecoztli (*yellow*)

bean field *n.* etlah

bean paste *n.* etextli

bean pod *n.* ecacahuatl

bear children *iv.* tlacachichua (*Preterit: onitlacachiuh*)

beard *n.* camatzontli, tentzontli

bearded *adj.* tentzoyoh

beardless *n.* tlalhuatic

beast *n.* tecuani

beat in a game *tv.* tlani (*Preterit: onitetlan*)

beautiful *adj.* cualneci, cualnezqui, cualnezca, quetzalli, quetzaltic, xochitic, yectli

beauty *n.* chipahuacayotl, cualnexiliztli, cualnezcayotl, yecyotl

because *conj.* ipampa

become *reflex. v.* mochihua (*Preterit: oninochiuh*)

become a father *iv.* tahtia (*Preterit: ontahtih*)

bed *n.* onoyan, tlapechtli

bedbug *n.* texcan, calxomilin

bedroom *n.* cochiantli, cochihuayan, cochihualoyan, cochiloyan

bedspread *n.* camaixquemitl, camaixquemmitl, pepechtlapachiuhcayotl, tlachcahuipilzotl

bee *n.* cuauhnecuhzayolin, cuatlayacatl, pipiolin (*wild*), xicohtli

beef *n.* cuacohnacatl, cuacuahnacatl, huacaxnacatl

beef stew *n.* huacaxayotl

beehive *n.* cuauhnecomitl

beeswax *n.* xicohcuitlatl

beetle *n.* mayatl (*green*), pinacatl (*black stink bug*)

before *adv.* achtopa, achtotipa, ayamo

beg *tv.* tlatlauhtia (*Preterit: onitetlatlauhtih*)

beggar *n.* tlaihtlaniani, motlahtlayehuiani, motlahtlayehuih

begin *iv.* pehua (*Preterit: onipeuh*), tzinti (*Preterit: onitzintic*); *tv.* tzintia (*Preterit: onitlatzintih*)

beginning *n.* pehualiztli, ompehualiztli, quizayan, tetzonyotl, tzintiliztli

behind *n.* tzintli, tzintlantli; *prep.* icampa, icuitlapan, tlatepotzco

behold *inter.* izcah

being *n.* nemiliceh, yeliztli

belch *iv.* mehputza (*Preterit: onimehputz*), moitzputza (*Preterit: onimoitzputz*)

belief *n.* tlaneltoquilizli, neltoquiliztli

believe *tv.* neltoca (*Preterit: onitlaneltocac*)

believer *n.* tlaneltocani

bell *n.* coyolli, tzilin, tzilli

bell-like *adj.* tzilictic (*sound*)

bell-ringer *n.* tlatziliniani, tlatztitzilitzani

belly *n.* ihtitl, ihtetl

belong to *iv.* tetech pohui (*Preterit: tetech onipouh*)

beloved *adj.* tlazohtli

below *adv.* nechca, nechcapa, tlani, tlatzintla (*large area*), tlatzintlan (*large area*), tlacxitla (*small area*)

bellow *iv.* cuacuauhchoca (*Preterit: onicuacuauhchocac*)

belt *n.* cuitlalpicayotl, cihuanelpiloni (*for women*), nelpiloni

bend *tv.* cueloa (*Preterit: onitlacueloh*); *iv.* cueloa (*Preterit: onicueloh*)

benevolence *n.* tlacayotl

benign *adj.* tlatlacatl

bereaved *adj.* yollotoneuhqui

bereavement *n.* yollotonehualiztli

best *iv.* tlacempanahuia (*Preterit: otlacempanahuih*)

better *adj.* oc ye cualli, cachi cualli

bib *n.* tencualaconi
bible *n.* teotlahtolli
biceps *n.* ahcolnacayotl
bid *n.* huallaaquiliztli, tlaahcoquetzaliztli;
    tv. ahcoquetza (*Preterit: onitlaahcoquetz*),
    huallaaquia (*Preterit: onihuallaaquih*)
bidder *n.* huallaaquiani, tlaahcoquetzani
big toe *n.* tohueixopil, xopiltecuhtli
big-eared *adj.* nacazhueyac
bile *n.* chichicatl
bilingual *adj.* ometlahtoleh, ometlahtolloh
bilingualism *n.* ometlahtollotl
billiard table *n.* telololtopehualitztlapechtli
biography *n.* nemilizamatl
biologist *n.* yolizmatini
biology *n.* yolizmatiliztli
bird *n.* tototl
birth *n.* tlacatiliztli
birthday *n.* ilhuitl, tlacatilizilhuitl, netlacatpapaquiliz,
    xihuaxetiliztli
birthplace *n.* quizcan, yolcan
bisexual *n.* tecuilontiani
bishop *n.* teoyoticatlahtoani
bite *n.* tetlanquichiliztli, tlanquechiliztli, tlaquehtzomaliztli,
    tecualiztli
bite *tv.* quetzoma (*Preterit: onitlaquetzon*), tlacuahcua
    (*Preterit: onitlacuahcuah*)
biting *adj.* tencuahcuah
bitter *adj.* chichic
bitterness *n.* chichializtli
black *adj.* tliltic, tlilli, yapalli, yapaltic
black bean *n.* ecapotzitl, tliletl

blackbird *n.* tzanatl, tzinitzcan
blackboard *n.* huapallahcuilolhuaztli, huapallahcuilolli,
    tepatlahcuiloni, tlahcuilolhuaztli, tlahcuilolhuapalitl
blacken *iv.* tlilihui (*Preterit: onitliliuh*), tlilehui
    (*Preterit: onitlileuh*)
blackness *n.* tlilihuiliztli, tlilehuiliztli
blacksmith *n.* tepuzpitzqui; ~ **shop** *n.* tepuzpitzcoyan
bladder *n.* axixtecomatl, tlapiazcomitl, tlapiaztecomatl
blanket *n.* cuachtli, quemitl, quemmitl
bleed *iv.* ezquiza (*Preterit: oniezquiz*); ~ **from the nose**
    iv. yacaezquiza (*Preterit: oniyacaezquiz*)
blender *n.* tepuzmolcaxitl, tepuzyollotlatexoni,
    tepuztlatzoaloni, tepuztlatexoni, tlatexoni
bless *tv.* yectenehua (*Preterit: onitlayecteneuh*), teochihua
    (*Preterit: oniteteochiuh*)
blessing *n.* teteochihualiztli
blind *adj.* ixpopoyotzin, ixpopoyotl, popoyotl, ixpahpaltic;
    to be ~ *iv.* ixpopoyoti (*Preterit: oniixpopoyotic*)
blindness *n.* ixpopoyotiliztli
blister *n.* totomoniliztli, xittomoniliztli
blond *adj.* cuatlecoz
blood *n.* eztli, yeztli
bloody *adj.* ezzoh
bloom *iv.* xotla (*Preterit: onixotlac*), cueponi
    (*Preterit: onicuepon*)
blossom *iv.* cueponi (*Preterit: onicuepon*)
blouse *n.* huipilli, quechquemitl
blow *tv.* pitza (*Preterit: nitlapitz*)
blow on a fire *iv.* tlepitza (*Preterit: onitlepitz*)
blow one's nose *reflex. v.* itzomia (*Preterit: oninitzomih*)
blue *adj.* texohtli, texotic, xippalli, xoxoctic
bluebird *n.* xiuhtototl

bluish green *adj.* matlalin, matlalli
boar *n.* coyametl
board *n.* huapalli
boast *iv.* ahuillahtoa (*Preterit: onahuillahtoh*)
boat *n.* acalli
bobcat *n.* ocotochin
body *n.* tonacayo, tlacayotl
body fluid *n.* chiahuiztli
boil *n.* nanahuatl, ixocuilin, tzotzotl; *iv.* pozoni
     (*Preterit: opozon*); *tv.* pozonia (*Preterit: onitlapozonih*)
boiled *adj.* pozonqui
boldness *n.* netlapaloliztli
bolt *n.* tepuztlatzacualoni
bomb *n.* axitontli
bone *n.* omitl, omitetl, pitztli
book *n.* amoxtli; **sacred ~** teoamoxtli
book cover *n.* amoxquiliuhcayotl
book margin *n.* amoxtentli
book title *n.* amoxmachiotl, amoxtocaitl
book vendor *n.* amoxnamacac
bookcase *n.* amoxtlatiloyan
bookkeeping *n.* tlapohualiztli
bookstore *n.* amacalli, amanamacoyan, amoxnamacoyan
border *n.* altepecuaxochtli, tlaltzontli
born *iv.* tlacati (*Preterit: onitlacatic and onitlacat*), piltia
     (*Preterit: onipiltih and onipiltiac*), yoli (*Preterit: oniyol*)
boss *n.* tlayecanquetl
botany *n.* xiuhtlamatiliztli
bother *tv.* xiuhtlalia (*Preterit: onitexiuhtlalih*)
bottle *n.* tehuiltecomatl
bottom *n.* tzintli
boundary *n.* altepecuaxochtli

bouquet *n.* xochtlalpictli
bow *n.* acalyacatl (*boat*); tlahuitolli (*weapon*);
    tetzauhtalcololli (*ribbon*), tetzontlacololli (*hair*);
    iv. toloa (*Preterit: onitoloh*)
bowing *n.* tololiztli
bowl *n.* caxitl
bowlegged *adj.* metzcacaltic
box *n.* cuauhpetlacalli, toptli
boy *n.* telpocatl, telpochtli (*Plural: telpopochtin*)
bracelet *n.* maquiztli, macuextli
brag *iv.* ahuillahtoa (*Preterit: onahuillahtoh*)
braggart *n.* ahuiillahtoani
braid *n.* tlaxochpitzactli, xinapal
brain *n.* cuatextli, cuayollotl
branch *n.* cuauhmaitl, maitl
branding iron *n.* tepuzmachiyotiloni
brave *adj.* tiacauh, yolchicahuac, yollohuapahuac
bravery *n.* yollotiliztli
brazier *n.* tlecuazco
bread *n.* pantzi, pantzin, caxtillantlaxcalli
breadth *n.* coyahualiztli, patlahualiztli
break *tv.* pohpoztequi (*Preterit: onitlapohpoztec*);
    iv. tlapani (*Preterit: otlapan*), poztequi (*Preterit: opoztec*)
break in *tv.* tlayancuilia (*Preterit: onitlayancuilih*)
break money *tv.* cayaniya (*Preterit: onitlacayanix*)
break something *tv.* xamania (*Preterit: onitlaxamanih*),
    poztequi (*Preterit: onitlapoztec*)
breakfast *n.* almahzalli, neuhcayotl, tenizaloni; **have ~**
    iv. teniza (*Preterit: oniteniz*), tlaitia (*Preterit: onitlaitih*)
breast *n.* chichihualli, elchiquihuitl
breath *n.* iihyotl
breathe *reflex. v.* iihyotia (*Preterit: oniniihyotih*)
breathless *adj.* ohuihcaiihyotini

bribery *n.* tenzolhuiliztli
brick *n.* xamixcalli
bricklayer *n.* tepanchiuhqui
bride *n.* cihuahtla
bridge *n.* apantli
bridle *n.* mazatenilpicatl, tepuzenmecayotl
brilliance *n.* tlanextiliztli, tlanextli
brimstone *n.* tlequihquiztlalli
brine *n.* iztaayotl
bring *tv.* hualhuica (*Preterit: onitlahualhuic*)
bring down *tv.* xitinia (*Preterit: onitexitinih*)
broad *adj.* coyahuac, coahualli, patlahuac, patlachtli
broil *tv.* tlehuatza (*Preterit: onitlehuatz*),
    ixca (*Preterit: onitlaxcac*)
broken *adj.* poztecqui, poztehqui, tlapanqui, xitic, xitinqui
brook *n.* atoyapitzactli
broom *n.* izquiztli, ochpahuaztli, popotl, tlachpahuaztli,
    izquiztepiton (*small*)
brothel *n.* ahuiancalli, netzinnamacoyan
brother *n.* teachcauh (*older*), teiccauh (*younger*)
brother-in-law *n.* textli (*man's*); huepulli (*woman's*)
brown *adj.* chocolatic
brownish *adj.* poctic
brush *n.* tlachichiconi, xolhuaztli (*for clothes*), xelhuaztli
brushstroke *n.* tlapalanalolli
brutal *n.* tlacamazatl
brutality *n.* tlacamazayotl
bubble *n.* momolocatl, popolochtli; **water ~** axitontli
bucket *n.* atlacoani
bud *iv.* cueponi (*Preterit: onicuepon*), mimilihui
    (*Preterit: omimiliuh*)
build *iv.* calquetza (*Preterit: onicalquetz*), calmana
    (*Preterit: onicalman*)

building *n.* hueicalli, tlazalolli
bull *n.* cuacuahueh
bullet *n.* tlequihquiztelolohtli, tlequihquiztelolotl
bullfight *n.* cuacuamminalolli
bullfighter *n.* cuatilanmicalini
bully *n.* tlacamixpoloc
bum *n.* xolopihtli
bumblebee *n.*xicohtli
bunch *n.* centlaantli
bunion *n.* xopilonquizac
burial *n.* tetoquiliztli
burn *iv.* tlatla (*Preterit: onitlatlac*)
burst *iv.* ititlapohui (*Preterit: onititlapouh*)
bury *tv.* quimiloa (*Preterit: onitequimiloh*), toca
     (*Preterit: onitlatocac*)
bus *n.* tehuiconi, tepuzcalmimilolli
bush *n.* tacatl
business *n.* tequiyotl
business card *n.* tocaihcuilolamatl, amatocaihcuilolli
bust *n.* tecuacuilli (*statue*)
busy *iv.* **be ~** tequipachoa (*Preterit: onitequipachoh*),
     tequipan ca (*Preterit: tequipan onicatca*)
but *conj.* tel, yeceh
butcher *n.* nacamacani
butcher shop *n.* nacamacoyan
butter *n.* cuacuachiahuizzotl
butterfly *n.*papalotl
buttock *n.* tzintamalli, tzintlantli, tonacayocan
button *n.* totomoliuhqui; **set of ~** totomoliuhca
buy *tv.* cohua (*Preterit: onitlacouh*)
buyer *n.* tlacohuani, tlacouhqui, tlacohcouhqui
buying *n.* tlacohualiztli
buzz zozoloca *iv.* (*Preterit: onizozolocac*)

buzzing *n.* zozolocaliztli
by *suff.* –titlan
by means of *suff.* –pal

C
cabbage *n.* coloix
cabin *n.* tlapixcacalli
cable *n.* tlahuilchicahualizmecatl
cacao bean *n.* cacahuatetl
cactus *n.* nohpalli
cactus fruit *n.* nochtli
cadaver *n.* micquetl
cage *n.* cuauhcalli, huauhcalli
cake *n.* yoltextlaoyotl
calendar *n.* ilhuitlapohualli, tonalamatl, tonallapohualoni
calf *n.* cotztli, cotztetl (*leg*); ~ **muscle** cotztetl;
    cuacuauhuehconetl (*cow*), cuacuauhconetl
callus *n.* chacayolli
calm *n.* cehuiliztli; *tv.* cehuia (*Preterit: onitecehuih*)
calm down *reflex. v.* cehuia (*Preterit: oninocehuih*),
    cuetlani (*Preterit: onicuetlan*)
calmly *adv.* matca
camera *n.* tlaixcopinaloni, tlahuilixiptla, achiuhtequixtiloni
canal *n.* apantli
canary *n.* polantototl
cancer *n.* huey cualocatl
candle *n.* xicohcuitlaocotl
candleholder *n.* tlepiaztli
cane *n.* macpatopilli, topilli
cane syrup *n.* ohuanecuhtli
canopy *n.* cuachcalli
canvas *n.* ichcatlazuptli

canyon *n.* atlahuitl

cap *n.* cuamatlatl

capability *n.* huelitiliztli

cape *n.* cuachtli, tilmahtli

capital *n.* altepanayotl, tecuacan

captive *n.* malli, tlaantli

capture *tv.* ana (*Preterit: onitean*), ma (*Preterit: onitlamah*)

car *n.* calmimilolli, nehnemiliztepuzcalli, tepuzcahuahyo

card game *n.* amapatoliztli

cardinal *n.* chiltototl (*bird*)

cardiologist *n.* yollotepahtiani

care *n.* nematiliztli

carefully *adv.* mihmatca, mahmatca; **very ~** mahmatcatzin

caress *n.* texoxocoyomatiliztli; *tv.* xochihuia
    (*Preterit: onitexochihuih*)

carnation *n.* texaxochxochitl

carnival rides *n.* tepuzneahuiltiloni

carpenter *n.* cuauhxinqui, cuauhtlachihchiuhqui

carpenter shop *n.* cuauhximaloyan

carpentry *n.* cuauhximaloyotl, cuauhxmaliztli

carpet *n.* tilmahicxipehpechtli

carrier *n.* tlamamah, tlameme, tlazacani, tlazazacani

carrot *n.* caxtillan camohtli

carry *tv.* huica (*Preterit: onitlahuic*), itqui
    (*Preterit: onitlatquic*), mama (*Preterit: onitlamamah,
    onitlamamac*), zazaca (*Preterit: onitlazazacac*)

carry on one's back *tv.* tepotzmama
    (*Preterit: onitlatepotzmamah*)

carry water *tv.* atlacui (*Preterit: oniatlacuic*)

cart *n.* cuauhtemalacatl

cartilage *n.* cecelicayotl

case *n.* quimiloloni

cassava *n.* cuauhcamohtli

cassette recorder *n.* caquilizcopinaloni

cassock *n.* yappaleopixnequentiloni

castrate *tv.* atecui (*Preterit: oniteatecuic*), atequixtia
   (*Preterit: oniteatequixtih*)

cat *n.* mizton

cataract *n.* ixtotolicihuiliztli

caterpillar *n.* payatl, huahuatl

catfish *n.* coatetl, tentzonmichin

cause *n.* pehualiztli

causeway *n.* caltzalantli

caution *n.* nematiliztli

cave *n.* oztotl

caviar *n.* ahuauhtli

cedar *n.* ahuehuetl, oyametl

ceiba tree *n.* pochotl, ichcacuahuitl

celibacy *n.* ahnenamictiliztli

cellar *n.* tlallancalli, occalli

cemetery *n.* tetocoyan

center *n.* yollohco, yollotl, yollohtli, ollotl;
   civic ~ altepeyollohtli

centipede *n.* centzummayeh

Central America *n.* Nolpopocayan

century *n.* macuilpoalxiuhcayotl

ceremony *n.* tlateomatiliztli

certainly *adv.* ca yeh, tlacahzo, yeh

certainty *n.* neltiliztli

chain *n.* tepuzmecatl

chair *n.* icpalli, ocoicpalli (*made of pine*)

chalk *n.* tizatl

chalkboard *n.* tlahcuilolhuapalitl, huapallahcuilolhuaztli,
   huapallahcuilolli

chameleon *n.* cuemitl, tapayaxin

chance *n.* zanoquiztli; **by ~** zanoquiztica
change *n.* xeltic (*money*); *tv.* papatla (*Preterit: onitlapapatlac*), patla (*Preterit: onitlapatlac*);
    ~ one's mind *iv.* yolcuepa (*Preterit: oniyolcuep*)
chaos *n.* teixneloliztli
chapel *n.* ayauhcalli
chaps *n.* cuetlaxmaxtlatl
chapter *n.* amoxxexeloliztli
character *n.* yelizyotl, nemiliztli
characteristic *n.* tlamanitiliztli
charcoal *n.* tecolli
charlatan *n.* mopouhcatlahtoani
charm *tv.* xochihuia (*Preterit: onitexochihuih*)
chatter *n.* papallotl; *iv.* papalchihua (*Preterit: onipaplachiuh*),
    tlatlahtoa (*Preterit: onitlatlahtoh*),
    chachalaca (*Preterit: onichachalacac*)
chayote fruit *n.* chayothli
cheap *adj.* ahmo patiyoh
cheek *n.* cantli, camapantli; **having big cheeks** *adj.* cantetetic
cheer *tv.* paccatzatzilia (*Preterit: onitepaccatzatzilih*)
cheese *n.* chichihualayotetzauhtli, tlatetzauhtli
    chichihualayotl
cherimoya *n.* ilamatzapotl (*fruit*)
cherry *n.* capolin, capulin
chess *n.* cuappatolli, cuauhpatolli
chest *n.* elpantli
chew *tv.* tlacuahcua (*Preterit: onitlacuahcuah*)
chewing gum *n.* tzictli
chick *n.* piotl
chicken *n.* cuanaca
chicken coop *n.* pioxcalli, poyoxcalli, piocalli
chief *n.* tiacauh, tlayacanqui, teyacanqui
child *n.* conetl (*Plural: coconeh*), oquichpilli,
    pilli (*Plural: pipiltin*)

childbirth *n.* mixihuiliztli
childhood *n.* piltian
childishness *n.* coconeyotl, pipillotl
childlike *adj.* pilloh, coneyoh
Chile *n.* Chillaltohcayotl
chili *n.* chilli; **season with ~** *tv.* chillotia
  (*Preterit: onitlachillotih*)
chimney *n.* tlecalli
chin *n.* tenchalli
chip *n.* cuauhhuiztic
chipmunk *n.* motohtli
chirp *iv.* chachalaca (*Preterit: onichachalacac*)
chisel *n.* tepuztlacuihcuiloni, huiteconi
chocolate *n.* chocolatl
choke on food *iv.* tlacualmihmiqui (*Preterit:*
  onitlacualmihmic)
chomp *reflex. v.* tencapania (*Preterit: ninotencapanih*)
chore *n.* cemilhuitequitl
chronicle *n.* nemilizamatl, nemiliztlahcuilolli
chronicler *n.* nemiliztlahcuiloani, xiuhtlachcuiloh
chubby *adj.* chamahuac
church *n.* teocalli, teopantli, teopixcalli
cicada *n.* chiquilichtli
cigar *n.* tenchichinalpocyo, tenpopocalotl
cigarette *n.* amacayetl, tlachichinolli, tempopocaloni,
  tenchichinaloni
cilantro *n.* culanto
cinema *n.* ixiptlayolin
circle *n.* yahualli
circumcise *tv.* xipincuayotequi
circumcision *n.* texipinehuayotequiliztli
cistern *n.* atecochtli

citizen *n.* altepetlacatl

city *n.* altepetl, huey altepetl, totecuacan

city gate *n.* hueyaltepecalaconi

civility *n.* nematcayotl

clapping *n.* cacapaca

clarify *tv.* nextia (*Preterit: onitlanextih*)

clarity *n.* tlanextli, tlanextiliztli

clay *n.* tlalzacuhtli, zoquitl

clay jug *n.* zoquitecomatl

clay mask *n.* zoquixayacatl

clay pot *n.* temetztli, xoctli

clay rattle *n.* cacalachtli

clay statue *n.* zoquiteixiptla

clean *adj.* chipahuac; **be ~** *iv.* chipahua
    (*Preterit: onichipahuac*)

cleanliness *n.* chipahualiztli

clear *adj.* naltonac, naltoctic; **be ~** *iv.* naltona
    (*Preterit: onaltonac*)

clergy *n.* teopixcayotl

clerical garb *n.* teopixcatlatquitl

cliff *n.* tepexitl

clitoris *n.* zacapilli

clock *n.* cahuitepuztamachihualoni, tepuztetzahuitl

clod *n.* taltetl, zacatzontetl

cloddy *adj.* tlalteyoh

clog *n.* cuauhcactli

close *tv.* tzacua (*Preterit: onitlatazauc*); **~ one's eyes**
    reflex. v. ixpiqui (*Preterit: oninixpic*)

close one's mouth *reflex. v.* tempiqui (*Preterit: oninotempic*)

close relative *n.* cetlacayotl

closet *n.* tlatquipialoyan

cloth *n.* cuachtli, tatapahtli

clothes *n.* tzotzomahtli

clothesline *n.* tlazohualoyan
clothing *n.* quemitl, quemmitl, tlaquemitl, tlaquemmitl
cloud *n.* mixtli
cloudy *adj.* mixtentoc, tlamixtemi
clove *n.* caxtillanchilli, clavo
clown *n.* tehuehuetzquitiani, tetlahuetzquitiani, tetlahuehuetzquitih
clue *n.* iximachiyotl
clump *n.* zoquitelolohtli
cluster *n.* centlaantli
coal *n.* teotetl, tlexochitl (*hot*)
cockroach *n.* cacalachin, calachin, calayotl, tlapitzoto
collar *n.* quechtetl
comedian *n.* tehuehuetzquitiani, tetlahuetzquitiani
comic *n.* tehuehuetzquitiani, tetlahuetzquitiani
complete *adj.* cemahcic
cocoon *n.* calocuilin, cochipilotl, tecilli
coffee *n.* acochcayotl, cafetzin
coffer *n.* tepuzpetlacalli, toptli
coin *n.* tlacohualoni
cold *n.* tzompilli (*illness*); *adj.* cecec; **be ~** *iv.* cecmiqui
   (*Preterit: onicecmic*); **have a ~** *iv.*
tzompilihui (*Preterit: onitzompiliuh*),
   tzompilahui (*Preterit: onitzompilauh*)
collar *n.* quechtli
collarbone *n.* quechcuahyotl
college *n.* calmecac, telpochcalli
colon *n.* cuitlaxcoltomactli
color *n.* tlapalli; (**to**) **~** *tv.* pa (*Preterit: onitlapah*)
column *n.* temimilli
comb *n.* tzicahuaztli, tzocohuaztli; *tv.* pepetla
   (*Preterit: onitepepetlac*)

come *iv.* huallauh (*Preterit: onihualla*), huitz
(*Preterit: onihuitza*)
comet *n.* xihuitl, popocacitlalin
comfortable *adj.* cialtic
comma *n.* tlahuazancoliuhqui
command *tv.* nahuatia (*Preterit: onitlanahuatih*)
commander *n.* tlacatecatl, yaoquizcayacanqui,
yaoquizcateyacanqui
commerce *n.* tlanamaquiliztli
common sense *n.* cemaxcanehmatiliztli, ixtli nacaztli
communal property *n.* cemaxacatl, nepantlaquitl
communal work *n.* coatequitl
community *n.* tlacanechicoltin, tlacanechicoltiloyan (*place*),
altepenechicoltin, altepenechiconyotl
compact disc *n.* caquilizcopinaloni in tonameyotica
compadre *n.* compaletzin
companion *n.* pohtli, tehuicatinemini
company *n.* tehuampoyotl
comparison *n.* machiotlahtolli
compass *n.* nehuehcatlachialoni
compassion *n.* icnohuahcayotl, tlacayotl, tetlaocoliliztli
compassionate *adj.* icnohuah, icnoyoh; **be ~** *iv.* icnoitta
(*Preterit: oniteicnoittac*)
competency *n.* huelitiliztli
competent *adj.* hueliti
completely *adv.* centetica
compliment *n.* tepehpetlaliztli
compose *iv.* cuicayocoya (*Preterit: onicuicayocox*), tlatlalia
(*Preterit: onitlatlalih*)
composer *n.* tlatlaliani
composition *n.* cuicapiquiliztli, tlatlaliliztli
compress *tv.* tilinia (*Preterit: onitlatilin*)
computer *n.* tlahuipanaloni, ilnamiquiliztepuztli

conceit *n.* nehuimatiloni
conceive *iv.* tlacachihua (*children*), yocoya
 (*Preterit: onitlayocox*)
concerned *adj.* nentlamatini, nentlamatqui; **be ~**
 iv. nentlamati (*Preterit: oninentlamat*)
concerning *prep.* –itech
concert *n.* tozquinamiquiliztli (*choral*), tecuicanamiquiliztli
 (*song*), tetlatzotzonaliztli
concert hall *n.* tlapitzaloyan
conclude *tv.* cencahua (*Preterit: onitlacencauh*)
condemn *tv.* miquiznahuati (*Preterit: onitemiquiznahuatih*)
condition *n.* yuh quizaliztli; **In what ~?** *interr. adv.* Quenamih?
condolence *n.* nematihuantlanextilli, nematihuannextiloni;
 express ~ *tv.* nematihuannextia
 (*Preterit: onitenematihuannextih*)
conference *n.* mononotzaliztli, tetechnetemachiliztli
confession *n.* neyolcuitiliztli
confidence *n.* tlacuauhtlamatiliztli
confused *adj.* cuayolcueptoc; **be ~** *reflex. v.* cuatlapololtia
 (*Preterit: oninocuatlapololtih*)
confusion *n.* tepoliuhtitlzalililiztli, cuatlapoliliztli, chalaniliztli
congratulate *tv.* quinopiltia (*Preterit: onicnopiltih*)
conjugation *n.* tetocapatlachihualnepanoliztli
conjunction *n.* tlacentlaliloni, tlanechicoltiquetl
conquer *tv.* poloa (*Preterit: onitepoloh*)
conqueror *n.* tepehuah
conquest *n.* tepehualiztli
conscience *n.* neyoliximachiliztli
consenting person *n.* ceani
consequence *n.* mochihualiztli
consequently *adv.* anca
consolation *n.* neyolalaliliztli
console *tv.* yollalia (*Preterit: oniteyollalih*)

consonant *n.* icacaquiztli
constable *n.* topileh
constitution *n.* nahuatillaliliztli
construct *tv.* quechilia (*Preterit: onitlaquechilih*)
construction materials *n.* texamicalquetzallotl
container *n.* caxcomulli, petlacalli, tecomatl
contaminate *tv.* mahua (*Preterit: onitemauh*)
contamination *n.* temahualiztli
contentment *n.* yocoxcayotl
contest *n.* neixnamiquiliztli
continence *n.* nematcatlahuanaliztli
contract *n.* netennonotzaliztli, netentotoquiliztli,
  tlanecuiloliztli
contradict *tv.* tlahtolilochtia (*Preterit: onitetlahtolilochtih*)
contradiction *n.* tetlahtolilochtiliztli
convent *n.* cihuateopixcacalli
convention *n.* mononotzaliztli
conversation *n.* nonochiliztli, zanilli
converse *tv.* nonotza (*Preterit: onitenonotz*
convert *n.* monemilizcuepqui
convict *n.* tecaltzacuilli, tetlatzacuilli
conviction *n.* tlaneltoquiliztli
convince *tv.* cealtia (*Preterit: onitecealtih*)
cook *n.* tlacualchihuani, tlacualchiuhqui; *tv.* tlacualchichihua
  (*Preterit: onitlacualchiuh*), pozonia (*Preterit: onitlapozonih*)
cooked *adj.* tlehuacqui
Copan *n.* Cuba
copper *n.* tepoztli
copper vessel *n.* tepuzcaxitl
coppery *adj.* pipinqui
copy *n.* tlaixcopinalli, neixcuitilamatl, tlacopintli,
  tlamachiyotilamatl, tlaquixtilli; *tv.* copina
  (*Preterit: onitlacopin*), quixtia (*Preterit: onitlaquixtih*)

copy machine *n.* tlaixcopinaloni
coral *n.* tapachtli
coral snake *n.* inantzicatl
cork *n.* tentzacua, cuauhzonectli
corkscrew *n.* tepuzcoliuhqui
corn *n.* elotl (*fresh ear*); cintli, centli (*dried ear*);
    izquitl (*toasted*); tlaolli (*dried kernel*); xilotl (*tender ear*);
    pinolli, tlaoltextli (*ground*)
corn cob *n.* olotl
corn dough *n.* nextamalli, nixtamalli, tlaoltextli
corn flour *n.* pinolli
corn fungus *n.* cuitlacochtli, cuitlacochin
corn grinder *n.* tezqui (*person*)
corn gruel *n.* atolli
corn husk *n.* totomochtli
corn plant *n.* toctli, ohuatl
corn stalk flower *n.* miahuatl
corn silk *n.* tlaoltzontli, elotzontli
corn syrup *n.* ohuanecuhtli
corn tassel *n.* elotzontli
corner *n.* tlaxomolli, xomolli
corpse *n.* micquetl
corpulent *n.* tlaqueh
corral *n.* tenpacalli
correct *adj.* melac, melahuac, yectli
correctness *n.* melahuacayotl, yectiliztli, yecyotl
corridor *n.* callampa, caltenyo
corrupt *adj.* tlayolmalacacholli; *tv.* xapotla
    (*Preterit: onitexapotlac*)
corruption *n.* ahuilquizaliztli
cost *n.* ipatiuh

cotton *n.* ichcatl; ~ **tree** ichcacuahuitl
cough *n.* tlatlaciztli; *iv.* tlatlaci (*Preterit: onitlatlaz*)
counsel *tv.* tlahtolmaca (*Preterit: onitetlahtolmacac*),
    nohnotza (*Preterit: onitenohnotz*)
count *n.* pohualiztli, tlapohualiztli; *tv.* pohua
    (*Preterit: onitlapouh*)
countenance *n.* ixconexiliztli
counter *n.* cuauhtlapechnamaconi (*store*); tlapouhqui
    (*numbers*)
country *n.* tlalnantli
courage *n.* oquichyollohtli, yollotiliztli
courageous *adj.* yollohuapahuac
course *n.* temachtiliztli (*act of teaching*), nemachtiliztli
    (*act of learning*)
court *tv.* teyolahcocui (*Preterit: oniteyolahcocuic*),
    teyollotlapana (*Preterit: oniteyollotlpan*), teyollotlapana
    (*Preterit: oniteyollotlpan*)
courteous *adj.* tecpiltic
courtesan *n.* ahuiani
courtesy *n.* nematcayotl
cover *n.* cuachtli, pepechtli, tzaccayotl; *tv.* quimiloa
    (*Preterit: onitlaquimlioh*)
covering *n.* piccatl
cow *n.* cihuacuacuahueh, huacax, cuacuahueh
cowardice *n.* mauhcatlacayotl, nemauhtiliztli, yollamiquiliztli
cowardly *adj.* ahmo tlapaltic, yollamicqui
cowboy *n.* cuacuappixqui, cuacuahpixqui
coyote *n.* coyotl, ixtlacchichi
crab *n.* atecuicihtli, tecuicihtli
crack *iv.* pitzini (*Preterit: opitzin*)
cracked *adj.* xamactic, xamanqui
cradle *n.* cozolli

crafty *adj.* quimatini, tlatlamachiani
cramp *n.* cotziliztli, cotztziliztli, cotzilli,
   cuehcuelihuiztli, huapahualiztli;
   iv. cuehcuelihui (*Preterit: onicuehcueliuh*),
   cecuappitzahui (*Preterit: onicecuappitzauh*),
   huapahua (*Preterit: onihuapahuac*)
crank *n.* matzitzquiloni
crate *n.* cuauhcalli, huacalli
craving *n.* tentlacihuiztli
crawl *iv.* ixacanehnemi (*Preterit: onixacanehnen*)
crazy *adj.* yollotlahueliloc
creak *iv.* nanatzca (*Preterit: oninanatzcac*)
cream *n.* ichiaya in chichihualayotl
crease *n.* tlapoztectli
create *tv.* yocoya (*Preterit: onitlayocox*)
creation *n.* tlachihualli
creature *n.* xolotl
cress *n.* mexixquilitl
crib *n.* cozolli
cricket *n.* chopilin
crime *n.* tetzauh tlatlacolli
criminal *n.* tetzauh tlahtlacoani
cripple *n.* huelatzin, huelantli, huehuelatzin xocue
crippled *adj.* metzcotoctic
criticize *iv.* tlatenehua (*Preterit: onitlateneuh*)
crocodile *n.* cipactli
crooked *adj.* malinqui
cross *n.* coloz, cocoltzin, colotzin, cuauhmahmazohualticoni,
   cuauhmahmazouhqui; *iv.* pano (*Preterit: onipanoc*)
cross-eyed *adj.* ixcuepoctic, ixcueponqui, ixtetziltic, ixchicotic
crossing *n.* panoayan, panoliztli (*action*)
crossroads *n.* ohmaxac, ohmaxalli, ohmaxalco, ohtlamaxac,
   ohtlamaxalli

crotch *n.* maxactli, maxatl, queztli

crow *n.* cacalotl

crowd *n.* miec tlacatl

crown *n.* copilli

crucifix *n.* cuauhmahmazouhticatzin

crucifixion *n.* temahmazohualtiliztli

crucify *tv.* temahmazohualtia (*Preterit: onitemahmazohualtih*)

crude *adj.* tentlahueliloc (*language*)

cruel *adj.* yollocococ, tlacamazatl

cruelty *n.* ahtlacayotl, tlacamazayotl

crumb *n.* quequexolli, tlapactli, cotoctli

crumble *iv.* xihxitini (*Preterit: oxihxitin*)

crush *tv.* patlachohua (*Preterit: onitlapatlachouh*)

crushed *adj.* patlachtic

crust *n.* tlapactli

cry *iv.* choca (*Preterit: onichocac*); **make ~** *tv.* choctia (*Preterit: onitechoctih*)

cry loudly *iv.* choquiliztzatzi (*Preterit: onichoquiliztzatzic*)

crystal *n.* chipilotl, tehuilotl

cuckold *n.* tlaxintli

cultivate *iv.* milchihua (*Preterit: onimilchiuh*)

culture *n.* tlamatiliztli, yuhcatiliztli, tlamatiliztli

cunning *adj.* mahmauhqui

cup *n.* apilolli, tlahuanoni, tlahuantli

cupboard *n.* caxmanaloyan

curable *adj.* pahtiloni

cure *n.* pahtli; *iv.* pahtia (*Preterit: onitepahtih*)

cured *adj.* pahtic

curing *n.* tepahtiliztli

curled *adj.* cocolochtic

curly *adj.* cocolochtic, molochtic

current *adj.* axa, axan, axca, axcan

currently *adv.* quinaxcatica

curse *n.* teahcualihtoliztli, tlapactecalli
curtain *n.* tlmahtli, tlapilolcanahuac, tezcapetzticoni
curve *iv.* colihui (*Preterit: onicoliuh*)
curved *adj.* coliuhtoc, coltic
cushion *n.* cuachicpalli
custom *n.* tlamanitiliztli
cut *tv.* cotona (*Preterit: onitlacoton*), tequi
    (*Preterit: onitlatec*), xima (*Preterit: onitlaxin*); *n.* tlatectli
cut stone *iv.* texima (*Preterit: onitexin*)
cutting tool *n.* tletequiloni, tlateconi
cypress *n.* tlatzcan, ahuehuetl
cyst *n.* xoxalli
Czech Republic *n.* Checotlahtocayotl

D

dagger *n.* tepuzteixilihuani
daily *adv.* momoztlaeh, momoztlae, momoztla,
    cehcemilhuitica
dairy *n.* chichihualayonamacoyan, nemeyalnamacoyan
dam *n.* atlatzacuhtli
damage *tv.* ihtlacoa (*Preterit: onitlaihtlacoh*)
damp *adj.* cuechahuac
dampen *tv.* cuechahuia (*Preterit: onitlacuechahuih*)
dampness *n.* cuechahualiztli, cuechahuallotl
dance *reflex. v.* ihtotia (*Preterit: oninihtotih*)
dance hall *n.* nehtotiloyan
dancer *n.* mhtotiani, ihtotiani
dandruff *n.* cuaehuayotl, cuatequixquitl, cuatextli, cuatenextli
danger *n.* ohuihcayotl
dangerous *adj.* ohuih (*Plural: ohuihqueh*)
dare *reflex. v.* tlapaloa (*Preterit: oninotlapaloh*)

dark *adj.* tlayohuallo, tlayohualtic, popoyacpil
darken *tv.* tlillotia (*Preterit: onitlatlilloh*), tlilhuia
    (*Preterit: onitlatlilhuih*); *iv.* tlayohua (*Preterit: otlayohuac*)
darkness *n.* ayauhyotl, tlayohualli, mixtecomactli
date *n.* zoyacapulin (*palm*)
daughter *n.* cihuaconetl, cihuapilli, xoco (*youngest*)
daughter-in-law *n.* cihuamontli
dawn *n.* tlahuizicalli; **to ~** *impers. v.* tlathui (*Preterit: otlathuic*)
day *n.* ilhuitl, tlahcahtli, tonalli; **on the next ~** *adv.* imoztlayoc
day after tomorrow *adv.* huiptla
day and night *adv.* cemilhuitl ceyohual
day before yesterday *adv.* ye ohuiptla
Day of the Dead *n.* Miccailhuitl, mihcailhuitl
deaf *adj.* ahtlacaquini, nacaztapal, nacaztzatza
deafness *n.* nacaztzatzayotl
dear *adj.* tlazohtli
death *n.* miquiztli, miquiliztli; **time of ~** *n.* miquian,
    miquiztentli
debate *n.* neteyaotiliztli
debris *n.* tepicilli
debt *n.* tetlahuiquililiztli, netlacuilli, tetech tlaahcoliztli,
    tetech tlapoliuhtaliztli
deceased *adj.* micqui
deceitful *adj.* omeyolloh
deceive *tv.* ixcuepa (*Preterit: oniteixcuep*), xicoa
    (*Preterit: onitexicoh*)
decency *n.* nemalhuiliztli
decision *n.* nenotztli
decorate *tv.* tlacualnextia (*Preterit: onitlacualnextih*),
    tlamahuichihchihua (*Preterit: onitlamahuichihchiuh*)
decorated *adj.* tlayecchihchiuhtli
decrease *iv.* caxahua (*Preterit: onicaxahuac*)
deed *n.* tlamahuizolli

deer *n.* mazatl
defamation *n.* mahuizpopoliztli
defame *tv.* mahuizzopoloa (*Preterit: onitemahuizzopoloh*)
defeat *tv.* pehua (*Preterit: onitepeuh*)
defecate *reflex. v.* axixa (*Preterit: oninaxix*),
    reflex. v. momanahuia (*Preterit: oninomanahuih*)
defective *adj.* cotoctic
definition *n.* tlacemihtoliztli
degree *n.* tlamamatlatl
delay *n.* huehcahualiztli, nehuehcaualiztli; *tv.* huehcahua
    (*Preterit: onitehuehcauh*)
delicate *adj.* yamanqui
delicious *adj.* huelic, hueltic
demise *n.* xitiniliztli
demon *n.* tzitzimitl
dense *adj.* chamahuac
dentist *n.* tetlamcopinqui, tetlampahtiani, tetlampahtih
dentures *n.* tlantlacentlaliloni
departure *n.* ompehualiztli, quizaliztli, yaliztli
deprive *tv.* tlacencahualtia (*Preterit: onitetlacencahualtih*)
depth *n.* huehcatlanyotl
descend *iv.* emo (*Preterit: onitemoc*)
descent *n.* temoliztli
desert *n.* ixtlahuatl
deserter *n.* moteputztiani
deserve *tv.* macehua (*Preterit: onitlamaceuh*), ilhuilti
    (*Preterit: nolhuiltic*; *Takes the possessive prefixes*)
desirable *adj.* neconi; *n.* nequiztli
desire *n.* tlanequiliztli; *tv.* elehuia (*Preterit: onitlaelehuih*),
    nequi (*Preterit: onitlanec*); *reflex. v.* icoltia
    (*Preterit: oninotlacoltih*)
desk *n.* tlahcuilolhuapalitl, tlapechtlahcuiloni
despicable *adj.* tlatelchihualoni

despise telchihua (*Preterit: onitetelchiuh*)

destiny *n.* tlaciuhcayotl

destroy *tv.* xitinia (*Preterit: onitexitinih*)

devil *n.* mictlanchaneh, tlacatecolotl, xolopihtli

devious *adj.* omeyolloh

dew *n.* ahhuachtli, huichtli

dexterous *adj.* momaimatini, momaimatqui

dialogue *n.* zazanilli

diamond *n.* tlacuahuactecpatl

diaper *n.* conetzotzomahtli, conequimiliuhcayotl, maxtlatl

diarrhea *n.* apitzalli, noquiliztli, nalquizalli, nalquixtilli,
    tlanoquilli, tlecoacihuiztli; **have ~** *iv.* nalquixti
    (*Preterit: oninalquixtic*), apitza (*Preterit: onapitz*),
    noquia (*Preterit: onicnoquih*)

dice *n.* omipatolli (*game*)

dictionary *n.* tlahtolnezcayoamoxtli

die *iv.* miqui (*Preterit: onimic*); **~ in battle** *iv.* yaomiqui
    (*Preterit: oniyaomic*)

diet *n.* netlacualizcahualtiliztli

difference *n.* ahmoneneuhcayotl

different *adj.* ahmoneneuhqui

difficult *adj.* ohuih, tequiyoh

difficulty *n.* ohuihcayotl

dig *tv.* coyonia (*Preterit: onitlacoyonih*)

digest *n.* temohuia (*Preterit: onitlatemohuih*)

digestion *n.* tlatemohuiliztli

dignity *n.* mahuizzotl, pilticayotl

diligent *adj.* motlacuitlahui, tlacacqui

diminish *iv.* cuetlani (*Preterit: onicuetlan*)

dim-witted *adj.* tepochcoyotl

dine *reflex. v.* mocochcayotia (*Preterit: oninocochcayotih*)

dining room *n.* tlacualoyan

dining table *n.* tlacualtlapechtli, tlacualhuapalitl,
    tlacualontlapechtli

dinner *n.* cochcayotl, cochcayotilli, cochcayotl, **have ~**
    reflex. v. mocochcayotia (*Preterit: oninocochcayotih*)
diplomat *n.* hueitlahtocatitlantli
director *n.* teyecanani, teyecanqui, tlayacanqui
dirty *adj.* catzactic, catzahuac, tzoyoh; **~** *tv.* zolotia
    (*Preterit: onitlazolotih*)
dirty old man *n.* ahuilhuehue
disarray *n.* teixneloliztli
disaster *n.* ohui tepanchihualiztli, ohui tepan yaliztli
disc *n.* caquilizcaxitl (*recording*)
disciplined *n.* tlahuapahualli
discotheque *n.* nehtotiloyan
discourage *tv.* zotlahua (*Preterit: onitezotlahuac*)
discouraged *adj.* zotlauhqui
discover *tv.* nextia (*Preterit: onitlanextih*)
discovered *adj.* tlanextilli
discovery *n.* ixtlapohuiliztli, tlanextilli, nequittallo
discreet *adj.* yolizmatqui
discreetness *n.* nezcaliliztli
disguise *tv.* xayacayotia (*Preterit: onitexayacayotih*)
dish *n.* caxitl; molli (*meal*)
dismiss *tv.* totoca (*Preterit: onitetotocac*)
disobedience *n.* tzonteyotl
disobedient *adj.* ahtlacaquini, tzontetl; **be ~** *iv.* tzontetia
    (*Preterit: onitzontetix*)
disorder *n.* teixneloliztli
disperse *iv.* mani (*Preterit: oniman*); *tv.* xitinia
    (*Preterit: onitexitinih*)
display *n.* tlanextiliztli; *tv.* tlanextilia (*Preterit: onitetlanextilih*)
dispute *n.* tetlatzohuiliztli, tetlatzohuililiztli *tv.* tlatzohuilia
    (*Preterit: onitetlatzohuilih*)
dissolve *tv.* paatla (*Preterit: onitlapaatlac*)

distressed *adj.* yollotoneuhqui
ditch *n.* apantli
diverse *adj.* nepapan
divide *tv.* xeloa (*Preterit: onitlaxeloh*)
divided *adj.* xeliuhqui
divine *adj.* teoyoh
divinity *n.* teoyeliztli, teoyotl
divisible *adj.* xelihuini
division *n.* tlaxexeloliztli, xexeloliztli
divorce *n.* nemacahualtiliztli
divulge *tv.* machiztia (*Preterit: onictemachiztih*), ixpantilia
     (*Preterit: onicteixpantilih*)
dizzy *adj.* ixhuintic
docile *adj.* yolceuhqui, yollomachtilli
docility *n.* yolceuhcayotl
dock *n.* acaltecoyan
doctor *n.* tepahtiani, ticitl (*Plural: titicih*)
document *n.* amatl
dog *n.* chichi, itzcuintli; **hairless ~** xoloitzcuintli
doll *n.* nenetl
donkey *n.* axno, polo
door *n.* caltencuahuitl, caltentli, calacohuayan, quiahuatl,
     tlatzacuillotl
doorbell *n.* tepuzcacalachtli, tepuznenonotzaloni
doorway *n.* quiahuatl
dormitory *n.* cochiantli, cochihualoyan, cochihuayan
dose *n.* pahtliliztli
dot *n.* tliltetl
double *adj.* nepanotl
double chin *n.* quechnacayotl/quechtlacxollotl
doubt *n.* neyolpololiztli, yoltequipacholli; *reflex. v.*
     yoltzotzona (*Preterit: oninoyoltzotzon*), omeyollohua
     (*Preterit: oninomeyollohuac*)

dough *n.* textli
dove *n.* huilotl, cocohtli (*turtle*)
down *n.* tohmitl; *adv.* tlani
downcast *adj.* zotlauhqui
downfall *n.* xitiniliztli
downtown *n.* altepeyollohtli
downward *adv.* tlanihuic, tlanipa
drain ahuatza *iv.* (*Preterit: onahuatz*)
draw *tv.* tlilana (*Preterit: onitlatlilan*)
draw blood *tv.* zoa (*Preterit: onitezoh*)
drawing *n.* tlahuahuanilli, tlahcuilolhuahuanilli
dream *n.* cochtemictli, temictli; *iv.* cochtemiqui
    (*Preterit: onicochtemic*), temiqui (*Preterit: onitemic*);
    tv. cochitta (*Preterit: onitlacochittac*)
dress *n.* cihuatlatlatquitl; *reflex. v.* tlaquentia
    (*Preterit: oninotlaquentih*); *tv.* quemi (*onicquen*);
    quentia (*Preterit: onitequentih*); **~ well**
    reflex. v. yecquetza (*Preterit: oninoyecquetz*)
drill *n.* tlamamalihualoni, tlacoyoniloni;
    tv. mamali (*Preterit: onitlamamalihuac*),
    coyonia (*Preterit: onitlacoyon*)
drink *n.* tlahuantli, tlailli; *tv.* i (*Preterit: onitlaic*);
    ~ liquor heavily *iv.* tlahuana (*Preterit: onitlahuan*)
drip *iv.* pipica (*Preterit: opipicac*)
dripping *n.* pipicaliztli
drive *tv.* nehmeniliztepuzacalnemachilia
    (*Preterit: oninehnemiliztepuzacanelmachilih*)
drive away *tv.* totoca (*Preterit: onitetotocac*)
driver *n.* nehnemiliztepuzacalnemachiliani
drizzle *n.* mixatl
drone *n.* zozoloquiztli (*sound*)

drool *iv.* iztlameya (*Preterit: oniztlacmex*)
drop *n.* tlachipintli
dropsy *n.* atemaliztli, itixihuiliztli
drought *n.* huaquiliztli, huaquiztli, huaccayotl,
    tlalhuaquiliztli
drown *iv.* atoco (*Preterit: onatococ*)
drowned *adj.* atococ
drowning *n.* atocoliztli
drowsy *adj.* cochmiquini
drug *n.* tecochtlazantli
drugged *adj.* tecochtlazalli
drum *n.* huehuetl (*large vertical*), teponaztli (*small horizontal*),
    tlapanhuehuetl (*large bass*)
drunk *adj.* ihuintic octlahuanqui, tlahuanqui, xocomicqui,
    xocomihqui, xocomiquini; **be ~** *iv.* ihuinti
    (*Preterit: onihuintic*)
drunkenness *n.* neiihuintiliztli, ihuintiliztli, tlatlahuanaliztli
dry *adj.* huacqui; **be ~** *iv.* huaqui (*Preterit: ohuac*);
    ~ *tv.* tonalhuatza (*Preterit: onitlatonalhuatz*)
dryness *n.* huaquiliztli, huaquiztli, huaccayotl
duck *n.* canauhtli, patox, xomotl
dullard *n.* tehpochtli
dumb *adj.* nontli
dungeon *n.* ohuihcan, tecaltzacualoyan
duration *n.* nemiani
dust *n.* teuhtli
dust cloud *n.* teuhyotl
dusty *adj.* teuhtic
duty *n.* nahuatilli
dwarf *n.* tzapa, tzapatl
dwelling *n.* nemohuayan
dye *n.* tlapaloni; *tv.* pa (*Preterit: onitlapah*)
dynasty *n.* tlahtocamecayotl

E

eagle *n.* cuauhtli

ear *n.* nacaztli

ear doctor *n.* tenacazpahtih, tenacazpahtiani

ear plug *n.* zoquinacochtli (*clay*)

earache *n.* nacazcocoliztli

early *adv.* cualcan, ayacuel, ayaquemman

early in the morning *adv.* yohuatzinco, zancuel, ihciuhpan

earring *n.* nacazpilcayotl, nacochtli, pipilolli

earth *n.* tlalli, tlalticpac

earthenware *n.* tepalcatl, zoquitlatquitl

earthly things *n.* tlalticpaccayotl

earthquake *n.* tlaloliniliztli, tlalolin

earthworm *n.* tlalocuilin, cuetlaxcolli

earwax *n.* nacazcuitlatl

earwig *n.* maxalli

ease *n.* chihualiztli

east *n.* tlauhcampa, tonayan, tonayampa, tonatiuh iquizayan

eastern *adj.* tonatiuh iquizayancayotl

eat *tv.* cua (*Preterit: onitlacuah*);
    ~ **sweets** *reflex. v.* xochipoloa (*Preterit: oninoxochipoloh*);
    ~ **too much** *tv.* xixicuinoa (*Preterit: onitlaxixicuinoh*)

eclipse *n.* metztli cualo (*lunar*), tonatiuh cualo (*solar*)

edge *n.* tentli

edible *adj.* cualoni, mocuani

educate *tv.* tlacazcaltia (*Preterit: onitlacazcaltih*), izcalia
    (*Preterit: oniteizcalih*)

educated *adj.* quixtilpilli

education *n.* huapahualizltli, tehuapahualiztli

educator *n.* tlacazcaltiani

eel *n.* coamichin

effeminate *adj.* cihuatic, cihuayolloh

effort *n.* huapahualiztli, tlapalihuiztli, yolchicahualiztli
egg *n.* totoltetl; palancatotoltetl, totoltepalan (*rotten*)
egg porridge *n.* totoltemolli
egg white *n.* totoltetl iiztaca
egg yolk *n.* totoltetl icuztica
eggshell *n.* totoltecacalli
eight *num.* chicuei
elbow *n.* molicpitl
election *n.* teixquetzaliztli, tepehpenaliztli
elector *n.* tepehpenani
electric current *n.* tlahuilmeyallotl
electricity *n.* tlahuitequiliztletl
elegance *n.* pilticayotl
elegant *adj.* piltic, tlayecchihchiuhtli
eleven *num.* matlactli once
eloquent *adj.* cualnezcatlahtoani
embark *reflex. v.* moacalaquia (*Preterit: oninoacalquih*)
embarrassed *iv.* pinahua (*Preterit: onipinahuac*)
embarrassment *n.* pinahualiztli, pinahuiztli
embassy *n.* tlahtohcatetitlaniliztli
ember *n.* tlecuezallotl
embrace *reflex. v.* macochoa (*Preterit: oninoimacochoh*)
emerald *n.* quetzalitztli
emptiness *n.* yuhcatlayotl
empty *adj.* cacticac; *tv.* noquia (*Preterit: onitlanoquih*),
    yuhticahua (*Preterit: onitlayuhticauh*)
empty space *n.* cacticacayotl
enamor *tv.* teyolehua (*Preterit: oniteyoleuh*), teyollotlapana
    (*Preterit: oniteyollotlpan*)
encircle *tv.* yahualoa (*Preterit: onitlayahualoh*)
enclose *tv.* tzacua (*Preterit: onitlatzauc*)
enclosure *n.* chinamitl
encounter *n.* tenamiquiliztli

encourage *tv.* izcalia (*Preterit: oniteizcalih*)

encyclopedia *n.* centlamatilizamoxtli

end *n.* tlamiliztli, tzonquizcayotl; *iv.* tzonquiza
    (*Preterit: onitzonquiz*)

endless *adj.* aictlanqui

enema *n.* tepahnamaconi, tetzimpahnamaconi

enemy *n.* yaotl, teyaouh

energy *n.* oquichyollohtli

engineer *n.* tepuzyollomatini (*mechanical*), tlaltamachihuani,
    tetepetlacoyoniani (*civil*)

engineering *n.* tepuzyollomatiliztli (*mechanical*),
    tetepelacoyoniliztli (*civil*)

England *n.* Anglitlalli

English *n.* Anglitlaltecatl (*person*); Anglitlallahtolli (*language*)

engrave *tv.* tlapalaquia (*Preterit: onitlatlapalaquih*),
    tetlahcuiloa (*Preterit: onitetlahcuiloh*)

engraving *n.* tetlahcuilolli, tetlacuicuilli

enjoy *tv.* pactia (*Preterit: onicpactih*)

enjoyment *n.* yolpaquiliztli

enliven *tv.* yolmaca (*Preterit: oniteyolmacac*)

enough *adv.* ixachi, ye ixquich

enroll *tv.* tocaihcuiloa (*Preterit: onitetocaihcuiloh*), tocatlalia
    (*Preterit: onitetocatlalih*)

entangled *adj.* pahzoltic

enter *iv.* calaqui (*Preterit: onicalac*)

entertainment *n.* neahuiltiliztli

enthusiasm *n.* neyolehualoni

entirely *adv.* cenquizca, huelcen

entrails *n.* eltzaccatl

entrance *n.* calaquiliztli (*act of*); caltentli (*door*), quiahuatl,
    calixtli

envious *adj.* moxicoani

envoy *n.* titlantli

envy *n.* chahualiztli, nexicoliliztli, nexicoliztli, nexicolli;
   reflex. v. xicoa (*Preterit: oninoxicoh*)
epidemic *n.* matlazahuatl
epilepsy *n.* mimiquiliztli; *iv.* **have ~** mimiqui
   (*Preterit: onimimic*)
epitaph *n.* miccatlahcuilolmachiotl
equal *adj.* nehneuhqui
equality *n.* nehneuhcayotl
equalize *tv.* namictia (*Preterit: onitlanamictih*)
equally *adv.* nehneuhca
erase *tv.* ixchihchiqui (*Preterit: onitlaixchihchic*), poloa
   (*Preterit: onitlapoloh*)
eraser *n.* tlapohpoaloni, tlapohpolhuaztli
erect *adj.* ihcac, ixmelactic; *tv.* quetza (*Preterit: onitlaquetz*)
erection *n.* tlacuahtililiztli; **have an ~** *iv.* tlacuauhtilia
   (*Preterit: onitlacuauhtilih*)
errand boy *n.* topilli
error *n.* neixpololiztli, tlacuapololiztli
escalator *n.* tepantleconi, tepantemoni
escape *iv.* maquiz (*Preterit: onimaquiz*)
esophagus *n.* cocotl, cocohtli, yolloixtli
especially *adv.* caccencaye, ilhuiceh
essential *adj.* ahhuelcahualloh
esteem *n.* tlatenyotiliztli
esteemed *adj.* huehcapan iuhqui
etched in stone *adj.* tetlahcuilolli
eternally *adv.* cemmanca
eternity *n.* cemihcayotl
ethics *n.* cualinemoani
ethnic group *n.* nepapan tlacah
euphoric *adj.* yuhqui ihuintic
Europe *n.* Eutlocpa
European *n.* tonatiuh icalaquiyantlacatl

even if *adv.* mazannel
evening *n.* teotlac (*early*), yohualli (*late*); **good ~**
Quen oteotlatihuac
event *n.* nechihualiztli, omochiuh
everyday *adv.* cecemilhuitica, momoztla
everywhere *adv.* nohhuian, nohhuiyan
evident *adj.* iximachoni, nezqui, paninezqui, neci
evil *adj.* tlahueliloc; *n.* poyotl
exact *adj.* motlahtolneltiani
exactly *adj.* netlahtolneltiliztica
exactness *n.* motlahtolneltiliztli
exam *n.* tlamachtilyehyecoliztli
examine *iv.* ixpetzoa (*Preterit: oninixpetzoh*), ixyehyecoa
(*Preterit: onitlaixyehyecoh*)
example *n.* neixcuitilli, xiyotl
exception *n.* tlanoncuaquixtilli
excitement *n.* neyolehualoni
excrement *n.* cuitlatl, axixtli
excretion *n.* cuitatl
excuse *n.* netlanehuiliztli
excuse me *interj.* xinechtlapopolhui; teixcotzinco
(*reverential*), mixpantzinco (*reverential*), mixpan;
when passing behind someone: micampa, micampatzinco
(*reverential*); *when passing to the side of someone:*
mocecac, mocecactzinco (*reverential*)
executioner *n.* miquiztequipaneh, tequechcotonani
executor *n.* itech necahualotiuh
exempt *adj.* ahnempehualtilloh
exemption *n.* ahnempehualtiliztli
exercise *n.* neyehyecoliztli; *reflex. v.* moyehyecoa
(*Preterit: oninoyehyecoh*)
exist *iv.* mani (*Preterit: omanca*)
existence *n.* nemiliztli

exit *n.* quixohuayan

exonerated *adj.* moquixtih, motemaquixtih

expensive *adj.* cencapatiyoh patiyoh, tlazohtli;
 be ~ *iv.* tlazohti (*Preterit: otlazohtic*)

experience *n.* nemilizzotl, tlamatiniyotl

explain *tv.* tlahtolmelahua (*Preterit: onitlahtolmelauh*),
 melahuacaihtoa (*Preterit: onicmelahuacaihtoh*)

explain clearly *tv.* melahuacaihtoa
 (*Preterit: onitlamelahuacaihtoh*)

explanation *n.* tlahtolmelahualiztli, melahuacaihtoliztli

explode *iv.* tlecueponi (*Preterit: onitlecuepon*)

explosion *n.* tlecueponilli, tlanextiliztli

express *tv.* nezcayotia (*Preterit: onitlanezcayotih*)

extract *tv.* copina (*Preterit: onitlacopin*), quixtia
 (*Preterit: onitlaquextih*)

exuberance *n.* pactinemiliztli

exuberant *adj.* pactinemi

eye *n.* ixtololohtli, ixtelolohtli, ixtli

eye disease *n.* ixcocoliztli

eye doctor *n.* teixpahtiani

eyeball *n.* ixtetl

eyebrow *n.* ixcuamulli, ixcuahmolli, ixtohmitl, tocochia

eyeglasses *n.* ixtezcaticoni, ixtezcatl, tehuiloixtli

eyelash *n.* tocochia, cochiatl, ixtzontli, ixpilli

eyelid *n.* ixtentli, ixehuatl, ixcuatolli

F

fable *n.* zanilli

fabric *n.* cuachtli

façade *n.* calixco

face *n.* ixtli, xayacatl

face down *adv.* ixaca

facial features *n.* ixconexiliztli
facial hair *n.* camatzontli, ixtzontli
fact *n.* nechihualiztli
factory *n.* tlachihualoyan, tlachiuhcan
faculty *n.* huelitiliztli
fagot *n.* cuauhtlalilli
fail *iv.* nenquiza (*Preterit: oninenquiz*), nenti
 (*Preterit: oninentic*)
failure *n.* nenquizaliztli
faint *adj.* zotlauhqui; *iv.* yolmiqui (*Preterit: oniyolmic*),
 iv. zotlahua (*Preterit: onizotlahuac*)
fainting *n.* zotlahualiztli
fair *adj.* yolmelahuac
faith *n.* tlaneltoquiliztli (*belief*), neltoquiliztli (*belief*),
 tlacuauhtlamatiliztli (*confidence*)
faithful *adj.* nehuelyollotiloni
falcon *n.* huactli, tlohtli
fall *n.* tonalco (*season*); xitiniliztli (*descent*); *iv.* huetzi
 (*Preterit: onihuetz*), tepehui (*Preterit: onitepeuh*),
 xitini (*Preterit: onixitin*)
fallen *adj.* xitinqui
falsely *adv.* tlapic
fame *n.* itauhcayotl, tauhca, tenyotl
family *n.* cencalli, cenyeliztli
famine *n.* mayanaliztli
famous *adj.* tenyoh
fan *n.* ehecacehuaztli
fang *n.* coatlantli
far *adj.* huehca; *adv.* huehca; *adv.* huehcapa (*from afar*)
fare *n.* hualpatiuhtli
farm worker *n.* miltequitqui, miltequitini, tlalmaitl
farmer *n.* millacatl, milpanecatl, milpan tlacatl, tlalchiuhqui
farsighted *adj.* huehcatlachiani

fart *n.* neyexiliztli; *reflex. v.* yexi (*Preterit: oninyex*)

fast *n.* ihyohuiliztli, nezahualiztli, nacacahualiztli (*from meat*); *iv.* nacacahua (*Preterit: oninacacauh*); *reflex. v.* zahua (*Preterit: oninozauh*); *adj.* painalli

fat *n.* ceyotl; *adj.* chamahuac, nacayoh, tomahuac; **be ~** *iv.* tomahua (*Preterit: onitomahuac*)

fatal *adj.* temictih

fate *n.* tlaciuhcayotl

father *n.* tahtli

father-in-law *n.* montahtli

fatigue *n.* ciammiquiliztli, ciahuiliztli, ciciyahuiztli

fatigued *adj.* patzmicqui

fault *n.* tlahtlacolli

favor *n.* ilhuilli, tepalehuiliztli, tetlatlauhtilli

fawn *n.* mazaconetl

fear *iv.* mahui (*Preterit: onimauh*); *tv.* imacaci (*Preterit: onteimacaz*); *n.* temahmauhtiliztli (*felt by others*), nemahmauhtiliztli (*felt by oneself*)

fearful *adj.* mauhqui

fearless *adj.* tiyacauhqui

feather *n.* ihhuitl, atlapalli

feathered *adj.* tlapotonilli

feature *n.* tlamanitiliztli

feces *n.* axixtli, cuitlatl

feeble *adj.* cuanhuacqui; **be ~** cuanhuacqui (*Preterit: onicuanhuac*)

feed *tv.* tlacualtia (*Preterit: onitetlacualtih*)

feeding *n.* tetlacualtiliztli

feel well *reflex. v.* mohuelmati (*Preterit: oninohuelmat*)

feeling *n.* nematihuani

feigning *n.* tlacaittaliztli

fellow countryman *n.* cecnitlacapohui

female *n.* cihuatl

female secretion *n.* cihuaayotl
fermented drink *n.* octli, tepach
fern *n.* ocopetlatl
ferociousness *n.* tecuanyotl
ferret *n.* zacotl
fertile land *n.* atoctli
fertilize *tv.* zoquipachoa (*Preterit: onitlazoquipachoh*)
fetter *tv.* mailpia (*Preterit: onitemailpix*)
fever *n.* totoniyalotl, tlepopocaliztli, totoniliztli, totonillotl;
    ~ **and chills** *n.* atonahuiztli; **have ~** *iv.* atonahui
    (*Preterit: onatonauh*)
fever medicine *n.* totoncapahtli
feverishness *n.* totonilizzotl
fiancée *n.* cihuahtla
fiber *n.* ichtli
fickle *adj.* yollocuecuepqui
fickleness *n.* yollocuepcayotl
fiction *n.* tlapiquiliztli
field *n.* ixtlahuatl, milli
field hand *n.* tlalmaitl
fiery *adj.* tleyoh
fifteen *num.* caxtolli
fig *n.* hicox
fig tree *n.* amacuahuitl
file *n.* tepuzichiconi (*tool*), tepuzteconi (*tool*); huipantli (*row*)
    tv. tepuzpetlahuia (*Preterit: onitepuzpetlahuih*)
fill *tv.* temitia (*Preterit: onitlatemitih*)
filth *n.* tlahzolli, tzotl, pitzoyotl, pitzoyutl
finally *adv.* auh yequene, yequene, yehqueneh, auh
    yehqueneh, za yeh queneh, zatlatzonco, iccen
fine *adj.* canahuac, piltic
finesse *n.* canahuacayotl
finger *n.* mahpilli

fingernail *n.* iztetl

finicky *adj.* acocollapaliuhqui

finish *iv.* tlami (*Preterit: onitlan*), tzonquixtia
    (*Preterit: onitlatzonquixtih*), tlacencahua
    (*Preterit: onitlacencauh*)

finished *adj.* tzonquizqui

fire *n.* tletl; **start a ~** *tv.* tletlalia (*Preterit: onitletlalih*);
    catch ~ *iv.* xotla (*Preterit: onixotlac*)

fire moth *n.* tlepapalotl

fire shovel *n.* tlemaco

firearm *n.* tlequihquiztli

firefly *n.* copitl, icpitl, tlahuilzayulin, popoquihtli, popoyecatl,
    xoxotlani

fireplace *n.* tlecuilli

firewood *n.* tlatlatilcuahuitl

fireworks *n.* tlatoltecahuiltitletl

firm *adj.* chicactic, tlapaltic, mahcic

firmness *n.* mahciconi

first *adj.* inic centetl; *adv.* achto, achtopa

firstborn *n.* yacapantli

fish *n.* michin; *tv.* michpihpiloa (*Preterit: onimichpihpiloh*)

fish egg *n.* michtetl, michpilli

fish market *n.* michnamacoyan

fish scale *n.* michehuatl, michincayotl

fish vendor *n.* michnamacac

fishbone *n.* michomitl, michomitetl

fisherman *n.* michmani, michacini, michpihpiloani

fishing *n.* michaxiliztli, michmaliztli

fishing pole *n.* coyolacatl

fishpond *n.* michacaxitl

fist *n.* mapichtli, maololli, matzolli

five *num.* macuilli

fix *tv.* yectilia (*Preterit: onitlayectilih*), tlacencahua
   (*Preterit: onitlacencauh*), cualtilia (*Preterit: onitlacualtilih*)
flag *n.* pamitl, pantli, cuachpamitl
flame *n.* tlecuezallotl, tlenenepilli, tlecomoctli, tlepapalotl,
   tlemiahuatl, tlemiyahuatl
flamingo *n.* quecholli
flank *n.* itzcalli
flap *reflex. v.* papatlatza (*Preterit: oninopapatlaz*)
flash *iv.* tlapetlani (*Preterit: otlapetlan*)
flat *adj.* canahuac
flatter *tv.* chachamahua (*Preterit: onitechachamauh*)
flatterer *n.* tepehpetlani
flattering *adj.* tepehpetlani
flattery *n.* techachamahualiztli, techachamahuiliztli,
   tepehpetlaliztli
flatulence *n.* iyelli
flatulent *adj.* miexini
flavor *n.* huelicayotl, hueliliztli
flea *n.* tecpin
flee *iv.* choloa (*Preterit: onichocac*)
fleece *n.* tohmitl
flesh *n.* nacayotl, tonacayo
flight *n.* patlaniliztli, patlanilli
flint *n.* tecpatl
flock *n.* centlamantinyolqueh
flood *n.* atemillotl; *tv.* atemia (*Preterit: onitlaatemih*)
flooded *adj.* atenqui; **be ~** *reflex. v.* atemia
   (*Preterit omatemih*)
floor *n.* tlalpantli
florist *n.* xochnamacac
flour *n.* textli
flow *iv.* meya (*Preterit: omex*), moloni (*Preterit: omolon*)

flower *n.* xochitl
flower shop *n.* xochinamacoyan
flower vase *n.* xochicomitl
flower vendor *n.* xochinamacac
flowerpot *n.* xoxhicomitl, xochtoconi
flowery *adj.* xochiyoh
flu *n.* yacatzompilihuiztli
fluorescent *adj.* naltic
flute *n.* tlapitzalli, zozoloctli
flutist *n.* zozolocpitzqui
flutter *reflex. v.* papatlatza (*Preterit: oninopapatlaz*)
fly *n.* zayolin; *iv.* patlani (*Preterit: onipatlan*)
flying saucer *n.* patlanizcaxitl
flyswatter *n.* yecacehuaztli
foam *n.* popozoctli, pozolli, pozoncayotl; ~ *iv.* popozoca
    (*Preterit: opopozocac*)
foamy *adj.* pozonalloh, pozonilloh
fodder *n.* mazatlacualli
fog *n.* ayahuitl, yauhtli
fold *n.* tlapoztectli; *tv.* pohpoztequi (*Preterit: onitlaphopoztec*),
    xolochoa (*Preterit: onitlaxolochoh*); *tv.* cueloa (*Preterit:*
    onitlacueloh)
follow *tv.* toca (*Preterit: onitetocac*); ~ **a road** ohtoca
    (*Preterit: oniohtocac*); ~ **an example** *reflex. v.* xiyotia
    (*Preterit: oninoxiyotih*)
fontanel *n.* cuaxicalmonamicyan
food *n.* tlacualli, tlemolli
fool *n.* xolopihtli
foolish *adj.* tlaixtomahuac
foolishly *adv.* xolopihtica
foolishness *n.* aquimamachiliztli, pipillotl xolopihnemiliztli,
    xolopihyotl

foot *n.* icxitl; tlacxitamachiloni (*measure*), xotamachihualoni;
  centlacxitl (*verse meter*); **at the ~ of** *loc. suff* -icxitlan
footprint *n.* icximachiyotl, icxipetlalli
for *prep.* ica
for a while *adv.* huecauhtica
for that reason *adv.* yeh ica
force *n.* tlacuahualiztli
forcefully *adv.* tlacuauh
forearm *n.* matzotzopaztli
forehead *n.* ixcuaitl, ixcuatl, ixcuatetl
foreign language *n.* pinotlahtolli; **speak a ~** *iv.* pinotlahtoa
  (*Preterit: onipinotlahtoh*)
foreigner *n.* huehca tlacatl, huehca chaneh, pinotl
foreseen *adj.* achtopaneitalli
foresight *n.* achtopaneittaliztli
foreskin *n.* xipintli
forest *n.* cuauhtlah, cuauhcamac
foretell *tv.* yolteohuia (*Preterit: onitlayoltohuih*);
  iv. mecatlapohua (*Preterit: onimecatlapouh*)
forever *adv.* iccemmaniyan
forget *tv.* ilcahua (*Preterit: onitlailcauh*)
forgetfulness *n.* tlalcahualiztli, ilcahualiztli
forgive *tv.* pohpolhuia (*Preterit: onitetlapohpolhuih*)
forgiven *adj.* tetlapohpolhuilli
forgiveness *n.* tetlapohpolhuiliztli, pololocayotl
form *n.* yuhcatiliztli, yuhcayotl
formerly *adv.* yenepa (*in ancient times*)
formula *n.* tlamantlahtolmachtiloni
fornicate *iv.* ahuilnemi (*Preterit: onahuilnen*)
fornication *n.* ahuilnemiliztli
fornicator *n.* ahuilnenqui
fortuitous *adj.* zanoquiztic

fortuitously *adv.* zanoquiztica
fortune-teller *n.* mecatlapouhqui
forum *n.* tecuhtlahtoloyan
foundation *n.* tzintiliztli, tzintli, nelhuayotl; **~ of a building**
    n. xopechtli, xopetlatl
founder *n.* tlatzintiani
fountain *n.* ameyalli
four *num.* nahui
four hundred *num.* centzontli
fourteen *num.* matlactli onnahui
fox *n.* capizcayotl, cuectli
foyer *n.* calixtli
fraction *n.* cotoncayotl
fragile *adj.* ahchicahuac
fragment *n.* cotoncayotl, cotoctli
frame *n.* cuauhyahualoni, tlanacaztli
France *n.* Galian
fraud *n.* tequelonmaltiliztli
freckle *n.* neixihtlacoliztli
freckly *adj.* yayapalectic, tlitlilectic
free *tv.* maquixtia (*Preterit: onitemaquixtih*);
    adj. tlacaxoxouhqui
free time *n.* cacticacayotl
free will *n.* nenomahuiliztli, neyocoyaliztli, yoliuhyaliztli
freedom *n.* tlacaxoxouhcayotl, tlacaconemiliztli
French *n.* Galian chaneh, Galitlaltecatl; Galian tlahtolli
    (*language*)
frequent *adj.* tlaicxitocac; *adv.* tlaicxitocatica;
    ~ *tv.* tlaicxitoca (*Preterit: onitlaicxitocac*)
frequently *adv.* achica, zantequi
fresh *adj.* celic, celtic
freshness *n.* celticayotl

friction *n.* netelohchiquiliztli
fried *adj.* tlatzoyonilli, tzoyonqui
fried beans *n.* etlacualli
friend *n.* icniuhtli, pohtli, yolicniuhtli (*dear*)
friendship *n.* icniuhyotl
frightened *adj.* momauhtiani
frightful *adj.* temauhtih
frog *n.* cueyatl, caca, calatl
frolic *iv.* paccaahuiltia (*Preterit: onipaccaahuiltih*),
    pahcaahuiltia (*Preterit: onipahcaahuiltih*)
froth *n.* popozoctli
frown *reflex. v.* ixcuahmolquehquetza
    (*Preterit: oninixcuahmolquehquetz*)
fruit *n.* xochihcualli, xochicualli, xocotl
fruit pit *n.* xocoyollohtli
fruit tree *n.* xochihcualcuahuitl, xochicualcuahuitl
fry *tv.* tzoyonia (*Preterit: onitlatzoyonih*)
frying pan *n.* tepuzcaxpetzoyoniloni
fuel *n.* tlatlatiloni
fugitive *n.* choloani, motlaloani, miyanani
full *adj.* pachiuhqui, tenqui
full moon *n.* omahcic metztli
fun *n.* teaahuililiztli; **have ~** *tv.* teaahuilia
    (*Preterit: oniteaahulih*)
funeral *n.* miccatlatlatlauhtiliztli
funnel *n.* caxpializtli
fur *n.* tohmitl
furious *adj.* aacqui, zomaleh
furniture *n.* chantlatquitl, icpalalli
furrow *n.* cuemitl
furry *adj.* tohmiyoh
future *n.* moztlacayotl, in yez; **~ tense** tlen panoz cahuitl
fuzz *n.* tohmitl

G

gadabout *n.* ohcalnehnenqui, papal

gadfly *n.* temolin

gag *n.* tenenepilpacholoni; *tv.* tenenepilcuappachoa
    (*Preterit:* onitenenepilcuappachoh)

gain *n.* tlacnopilhuiliztli; ~ **weight** *reflex. v.* nacayotia
    (*Preterit:* oninonacayotih)

gallery *n.* mahuichichiuhcalli

gambler *n.* patoani

game *n.* ahuelli, neahuiltiliztli, mahuiltiliztli, neahuiltiloni

gander *n.* atlatlalacatl, concanauhtli, zoquicanauhtli

garden *n.* quilmilli, xochichinancalli, xochitepancalli, xochitla

gardener *n.* xochipixqui, xochitocani

gargle *iv.* tozcapapaca (*Preterit:* onitozcapapacac)

gargling *n.* tozcapapaconi

garlic *n.* caxtillan xonacatl, axox, caxtillan ajo, caxtillan axox

garter *n.* metzilpicayotl

gasoline *n.* techiahuacatlatlatiloni

gasp *iv.* ihcica (*Preterit:* onihcicac)

gate *n.* quiahuatl

gather *tv.* ololohua (*Preterit:* onitlaololouh)

gauze *n.* tocapeyotl

gelatin *n.* necuhtlachihchihualpitzac

general *n.* tlacatecatl, yaoquizcatlahtoani

generally *adv.* nohuianyotica

generation *n.* tlatlacatililiztli

generosity *n.* yolhueiliztli

generous *adj.* yollopiltic

gentleness *n.* cencatlacayotl, icnohuacayotl

gentle *adj.* cencatlacatl, icnoyoh

gentle of heart *adj.* yolyamanqui

gentleman *n.* piltic

gentleness *n.* yolceuhcayotl
gently *adv.* yocoxca
German *n.* Alamanecatl
Germany *n.* Alamanian
gesture *n.* nenemmictiliztli
get fat *reflex. v.* tomahua (*Preterit: oninotomahuac*)
get married *reflex. v.* monamictia (*Preterit: oninonamictih*)
get up *reflex. v.* ehua (*Preterit: oninehuac*)
get well *iv.* pahti (*Preterit: onipahtic*)
giant *n.* quinametl, tlacahueyac
giddiness *n.* necuahuihuintil
gift *n.* huentli, nemactli, tlauhtli, tlamanalli
ginger *n.* caxtillanchilli
girdle *n.* nelpiloni
girl *n.* ichpochtli (*Plural: ichpopochtin*)
give *iv.* maca (*Preterit: onitlamacac*)
give away *tv.* tetlocolia (*Preterit: onitetlocolih*)
give birth *iv.* mixihui (*Preterit: onimixiuh*)
gizzard *n.* aitztetl
glass *n.* tehuilotl, teitzlti, tezcatl; tlahuantli (*drinking*)
globe *n.* xiquipilacoquizaloni
gloomy *adj.* talyohualloh
glossy *adj.* tehuiltic
glottal stop *n.* ihyotzecoliztli
glove *n.* maehuatl, mapiccatl, matlapechtli
glue *n.* tzacuhtli, tzauctli; *tv.* zaloa (*Preterit: onitlazaloh*)
glutton *n.* cococoyactli, camacoyactli, cuetzpal, tlacahzolli, xixicuin, teztlatic
gluttony *n.* xixicuiyotl
glyph *n.* machiyohcuilollotl
go *iv.* yauh (*Preterit: oniyauh*), ya (*Preterit: oniya*)
go about *iv.* nehnemi (*Preterit: oninehnen*)
goal *n.* ahcitiliztli

goat *n.* cuacuauhtentzoneh
goblet *n.* tlahuantli
god *n.* teotl (*Plural: teteoh*); **Oh, my God!** *interj.* tlacahzo!
godchild *n.* teoconetl
godfather *n.* teoticatahtli, teotahtli
godmother *n.* teoticanantli, teonantli
goiter *n.* quechpalaniliztli
gold *n.* teocuitlatl
gold chain *n.* teocuitlamecatl
gold mine *n.* teocuitlaoztotl
golden *adj.* teocuitlayoh
goldfinch *n.* tzocuil
good *adj.* cualli, yectli
good afternoon *interj.* nocomatzin, teotlactzin,
    teotlaquiltih (*late*)
good evening *interj.* nocomatzin, teotlaquiltih,
    quen otimoteotlaquilti
good fortune *n.* netlamachtilli
good looking *adj.* yecnacayoh
good morning *interj.* nocomatzin, tlahcatzin
good night *interj.* yohuaquiltihtzino
good voice *adj.* yectaltoleh
goodness *n.* cuallotl, yectiliztli, yecyotl
goose *n.* atlatlalacatl, concanauhtli, zoquicanauhtli
gopher *n.* tozan
gossip *n.* tlatenehualoni; *iv.* papalchihua
    (*Preterit: onipapalchiuh*), tlatenehua
    (*Preterit: onitlateneuh*)
gossiper *n.* papal, ohcalnehnenqui
gourd *n.* huaxin, xicalli, xicaltecomatl
gout *n.* coacihuiztli; **suffer from ~** *iv.* coacihui
    (*Preterit: onicoaciuh*)

govern *iv.* itqui (*Preterit: onitlatquic*), pachoa
 (*Preterit: onitepachoh*)
government *n.* tecpanicatl, tecemitqui, teyacanaliztli,
 tecemitqui
grab *tv.* cui (*Preterit: oniccuic*)
grace *n.* huelnexiliztli
grade *n.* tlamamatlatl
gradually *adv.* iyolic
grain *n.* tetl
grammar *n.* netlahtoltemachtiloni, netlahtolmachtiloni,
 tlahtolnahuatilli
granary *n.* cuezcomatl
grandchild *n.* ixhuiuhtli, teixhui, teixhuiuh
granddaughter *n.* cihuaixhuiuhtli, ixhuiuhtli
grandfather *n.* colli
grandmother *n.* cihtli
grandparent *n.* colli
grandson *n.* oquichixhuiuhtli, ixhuiuhtli
grant *reflex. v.* nemactilia (*Preterit: oninonemactilih*)
grape *n.* xocomecayollotl
grapevine *n.* xocomecatl, caxapo
grasp *tv.* cui (*Preterit: oniccuic*)
grass *n.* zacatl
grasshopper *n.* chapulin
grassland *n.* zacamilli
grassy reed *n.* tolin
grateful *adj.* motlazohcamatini, motlazohmatini
gratis *adj.* tenemmaco; *adv.* tenemmacatica
gratitude *n.* netlazohcamatiliztli
grave *n.* miccacoyoctli, miccatlacoyoctli, mihcacoyoctli,
 mihcatlacoyoctli, tecochtli, tlaxapochtli
gravedigger *n.* miccaquimiloani, mihcaquimiloani
gravel *n.* xaltetl, tepecilli

gray *adj.* nextic, tizatl
gray hair *n.* cuaiztalli, tzoniztalli, tentzoniztalli (*beard*)
gray-haired *adj.* tzoniztac
grease *n.* ceyotl
greasy *adj.* chiyahuac
great-grandchild *n.* icuhtontli, mintontli
great-granddaughter *n.* icuhtontli
great-grandfather *n.* achtontli
great-grandmother *n.* piptontli
great-grandson *n.* icuhtontli
greatness *n.* hueicayotl
grebe *n.* acacalotl
Greece *n.* Helenoyan
greed *n.* tlaelehuiliztli
Greek *n.* Helenoyan chaneh
green *adj.* quiltic, quilitl, xoxoctic, xoxouhqui
green bean *n.* exotl
greet *tv.* tlahpaloa (*Preterit: ontetlahpaloh*)
greeting *n.* tetlahpaloliztli, tetlahpalolli
greyhound *n.* anquichichi, aminitzcuintli
griddle *n.* comalli
grief *n.* nentlamatiliztli
grill *tv.* tlehuatza (*Preterit: onitlatlehuatz*)
grimace *n.* nenemmictiliztli
grimy *adj.* chiyahuac
grind cuechohua (*Preterit: onitlacuechouh*), cuechoa
    (*Preterit: onitlacuechoh*), teci *tv.* (*Preterit: onitlatez*)
grinder *n.* texalli (*stone*)
grinding *n.* texiliztli
grippe *n.* yacatzompilihuiztli
groan *n.* quiquinaquiliztli, tenaliztli; *iv.* quiquinaca
    (*Preterit; oniquiquinacac*), tena (*Preterit: onitenac*)

groin *n.* quexalli
grooved *adj.* acaltic
ground *adj.* cuechtic
grove *n.* cuacuauhtl
grow *iv.* huepahue, mimilihui (*Preterit: omimiliuh*), tlapihuia
  (*Preterit: onitlapihuih*)
grow fat *iv.* chamahua (*Preterit: onichamahuac or*
  onichamauh); *reflex. v.* nacayotia
  (*Preterit: oninonacayotih*)
grow hair *iv.* tzonquiza (*Preterit: onitzonquiz*)
grown-up *n.* cuahcuauhtic
gruel *n.* atolli, comic atolli, totonca atolli
guacamole *n.* ahuacamolli
guard *n.* tlachixqui, tepixqui, tlapixqui; *tv.* pia
  (*Preterit: onitlapix*)
guardian *n.* tepixqui, tlapixqui
guava *n.* xaxocotl, xalxocotl, xoxocotl
guess *tv.* nahualcaqui (*Preterit: onitenahualcac*)
guest *n.* tecochtli, tecelilli, tepancochqui
guitar *n.* mecahuehuetl, caxtilhuehuetl
guitarist *n.* mecahuehuetzotzonani, mecahuehuetzotzonqui
gulf *n.* aitectli
gums *n.* quehtolli
gun *n.* tlequihquiztli
gunpowder *n.* tlequihquiztlalli

H

habit *n.* tetechnematiliztli
hail *n.* tecihuitl; **to ~** *impers. v.* tecihuitl huetzi
  (*Preterit: tecichuitl ohuetz*)
hair *n.* tzontli, camatzontli (*facial*), metztzontli (*leg*)

hairbrush *n.* tzonhuaztli, xolhuaztli, xelhuaztli, cuaxilhuaztli
haircut *tv.* xima (*Preterit: onitexin*)
hairless *adj.* ahtomiyoh
hairless dog *n.* xoloitzuintli
hairnet *n.* cuamatlatl
hairy *adj.* tohmiyoh
half *n.* centlahco, tlahco
hall *n.* nenonotzaloyan (*meeting*)
hallway *n.* calmelactli
ham *n.* pitzometzhuatzalli
hamlet *n.* cacallan, cahcallahtli
hammer *n.* tepuztlatehuioni/tepuztlatetzotzonaloni
hammock *n.* chitahtli
hand *n.* maitl
handcuff *n.* nemailpiloni; mailpia (*Preterit: onitemailpix*)
handful *n.* centlamapictli, centlamohtzolli
handicap *n.* matepuyotl
handicapped *adj.* ahhuelitilli
handkerchief *n.* neyacapohpolohuani (*nose*),
    nexayacapohpoloani (*face*), pahyo
handle *n.* matzitzquiloni, nepiloloni; *tv.* tlamachia
    (*Preterit: onitlatlamchih*)
handsome *adj.* cualnezquentic
hang *tv.* piloa (*Preterit: onitlapiloh*)
hanging *adj.* pilcac
hangnail *n.* iztetzintli
hangover *n.* neocuiliztli; **have a ~** *reflex. v.* ocuia
    (*Preterit: oninocuih*)
happen *reflex. v.* mochihua (*Preterit: omochiuh*)
happily *adv.* pacca, pahca
happiness *n.* ahuiliztli, pacyotl, paquiliztli, quicempaccayotl,
    quicempahcayotl, tlacempahcayotl

happy *adj.* paquini, pacqui, pahqui; **be ~** *iv.* paqui
 (*Preterit: onipac*), *iv.* ahuia (*Preterit: onahuix*),
 huellamati (*Preterit: onihuellamat*),
 yolpaqui (*Preterit: oniyolpac*)
hard *adj.* opahuac, tepiztic, tetic
hardness *n.* teticayotl
hardware *n.* tepuztlatquitl
hare *n.* cihtli
harm *tv.* ihtlacoa (*Preterit: onitlahtlacoh*)
harp *n.* mecahuehuetl
harpist *n.* mecahuehuetzotzonani, mecahuehuetzotzonqui
harvest *iv.* pixca (*Preteri: onipixcac*); *n.* pixquitl
hat *n.* cuacehualoni, necuacehualpatlahuac, ecahuiloni
hate *tv.* cocolia (*Preterit: onitecocolih*), telchihua
 (*Preterit: onitetelchiuh*)
haughty *adj.* mopohuani
haul *tv.* tilana (*Preterit: onitlatilan*)
have *tv.* pia (*Preterit: onitlapix*)
hawk *n.* tlohtli, cuixin
hay *n.* mazatlacualli, polozacatl, zacatextli
he *pron.* yeh, yehhuatl, yehuatl
head *n.* cuaitl, tecomatl, tzontecomatl; totzontlan (*bed*)
headache *n.* tzonteconcocoliztli, tzonteconcocolli;
 give a ~ *tv.* tzonteconehua (*Preterit: onitetzonconeuh*)
headdress *n.* tzoncalli, tzonicpalli
heal *iv.* tetzolihui (*Preterit: otetzoliuh*)
healing *n.* pahtiliztli
health *n.* paccayeliztli, pahcayeliztli, pactinemiliztli
healthful *adj.* pahtiloni
healthy *adj.* pacayeliceh, pahtic; **be ~** *iv.* pactinemi
 (*Preterit: onipactinen*)
heap *n.* centlalilli, ololli
hear *tv.* caqui (*Preterit: onitlacac*)

heard *adj.* tlacactli
hearing *n.* tlacacoyan
heart *n.* yollotl, yollohtli, yollolohtli, yolli
heartburn *n.* xocoyaliztli
hearth *n.* tlecuilli, tlexictli
heat *n.* tonalli, tonalmiquiliztli (*extreme*), totoniliztli, totonillotl; *tv.* totonia (*Preterit: onitlatotonih*)
heater *n.* callatotoniloni, tlatotoniloni
heaven *n.* ilhuicatl, nelhuicac, nelhuicactli, tlalocan
heaviness *n.* etiliztli
heavy *adj.* etic, yetic
hedge *n.* chinamitl
heel *n.* quequetzolli, cacpehuallotl (*shoe*)
height *n.* huehcapancayotl, octacayotl
heir *n.* tlacacahuililotiuh
helicopter *n.* tepuzmoyotl
hell *n.* mictlan
hello *interj.* niltze, panolti, panoltihtzino (*reverential*)
helm *n.* acahuelteconi
helmet *n.* tepuzcuacalalahtli
help *tv.* palehuia (*Preterit: onitepalehuih*)
helper *n.* tlapalehuiani
hemorrhoids *n.* menexualiztli, xochicihuiztli
hence *adv.* anca
hen turkey *n.* totolin
henhouse *n.* totolcalli
her *poss.* i-
herb *n.* xihuitl
herb root *n.* xiuhnelhuatl
herbalist *n.* pahixmatqui, xiuhpahnamacac
herd *n.* centlamantinyolqueh, centlamantin
here *adv.* nican; ici, izca, izcatqui (*here is, behold*), iz
heritage *n.* tetlacacahuililli

hermit *n.* tlamaceuhqui
hermitage *n.* teocaltontli
hero *n.* tenyoh
heroine *n.* cihuatenyoh
heron *n.* aztatl
herself *reflex.* mo-
hesitate *reflex. v.* omeyollohua (*Preterit: oninomeyollohuac*)
hesitation *n.* omeyollohualiztli
hey! *interj.* netle
hiccup *n.* tzicunoliztli; *iv.* tzicunoa (*Preterit: onitzicunoh*)
hidden place *n.* tlachicoyan
hide *n.* cuetlaxtli, ehuatl, mazaehuatl; *tv.* tlatia
     (*Preterit: onictlatih*)
hierarchy *n.* teopixcatlahtocapillotl
hieroglyph *n.* machiyohcuilollotl
high *adj.* cuauhtic, cuahcuauhtic, hueyac, huecapantic, tlacpac
high sea *n.* ahuecatlan, amictlan, aoztoc
highway *n.* hueyohtli
hill *n.* tepetl, tlachiquilli, tlatilli
himself *reflex.* mo–
hinder *tv.* elleltia (*Preterit: oniteelleltih*), tlacahualtia
     (*Preterit: onitetlacahualtih*)
hindrance *n.* teelleltilizlti, tetlacahualtiliztli
hip *n.* cuappantli, cuitlaxayacatl, nacayocantli
hipbone *n.* quiztepulli
hire *reflex. v.* tlaquehuia (*Preterit: oninotetlaquehuih*)
his *poss.* i–
hissing *n.* zozoloquiztli
historian *n.* nemiliztlahcuiloani, xiuhtlachcuiloh
history *n.* ihtoloca (*oral*), nemilizamatl (*written*),
     nemiliztlahcuilolli (*written*); nemiliztlahtollotl (*oral*),
     tlahtollotl (*oral*)
hither *adv.* nicancopa

hoarse *adj.* tozcananalca
hoax *n.* tecanetopehualiztli
hobby *n.* neahuiltiliztli
hodgepodge *n.* machontequixtinenelli
hoe *n.* tlaltepuztli, tepuzhuictli
hole *n.* tlacoyoctli, coyoctli, tlacomolli, tlaxapochtli
holiday *n.* ilhuitl, ilhuitl pieloni
Holland *n.* Hollalpan
home *n.* chantli
homeland *n.* tlalnantli, tetlacatyan, tetlalpan
homeless *adj.* zannen nenemi, xomulco caltech nemini
homeowner *n.* chaneh
homework *n.* caltequitl
homosexual *n.* cuiloni (*passive sexual partner*), tecuilontiani
  (*active sexual partner*)
honest *adj.* mimatqui, melahuac, yolmelahuac
honesty *n.* nematiliztli, nemalhuiliztli
honey *n.* necuhtli, cuauhnecuhtli
honeycomb *n.* mimiyahuatl, panatl
honor *n.* mahuiztli, teciyotl; *tv.* mahuiztilia
  (*Preterit: onitemahuiztilih*)
honorable *adj.* mahuizzoh
hoof *n.* xotlapalli
hook *n.* acatepuzotl, chicolli, coyolli
hope *n.* netemachiliztli, techializtli, tlacuauhtlamatiliztli
hopefully *adv.* mayecuele, macueleh
horn *n.* cuacuahuitl
hornpipe *n.* xololohtli
horrible *adj.* temahmauhtih
horrify *tv.* yollamictia (*Preterit: oniteyollamictih*)
horror *n.* neyolmiquiliztli
horse *n.* cahuahyo, capayo, caxtillammazatl, mazanenemi
horsefly *n.* temolin

horseshoe *n.* tepuzcactli

hospice *n.* teceliloyan

hospitable *adj.* tecelilloh

hospital *n.* cocoxcacalli, cocoxcacalco

hospitality *n.* tecelillotl

host *n.* tecoanotzqui; teoyotlamanalli (*Eucharist*), tlaxcalhuentli (*Eucharist*)

hostile *adj.* teyaouh

hostility *n.* teyaochihualiztli

hot *adj.* cococ (*spicy*), comonqui, totonqui;
    be ~ *iv.* tlemiqui (*Preterit: onitlemic*), tonalmiqui
    (*Preterit: onitonalmic*), tlequiza (*Preterit: onitlequiz*);
    become ~ *iv.* totonia (*Preterit: onitotonih and onitotonix*)

hot coal *n.* tlexochitl

hot sauce *n.* chilmolli

hot stone *n.* tlexictetl (*for heating steam bath*)

hot water *n.* atotonilli

hotel *n.* axihuayan, oztomecacalli, nehnencachialoyan

hour *n.* cahuitl, imman; **at this ~** *adv.* immanin

house *n.* calli

household *n.* cencalli

how *adv.* quenin

however *adv.* immanel, intlanel

How is it possible? *adv.* quemmach

How long? *adv.* quexquichcauh

How many? *interr pron.* quezqui

How many times? *adv.* quezquipa

How much *adv.* quexquich

How often? *adv.* quezquipa

howl *iv.* tlahuahualoa (*Preterit: onitlahuahualoh*), tecoyohua (*Preterit: onitecoyouh*)

hue *n.* tlapalnamictiliztli

hug *n.* tenahuatequiliztli; *tv.* nahuahtequi
  (*Preterit: onitenahuahtec*),
  pachoa (*Preterit: onitepachoh*)
human *adj.* tlacatl
human nature *n.* tlacayeliztli
humanity *n.* tlacayotl
humble *adj.* mocnomatini
humid *adj.* cuechahuac
humidity *n.* cuechahualiztli, cuechahuallotl
humiliate *tv.* tlanitlaza (*Preterit: onitetlanitlaz*)
humiliating *adj.* pinauhtic, necnimatic
humiliation *n.* teicnotecaliztli
humility *n.* necnotecaliztli, pechtequiliztli
hummingbird *n.* huitzilin, huitzitzilin
hump *n.* teputzotl
hunchback *n.* tepotzohtli
hunchbacked *adj.* tepotzoh, teputzoh
hunger *n.* apiztli, mayanaliztli, mayantli, teocihuiliztli
hungry *adj.* teocihuini, teociuhqui; **be ~** *iv.* mayana
  (*Preterit: onimayan*), teocihui (*Preterit: oniteociuh*),
  tolina (*Preterit: onitolinac*)
hunter *n.* tlaminqui, tlamani
hurry *n.* iciuhcayotl, ihcihuiliztli, teihcihuitiliztli; *iv.* ihcihui
  (*Preterit: onihciuh*)
husband *n.* namictli, tenamic, teoquichhui
husky *adj.* tlachicauhtli
hut *n.* xahcalli, zacaxahcalli (*grass*)
hydrophobia *n.* tecuancocoyaliztli
hygiene *n.* chipahualiztli
hymn *n.* teocuicatl
hypocrisy *n.* tlacaittaliztli, tlacaihtaliztli
hypocrite *n.* moyectocani, mocuallapiquiani

hypothetical *adj.* zazanca
hypothesis *n.* tlanenehuiliztli

I

I *pron.* neh, nehhua, nehhuatl, ni–
ice *n.* cetl
ice cream *n.* cehpayahuitl
ice-cream parlor *n.* cehpayauhnamacoyan
icicle *n.* acectli
idea *n.* tlanemililiztli; tlatlaliliztli
identical *adj.* neneuhqui
identification card *n.* tocaihcuilolamatl, amatocaihcuilolli
identify *tv.* neneuhtia (*Preterit: onitlaneneuhtih*)
identity *n.* tlaneneuhtililiztli
idiosyncrasy *n.* yuh quiztli
idiot *n.* ahquimati
idle *adj.* nennenqui; **be ~** *reflex. v.* zoquiahuiltia
     (*Preterit: oninozoquialhuiltih*)
idol *n.* tecuacuilli
idolize *tv.* teotoca (*Preterit: onitlateotocac*)
if *conj.* intla, tla
ignorance *n.* ahmomachiliztli
ignorant *adj.* ahtle quimati, ahtlematini
iguana *n.* cuahuito, huehuetzpalin, huetzpalin
illegal *adj.* ahtlatecpanalli
illegitimate child *n.* tepalconetl
illicit *adj.* ahmo monequi, ahneconi
illness *n.* cocolli
illuminate *tv.* tlanextia (*Preterit: onitlanextih*)
illuminated *adj.* tlatlanextilli
illusion *n.* techializtli
illustrator *n.* tlatlilanqui

image *n.* ixiptla, ixiptlayotl, teixiptla
imaginary *adj.* tlalnamico
imagination *n.* neyolnotzaliztli
imitable *adj.* tlaquixtiloni, yecalhuiloni
imitate *tv.* quixtia (*Preterit: onitequixtih*), nemiliztoca
    (*Preterit: onitenemiliztocac*), tetlayehyecalhuia
    (*Preterit: onitetlayehyecalhuih*)
imitation *n.* tlaquixtiliztli, tetlayehcalhuiliztli
imitator *n.* tlaquixtiani, tetlayehyecalhuiani
immediately *adv.* nimanic, zan niman
immense *adj.* cencahueyac
immodest *adj.* ahpinahuani, ahpinauhqui
immodesty *n.* ahpinahualiztli
immoral *adj.* ahcualnenqui
immortal *adj.* ahmiquini
immortality *n.* aic miquiliztli, cemihcac yoliliztli
impatience *n.* cualancayotl, talhuellotl
impatient *adj.* cualanini, tlahueleh
impenetrable *adj.* ahhueltlaaquic
imperceptible *adj.* ahhuelitalloh
imperfect *adj.* cotoctic
importance *n.* moneconi
important *adj.* cenca cualtic
impossible *adj.* ahhuelli
impostor *n.* teiztlacahuiani
impotence *n.* tzimmiquiliztli
impotent *adj.* totomicqui (*masc.*), tzimmicqui (*fem.*)
impractical *adj.* ahhuelchihualloh
impregnate *tv.* otztia (*Preterit: oniteotztih*)
improper *adj.* ahtetlatqui
improvisation *n.* iciuhca tlachihualiztli
improvise *tv.* iciuhca tlachihua (*Preterit: iciuhca onitlachiuh*)
impunity *n.* ahnempehualtiliztli; **with ~** *adv.* ahnempehualiztica

in *prep.* ipan; *suff.* –pan
in a minute *adv.* aocmo huecauh
in blossom *adj.* xotlac
in love *adj.* moyoleuhqui, moyollopanqui
in many places *adv.* mieccan
in the middle of *suff.* –nepantlah, –tzalan
in the past *adv.* ye nepa
in the road *adv.* ohtlica, ohtlipan
in vain *adv.* nen, nempanca, nenya
incapacity *n.* matepuyotl
incense *n.* copalli, popochtli, tlenamactli
incense burner *n.* tlecaxitl
incense ladle *n.* tlemaitl
incense vessel *n.* popochcomitl
incest *n.* tehuanyollatlacolli, tehuanyoltlatlacolli
inch *n.* cemmahpilli, inicatohueimapil
incident *n.* tepan hualahcic
inconsistent *adj.* yolnentic
inconvenience *n.* ahtetechmonequiliztli
inconvenient *adj.* ahtetechmonecoc
incorrigible *adj.* yollotetic
increase *tv.* miequilia (*Preterit: onitlamiequilih*),
    tlapihuilia (*Preterit: onitlahtlapihuilih*);
    iv. tlapihui (*Preterit: onitlapihuih*)
incredible *adj.* ahhuelneltococ
incurable *adj.* ahtepahtic
indebted *adj.* motlacuih; **be ~** *reflex. v.* motlacuia
    (*Preterit: oninotlacuih*)
indecency *n.* ahmimatcanemiliztli
indecent *adj.* ahmimatcanenqui
indecisive *adj.* cototzic
indecisiveness *n.* cototzyotl
indefinite *adj.* ahihuianyoh

indefinitely *adv.* ahihuianyotica
indelible *adj.* ahtlapololloh
independence *n.* tlacaxoxouhcayotl, cenitlacaxellotl
independent *adj.* tlacaxoxouhqui, cecnimani
index *n.* amoxmachiotl
indicate *tv.* tlacaquitia (*Preterit: onitlacaquitih*)
indication *n.* tetlacaquitiliztli
indifference *n.* ilihuiztli
indifferent *adj.* ilihuizqui
indigenous *n.* macehualli
indigestion *n.* atemoliztli, temamatiliztli
indignation *n.* cualaniliztli
indirect *adj.* ahmelactic
indirectly *adv.* ahmelahuaca
indiscreet *adj.* ahixtlamatqui
indispensable *adj.* ahhuelcahualloh
industrious *adj.* motlacuitlahui
inexhaustible *adj.* ahtlatzonquixtilloh
inexpensive *adj.* ahmo patiyoh
infant *n.* conechichilli
infect *tv.* mahua (*Preterit: onitemauh*)
infected *adj.* temahualli
infection *n.* palaxtli, temahualiztli
infectious *adj.* temahuac
inferior *adj.* tlahcotepiton
infested with flies *iv.* zayolloa (*Preterit: ozayolloac*)
infested with lice *adj.* atempach
infidelity *n.* ahitechnecahualiztli; *marital* tepanyaliztli
infinite *adj.* ahtlamiliztica
infinity *n.* ahpohualiztli
inflammation *n.* pozahuiliztli
inflate *tv.* pozahua (*Preterit: onitlapozahuac*)

influence *n.* tepantlahtollotl; *tv.* tepantlahtoa
   (*Preterit: onitepantlahtoh*)
inform *tv.* machiltia (*Preterit: onitemachiltih*),
   machiztia (*Preterit: onitemachiztih*),
   tlahtolmelahua (*Preterit: onitlahtolmelahuac*),
   nahuatia (*Preterit: onitenahuatih*)
information *n.* temachiltiliztli, tlahtolmelahualiztli,
   tlayolmelahualiztli
informed *adj.* machizeh
ingenuity *n.* tlachializtli
ingredient *n.* tlamannenellotl, itlanahnamic
ingrown nail *n.* iztecocoliztli
inhabitant *n.* nemini
inheritance *n.* tetlacacahuililli, tlatquitl
initial *adj.* tlatzintiani, pehuani
initiate *tv.* tzintia (*Preterit: onitlatzintih*)
initiative *n.* tlatzintiloni
initiator *n.* tlatzintiani
inject *tv.* pahyacahuitzmina (*Preterit: onitepahyacahuitzmin*),
   tzopinia (*Preterit: onitetzopinih*)
injection *n.* tlatzopiniliztli, nepahyacahuitzminallotl
injustice *n.* ahcualtiliztli, ahmomelahualiztli
ink *n.* tlilli
inkwell *n.* totolacatecomatl
inn *n.* cochihuayan, nehnencachialoyan
innkeeper *n.* nehnencachixqui, tecochitiani
innocence *n.* ahtlatlacoliztli
innocent *adj.* yectli, ahtlahtlacoleh
innuendo *n.* netlahtoltequipacholiz
insane *adj.* ahmimati, xolopihtli, yollococoxqui
insanity *n.* yollotlahuelilocatiliztli
inscription on stone *n.* tetlahcuiloliztli
insect *n.* yolcatontli

insect bite *n.* moyococotl
insensitive *adj.* tlaixtomahuac
insensitivity *n.* tlaixtomahualiztli
insert *tv.* calaquia (*Preterit: onitlacalaquih*)
inside *prep.* ihtic
insipid *adj.* ahtzopelic
insomnia *n.* ixtozotl
inspection *n.* tlacuitlahuiloliztli
inspector *n.* mocuitlahuiani
inspiration *n.* teyolihtectiliztli
instant *n.* zancuelachic
instinct *n.* yuhqui yeliztli
instruction *n.* nemachtiliztli
insult *n.* tetlahtolpinahuiliztli, tetlahtolpinauhtiliztli,
    tetelchihualiztli; *tv.* tetelchihua (*Preterit: onitetelchiuh*),
    tetlahtolpinauhtia (*Preterit: onitetlahtolpinauhtih*)
intact *adj.* cenquizqui
integrity *n.* motquihtaliztli
intelligent *adj.* yolloh
intention *n.* yuhcateyollo
intentional *adj.* yuhcateyolqui
interest *n.* tlaixnextiliztli
interesting *adj.* cualtic, cencacualtic, tlaixnextoc
interior *n.* ihtitl
interpreter *n.* nahuatlahtoh, nahautlahtolcuepani,
    tlahtolcuepani
interrogate *tv.* tlatlania (*Preterit: onitetlatlanih*),
    tlahtolana (*Preterit: onitetlahtolan*),
    tlahtoltia (*Preterit: onitetlahtoltih*)
interrogation *n.* tetlahtolanaliztli
interrogator *n.* tetlahtolanani
interrupt *tv.* tlacahualtia (*Preterit: onitetlacahualtih*)
interruption *n.* tetlacahualtiliztli
intersection *n.* ohmaxac, ohmaxalli, ohmaxalco, ohtlamaxac,
    ohtlamaxalli

interval *n.* cecancahuitl, tlacoyonililli, tlacoyoyan
interview *n.* tetlahtolanaliztli; *tv.* tetlahtolana
    (*Preterit: onitetlahtolan*)
interviewee *n.* tlatlahtolantli
interviewer *n.* tetlahtolanani
intestinal obstruction *n.* temamatiliztli (*empacho*)
intestine *n.* cuitlaxcolli; **large ~** cuitlaxcoltomactli;
    small ~ cuitlaxcolpitzactli
intimate *adj.* yolicniuh
intolerable *adj.* ahyecolic
intolerance *n.* ahyecoliztli
intolerant *adj.* ahyecoltoc
intoxicating *adj.* teihuintih
intricate *adj.* ixneliuhqui
introduce *tv.* tlaaquia (*Preterit: onitlaaquih*)
introduction *n.* tlaaquiliztli
intruder *n.* ichtacacalac
invade *tv.* ixpehualtia (*Preterit: oniteixpehualtih*)
invader *n.* teixpehualtiani
invasion *n.* teixpehualiztli
invent *tv.* nextia (*Preterit: onitlanextih*); yocoya
    (*Preterit: onitlayocox*)
invention *n.* tlatlalilli, tlayocoxtli
inventory *n.* tlacentlalilamatl
investigate *tv.* nepanoa (*Preterit: onitlanepanoh*)
investigation *n.* tlanepanoliztli
invisible *adj.* ahhuelittoc
invitation *n.* tecoanotzaliztli, tetlalhuiliztli, tlahuentiliztli
invite *tv.* coachihua (*Preterit: onitecoachiuh*), coanotza
    (*someone to eat*) (*Preterit: onitecoanotz*)
involuntarily *adv.* ahcializcopa
involuntary *adj.* ahciani

iron *n.* tepuztlazohualoni, tlaixmelahualoni (*clothes*);
    tliltic tepuztli (*mineral*); *iv.* tepuztlazohua
    (*Preterit: onitepuztlazouh*)
irregular *adj.* ahahuatilpiani
irregularity *n.* ahahuatilpializtli
irritable *adj.* patzmicqui
island *n.* hueyapancatlalli; *n.* tlalhuactli
it *pron.* yeh, yehhuatl, yehuatl
it doesn't matter *adv.* zazo
it hurts *impers. v.* tonehua (*Preterit: otoneuh*)
it is day *impers. v.* ithui
it is said *impers. v.* mihtoa (*Preterit: omihtoh*), motenehua
    (*Preterit: omoteneuh*)
itch *n.* cuecuetzocaliztli, xiyotl; *iv.* cuecuetzoca
    (*Preterit: onicuecuetzocac*), yoyomoca
    (*Preterit: oniyoyomocac*)
itching *n.* yoyomiquiliztli
itinerary *n.* neohtlamachtiloni
its *poss.* i-
itself *reflex.* mo–
ivory *n.* tlanomitl

J

jade *n.* chalchihuitl, xochitapachtli (*finest*)
jaguar *n.* ocelotl, tecuani
jail *n.* cuauhcalli, huauhcalli, teilpiloyan
jailer *n.* cuauhcalpixqui
jam *n.* necuhtlachihchihualtic
Japan *n.* Niponian
Japanese *n.* Niponian chanehl; Niponiantlahtolli (*language*)

jaw *n.* camachalli
jawbone *n.* camachalcuauhyotl, camachalomitl
jealous *adj.* chahuatic; **be ~** *iv.* chahuati (*Preterit: onichahuatic*)
jealousy *n.* nexicolli, nexicoliztli
jelly *n.* necuhtlachihchihualtic
jest *iv.* cemanallahtoa (*Preterit: onicemanallahtoh*)
jet *n.* iciuhca tepuztototl
jewel *n.* cozcatl
jewelry store *n.* teocuitlacozcanamacoyan
Jewish *adj.* Xotiyo
jicama *n.* xicamatl
jimsonweed *n.* tlapatl
job *n.* tequitl
joint *n.* zaliuhyantli, zahzaliuhyantli, huihuilteccantli
jointly *adv.* netloc
joke *n.* camanalli, tecanetopehualiztli, zazanilli,
    quehqueloliztli; *iv.* cemanallahtoa
    (*Preterit: onicemanallahtoh*)
jokester *n.* ahuiillahtoani
journalist *n.* amatlaixpanhuiani
journey *n.* ohtlatocaliztli
joy *n.* cemelli, pacyotl, paquiliztli, yolpaquiliztli
joyful *adj.* pacqui
joyfully *adv.* pacca
judge *n.* tecuhtlahtoh, tetlamachiani, tlailotlac
judgment *n.* tlacaquiliztli, yuh nematiliztli;
    tetlatzontequiliztli (*law*)
jug *n.* comitl, tecomatl
juice *n.* ayotl, patzcatl, tlapatzquitl, **orange ~** naranjayotl;
    meat ~ *n.* nacatlapalollotl, nacatlapatzcaayotl,
    nacatlapalollotl
juicy *adj.* ayoh

jump *n.* panchololiztli; *iv.* patlantiquiza
    (*Preterit: onipatlantiquiz*) *iv.* pancholoa
    (*Preterit: onipancholoh*)
just *adj.* yolmelahuac
just a litlle *adv.* zan tepitzin
justice *n.* tlamelahuacachihualiztli, tlamelahuacachihualiztli

K

kettle *n.* tepuzapaztli
key *n.* tlahtlapoaloni, tepuztlatzacualoni, tlatlapoloni
kick *n.* tlaxopehualli, tlaxopeuhtli; *tv.* xopehua
    (*Preterit: onitexopeuh*)
kid *n.* chamatl
kidney *n.* yoyomoctli, cuitlacaxiuhyantli, necoctetencatl
kill *tv.* mictia (*Preterit: onitemictih*)
kind *n.* cehcentlamantli iyelic; *adj.* tecemicniuh
kindness *n.* tecemicniuhyotl
kinship *n.* cihuahuanyolcayotl, huayolcayotl
kiss *tv.* tempitzoa (*Preterit: onitetempitzoh*), tennamiqui
    (*Preterit: onitetennamic*), pitzoa (*Preterit: onitepitzoh*)
kitchen *n.* tlacualchihualoyan, tlacualchiuhcan
kite *n.* papalotl
knapsack *n.* quimilli
knead *tv.* xacualoa (*Preterit: onitlaxacualoh*)
knee *n.* tetepontli, tlancuaitl
kneel *reflex. v.* motlancuaquetza (*Preterit: oninotlancuaquetz*)
knife *n.* itztli, tezoaloni
knit *iv.* ihquiti (*Preterit: onihquit*), tzahua
    (*Preterit: onitzauh*)
knock *iv.* tlatzacuillotzotzona (*Preterit: onitlatzacuillotzotzon*),
    tzotzona (*Preterit: onictzotzon*),
    tlacuahuitequi (*Preterit: onitlacuahuitec*)

knock-kneed *adj.* metzcacaltic
knoll *n.* tlamimilolli
knot *n.* ilpicayotl
know *tv.* tlamati (*Preterit: onitlamach*); ~ **well**
   iv. nalquizcamati (*Preterit: onitlanalquizcamat*)
knowledge *n.* machiliztli, tlamachilizlti, tlilli tlapalli
knowledgeable *adj.* machizeh
known *adj.* iximachoni, macho; **well-** ~ nohhuian macho
knuckle *n.* cecepoctli

L

labia *n.* piccatl
labor *n.* tlailiztli
laboratory *n.* tlamantlaneltiloyan
laborer *n.* tepaltequitqui, tequipanoani, tequitqui
lachrymal *n.* ixcuilchilli
lack *n.* yuhcatlatiliztli, netoliniliztli
lacquer *n.* tlaixpetzoni
ladder *n.* cuauhecahuaztli, mamatlatl
lake *n.* amaitl, huey atezcatl
lamb *n.* ichcatl
lame *n.* metzcocoxqui,metzcotoctic, xocue
lamp *n.* netlahuililoni
land *n.* tlalli; ~ **of** *suff.* –tlan
language *n.* tlahtolli, hueltetlahtol; **foreign** ~ *n.* pinotlahtolli;
   foul ~ *n.* pitzotlahtolli
lantern *n.* tlahuilcalli
lap *n.* cuexantli, cuixantli
lard *n.* chiyahuacayotl, mantecayotl
large *adj.* huei
larynx *n.* tozcapanoloni
last year *adv.* monamiccan

latch *n.* tepuztlatzacualoni
late *adv.* ye tlahca
later *adv.* huehcauhpa, yatepa, zatepan, quintepan
laugh *iv.* huetzca (*Preterit: onihuetzcac*), huehuetzca
    (*Preterit: onihuehuetzcac*); **make people ~** *tv.* xochhuia
    (*Preterit: onitexochhuih*)
laughing stock *n.* texochhuiani
laughter *n.* huetzquiztli
laundromat *n.* tlapacoyan
laurel *n.* ecapahtli
law *n.* nahuatilli, tenahuatilli; tepaltlahtoliztli (*profession*)
lawmaker *n.* nahuatillaliani
lawyer *n.* tepantlahtoani
laxative *n.* noquiloni, tlanoquiloni, tetlanoquililoni,
    tepahnamaconi, tetzimpahnamaconi
laziness *n.* tlatzihuiliztli, tlatziuhcayotl
lazy *adj.* tlatziuhqui; **be, feel ~** *iv.* tlatzihui
    (*Preterit: onitlatziuh*)
lead *n.* temetztli (*metal*); *tv.* yacana (*Preterit: oniteyacan*)
leader *n.* teyacanani, teyecanqui
leaf *n.* izhuatl, quilmaitl
lean *adj.* ahmo nacayoh
leap *iv.* patlantiquiza (*Preterit: onipatlantiquiz*)
learn *tv.* zaloa (*Preterit: onitlazaloh*)
learning *n.* nemachtilli
leather shoe *n.* cuetlaxcactli
leather strap *n.* cuetlaxmecatl, ehuamecatl
leathery *adj.* cuetlaxtic
leave *iv.* quiza (*Preterit: oniquiz*); **~ with haste**
    iv. patlantiquiza (*Preterit: onipatlantiquiz*)
leave behind *tv.* cahua (*Preterit: onitlacauh*)
leaven *n.* xocotextli
leaving *n.* quetzaliztli

lecherous *n.* ahuilnenqui
lechery *n.* ahuilnemiliztli
leech *n.* acuecueyachin
left *adj.* ichpochtli
left hand *n.* opochmaitl, opochtli, pochmaitl, pochtli
left-handed *adj.* opochmayeh
left side *n.* opochtli
leftovers *n.* tencahualli (*from a meal*)
leg *n.* metztli, xotl; cuauhicxitl (*table*)
leg hair *n.* metztzontli
leg nerve *n.* metztlalhuatl
legend *n.* nemiliztlahtollotl
legging *n.* cotztlapachoni
lemon *n.* xocotl limón
lend *tv.* tlatlacuiltia (*Preterit: onitetlatlacuiltih*), tlatlaneuhtia
    (*Preterit: onitetlatlaneuhtih*)
lender *n.* tetlatlacuiltiani, tetlatlaneuhtiani
length *n.* hueyacayotl
lens *n.* ixtezcatl
lentil *n.* epatzactli; pitzahuac etl
leprosy *n.* nanahuatl
less *adv.* occenca ahmo
lesson *n.* nemachtiliztli, temachtilli
let go of *tv.* macahua (*Preterit onitlamacauh*)
letter *n.* amatlahcuilolli (*mail*); tlahcuilolli (*alphabet*)
letterhead *n.* amaihcuiloliztli
level *n.* melauhcaittaloni; *adj.* ixmanqui; *tv.* ixmana
    (*Preterit: onitlaixman*)
lever *n.* cuammitl
liar *n.* iztlacatini, tlapicqui, tlapihqui, tlapictlahtoani
liberate *tv.* temaquixtia
liberation *n.* temaquixtiliztli
liberator *n.* temaquixtiani, temaquixtihqui

liberty *n.* temaquixtiliztli, tlacaxoxouhqui
library *n.* amoxcalli, amoxpialoyan
license *n.* temacahuiliztli, tlamacahuiliztli
licentious *adj.* mixtlapaloani
licentiousness *n.* tlalticpaccayotl
lick *tv.* pahpalohua (*Preterit: onitlapahpalouh*), papaloa
    (*Preterit: onitlapapaloh*)
lid *n.* tzaccayotl, tentli
lie *n.* iztlacatiliztli, iztlacatlahtolli, tlaixcuepalli;
    iv. tlapictlahtoa (*Preterit: onitlapictlahtoh*),
    iztlacati (*Preterit: oniztlacat*)
lie down *iv.* onoc (*Preterit: ononoya and ononoca*),
    reflex. v. teca (*Preterit: oninotecac*)
life *n.* nemiliztli, yoliztli
lift *tv.* tlehcahuia (*Preterit: onitlatlehcahuih*), tlehcoltia
    (*Preterit: onitlatlehcoltih*)
light *n.* tlahuilli, tlanexillotl, tlanextiliztli, tlanextli;
    to ~ *tv.* tlacuiltia (*Preterit: onitlacuiltih*);
    adj. canahuac, ehcauhtic (*weight*)
light bulb *n.* electzontlanexpeuhcayotl
light-headed *adj.* cuaihuintic
lightning *n.* tlapetantli, tlapetlaniliztli; *iv.* tlapetlani
    (*Preterit: otlapetlan*)
lightning rod *n.* tepuztlahuiteconi
like *adv.* yuh, yuhqui, yuhquin, yohque, ihqui, iuhqui, iniuh
    iniuhqui; *suff.* –copa, –teuh
likewise *adv.* neneuhca
lily *n.* tzacuxochitl
lime *n.* xocotl lima
limestone *n.* tenextetl, tenextli
limestone water *n.* nexayotl
limit *n.* tlaltzontli
limp *iv.* queznecuiloa (*Preterit: oniqueznecuiloh*)

line *n.* huipantli
lineage *n.* mecayotl, tlacamecayotl
linguist *n.* tlahtolmatini
linguistics *n.* tlahtolmatiliztli
link *n.* tepuzchicolli
lioness *n.* cihuamiztli
lip *n.* tentli, xipalli, tenxipalli
liquid *n.* atl
liquidambar *n.* ocotzotl
liquor *n.* xolopihayotl
lisp *iv.* tentzitzipitlahtoa (*Preterit: onitentzitzipitlahtoh*),
    nenempochtlahtoa (*Preterit: oninenempochtlahtoh*)
listener *n* nacazeh
lithographer *n.* teihcuiloani
lithography *n.* teteihcuiloliztli
litigant *n.* monomateixpahuih
little *adv.* achi, zan tepitzin
little bit *adv.* achiton
little girl *n.* ichpocaconetl
liturgy *n.* teomahuizmelahualoni
live *iv.* nemi (*Preterit: oninen*); yoli (*Preterit: oniyol*)
liver *n.* elli, yelli, eltapachtli
living room *n.* calchialoyan, celiloyan
lizard *n.* cuetzpalin
load *n.* tequitl, tlamamalli
loaf *n.* tlaxalcalcentetl, yoltexpahuacentetl
loafer *n.* nennenqui
loan *n.* netlanehuiliztli, netlacuilli, tetlatlanuehtiliztli,
    tetlatlaneuhtiloni
lobby *n.* calixtli
lock *n.* tepuztlatzacualoni
locomotive *n.* tepuztlahuilanani
lodging *n.* tlaceliloyan

loin *n.* tomiyahuayocan, tocoyonya

loincloth *n.* maxtlatl, maxtli

loneliness *n.* cactimaniliztli

long *adj.* hueyac, melactic

long-legged *adj.* xohuiac

long-stemmed *adj.* xohueyac

longing *n.* neteelehuiliztiliztli

look *iv.* tlachia (*Preterit: onitlachix*)

look beautiful *iv.* cualneci (*Preterit: onicualnez*)

look for *tv.* temoa (*Preterit: ontlatemoh*)

loom *n.* ihquitihualoni, ihquitiloni

loose *adj.* caxanqui; **become ~** *iv.* caxani
(*Preterit: onicaxan*)

loosen *tv.* caxania (*Preterit: onitlacaxanih*)

lord *n.* tecuhtli (*Plural: tetecuhtin*), teuctli (*Plural: teteuctin*)

lordship *n.* tecuhyotl, tlahtohcayotl

lose *iv.* poloa (*Preterit: onipoloh*)

lost *adj.* poliuhqui

lottery *n.* tetlatlamaniloni

loud *adj.* huelcaquiztilloh

loudmouthed *adj.* tzatzini

louse *n.* metolin

love *n.* tetlazohlaliztli; *tv.* tlazohtla (*Preterit: onitetlazohtlac*);
~ one another *reflex. v.* nepantlazohtla
(*Preterit: otitonepantlazohtlac*); **fall in ~**
reflex. v. yolahcocui (*Preterit: oninoyolahcocuic*)

loveable *adj.* tlazohtlaloni

lover *n.* tlazohtlaliceh, mecatl

lower *tv.* temohiia (*Preterit: onictemohuih*)

lower body *n.* tzintli

lowest *adj.* tzocotontli

loyal *adj.* nehuelyollotiloni

luck *n.* netlatlamaniliztli, tonalli

lullaby *n.* cozolcuicatl
lumber *n.* cuahuitl
lumberyard *n.* cuauhnamacoyan, huapalnamacoyan
lump *n.* nanahuatl
lunch *n.* nepantlahyotl, tenizaloni
lung *n.* zazanactli
lust *n.* ahuilnemiliztli
lye *n.* nexatl
lying down *adj.* huetztoc, motecac
lynch *tv.* ixili (*Preterit: oniteixil*)
lynching *n.* teixiliztli
lynx *n.* cozantli, tlacomiztli

M

macaw *n.* alo
machete *n.* tepuzmactli
machine *n.* tepuzteyolehualoni
madman *n.* yolpoliuhqui
madness *n.* xolopiyotl, cuatlapoliliztli
maggot *n.* nacaocuilin
magician *n.* xochihuah
magistrate *n.* tecuhtlahtoh
magnet *n.* tlaeltiloni, tlaihiyoanani tetl, tlaahcocuini tetl
magnolia *n.* yolloxochitl, yollohxochitl
maguey *n.* metl; mexcalli (*cooked*); mezotl (*dried*)
maguey juice *n.* necuatl (*unfermented*); octli (*fermented*)
maguey juice collector *n.* tlahchiquini
maguey plant *n.* toctli
maguey sap *n.* meolli
maguey shoot *n.* meyollohtli
maguey stalk *n.* quiotl
maguey thread *n.* ichtli

maguey worm *n.* meocuilin

mahogany *n.* ayacachcuahuitl, cuauhayacachtli

maiden *n.* ichpocatl, ichpochtli

mail carrier *n.* painani

mailbox *n.* amatlahcuilolqxiquipilli

maimed *adj.* machotoc

mainland *n.* cemantoctlalli

majestic *adj.* cenquizca mahuiztic

majesty *n.* cenquizca mahuizzotl

make *tv.* chihua (*Preterit: onitlachiuh*), yocoya
    (*Preterit: onitlayocox*)

make an incision *tv.* xoxotla (*Preterit: onitexoxotlac*)

make fun of *reflex. v.* quehqueloa (*Preterit: oninoquehqueloh*)

make tamales *tv.* tamaloa (*Preterit: onitamaloh*)

make tortillas *tv.* tlaxcaloa (*Preterit: onitlaxcaloh*)

maker *n.* tlachihualeh, tlachiuhqui

makeup *n.* xahualli, axin

malaria *n.* tonahuiztli

male *adj.* oquichtli

male genitalia *n.* oquichnacayotl

mamey *n.* tezontzapotl

man *n.* oquichtli

manacle *n.* nemailpiloni; mailpia (*Preterit: onitemailpix*)

manage *tv.* pachoa (*Preterit: onitepachoh*), yacana
    (*Preterit: oniteyacan*)

mane *n.* ixcuatzontli, quechtzontli

maneuver *n.* machiuhcayotl, tlamatequipanoni; *tv.* machihua
    (*Preterit: onitlamachiuh*)

manger *n.* mazatlacualtiloyan, mazacualoyan,
    cahuahtlacualoyan

manifest *tv.* nextia (*Preterit: onicnextih*), nextilia
    (*Preterit: onictenextilih*)

manifestation *n.* nexiliztli

manipulate *tv.* tlamacuecuetzoa (*Preterit: onitlamacuecuetzoh*)
manipulator *n.* tlacamacuecuetzoani
mannequin *n.* cuauhtlatlaquitamachihualli
manner *n.* yuhcayotl
manners *n.* nematcayotl
manufacture *tv.* chihua (*Preterit: onitlachiuh*);
   n. nechihchihualiztli
manuscript *n.* matlahcuilolli
many *adj.* ixachtin, ixaxhintin (*Singular: ixachi*)
many times *adv.* miecpa
map *n.* cemanahuactlalmachiotl (*world*)
marble *n.* tezcalli
march *n.* neohtlatocaliztli; *iv.* ohtlatoca (*Preterit: onohtlatocac*),
   ohtoca (*Preterit: oniohtocac*)
mare *n.* cihuacahuayo
margin *n.* tentli
marigold *n.* cempohualxochitl
mark *n.* machiyotl, tlamachiyotl; *tv.* machiyotia
   (*Preterit: onitlamachiyoh*)
marketplace *n.* tianquiztli
marksmanship *n.* tlamelauhcaittaloni
marriage *n.* nemactiliztli, nenamictiliztli
married *adj.* oquichhuah (*fem.*), cihuahuah (*masc.*),
   momanepanohqui
marrow *n.* omiceceyotl
marsh *n.* zoquiatl
martyr *n.* imiquiztica tlaneltiliani
marvel *n.* tlamahuizolli
marvelous *adj.* tlamahuizoltic
mask *n.* xayacatlachihchihualli, xayacatl
mason *n.* calchiuhqui, tepanchiuhqui
masturbate *reflex. v.* mahuia (*Preterit: oninomahuih*),
   matoca (*Preterit: oninomatocac*)

mat *n.* petlatl, zotolpetlatl (*palm leaf*)
maternal *adj.* tenanyoh
mathematician *n.* tlapohualmatini
mathematics *n.* tlapohualmatiliztli
mattress *n.* cuachpepechtli, pepechtli, pehpechtli,
    cuachpehpechtli
mature *n.* omahcic
maturity *n.* mahciticayotl
mausoleum *n.* tecochtlayecchiuhtli
maybe *adv.* ahzo
mayor *n.* tetlatzontopileh, tlahtocateixiptla
meal *n.* tlemolli
mealtime *n.* tlacualizpan
mean *tv.* nezcayotia (*Preterit: onitlanezcayotih*)
meaning *n.* tlahtolnezcayotl
meanwhile *adv.* in oquiz
measure *tv.* tamachihua (*Preterit: onitlatamachiuh*)
measurement *n.* tamachiuhcayotl
measuring stick *n.* octacatl
meat *n* nacatl
meat dish *n.* nacamulli
meat pie *n* nacatlaoyotl
meat stew *n.* nacaayotl
mechanism *n.* tlacotonxexelhuiliztli
medal *n.* tepuzmachiyopilcac
medicine *n.* pahtli (*remedy*), pahmatiliztli (*science*);
    ticiyotl (*art of healing*)
mediocre *adj.* tlahconemini
mediocrity *n.* tlahconemilizzotl
meditation *n.* neyolnonotzaliztli
medium *n.* zan tlahco
meek *adj.* tlacaciuhqui
meekly *adv.* yocoxca

meekness *n.* tlacaciuhcayotl
meeting *n.* mononotzaliztli, tenamiquiliztli
melancholy *n.* ahtleyecyotl
melt *iv.* pati *(Preterit: opat)*
memento *n.* necauhcayotl
memo book *n.* amoxneihcuiloni
memorable *adj.* tlalnamictli
memorandum *n.* tlalnamiconi
memory *n.* tlalnamiquiliztli
menstruate *reflex. v.* metzhuia *(Preterit: oninometzhuih)*
menstruation *n.* cihuacocolli
mental *adj.* tlalnamiquilli
mention *n.* teilnamiquiliztli; *tv.* teilnamiqui
    (Preterit: oniteilnamic)
meow *tv.* tlatzomia *(Preterit: onitlatlatzomih)*
merchandise *n.* nanauhtli
merchant *n.* pochtecatl, oztomecatl, tlanamacac
merciful *adj.* tetlaocoliani, teicnottani
mercy *n.* icnoyohualiztli, netoliniztli, teicnoittaliztli
mermaid *n.* cihuatlacamichin
mescal *n.* mexcalli
mesquite *n.* mizquitl
message *n.* netitlaniliztli
messenger *n.* titlantli, topilli
mestizo *adj.* itlacauhnelonqui
metal *n.* tepoztli
metallic *adj.* chictlapanqui
metaphor *n.* machiotlahtolli
method *n.* nehnemilizohtli, ohtoquiliztli, ohtlamachiliztli,
    ohtlamatiliztli
Mexican *n.* Mexihcatl, Mexihcatlacat
Mexico *n.* Mexihcol

midday *n.* nepantla tonalli, nepantla tonatiuh, tlahcotonalli, tlahcotonatiuh

middle *n.* nepantlahtli, ollotl

middle-aged woman *n.* yollococihuatl

middle finger *n.* mapilhueyacatl

midnight *n.* tlahcoyohuan, yohualnepantla, tlahcoyohualli, tlahcoihualli

migration *n.* quizaliztli

mild *adj.* tlayamanilli, yamanqui

mildew *n.* amumuxtli

mildness *n.* tlayamaniliztli, yolceuhcayotl

milk *n.* chichihualayotl

mill wheel *n.* matexoani

mind *n.* ilnamiquilizyotl, tlalnamiquiliztli, tlalnamiquiloni

mine *n.* tlaloztotl

mineral *n.* oztocayotl

miracle *n.* tlamahuizolli

miraculous *adj.* tlamahuizoltic

miraculously *adv.* tlamahuizoltica

mire *n.* tlalxayotl, zoquiatl

mired *adj.* zoquiacqui

miscellaneous *adj.* tlamanenel

misery *n.* icnoyotl, tzotzocayotl

misfortune *n.* aompayotl, nenquizaliztli

mist *n.* ayahuitl, yauhtli

mistake *n.* neixpololiztli, tlacuapololiztli

misty *adj.* ayauhtic

mix *tv.* neneloa (*Preterit: onitlaneneloh*), cenneloa (*Preterit: onitlacenneloh*)

mixed *adj.* tlanelolli

mixture *n.* tlanenelolli

moan *iv.* tena (*Preterit: oniten*)

mock *iv.* quehqueloa (*Preterit: oninoquehqueloh*)

mockery *n.* quehqueloliztli

model *n.* octacatl, neixcuitilli

modern *adj.* axa, axan, axca, axcan, quin onez, quinez

modesty *n.* ihuianyotl, yocoxcayotl

moist *adj.* cuechahuac

moisten *tv.* tlapaloa (*Preterit: onitlapaloh*), cuechahuia
(*Preterit: onitlacuechahuih*)

moisture *n.* cuechahualiztli, cuechahuallotl

molar *n.* tlancochtli

molasses *n.* necuilacatztli, necuhtlatzoyonilli

mold *n.* amumuxtli (*mildew*); huapallotl (*frame*)

moldy *adj.* poxcauhqui; **become ~** *iv.* poxcahui
(*Preterit: opoxcauh*)

mole *n.* tlacihuiztli (*skin*)

moment *n.* zan ixquichcacahuitl, zan achitonca;
at this ~ *adv.* ihcuaquinon

momentarily *adv.* zanachiltica

momentary *adj.* zanachic

monastery *n.* teopixcacalli

money *n.* tomin

monkey *n.* ozomahtli

monster *n.* tlacacemele, xolotl

month *n.* metztli

monthly *adj.* cehcemmetztli; *adv.* cehcenmetztica

moon *n.* metztli

moonlight *n.* metztonalli

moral *adj.* yecnemi

morality *n.* yecnemiliztli

more *adv.* ocachi

morning *n.* yohuahtzinco, ihuahtzinco, huatzintica,
tlahuizcalpan, tlaneci

morning star *n.* huey citlalin

morpheme *n.* achitlahtolli

morsel *n.* ihtacatl, cotoctli

mortal *adj.* miquini

mortar *n.* tenexzoquitl, tenexpololli

mortgage *n.* teyollaliztli

mortuary *n.* miccatechan, mihcatechan

mosquito *n.* moyotl, yoyoliton

moss *n.* amumuxtli

moth *n.* chahuapapalotl, papalotontli, yohualpapalotl, tilmahocuilin (*clothes*)

mother *n.* nantli

motherhood *n.* nanyotl

mother-in-law *n.* monnantli

motive *n.* neyolehualoni

motor *n.* tepuztlaolininiloni, tepuzyollotl

mound *n.* potzalli, putzalli

mountain *n.* tepetl

mountain lion *n.* miztli

mountain peak *n.* tepeticpac

mountain range *n.* tepetla

mourner *n.* miccahuah, miccatilmahhuah

mourning *n.* miccahuahcayotl, mihcacahuahcayotl

mouse *n.* quimichin

mouth *n.* camatl

move *tv.* olinia (*Preterit: onitlaolinih*),
   iv. olini (*Preterit: oolin and oolinqui*);
   ~ **out of a home** *iv.* calcahua (*Preterit: onicalcauh*)

movement *n.* olin, olintli

movie theater *n.* ixiptlayollan, ixiptlayolin

much *adj.* miec (*Plural: miequintin*), ixachi (*Plural: ixachtin, ixachintin*); *adv.* achi, cenca, miac, miec

mucus *n.* yacacuitlatl, yacatolli

mud *n.* tlalxayotl, zoquitl

muddy *adj.* zoquitic, zoquiyoh; **be ~** *iv.* zoquiti
 (*Preterit: onizoquitic*)
mule *n.* yolitl
multi-colored *adj.* cuicuiltic
multiply *iv.* tlapihuia (*Preterit: onitlapihuih*); *tv.* tlapihuilia
 (*Preterit: onitlahtlapihuilih*)
mummy *n.* micquitlahuatztli
mumps *n.* quechpalaniliztli
mundane *adj.* tlacticpaccayotl
murmur *n.* chachalacaliztli
muscle *n.* ahcoltetl
mushroom *n.* nanacatl, nahnacatl, xoletl
music *n.* tlatzotzonalli
musician *n.* tlatzotzonqui
mustache *n.* atliatl, tentzontli
mustachioed *adj.* tentzoyoh
mute *adj.* nonohtli, nontli
mutually *adv.* nepanotl
my *pos.* no–
myself *reflex. pron.* nino-
mystery *n.* ahteixaxiliztli

N
Nahuatl *n.* nahuatlahtolli, mexihcatlahtolli;
 speak ~ *iv.* nahuatlahtoa (*Preterit: oninahuatlahtoh*);
 in ~ *adv.* macehualcopa, mexihcatlahtolcopa,
 mexihcacopa, nahuatlahtolcopa, nahuacopa
Nahuatl culture *n.* nahuatlamatiliztli
Nahuatl speaker *n.* nahuatlahtoani, nahuatlahtoh
nail *n.* tepuztlaxichtli, tlatepuztoconi; *tv.* tlatepuztoca
 (*Preterit: onitlatepuztocac*)
naked *adj.* nacatetl

name *n.* tocaitl, tocayotl, tocahtli; *tv.* tocayotia
    (*Preterit: onitetocayotih*)
namesake *n.* tocayoh
nap *iv.* ixcocochi (*Preterit: onixcoch*)
nape *n.* quechcochtetl, quechcochtli, quechtepolli
napkin *n.* pahyo, tempohpoaloni, netempohpoloani,
    tempohpoalamatl, tlacualtzohtzomahtli
narcotic *n.* tecochtlazantli
narration *n.* zazanilli
narrator *n.* tlapouhqui, tzoltic
narrow *adj.* pitzahuac, copitztic
nasal *adj.* yacapani
nation *n.* cecnitlacah, tlalnantli; **foreign ~** *n.* huehca tlalli
national *adj.* cecnitlacayoh
national anthem *n.* tlalnancuicatl
nationality *n.* cecnitlacatiliztli
native language *n.* macehuallahtolli
natural *adj.* zanyeyuhqui, yuh quiz
naturally *adv.* yuhyotica
nature *n.* teyeliztli, yelizyotl
nausea *n.* nezotlaliztli
navel *n.* xictli
navy blue *n.* yahuitl
near *suff.* –nahuac, –tloc
nearsighted *adj.* zaniztlachiani
necessary *adj.* neconi; **be ~** *iv.* monequi (*Preterit: omonec*)
necessity *n.* monequiliztli
neck *n.* quechtli, quechtetl
necklace *n.* cozcatl, coztli
need *n.* tetech monequiliztli; **have ~** *iv.* monequi
    (*Preterit: omonec*)
needle *n.* tlahtzomaloni, omitl (*bone*), omitetl
negation *n.* ahnecuitiliztli

neglect *tv.* ixcahua (*Preterit: onitlaixcauh*)
negligence *n.* tlaahuilcahualiztli
negligent *adj.* ixquimilli
neighbor *n.* calehcapohtli, nocalehcapo, nocalnahuac tlacatl, milehcapohtli (*farm*)
neighborhood *n.* calpulli, chinamitl, tlaxilacalli
neither *adv.* amono
nephew *n.* machtli
nephrite *n.* quetzalitztli
nerve *n.* tlalhuatl
nervous *adj.* tlalhuatic, tlalhuayoh
nervousness *n.* tlalhuayotl
nest *n.* tapahzolli
net *n.* matlatl
Netherlands *n.* Netellalli
never *adv.* aic
nevertheless *conj.* yeceh, maciuhqui
new *adj.* celtic, yancuic; *n.* yancuiliztli (*something*)
newborn *n.* coneatl, conechichilli
newspaper *n.* amatlaixpanhuiloni
next to *loc. suff.* –nahuac, –titlan, –tloc
nickname *n.* ontetocaitl
niece *n.* machtli
night *n.* yohualli; **good ~** ma cualli yohualli
night before last *n.* yalhua yohuac, yalhua yohualli, yalhua ihualli
nightfall *impers. v.* tlayohua (*Preterit: otlayohuac*)
nighttime *adv.* ye tlayohuac
nightly *adv.* cehcenyohuac
nine *num.* chicnahui
nipple *n.* chichihualyacatl, nechichitiloni
nit *n.* acelin
no *adv.* ahmo; maca, macahmo, macamo, mahcamo (*used in negative commands*)

no one *pron.* ayac

nobility *n.* pillotl, pilticayotl

noble *n.* pilli (*Plural: pipiltin*); *adj.* piltic

nod in agreement *iv.* ixcueloa (*Preterit: onixcueloh*)

noise *n.* chachalaquiztli, zozolocaliztli

nomadic *n.* nehnenqui

nonsense *n.* aquimamachiliztli

noon *n.* nepantla tonalli, nepantla tonatiuh, tlacotonalli, tlacotonatiuh

nor *adv.* amono

north *n.* mictlampa

nose *n.* yacatl, yacahtzolli; **blow one's ~** *reflex. v.* itzomia (*Preterit: oninitzomih*)

nose hair *n.* yacatzontli

nostril *n.* yacatzolcoyoc

not *neg.* ahmo

not working *adj.* xitic, xitinqui

not yet *adv.* ayamo, oc

notary public *n.* tecuhtlahcuiloh

notary's office *n.* tecuhtlahcuiloloyan

notebook *n.* amoxneihcuiloni, izhuaamoxtli, tlalnamiconi, amoxtli

nothing *pron.* ahmitla, ahmotlein, ahtle, ahtlein, axtlen

notice *n.* netlahtolmelahualo

noun *n.* tocaitl

nourish *tv.* tlacualillotia (*Preterit: onitlacualillotih*)

nourishment *n.* tonacayotl, yolcayotl

novelty *n.* yancuiliztli

now *adv.* axcan, axca, immanin

nowhere *adv.* ahcan

null and void *adj.* inayacpatiyoh

numb *adj.* cepouhqui; **become ~** *iv.* cepohui (*Preterit: onicepouh*)

number *n.* tlapohualmachiyotl, tlapohualizmachiyotl,
   tlahcotompohualoni
numbering *n.* tlapohualiztli
numbness *n.* cepohualiztli
nun *n.* cihuateopixqui
nurse *iv.* tlachichitia (*Preterit: onitlachichitih*)
nutrition *n.* tlacualillotiliztli
nutritious *adj.* tlacualillotqui

O

oak *n.* ahuacuahuitl, ahuatl
obedience *n.* tetlacamatiliztli
obese *adj.* cuitlananacatic
obesity *n.* cuitlananacatzcayotl
obey *tv.* tlacamati (*Preterit: onitetlacamat*)
obituary *n.* amoxmiccacuiloni
object *n.* tlamantli
objective *n.* ahcitiliztli
oblivion *n.* ilcahualiztli
obscenity *n.* pinauhtlahtolli, tlahuelihtolli, tlahuellahtoli
observation *n.* tlachializtli
observatory *n.* nextiloyan, tlachialoyan
observe *iv.* tlachia (*Preterit: onitlachix*)
obsidian *n.* itztli
obstacle *n.* teelleltilizlti, tetlacahualtiliztli
obvious *adj.* paninezqui
occupation *n.* tequitl, tlachihchiuhcayotl
occur *reflex. v.* mochihua (*Preterit: omochiuh*)
occurrence *n.* nechihualiztli, omochiuh
ocean *n.* huey atl, ilhuica atl, teoatl
of course *adv.* zan queh

offend *tv.* tlatlacalhuia (*Preterit: onitetlatlacalhuih*),
   tv. yolihtlacoa (*Preterit: oniteyolihtlacoh*)
offense *n.* tetelchihualiztli, tlahtlacolli
offer *tv.* mana (*Preterit: onitlaman*), *tv.* manilia
   (*Preterit: onitetlamanilih*)
offering *n.* tlamanalli
office *n.* tlecopatl, tequipan
offspring *n.* tlatlacatililli
often *adv.* achica, zan tequi
oh! *interj.* ecue, tlacace
oil *n.* chiahuacayotl, chiahuiztli, xochiyotl
oily *adj.* chiahuizzoh
ointment *n.* oxitl tlanechicolpahtli
old *adj.* huehueh (*Plural: huehuetqueh*), zozoltic;
   grow ~ *iv.*huehuehquiza (*Preterit: onihuehuequiz*)
old age *n.* huehueliztli, huehuetcayotl; huehuetilizltli (*masc.*),
   heuhuehyotl (*masc.*); ilamayotl (*fem.*), ilamatiliztli (*fem.*)
older *n.* tiachcatl
Olmec *n.* Olmecatl
omen *n.* tetzahuitl, tetzahuiliztli
omission *n.* tlacauhtli
omit *tv.* tlacahua (*Preterit: onitlacauh*)
on *prep.* ipan
on account of *suff.* –pampa
on all sides *adv.* nohuiyan
on both sides *adv.* necoc
on earth *adv.* tlalticpac
on the ground *adv.* tlalchi, tlalpan
on the other side *loc. suff.* –nal, nalco
once *adv.* ceppa
once upon a time *adv.* iczan
one *num.* ce

one-eyed *adj.* ixcapitztic
one-handed *adj.* matepultic
onion *n.* xonacatl
only *adv.* zan, zaniyoh
ooze *tv.* timalquiza (*Preterit: onitimalquiz*)
oozing *n.* netimalquizaliztli
opal *n.* huitzitziltetl
open *adj.* tlapouhqui; *tv.* tlapoa (*Preterit: onitlahtlapoh*),
    tlapohua (*Preterit: onitlahtlapouh*); *iv.* tlapohui
    (*Preterit: onitlapouh*)
opening *n.* coyonca
ophthalmologist *n.* teixpahtih, teixpahtiani
opinion *n.* tlacaquiliztli, yuh nematiliztli
opossum *n.* tlacuatzin, tlachuihcuilotl
opponent *n.* tenamiquini
opportunity *n.* cualcancayotl, immanyotl, ipanyotl
opposition *n.* tzonteyotl
or *conj.* ahnozo, ahnoce, nozo
orange *n.* lalanxol, naranjo xocotl, alaxox; *adj.* xochipalli (*color*)
orchard *n.* quilmilli
order *n.* tenahuatilli; *tv.* tlanahuatia (*Preterit: onitlanahuatih*)
organ *n.* ehuatlapitzalhuehuetl
organist *n.* ehuatlapitzaltzotzonqui
organization *n.* tlahuipanaliztli
organize *tv.* huipana (*Preterit: onitlahuipan*)
orgy *n.* tlatlahuanallotl
origin *n.* amoxollal, pehualiztli, peuhcayotl, quizayan
originating from *adj.* cayotl
oriole *n.* xochitototl, coztictototl
orphan *n.* icnotl, icnotlacatl
orphanage *n.* icnopilloyan, icnoyocan
orphanhood *n.* icnopillotl, icnoyotl, icnotlacayotl
osteoporosis *n.* omitiliztli

Otomi *n.* Otomitl
our *poss.* to–
ourselves *reflex.* tito–
outing *n.* paxalolli
outrage *tv.* tetelchihua (*Preterit: onitetelchiuh*)
outside *adv.* callampa, callan, quiyahuac;
    tv. **take ~** callanquixtia (*Preterit: onitlacallanquixtih*)
outskirts *n.* tenanquiahuatl
oven *n.* texcalli
overrun *iv.* moloni (*Preterit: onimolon*)
overthrow *tv.* xitinia (*Preterit: onitexitinih*)
owl *n.* tecolotl, chichtli
owner *n.* tecohtli
ox *n.* cuacuahueh
oyster *n.* eptli

P
pack *n.* quimilli
package *n.* quimilli
pact *n.* nenahualiztli
pagan *n.* tlateotocani
page *n.* amaizhuatl
pain *n.* cocolli; **feel ~** *iv.* chichinaca (*Preterit: onichichinacac*)
paintbrush *n.* tlapalanaloni
paint *n.* tlapalli; *tv.* tlapalaquia (*Preterit: onitlatlapalaquih*),
    tlapaltia (*Preterit: onitlapaltih*); *tv.* pa (*Preterit: onitlapah*)
painting *n.* tilmahtlahcuilolli, tlapalaquilli, tlahcuilolli;
    tlatlapalaquiliztli (*act of*)
palace *n.* tecpancalli, tecpan
palate *n.* copactli, camatapalli
pale *adj.* iztalectic
paleness *n.* iztlaectiliztli

palm *n.* macpalli (*of the hand*)
palm date *n.* zoyacapolin
palm grove *n.* zotollah
palm leaf *n.* zoyachiquihuitl
palm tree *n.* zotolin, zoyatl
palsy *n.* cohuacihuiliztli, nacayomihmiquiliztli
pamper *tv.* ahahulia (*Preterit: oniteahahuilih*), xocoyomati
   (*Preterit: onitexocoyomat*)
pamphlet *n.* amatlahcuilolnextiloni
pan *n.* tepuzcomitl
pant *iv.* ihcica (*Preterit: onihcicac*)
pantry *n.* caxmanaloyan
pants *n.* metztlaquemitl
paper *n.* amatl
parakeet *n.* quiltototl, coyotzin
paralysis *n.* coacihuiztli; **suffer from ~** coacihui *iv.*
   (*Preterit: onicoaciuh*)
paralyzed *adj.* cuauhpitztic
parchment *n.* ehuaamatl
pardon *n.* tetlapohpopolhuiliztli
parent *n.* pilhuah, tenan tetah
parenthesis *n.* yahualmachiotl, yahualmachiotlahcuilolli
park *n.* xochitepancalli
parrot *n.* cochotl, ococuizalli, quiltototl, toztli (*yellow headed*)
partridge *n.* tepezolin
party *n.* teicniuhnechicoliztli
pass *iv.* pano (*Preterit: onipanoc*)
passenger *n.* panoni
passion *n.* neyolcocoltiliztli
paste *n.* tzacuhtli, tzauctli; *tv.* zaloa (*Preterit: onitlazaloh*)
past tense *n.* opanoc cahuitl
pastime *n.* neellelquixtiliztli
patch *n.* quilmilli (*vegetable*)

paternal *adj.* tetahyoh
path *n.* ohpitzactli, ohtli
pathetic *adj.* tetlaocoltih
patience *n.* tlapacaihiyohuiliztli
patient *adj.* moyollotepitztiliani; **be ~**
   reflex. v. moyollotepitztilia (*Preterit: oninoyollotepitztilih*)
patio *n.* caltenco, ithualli
patrimony *n.* huehhuetlatlaquitl, tlatquitl
patriot *n.* neyolcantlazohtlani, teaxcapantlazohtlani
patriotism *n.* neyolcantlazohtlaliztli, teaxcapantlazohtlaliztli
pause *n.* nehuehcauiliztli; *reflex. v.* huehcahua
   (*Preterit: oninohuehcauh*)
pay *n.* tlaxtlahuilli; *tv.* patcayotia (*Preterit: onitlapatcayotih*),
   tv. ixtlahua (*Preterit: onitetlaxtlauh*), tlaxtlahuia
   (*Preterit: onitetlaxtlahuih*); **~ tax** *iv.* tlacalaquia
   (*Preterit: onitlacalaquih*)
payment *n.* ilhuilli
peace *n.* paccanemiliztli, pahcanemiliztli, tlamatcanemiliztli,
   tlacaconemiliztli, yocoxcayotl
peaceful person *n.* yocoxcatlacatl
peacefully *adv.* matca
peach *n.* durazno; **~ tree** durazno cuahuitl
peacock *n.* quetzaltototl
peanut *n.* cacahuatl, tlalcacahuatl
pearl *n.* eptli
peasant *n.* altepemaitl, millacatl, milpanecatl, milpan tlacatl
pebble *n.* atoyatetl, xaltetl
peccary *n.* coyametl
peck *n.* tetemminaliztli; *tv.* temmina (*Preterit: onitetemmin*)
peculiarity *n.* yuh quiztli
pediatrician *n.* coconeh intepahticauh, coconeh impahticauh
peel *tv.* xipehua (*Preterit: onitlaxipeuh*)
pen *n.* tlahcuiloloni (*writing*), tepancalli (*enclosure*)

pencil *n.* cuauhtlahcuiloloni, teconalli
pencil holder *n.* cuauhtlahcuilolcalli
pencil sharpener *n.* cuauhtlacuilolchichiquiloni,
   teconalchichiquiloni
penis *n.* tepolli, tepulli
penitentiary *n.* tetlatzacuilcalli, tetlatzacuiloyan
pentagon *n.* macuilcampa
people *n.* macehualtin, tlacah
pepita *n.* pitztli
pepper (*hot*) *n.* chilli; Caxtillan chilli (*black*)
perceptive *adj.* yolizma
perfect *adj.* cemahcic, cenquizqui, tzompatic, tzontic;
   tv. cencahua (*Preterit: onitlacencauh*)
perfection *n.* tlacencahualiztli
perfectly *adv.* cenquizca
perforate *tv.* coyonia (*Preterit: onitlacoyonih*), mamali
   (*Preterit: onitlamamalihuac*)
perforated *adj.* coyonqui
performance *n.* nexiptlatiliztli
perfume *n.* xochitlenamactli, popochtli
perhaps *adv.* ahzo, in ahzo, cuix, mach, quimmach,
   quilmach, ach, hueliz
perhaps not *adv.* acanozomo
period *n.* tliltetl (*punctuation*); cahuipanahuilo (*time*)
perish *iv.* polihui (*Preterit: onipoliuh*), xitini
   (*Preterit: onixitin*)
perishable *adj.* polihuini
perplexed *adj.* nequetzalli
perplexity *n.* nequetzaliztli
person *n.* tlacatl
personality *n.* tlacayotl
perspiration *n.* itonilli, tlacaipotoctli, tzocuitlatl, tzotl, tzoyotl
perspire *iv.* itonia (*Preterit: oniitonih*), itoni (*Preterit: oniiton*)

persuade *tv.* cealtia (*Preterit: onitecealtih*)

pestilence *n.* temoxtli ehecatl

pettiness *n.* tzotzocayotl

peyote *n.* peyotl

pharmacist *n.* pahchihchiuhqui, pahpiani

pharmacy *n.* pahcalli, pahnamacoyan

pheasant *n.* coxolihtli

philosopher *n.* tlamatiliztlazohtlani, tlamatini

philosophy *n.* tlamatiliztlazohtlaliztli

phlegm *n.* tozcacuitlatl, tozcayacacuitlatl

phoneme *n.* caquiztli

phonograph *n.* tepuzteyolehuallahtoloni

photograph *n.* teixiptlaamatl tlatlilquixtiloni;
    ~ *tv.* ixcopina (*Preterit: onitlaixcopin*),
    tetlilquixtia (*Preterit: onitetlilquixtih*)

photographer *n.* tetlilquixtiani

physician *n.* tepahtiani, tepahtih, ticitl (*Plural: titicih*)

pick *tv.* pehpena (*Preterit: onitlapehpen*)

pick fruit *tv.* xochicualcotona (*Preterit: onixochicualcoton*)

picture *n.* tlatlilquixtiloni

picturesque *n.* cuilolnezqui

pie *n.* tlaoyotl

piece *n.* centlatzayantli, cotoncayotl, tlahcotontli, cotoctli

pier *n.* acaltecoyan

pierce *iv.* coyonia (*Preterit: onitlacoyonih*)

pierced *adj.* coyoctic, coyonqui

pig *n.* pitzotl

pigeon *n.* huiloconetl

pigpen *n.* pitzocalli

pile *n.* centlalilli, ololli

pilgrim *n.* nehnencatzintli, ohtlatocani, yani

pilgrimage *n.* ohtlatocaliztli, nehnemiliztli, nehuentiliztli
    (*religious*)

pill *n.* pahtelolohtontli, telolohpahtli
pillow *n.* tzonicpalli, cuatlapechtli
pilot *n.* nemachiliani
pimple *n.* cocotl, ixzahuatl, nanahuatl, zahuatl, ixocuilin, tzotzotl; **have pimples** *iv.* cocoti (*Preterit: onicocotic*)
pimply *adj.* zahuayoh
pin *n.* tepuztilmazoani, tepuztlatlatzicoltiloni
piñata *n.* tlapanhuetzconi, tlateiniloni
pincers *n.* tepuztlaanoni
pinch *n.* tecotonaliztli; *tv.* cotona (*Preterit: onitecoton*)
pine *n.* ayauhcuahuitl
pine grove *n.* ocotla, ococuauhtla, ayauhcuauhtla
pine log *n.* ocotl
pine nut *n.* ococenyollohtli, ococuauhcecenton
pineapple *n.* matzahtli, ococentli, ococuauhcecenton
pinecone *n.* ococentli
pink *adj.* tlaztalehualli
pinkie finger *n.* mapiltontli, mapilxocoyotl
pinto bean *n.* zoletl
pipe *n.* huei cuauhcomitl
pistol *n.* tlequihquiztontli
pit *n.* tecochtli, yolloxocotl
pitiful *adj.* tetlaocoltih
pitcher *n.* xalo
pitchfork *n.* cuatlaltatzicoltiloni
pity *n.* tetlaocoliliztli
place *n.* yeyantli; (**to**) ~ *tv.* tema (*Preterit: onitlaten*), tlalia (*Preterit: onitlatlalih*)
place in front of *tv.* manilia (*Preterit: onitetlamanilih*)
place of birth *n.* tlacatiyan
place where *suff.* –yan
placenta *n.* cihuatlahyelli
plague *n.* chihuaiztli, matlazahuatl, totomonaliztli, chahuiztli

plain *n.* ixtlahuatl
plan *n.* tlayolapanallapictli
plane *adj.* ixmanqui
planer *n.* tenextlazaloloni, tlaaquiltetl
planet *n.* ahtlahuilcitlalin, ilhuicayotl
plant *n.* xochitl; *tv.* toca (*Preterit: onitlatocac*), pixoa
    (*Preterit: onitlapixoh*)
plant leaf *n.* xiuhizhuatl
plaster *n.* tezoquitl, tlalzacuhtli
plate *n.* caxitl, caxpechtli
platform *n.* cuauhxopehpechtli, tlalmantli, tlapechtli
play *iv.* paccaahuiltia (*Preterit: onipaccaahuiltih*),
    pahcaahuiltia (*Preterit: onipahcaahuiltih*;
    ~ music *iv.* cuicatia (*Preterit: onicuicatih*)
play an instrument *tv.* tzotzona (*Preterit: onitlatzotzon*)
play ball *reflex. v.* matotepehua (*Preterit: oninomatotepeuh*),
    iv. ollama (*Preterit: onollan*), ollamia (*Preterit: oninollamih*)
play cards *iv.* amapatoa (*Preterit: onamapatoh*)
playful *adj.* paccaahuiltini, pahcaahuiltini
plaza *n.* tianquiztli
pleasant *adj.* ixmahuiztic
please *interj.* mixpantzinco, nimitztlatlauhtia; *tv.* pactia
    (*Preterit: onitepactih*)
pleasurable *adj.* tehuellamachtih
pleasure *n.* ahuilli; **with ~** *adv.* ica paquiliztli, paquiliztica
pliers *n.* tepuzcuacualoni
plow *iv.* tlaxotla (*Preterit: onitlaxotlac*)
plowing *n.* tlaxotlaliztli
pluck a guitar *iv.* mecahuehuetzotzona
    (*Preterit: onimecahueuetzotzon*)
plug *n.* tentzacua
plum *n.* xocotl
plumb *n.* temetztepilolli

poem *n.* xochitlahtolli
poet *n.* cuicanitl, xochitlahtoani, cuicapixqui,
   tlahtolchichiuhqui, tlahtollaliani
poetry *n.* tlahtolchihualiztli, tlahtollaliliztli, xochitlahtolli,
   xochitl cuicatl
poinsettia *n.* cuitlaxochitl
point *n.* yacatl, huitztli
point of departure *n.* huelihcuac in huilohua
pointed *adj.* cuahuetztic, cuapintic, cuatohuitztic,
   cuayacapitztic
poison *n.* iztlactli
poisonous *adj.* iztlacyoh
Poland *n.* Polonian
pole *n.* cuauhacatl
police officer *n.* tlatecpanalpixqui, tlatecpanaltecuitlahuiani
Polish *n.* Polonian chaneh; Polonian tlahtolli (*language*)
polish *n.* tlanemachiliztli, *tv.* nemachilia
   (*Preterit: onitlanemachilih*), petzoa (*Preterit: onitlapetzoh*)
polished *adj.* ixpetlanqui, tehuiltic, petztic
polishing machine *n.* tlanemachililoni
politician *n.* quentecemitquiani, tecpantlapiquini
politics *n.* quentecemitquiliztli
pollution *n.* temahualiztli
polygamous *adj.* miectincihuapixqui
polygamy *n.* miectincihuapixcayotl
pool *n.* atlacuihuayan, acaxitl
poor *adj.* motolinia, motolinihqui; **be ~** *reflex. v.* tolinia
   (*Preterit: oninotolinih*)
popcorn *n.* izquitl
pope *n.* hueiteopixcatlahtoani
poplar *n.* pepeyolcuahuitl
popular *adj.* altepetlazotlalli
population *n.* cuitlapilli atlapalli

porcupine *n.* huitztlacuatl
pore *n.* ehuacoyoctli
pork *n.* pitzonacatl
porous *adj.* zonectic
porridge *n.* atolli, comic atolli, totonca atolli
portable *adj.* moliniani
portion *n.* centlatzayantli, cotoncayotl, tlacotontli
positive *adj.* melahuac, nelli
positively *adv.* neltihtica
possession *n.* axcaitl, tlatquitl
possibility *n.* hueltiliztli, huelitiliztli, chihualiztli
possibly *adv.* hueliyotica, hueliz, za yeh queneh,
   quimmach, ach
post *n.* cuauhtlaxillotl (*wood*)
post office *n.* iciuhcatitlancalli, painaltlecopatl,
   amatitlaniloyan
posterity *n.* quin tlacatiliztli
postpone *tv.* panahuiltia (*Preterit: onitlapanahuiltih*)
postponed *adj.* tlapanahuiltilli
pot *n.* comitl, xoctli, yecomitl (*boiling beans*)
pot maker *n.* conchiuhqui
potato *n.* papas
potato bug *n.* tlalconetl
potbellied *adj.* xiquitic
potion *n.* pahatliliztli
potsherd *n.* tepalcatl, tapacatl
potter *n.* zoquichiuhqui
pouch *n.* xiquipilli
poverty *n.* icnoyotl, icnotlacayotl, netoliniliztli
powder *n.* teuhtli
powdered *adj.* teuhyoh, cuechtic
power *n.* cualle, hueliyotl, huelitiliztli, hueliliztli
powerful *adj.* huelitini, hueliyoh, teputzeh, chicactic

practice *n.* yetlachihualiztli; *reflex. v.* moyehyecoa
  (*Preterit: oninoyehyecoh*)
praise *tv.* yectenehua (*Preterit: oniteyecteneuh*)
prank *n.* camanalli
pray *reflex. v.* teotlaitlania (*Preterit: oninoteotlaitlanih*)
preacher *n.* neltiliztenonotzani, neltiliztemachtiani
precious *adj.* tlazohtli
precious stone *n.* quetzalchalchihuitl (*blue or green*),
  tlazohtetl
precursor *n.* teyacantihqui, tlatzintiani
predecessor *n.* achtopahualla
predict *tv.* yolteohuia (*Preterit: onitlayoltohuih*);
  iv. mecatlapohua (*Preterit: onimecatlapouh*)
prediction *n.* tlaachtopaihtoliztli
prefer *tv.* nachcapanquetza (*Preterit: onitenachcapanquetz*),
  yacatticatlalia (*Preterit: oniteyacatticatlalih*),
  panahuiltia (*Preterit: onicpanahuiltih*)
preferable *adj.* tlapanahuiltilli, tlanachcapanquetzalli
preference *n.* tlapanahuiltiliztli, tlanachcapanquetzaliztli
prefix *n.* tlahtolpehualiztli
pregnancy *n.* otzyotl
pregnant *adj.* otztli, pilhuah; **be ~** *iv.* otztia (*Preterit: onotztih*)
prelate *n.* teopixcatlahtoani
premeditate *tv.* itztimotlalia (*Preterit: onitlaitztimotlalih*),
  nemilia (*Preterit: onitlanemilih*)
preparation *n.* tlacecencahualiztli
prepare *tv.* cecencahua (*Preterit: onitlacecencauh*)
prepare a cure *tv.* pahchihua (*Preterit: onioahchiuh*)
present *n.* axcancayotl (*time*); **~ tense** axcan cahuitl;
  tv. mana (*Preterit: onitlaman*), teixmachtia
  (*Preterit: onitetlaixmachtih*)
present as a gift *tv.* huentia (*Preterit: onitlahuentih*)

presentation *n.* teixpantlaliliztli, tlaixpantlaliliztli
preservation *n.* temaquixtiliztli
preservative *n.* temaquixtiloni
preserve *tv.* maquixtia (*Preterit: onitemaquixtih*)
presidency *n.* tepanihcaliztli
president *n.* cecnitlacahueitepachoani, huey tlahtoani
press *iv.* tepuztlazohua (*clothes; Preterit: onitepuztlazouh*)
pressure *n.* tlapacholiztli
pretend *tv.* tlapiqui (*Preterit: onitlapic*); ~ **to love someone**
    nahuallazohtla (*Preterit: onitenahuallazohtlac*)
pretend to be good *reflex. v.* yecnequi (*Preterit: oninoyecnec*)
pretty *adj.* cuacualtzin, ixcuacualtzin, tlayecchichiuhtli
prevent *tv.* elleltia (*Preterit: oniteelleltih*), tlacahualtia
    (*Preterit: onitetlacahualtih*)
previous *adj.* achtopanyauh, achtopapaneitalli
price *n.* ipatiuh, patitl, patiuhtli, patiyotl
prick *tv.* tzapinia (*Preterit: onitetzapinih*), tzopinia
    (*Preterit: onitetzopinih*)
prickly pear *n.* nochtli, coznochtli (*yellow*), xoconochtli
    (*bitter, green*)
pride *n.* nehueililiztli
priest *n.* teohuah, teopixqui, tlamacazqui
priesthood *n.* teopixacayotl
primacy *n.* huellayacanaliztli
prince *n.* tlahtocapilli
princess *n.* tlahtocacihuapilli
print *iv.* tepuztlahcuiloa (*Preterit: onitepuztlahcuiloh*)
print shop *n.* tepuztlahcuiloloyan
printer *n.* tepuztlahcuiloh (*person*); tepuztlahcuiloloni
    (*machine*)
printing press *n.* tepuztlacopinaloni
prison *n.* cuauhcalli, tetlatzacuilcalli, tetlatzacuiloyan
prisoner *n.* tecaltzacuilli, tetlatzacuilli, tlaantli, malli

privilege *n.* teicneliloni
privileged *adj.* tlacnelilli
probable *adj.* huelizyez, neltililoni
probably *adv.* huelizyeztica, in ahzo, tlaneltililiztica
proclaim *iv.* tecpoa (*Preterit: ontecpoh*)
proclamation *n.* tecpoyotlahtolli
produce offspring *tv.* tlacatilia (*Preterit: ontetlacatilih*)
profanity *n.* ahcuallahtolli, pinauhtlahtolli, tlahuelihtolli,
  tlahuellahtolli,pitzotlahtolli
profit *n.* tlaixnextiliztli
profitable *adj.* tlacnopilhuilloh
program *n.* amatequitl
project *n.* nelhuiliztli
promise *n.* nehtolli; *tv.* tenehua (*Preterit: onitlateneuh*),
  cemihtoa (*Preterit: ontlacemihtoh*)
prompt *adj.* painalli, iciuhcayoh, ihciuihcayoh
promptly *adv.* iciuhca, ihciuhca
pronoun *n.* tetocapatlahquetl
pronounce *tv.* tlatenquixtia (*Preterit: onitlatenquixtih*)
pronunciation *n.* tlatenquixtiliztli
proof *n.* tlaneltililiztli
prop *n.* tlaxillotl
property *n.* axcaitl
prophecy *n.* tlaachtopaitoliztli
prophet *n.* tlaachtopaihtoani
prosperity *n.* quicempaccayotl, quicempahcayotl,
  tlacempahcayotl, tlaipantililiztli
prostitute *n.* ahuiani, cihuacuecuech, motzinnamacani
prostitution *n.* netlaneuhtilizlti; **house of ~** *n.* netlaneuhtilizcalli,
  netzinnamacoyan
protect *tv.* xillanhuia (*Preterit: onitexillanhuih*);
  aquia (*Preterit: oniteaquih*)
protection *n.* teaquiliztli, temanahuiliztli

protector *n.* cuexaneh
proud *adj.* mopohuani, mopouhqui
prove *tv.* neltilia (*Preterit: onitlaneltilih*)
province *n.* huey altepetl
provisions *n.* itacatl, nemiliztlacualli
prudence *n.* nemachiliztli, nezcaliliztli
prune *tv.* xipehua (*Preterit: onitlaxipeuh*)
psychologist *n.* yolixmatini
psychology *n.* yolixmachiliztli
public *n.* teixpanyotl; *adj.* nohhuian macho
public service *n.* altepetequipanoliztli
public square *n.* altepeyollohco, tlayollohco
publication *n.* tetlanextiliztli
publicize *tv.* panotla (*Preterit: onitetlapanotlac*)
publicly *adv.* teixpan
puddle *n.* atezcatl
Puerto Rico *n.* Necuiltonolacalquixohuayan,
    Tlatquihuaacalquixohuayan
pull *tv.* tilana (*Preterit: onitlatilan*)
pull weeds *tv.* xiuhpopoa (*Preterit: onitlaxiuhpopoh*),
    xippopoa (*Preterit: onitlaxippopoh*)
pulley *n.* temalacatlatlehcahuiloni
pulque bar *n.* ocnamacoyan
pulque *n.* octli, necuhtli
pulse *n.* matlalhuayo itetecuicaca, tlalhuatl itetecuica,
    tlalhuatl itetecuicaca
pulverize *tv.* teuhtia (*Preterit: onitlateuhtih*)
puma *n.* miztli
pumpkin *n.* ayohtli
pumpkin seed *n.* ayohachtli, ayohhuachtli
punch *n.* tlaixtepinilli; *tv.* tepinia (*Preterit: onitetepinih*)
punish *tv.* tlatzacuiltia (*Preterit: onitlatzacualtih*),
    tetlacaquitia (*Preterit: onitetlacaquitih*)

punishable *adj.* tlatzacuiltiloni
punishment *n.* tetlatzacuiliztli, tetlacaquitiliztli, tetl cuahuitl
pupil *n.* ixnenetl (*of the eye*); tlamachtilli (*school*)
puppy *n.* itzcuinconetl
purchase *n.* tlacohualli; *tv.* cohua (*Preterit: onitlacouh*)
Purgatory *n.* nechipahualoyan, neyectiloyan
purification *n.* tlachipahualiztli
purifier *n.* tlachipahuani (*person*), tlachipahualoni (*device*)
purify *tv.* chipahua (*Preterit: onitlachipahuac*)
purity *n.* chipahuacayotl, motquihtializtli
purple *adj.* camohpalli, camohpaltic, camohpalli, yauhtic
purpose *n.* ahcitiliztli, nelhuiliztli
purslane *n.* canauhquilitl
pus *n.* palaniliztli, temalli; **filled with ~** *adj.* temalloh;
    be filled with ~ temalloa (*Preterit: otemalloac*)
push *tv.* matopehua (*Preterit: onitematopeuh*), topehua
    (*Preterit: onitetopeuh*)
put *tv.* tema (*Preterit: onitlaten*), tlalia (*Preterit: onitlatlalih*)
put in order *tv.* tlatecpana (*Preterit: onitlatecpan*)
put on one's shoes *reflex. v.* cactia (*Preterit: oninocactih*)
putrid *adj.* miquiziyaltic
pyramid *n.* tzacualli, tlachihualtepetl

Q

q-tip *n.* nenacaztahtaconi
quack *n.* mopouhcatlahtoani
quail *n.* zolin
quake *n.* olin; *iv.* olini (*Preterit: oolin and oolinqui*);
    impers. v. tlalolini (*Preterit: otlalolin*)
quarrel *n.* cocolli
quarry *n.* tequixtiloyan, tetlapanaloyan
quartet *n.* nauhcuicanimeh

receive *tv.* celia (*Preterit: onitlacelih*)

recent *adj.* yancuic

recently *adv.* yancuican, inici

reception *n.* teceliliztli

recite *tv.* tempohua (*Preterit: onitlatempouh*)

reckless *adj.* mixtlapaloani

recklessly *adv.* neixtlapaloliztica

recklessness *n.* nexitlapaloliztli

recognize *tv.* ixpehpena (*Preterit: oniteixpehpen*); ixmati
    (*Preterit: oniteixmat*)

recommend *tv.* tlahtolpalehuia (*Preterit: onitetlahtolpalehuih*)

recommendation *n.* tlahtolpalehuiztli

reconciliation *n.* nenonotzaliztli, nenotzaltiliztli

record player *n.* tepuzteyolehuallahtoloni

recreation *n.* neahuiltiliztli

rectory *n.* teopixcacalli

rectum *n.* yohhuicuitl

red *adj.* chiltic, chichiltic, eztic, tlapalli, tlatlactic, tlatlauhqui

red tomato *n.* xitomatl

reed *n.* acatl

reed basket *n.* zacatanahtli, zacapetlatanahtli

reflect *reflex. v.* quexquitzahuia
    (*Preterit: oninoquexquitzahuih*), yolmaxiltia
    (*Preterit: oninoyolmaxiltih*)

refrigerator *n.* tepuztlacualcehuiloni, tlacualitztiloni,
    tepuztlacualitztiloni, tepuztlaitztiloni

refuge *n.* nemaquixtiloyan

regarding *prep.* –tech

register *tv.* tetocaihcuiloa (*Preterit: onitetocaihcuiloh*),
    tocatlalia (*Preterit: onitetocatlalih*)

registration *n.* tetocaihcuiloliztli

registry *n.* amatlazontli

regress *iv.* tzinquiza (*Preterit: onitzinquiz*)

reject *tv.* xocoa (*Preterit: onitexocoh*)
relationship *n.* tehuayolcayotl (*blood*)
relative *n.* tehuanyolqui, nohuanyolqui, huanyolqui
release *tv.* toma (*Preterit: onitlaton*)
remains *n.* necauhcayotl, tlacahualli, tlacahuilli
remedy *n.* tlacualtiliztli, pahtli
remember *tv.* ilnamiqui (*Preterit: onitlalnamic*)
remembrance *n.* necauhcayotl
remove the crust *tv.* xipehua (*Preterit: onitlaxipeuh*)
renovate *tv.* yancuilia (*Preterit: onitlayancuilih*)
renovation *n.* tlayancuililiztli
rent *tv.* tlaquehua (*Preterit: onitlatlaquehuac*)
repair *tv.* nitlapahtia (*Preterit: onitlapahtih*), cualtilia
 (*Preterit: onitlacualtilih*), tlacencahua
 (*Preterit: onitlacencauh*)
repairperson *n.* tlacencahuani, tlacualtiliani
repent *reflex. v.* elleltia (*Preterit: oninoelleltih*), yolcocoa
 (*Preterit: oninoyolcocoh*)
repentance *n.* nelleltiliztli, neyolcocoliztli, neyolcuepaliztli
report *n.* tenehualiztli
representative *n.* ixiptlatl, titlantli
reprimand *tv.* nohnotza (*Preterit: onitenohnotz*)
reproach *tv.* tlayehualtia (*Preterit: onitetlayehualtih*)
reputation *n.* tenyotl
request *n.* tetlatlauhtiloni
research *n.* tlanelhuayotoquiliztli, tlahtolaxiltillotl;
 iv. tlanelhuayotoca (*Preterit: onitlanelhuayotocac*),
 tlahtolaxiltia (*Preterit: onitlahtolaxiltih*)
researcher *n.* tlanelhuayotocani, tlahtolaxiltiani
reside *reflex. v.* chantia (*Preterit: oninochantih*)
residence *n.* nemohuayan
resident *n.* calcatl, calqui, chaneh
residue *n.* cuitlatl, zoquiyotl

resin *n.* ohxitl
resolute *n.* yollotetl
resolution *n.* nelhuiliztli, nenotztli
resounding *adj.* huelcaquiztilloh
respect *n.* mahuiztli
rest *n.* cehuiliztli, cehuilli, necehuiliztli, tlacehuilizpan;
    iv. cehui (*Preterit: oniceuh*), cehuia (*Preterit: onicehuih*)
restaurant *n.* tlacualoyan
restlessness *n.* teamanaliztli
result *n.* mochihualiztli
resurgence *n.* nezcaliliztli
retraction *n.* netencuepaliztli
retreat *iv.* tzinquiza (*Preterit: onitzinquiz*);
    reflex. v. cuitlacuepa (*Preterit: oninocuitlacuep*)
return *n.* ilotiliztli; *iv.* iloti (*Preterit: onilot*), *reflex. v.* cuepa
    (*Preterit: oninocuep*)
reveal *tv.* nextia (*Preterit: onitlanextih*); ~ **oneself to**
    someone *reflex. v.* ittitia (*Preterit: oninoteittitih*)
revelation *n.* tlanextilli
revenge *n.* netzoncuiliztli
revere *tv.* imacaci (*Preterit: oniteimacaz*)
revered *adj.* huehcapan iuhqui
revolve *reflex. v.* mimiloa (*Preterit: oninomimiloh*)
reward *n.* tetlaxtlahuilli, ilhuilli; *tv.* tlaxtlahuia
    (*Preterit: onitetlaxtlahuih*)
rheum *n.* ixcuitlatl
rheumatism *n.* coacihuiztli; **suffer from** ~ coacihui *iv.*
    (*Preterit: onicoaciuh*)
rib *n.* omicicuilli
ribbon *n.* tzontlacololli (*hair*), tetzauhtlacololli
rich *adj.* axcahuah, tlatquihuah
ridge *n.* tepeixco
ridicule *tv.* huehuetzquilia (*Preterit: onitlahuehuetzquilih*)

ridiculous *adj.* tlahuehuetzqui (*person*), tlahuehuetzconi
   (*thing*)
rifle *n.* matlequiquiztli
right *adj.* yeccantli
right hand *n.* mayeccantli, mayectli, yecmaitl
righteousness *n.* melahuacayotl
rind *n.* ehuatl
ring *n.* maxitlaztli, maxotlaztli, tepuzyahualli, matepuztli;
   iv. tzilini (*Preterit: otzilin*); ~ **a bell** *iv.* tlatzilinia
   (*Preterit: onitlatzilinih*), tlatzitzilitza
   (*Preterit: onitlatzitzilitz*)
riot *n.* tehuicpanehualli
ripe *adj.* atoltic
ripeness *n.* atolticayotl
rise *iv.* tlehco (*Preterit: onitlehcoc*)
ritual calendar *n.* ilhuitlapohualamoxtli
rival *n.* tenamicqui
river *n.* atoyatl
road *n.* ohtli, ochpantli
roadrunner *n.* poxacuatl
roast turkey hen *n.* totollaehuatzalli
roast *tv.* tletema (*Preterit: onitlaten*)
roasted *adj.* tlaxquitl
robust *adj.* tlachicauhtli, tlapaltic
rock *n.* tetl; *tv.* neloa (*Preterit: onitlaneloh*)
rocky *adj.* teteyoh
rocky terrain *n.* tetetla, tetlahtli, tetellan
rod *n.* tlacotl, topilli
roe *n.* michpilli
role model *n.* octacatl
roll *reflex. v.* mimiloa (*Preterit: oninomimiloh*); *iv.* temimilo
   (*Preterit: onitemimiloc*)
roll a tortilla *tv.* ixpiqui (*Preterit: onitlaixpic*)

roll up *tv.* malacachoa (*Preterit: onitlamalacachoh*)
rolled-up *adj.* cocolochtic
romance language *n.* romatlahtolli
roof *n.* calcuaitl, tlapantli, tlacpaccayotl
roofing tile *n.* tapalcaxpichtli
rooster *n.* cayo
root *n.* nelhuatl, nelhuayotl, tlanelhuayotl
rope *n.* mecatl; (**to**) ~ *tv.* tzohuia (*Preterit: onotlatzohuih*)
rose *n.* caxtillanxochitl
rose-colored *adj.* tlaztalehualli
rose petal *n.* xochizhuatl
roster *n.* tocaamatl
rot *iv.* palani (*Preterit: onipalan*)
rotten *adj.* palanqui
round *adj.* mimiltic, mimiliuhqui, ololiuhqui, ololtic,
    tapayoltic, tolontic, yahualtic
roundness *n.* mimiliuhcayotl, ololiuhcayotl
row *n.* huipantli; *iv.* tlaneloa (*Preterit: onitlaneloh*)
rub *tv.* tlaxacualoa (*Preterit: onitlaxacualoh*)
rub on *tv.* oza (*Preterit: oniteoz*), tlamatelhuia
    (*Preterit: onitetlamatelhuih*)
rubber *n.* olli, pozolli, ulli
rubber-ball game *n.* ollamaliztli
ruby *n.* tlapalteoxihuitl
rudder *n.* acahuelteconi
ruin *tv.* zoloa (*Preterit: onitlazoloh*)
rumor *n.* tenehualiztli
rumormonger *n.* nenepilmaxaltic
rump *n.* tzintlantli
run *reflex. v.* tlaloa (*Preterit: oninotlaloh*); ~ **fast** *iv.* paina
    (*Preterit: onipain*)
rung *n.* tlamamatlatl
runner *n.* motlaloani

Russia *n.* Rusian
Russian *n.* Rusian chaneh; Rusiantlahtolli (*language*)
rust *n.* tepuzpoxcauhcayotl, tepuztlalli; *iv.* tepuztlaloa
    (*Preterit: otepuztlaloh*)
rusted *n.* tepuztlalloh
rusty *adj.* poxcauhqui; **become ~** *iv.* poxcahui
    (*Preterit: opoxcauh*)

S
sack *n.* coxtal, tlamamalxiquipilli
sacrament *n.* teyolmachiyotiliztli
sad *adj.* talocoxqui, yollotoneuhqui; **be ~** *iv.* tlaocoya
    (*Preterit: onitlaocox*), patzmiqui (*Preterit: onipatzmic*);
    reflex. v. yolcocoa (*Preterit: oninoyolcocoh*)
saddle *n.* pehpechtli
saddle blanket *n.* pehpechtli
sadenning *adj.* teopouhqui
sadness *n.* cuezolli, tlaocolli, tlaocoyaliztli, yollotonehualiztli
sage *n.* tlamatini, tlamatqui
sail *n.* acalcuahpamitl
sailor *n.* atlacatl
salamander *n.* axolotl
salary *n.* tlaxtlahuilli
saliva *n.* chihchitl, iztlactli, tenayotl
salivate *tv.* iztlaqui (*Preterit: onitlaiztlac*)
salt *n.* iztatl; *tv.* poyelia (*Preterit: onitlapoyelih*)
saltshaker *n.* iztacaxitl
salty *adj.* poyec, iztayo; **very ~** *adj.* poyelpahtic, iztachichic
salvation *n.* nemaquixtiliztli, temaquixtiliztli
same *adj.* neneuhqui, nehneuhqui
sameness *n.* neneuhcayotl
sand *n.* xalli, xalipicilli (*fine*)

sandal *n.* cactli, tacactli, tecactli, zotolcactli (*made of palm leaf*)

sandy ground *n.* xalla, xalpan

sapling *n.* cuauhpilli

sarape *n.* tilmahtli

sarcasm *n.* huiteyolihtlacoliztli

sarcastic *adj.* huiteyolihtlacoani

sash *n.* nelpiloni

satellite *n.* tepuzmetztli

satisfaction *n.* netlacamatiliztli, quicempactiliztli, tlayolpachihuiliztli

satisfied *adj.* pachiuhqui

satisfy *tv.* yoliuhtlalia (*Preterit: oniteyoliuhtlalih*), yolpachihuitia (*Preterit: oniteyolpachihuitih*)

sauce *n.* molli

sauce bowl *n.* molcaxitl

sauce grinder *n.* texolotl (*stone*)

sausage *n.* cuiyantlanacatentli, cuauhtlanchaneh

savannah *n.* zacatlah

save *tv.* maquixtia (*Preterit: onitemaquixtih*)

savior *n.* temaquixtiani. temaquixtihqui

savor *tv.* iztlaqui (*Preterit: onitlaiztlac*)

saw *n.* tlatequiloni, tlateconi

sawdust *n.* cuauhpinolli, cuauhtextli, cuauhcuechtli

say *tv.* ilhuia (*Preterit: oniquilhuih*), tenehua (*Preterit: onitlateneuh*)

saying *n.* tlahtolli

scab *n.* nexhuacayotl, xincayotl, zahuatl

scaffold *n.* tlepechtli

scale *n.* ehuatl

scalp *n.* cuaehuayotl, cuanacayotl

scar *n.* tetequilli

scare *tv.* mauhtia (*Preterit: onitemauhtih*)

scared *adj.* momauhtiani
scarf *n.* pahyo
scary *adj.* temauhtih
scatter *tv.* chayahua (*Preterit: onitlachayauh*)
schedule *n.* cahuitl
scholar *n.* amoxeh, amoxhuah, tlamatini
school *n.* calmecac, calmachtiloyan, nemachtiloyan,
    temachtiloyan, temachtilcalli, telpuchcalli
science *n.* tlaixmatiliztli, tlamachiliztli, tlamatiliztli
scientist *n.* tlaixmatini, tlaixmatqui, tlamatini
scissors *n.* tepuztlateconi, tlateconi, tlatequiloni
scorch *tv.* chinoa (*Preterit: onitlachinoh*)
scorpion *n.* colotl, acaltetepon
scrape *tv.* ihchiqui (*Preterit: onitlahchic*)
scraper *n.* tepuztlatextiloni
scratch with the nails *iv.* tlahuana (*Preterit: onitlahuan*)
scream *iv.* tztatzi (*Preterit: onotzatzic*)
scribe *n.* amatlahcuiloh, tlahcuiloh
scripture *n.* teoamoxtli
scrotum *n.* atexicolli, aloyotl
scrutinize *tv.* ixyehyecoa (*Preterit: onitlaixyehyecoh*)
scrutiny *n.* tlaixtemoliztli
sculpt *tv.* tlacuihccui (*Preterit: onitlacuihcuic*)
sculptor *n.* tlacuihcuic, tlacuihcuini
sculpture *n.* tlacuihcuiliztli
sea *n.* huey atl, ilhuica atl
sea lion *n.* amiztli
sea turtle *n.* ayotectli
seal *n.* nenecuilhuaztli, tecuilhuaztli
seamstress *n.* tlahtzonqui, tlahtzomani
search *tv.* temoa (*Preterit: ontlatemoh*)
season *n.* xiuhcahuitl
seat *n.* icpalli, tzinicpalli, yeyantli

secret *n.*ichtacayotl; *adj.* ichtacayoh
secretary *n.* amatlahcuiloh, tequitlahcuiloa, tequitlahcuiloh
secretly *adv.* ichtaca, ichteca
security *n.* tlacacoyeliztli
sedge *n.* tolin
sediment *n.* xachtli
seduce *tv.* xapotla (*Preterit: onitexapotlac*), xochihuia
   (*Preterit: onitexochihuih*)
seducer *n.* texapotla
see *tv.* itta (*Preterit: onitlaittac*), ihta (*Preterit: onitlaihtac*)
seed *n.* achtli, huachtli, chilachtli (*hot pepper*), xinachtli, pitztli
seem *iv.* neci (*Preterit: oninez*)
seemingly *adv.* yuhquimma
select *tv.* pehpena (*Preterit: onitlapehpen*)
self-esteem *n.* netlazohtlalizlti
selfishness *n.* neelehuiliztli, nexicolli
sell *tv.* namaca (*Preterit: onitlanamacac*), pochtecati
   (*Preterit: onipochtecatic*); ~ **cheaply** tlapihuilia
   (*Preterit: onitetlapihuilih*)
semen *n.* xinachyotl, oquichayutl, tlacaxinachtli, oquichotl
senate *n.* tecuhtlahtoliztli
senator *n.* tecuhtlahtoh
send *tv.* titlani (*Preterit: onitetitlan*)
sensation *n.* nematihuani
sensual *adj.* tlaelpaquini
sensuality *n.* tlaelpaquiliztli
sentence *n.* tetlatzontequiliztli; *tv.* tetlatzontequilia
   (*Preterit: onitetlatzonquilih*)
sentinel *n.* tlachixqui
separately *adv.* noncuah
separation *n.* nemacahualtiliztli
serenade *n.* yohualcuicatl, yohualcuicatlacaconi
serf *n.* tlacohtli

serfdom *n.* tlacohyotl
serious *adj.* nemalhuilli
seriousness *n.* nemalhuiliztli
sermon *n.* teotemachtilli, teteononotzaloni
serum *n.* chichihualixmexcayotl
servant *n.* coco, xolotl
servitude *n.* tequiyotl, tlacohyotl
settled *adj.* motlaliani, motlalih
seven *num.* chicome
sew *tv.* tlahtzoma (*Preterit: onitlahtzon*)
sewer *n.* atlacoyoctli (*drainage*)
sewing machine *n.* tepuztlahtzomaloni, tzomaliztepuztli,
    tepuztlamatzomaloni
sewn *adj.* tlahtzontli
sex *n.* nenepanoliztli, yuhquiznacayotl
sexual *adj.* yuh quiznacayoh; ~ **desire** *n.* tlanequiliztli
shadow *n.* cehualli, ecahuilli
shade *n.* cehualli, ecahuilli
shake *tv.* tzetzeloa (*Preterit: onitzetzeloh*)
shake hands *reflex. v.* momaquitzquia
    (*Preterit: oninomaquitzquih*)
shame *n.* pinahualiztli, pinahualiztli, pinahuiztli;
    with ~ *adv.* pinahuaca, pinauhtica
shameless *adj.* ahpinahuani, ahpinauhqui
shard *n.* tapalcatl, tepalcatl
sharp *adj.* teneh, tlatentilli
sharpen *tv.* tlatentia (*Preterit: onitlatenih*), yacahuitzoa
    (*Preterit: onitlayacahuitzoh*)
shatter *iv.* xamani (*Preterit: onixaman*)
shave *n.* neximaliztli; *reflex. v.* xima (*Preterit: oninoxin*);
    ~ **someone** *tv.* xima (*Preterit: ontexin*)
shawl *n.* pahyo
she *pron.* yeh, yehhuatl, yehuatl

shear *tv.* cuatezonoa (*Preterit: onitecuatezonoh*)
shed light on *tv.* tlanextia (*Preterit: onitlanextih*)
sheet *n.* tlaixpechotl
sheriff *n.* topileh
shell *n.* atzcalli, tecciztli (*conch*); eptli (*oyster*)
shellfish *n.* atlanchanehqueh
shepherd *n.* cuacuappixqui
shield *n.* chimalli
shin *n.* tetepontli, tlanitztli
shine *iv.* naltonahtimani (*Preterit: onaltonahtimanca*),
    petlani (*Preterit: onipetlan*); *tv.* petzoa
    (*Preterit: onitlapetzoh*)
shiny *adj.* ixpetlanqui, petztic
shipwreck *n.* acallapanaliztli
shirt *n.* coton
shiver *iv.* huihuitoca (*Preterit: onihuihuitocac*), papatlaca
    (*Preterit: onipapatlacac*)
shoe *n.* cactli, tecactli
shoe factory *n.* cacchihualoyan
shoe polish *n.* cactlilli (*black*)
shoe store *n.* cacnamacoyan
shoelace *n.* cacmecatl
shoemaker *n.* cacchiuhqui
shooting star *n.* cuitlapilyo citlalin
shopping *n.* tlacohualiztli
shore *n.* ilhuicaatentli
short *adj.* ahmo cuauhtic
shortly *adv.* aocmo huehcauh, zan cuel, zan cualcan, za ica
    in, zazan
shotgun *n.* matlequiquiztli
shoulder *n.* ahcolli, tepotztli, teputztli
shoulder blade *n.* ahcolchimalli
shout at *tv.* tetzahtzilia (*Preterit: onitetzahtzilih*)

shouting *n.* tetzahtzililiztli
shove *tv.* topehua (*Preterit: onitetopeuh*)
shovel *n.* tlaacanoni, huictli
show *tv.* tlanextilia (*Preterit: onitetlanextilih*)
shower *n.* netemalaciahualiztli
showing *n.* tlanextiliztli
shrimp *n.* chacalin
shrink *iv.* cototzahui (*Preterit: ocototzauh*)
shroud *n.* miccaquimiliuhcayotl, miccatequimilolli,
    mihcaquimiliuhcayotl, mihcatequimilolli
shrub *n.* tacatl
shy *adj.* temauhcaittani
sibling *n.* icuh
sick *adj.* cocoxqui; **be ~** *iv.* cocoya (*Preterit: onicocox*); *reflex.*
    v. mococoa (*Preterit: oninococoh*)
sickle *n.* tepuzotlapalhuaztli
sickly child *n.* tzipitl
sickness *n.* cocoliztli
side *n.* itzcalli, yomotlantli; **from the ~** *adv.* nacicic
side by side *adv.* centlapal
sideburn *n.* ixteliuhtzontli
siege *n.* tlayaoyahualoni; *tv.* yaoyahualoa
    (*Preterit: onitlayaoyahualoh*)
siesta *n.* tonayan cochiztli, tlahcotonatiuh cochiztli;
    take a ~ *iv.* tonayan cochi, tlahcotonatiuh cochi
    (*Preterit: tonayan or tlahcotonatiuh onicoch*)
sieve *n.* tlatzetzeloloni
sigh *n.* tzicunoliztli; *iv.* tzicunoa (*Preterit: onitzicunoh*)
sign *n.* machiyotl, nezcayotl; *reflex. v.* motcaihcuiloa
    (*Preterit: oninotocaihcuiloh*)
signal light *n.* tepuztlahuilmachiyotl
signature *n.* netocaihcuiloliztli
signify *tv.* nezcayotia (*Preterit: onitlanezcayotih*)

silence *n.* necahualiztli
silent *adj.* mocahuani, necauhtli; **be ~** *reflex. v.* mocahua
  (*Preterit: oninocauh*)
silently *adv.* necahualiztica
silk *n.* ocuilicpatl
silliness *n.* tlaixtomahualiztli
silly *adj.* tlaixtomahuac
silt *n.* tlalxayotl, zoquiatl
silver *n.* iztacteocuitlatl
silver mine *n.* iztacteocuitlaoztotl
similar *adj.* ixiuhqui
similarity *n.* quixnenehuiliztli
simple *adj.* centlaixtli, cemani
simplicity *n.* centlaixxotl, cemaniliztli, melahualiztli
simply *adv.* centlaixca, cemanca, melahuaca
sin *n.* tlahtlacolli; *tv.* ihtlacoa (*Preterit: onitlaihtlacoh,*
  onitlahtlacoh), pilchihua (*Preterit: onitlapilchiuh*)
since *conj.* yehica
sincere *adj.* yolmotquitiani
sincerity *n.* yolmotquitializtli
sinful *adj.* tlahtlacoloh
sing *iv.* cuica (*Preterit: onicuicac*)
singe *tv.* chinoa (*Preterit: onitlachinoh*)
singer *n.* cuicani
singing *n.* cuiquiztli; tzahtzilializtli (*of birds*)
single *n.* ahnamiqueh (*not married*)
sinister *adj.* ahmo melahuac, chicoyotl
sink *n.* tlapahpacoyan, nemahtequilcaxitl, tlapaconi,
  tlapohpohualoni; *iv.* actihuetzi (*Preterit: onactihuetz*)
sinner *n.* tlahtlacoani, tlapilchihuani
sip *n.* tlaltequiztli; *tv.* tlaltequi (*Preterit: onitlaltec*)
sister *n.* hueltiuhtli (*older*); teicuh (*younger*)
sister-in-law *n.* huepulli (*of a man*); huezhuaztli (*of a woman*)

sit down *reflex. v.* tlalia (*Preterit: oninotlalih*)
sit on one's heels *iv.* xoloca (*Preterit: onixolocatca*)
site *n.* onohuayan
sitting *adj.* motlaliani, motlalih
six *num.* chicuace
size *n.* tamachiuhcayotl, ixquichin
size up *tv.* cuecuepa (*Preterit; oniccuecuep*), iihta
  (*Preterit: oniquiihtac*)
skeleton *n.* miccacuahuitl, mihcacuahuitl
skeptical *adj.* ahneltocac
sketch *n.* tlatlilanaliztli; *tv.* tlilana (*Preterit: onitlatlilan*)
skill *n.* nematiliztli
skillful *adj.* ixtlamatqui
skillfully *adv.* mihmatca, mahmatca; **very ~** mahmatcatzin
skin *n.* ehuatl, ixehuatl (*facial*), topanehuayo, toehuayo
skinny *adj.* pitzahuac
skirmish *n.* neicaliliztli, neyaotlaliztli
skirt *n.* cueitl
skull *n.* cuaxicalli
skunk *n.* epatl, yepatl
sky *n.* ilhuicatl
skyscraper *n.* cencuauhticcalli
slab *n.* tepatlactli
slander *tv.* tlapiquia (*Preterit: onitetlapiquih*)
slap *n.* tecapactli; *tv.* tecapani (*Preterit: onitetecapan*)
slate *n.* tepetlatl (*stone*)
slave *n.* tlacohtli
slavery *n.* tlacohyotl
sleep *n.* cochiztli; *iv.* cochi (*Preterit: onicoch*)
sleeping quarters *n.* cochihualoyan
sleepwalker *n.* cochnenqui
sleepy *adj.* cochmiquini, tonalcochqui; **be ~** *iv.* cochmiqui
  (*Preterit: onicochmic*)

slender *adj.* piaztic, pitzahuac; **be ~** *iv.* pitzahua
    (*Preterit: onipitzahuac*)
slice *n.* tlacotontli, xoxotlalli; *tv.* xima (*Preterit: onitlaxim*)
slide *reflex. v.* alahua (*Preterit: oninalahuac*);
    n. nealahualoyan
slime *n.* tlalxayotl
sling *n.* tematlatl
slingshot *n.* tematlatl
slip *reflex. v.* alahua (*Preterit: oninalahuac*)
slip away *iv.* copini (*Preterit: onicopin*)
slippery *adj.* alactic, alahuac, alaztic, tepeztic
slope *n.* tepetlalli, tlehcoayan, tepeixco
slow *adj.* tancaxtic, yolic, motzicoani
slowly *adv.* ayaxcanyotica, ayaxcan, netzicoliztica, tlamach
slowness *n.* netzicoliztli
sluggish *adj.* motzicoani
sluggishness *n.* netzicoliztli
small toe *n.* xopilxocoyotl
smallness *n.* tepitoyotl
smallpox *n.* zahuatl
smear *tv.* zolotia (*Preterit: onitlazolotih*)
smear with mud *tv.* zoquialtia (*Preterit: onitlazoquialtih*)
smell *tv.* ihnecui (*Preterit: onitlahnecu*)
smile *n.* tenhuehuetzcaliztli; *iv.* ixhuetzca
    (*Preterit: oniixuetzcac*), tenhuehuetzca
    (*Preterit: onitenhuehuetzcac*)
smiling *adj.* ixhuetzqui
smirk *n.* nenemmictiliztli
smith *n.* tepuzpitzqui
smoke *n.* poctli, pocatl, pocyotl, ayahuitl; *iv.* popoca
    (*Preterit: onipopocac*); **~ cigarettes** *iv.* tlachichina
    (*Preterit: onitlachichin*)
smoked *adj.* poctic

smooth *adj.* peztic, tlamahtzin

snack *n.* cencamatl, tentlacihuiztli

snail *n.* cilin

snake *n.* coatl

sneeze *iv.* ecuxoa (*Preterit: onecuxoh*)

sneezing *n.* ecuxoliztli

snitch *n.* ichtacapitzani, ichtacateilhuini

snore *iv.* cochtotolca (*Preterit: onicochtotolcac*), zoloni
    (*Preterit: onizolon*), zozolca (*Preterit: onizozolcac*)

snow *n.* cehpayahuitl; *impers. v.* cehpayahuitl huetzi
    (*Preterit: cehpayahuitl ohuetz*), cehpayahui
    (*Preterit: ocehpayauh*)

snowfall *n.* pixahuiliztli

so *adv.* yuhqui (*in this manner*)

so much *adv.* ixquich

so that *conj.* inic

soak *tv.* ciyahua (*Preterit: onitlaciyauh*)

soaked *adj.* ciyahuac

soap *n.* xapo, amolli, tlapaconi, xapohtli

soapdish *n.* amolcaxitl

sob *iv.* tzicunoa (*Preterit: onitzicunoh*), choquiliztzahtzi
    (*Preterit: onichoquiliztzahtzic*)

sociable *adj.* tlacaicniuhtli

social *adj.* tlacaicniuhyoh

social gathering *n.* teicniuhnechicoliztli

society *n.* tlacaicniuhyotl

sock *n.* icxinequentiloni

sod *n.* cueptli, tlachcuitl, zacatzontetl

soft *adj.* tlamahtzin, yamactic, yamanqui, zoquitic

soil *tv.* zoquialtia (*Preterit: onitlazoquialtih*)

solace *n.* neyolaliliztli

soldier *n.* tiyahcauh, yaochiuhqui, yaoquizqui

sole *n.* cacxopetlatl (*shoe*), icxipehpechtli; icxopalli (*foot*), xocpalixtli, xocpalli

solemn *adj.* huey mahuiztic

solemnity *n.* hueicayotl, mahuizzotl

solid *adj.* chicactic, chicahuac, mahcic, tepitztic

solidity *n.* chicahualiztli, mahciconi

solitude *n.* cactimaniliztli, ayactlatlacatl

solution *n.* tlacualtiliztli

some day *adv.* quemmaniyan

someone *pron.* aca, aquin, te–

someone's *poss.* te–

something *pron.* itlah, tla–

something else *pron.* occe tlamantli

sometime *adv.* icah

sometimes *adv.* cehcehpa, quemman

somewhere *adv.* canah, cana

son *n.* oquichconetl, oquichpilli

son-in-law *n.* montli; ixhuiuhmontli (*great-son-in-law*)

song *n.* cuicatl

songbook *n.* cuicaamatl

soon *adv.* ihciuhca

soot *n.* calcuechtli, cuichtli, texcalcuichtli

sorcerer *n.* nahualli, chichtli

sorcery *n.* nahuallotl, nahualiztli

sore *n.* cocotl, palaxtli

sorrow *n.* tlaocolli

soul *n.* teyolitia, teyolia

sound *n.* caquiztli

sound wave *n.* caquilizmimilli

soundness *n.* chicahualiztli, mahciconi

soup tureen *n.* ciahualcaxitl

sour *adj.* xococ

source *n.* pehualiztli, meyalli

sourness *n.* xocoliztli, xocoyaliztli
south *adv.* huitztlampa
souvenir *n.* necauhcayotl
sow *tv.* pixoa (*Preterit: onitlapixoh*)
space *n.* tlacauhtli
spaceship *n.* cicitlaltepuzacalli
spacious *adj.* peltic
spade *n.* huictli
Spain *n.* Caxtillalpan
Spaniard *n.* Caxtillantlacatl, Caxtiltecatl
Spanish *n.* Caxtillantlahtolli (*language*); *adj.* Caxtillan;
    adv. **in ~** caxtillancopa
spark *n.* tlemoyotl, tlecuezallotl
sparrow *n.* molotl, teocaltototl
speak *iv.* tlahtoa (*Preterit: onitlahtoh*); **~ a foreign language**
    iv. pinotlahtoa (*Preterit: onipinotlahtoh*)
speak while asleep *iv.* cochtlahtoa (*Preterit: onicochtlahoth*)
spear *n.* tlacochtli
spear thrower *n.* ahtlatl
spearmint *n.* Caxtillan epazotl
specialist *n.* tlamah, tlamatqui, tlahmah, tlahmatqui
    (*physician*)
speech *n.* tlahtolli, tecpillahtolli (*formal*)
speed *n.* ihciuhcayotl, painaliztli
speedily *adv.* ihciuhca
speedy *adj.* ihciuhcayoh, painalli
spell *tv.* tempohua (*Preterit: onitlatempouh*), tenihtoa
    (*Preterit: onitlatenihtoh*); **cast a ~** *tv.* nahualhuia
    (*Preterit: onitenahualhuih*)
sperm *n.* xinachyotl, oquichayutl, oquichtotl
sphere *n.* ololli, tolontli
spherical *adj.* tolontic
spice *n.* tlanahnamic

spicy *adj.* cococ
spider *n.* tocatl
spiderweb *n.* tocatzahualli, tocazahualli
spin yarn *iv.* tzahua (*Preterit: onitzauh*)
spindle *n.* malacatl
spine *n.* cuitlapanteputzchichiquilli
spinster *n.* ahnamiqueh, ichpochcahualli, icnocihuatl
spire *n.* callapanhuetzian, teocallapanhuetzian
spirit *n.* yoliliztli, iihyotl
spiritual *adj.* iihyoh, teoyoh, yolilizoh
spirulina algae *n.* tecuitlatl
spit *iv.* chihcha (*Preterit: onichihchac*)
spleen *n.* elcomalli
splinter *n.* cuauhximalli, cuauhhuiztic
split *iv.* pitzini (*Preterit: opitzin*)
split in half *iv.* xelihui (*Preterit: oxeliuh*)
splitting hairs *n.* tzonocuilcualiztli
spoil *iv.* palani (*Preterit: onipalan*)
spoiled *adj.* palanqui
sponge *n.* zonecticulli
spongy *adj.* papatztic
spontaneously *adv.* nohmah
spoonful *n.* cecenxomahtli, cemacuahuitl, cenxomahtli
spotted *adj.* cuicuiltic
spouse *n.* tenamic
spout *n.* caxpializtli
spread *tv.* teca (*Preterit: onitlatecac*)
spread out *iv.* moloni (*Preterit: omolon*)
spring *n.* xopan, xopaniztli, xopantlah, xopaniztempan, (*season*); ameyalli (*water*)
sprinkle *tv.* chayahua (*Preterit: onitlachayauh*)
sprout *iv.* cueponi (*Preterit: onicuepon*)
spur *n.* tepuzhuitztli, cahuahyo itzapiniloca

spy *n.* ichtacatlachixqui, motepachihuih, tepipiani,
yaotlachixqui; *reflex. v.* pachihuia
(*Preterit: onicnopachihuih*)

squander *tv.* nenquixtia (*Preterit: onitlanenquixtih*)

square *n.* nauhcampa, tlanacazantli

squared *adj.* nauhcampa nacaceh

squash *n.* tlalayohtli (*wild*), tzilcayohtli (*bluish-green*)

squash flower *n.* ayohxochitl, ayoxochquilitl

squeeze *tv.* patzca (*Preterit: onitlapatzcac*)

squirrel *n.* chechelotl, chachalotl, cuauhtechalotl, motohtli,
techalotl, techelotl

stabbing pain *n.* tzitzicuincocoyaliztli

stable *n.* cahuahyocalli, cahuahcalli, mazacalli

staff *n.* topilli

stagger *reflex. v.* occampa olinia (*Preterit: occampa ninolinih*)

stain *n.* chichictli

staircase *n.* tlamamatlatl

stalk *n.* quiyotl, tlacotl

stalker *n.* tepipiani

stammer *iv.* elmimiqui (*Preterit: onelmimic*), eltzatzacui
(*Preterit: oneltzatzacuic*), poloni (*Preterit: onipolon*)

stamp *n.* amamachiotl, tecuilhuaztli; ihciuhcatitlanmachiyotl
(*postal*)

stand *iv.* ihcac (*Preterit: onihcaca*)

standing *adj.* ihcatoc

standard *n.* octacatl

stand up *reflex. v.* moquetza (*Preterit: oninoquetz*)

standing *adj.* ihcac

star *n.* citlalin, citlallin

starry *adj.* citlalloh

start a fire *iv.* tletlatlia (*Preterit: onitletlalih*)

stationary store *n.* amanamacoyan, amacalli

statue *n.* cuilli

stay *n.* nenactiliztli; *reflex. v.* nactia (*Preterit: oninonactih*)

steal *tv.* tlacuicui (*Preterit: onitlacuicuic*), ichtequi
(*Preterit: onitlaichtec*), nahualcui
(*Preterit: onitlanahualcuic*)

steam *n.* apocti, ihpotoctli

steam bath *n.* temazcalli; **take a ~** *reflex. v.* tema
(*Preterit: oninoten*)

steamed *adj.* xolonqui (*cooked*)

stem *n.* quiyotl, tlacotl

stench *n.* potoniliztli

step *n.* tlamamatlatl

stepchild *n.* tlacpaconetl

stepfather *n.* tlacpatahtli

stepmother *n.* chahuanantli, tlacpanantli

sterile *adj.* tetzacatl, tetzicatl

sterility *n.* tetzacayotl, tetzicayotl

stew *n.* ayotl, pozolli

steward *n.* calpixqui; **~ of a town festival** ilhuipixqui,
tlalhuipixqui

stewardship *n.* calpixcayotl

stick *n.* cuahuitl, tlacotl

sticky *adj.* zazaltic, tetzahuac

stiff *adj.* cuauhpitztic

still *adv.* nohmah, nohmatca, oc

still living *adj.* ocnemi

stimulate *tv.* yolacocui (*Preterit: oniteyolacocuic*), yolmaca
(*Preterit: oniteyolmacac*)

stimulation *n.* teyolahcocuiliztli

sting *n.* tetemminaliztli; *tv.* temmina (*Preterit: onitetemmin*)

stingy *n.* tzotzocatl

stink *iv.* potoni (*Preterit: onipoton*)

stinking *adj.* potonqui

stir *tv.* neloa (*Preterit: onitlaneloh*)

stirring *n.* olin

stitch *n.* centlazotl

stocking *n.* metznequentiloni

stomachache *n.* eltemiliztli

stomach *n.* ihtitl, ihtetl, ihtictli, xillantli, yoltitlan

stone *n.* tetl

stone cutter *n.* tetzotzonqui, texinqui, tetlapanqui, tetlapanani

stone grinder *n.* matetexoni, metlatl

stone stairway *n.* temamatlatl

stone wall *n.* tepamitl

stop *n.* nehuecauiliztli, nenactiliztli; *reflex. v.* huecahua
    (*Preterit: oninocauh*)

stork *n.* aztatl

storm *n.* atlatlacamahmaniliztli, amaniliztli

story *n* zanilli

stove *n.* tleamanalli

straight *adj.* melahuac, melactic, xitlahuac

straighten *tv.* melahua (*Preterit: onitlamelahuac*)

stranger *n.* huehca chaneh, huehca tlacatl, pinotl, chontalli

straw *n.* popotl

stream *n.* atoyapitzactli

street *n.* calhueyohtli, calohtli, caltzalantli, ohtli, ohcalli

strength *n.* tlapalihuiztli

stretch *tv.* tilinia (*Preterit: onitlatilinih*), tititza
    (*Preterit: onitlatititz*); *reflex. v.* (*yawn*) tititza
    (*Preterit: oninotititz*)

stretcher *n.* cuauhpantli

string *n.* icpatl, ichtli, mecatl, tepilolli

string bean *n.* epitzahuac

strip *n.* tlatentli

stroll *n.* paxalolli

strong *adj.* chicahuac, chicactic, oquichnacayoh, teputzeh, tlapaltic; **be ~** *iv.* huapahua (*Preterit: onihuapahuac*)

strongly *adv.* tlacuauh

stubborn *adj.* tzontetl; **be ~** *iv.* tzonteti (*Preterit: onitzontet*)

stubbornness *n.* aquimamachiliztli

student *n.* momachtiani

study *n.* nemachtiliztli, nemachtilli, tlaixmachiliztli; *reflex. v.* momachtia (*Preterit: oninomachtih*)

stuff *tv.* temitia (*Preterit: onitemitih*), ixhuitia (*Preterit: oniteixhuitih*)

stuffed *adj.* tenqui, ixhuic

stump *n.* tepuntic cuahuitl

stunned *iv.* cuayolhuinti (*Preterit: onicuayolhuintic*); *adj.* cuayolhuntic

stupid *adj.* ahyolloh, ixtecuecuech, tehpochtli, cantetic, yolquimil

stutter *iv.* elmimiqui (*Preterit: onelmimic*), eltzatzacui (*Preterit: oneltzatzacuic*), poloni (*Preterit: onipolon*)

stutterer *n.* elmimicqui

sty *n.* ixtomoniliztli

subjugate *tv.* panahuia (*Preterit: onitepanahuih*)

submerge *tv.* atlantema (*Preterit: onitlaatlanten*)

subside *iv.* cuetlani (*Preterit: onicuetlan*)

subsistence *n.* nencayotl

substitution *n.* neixiptlatiliztli

suburb *n.* altepemaitl, tenanquiahuatl

subway *n.* altepetepuzocuilin, tlallantepuztlahuilanalli

subway station *n.* altepetepuzocuilquixohuayan

subway train *n.* tlallantepuztlahuilanalli; tepuztlahuilanalli

success *n.* axiliztli, huel quizaliztli

successful *adj.* huel quizani

succession *n.* ontetoquiliztli

successively *adv.* tetoquiliztica

successor *n.* ontetoquiliani
suck *tv.* chichina (*Preterit: onitlachichin*), pipitzoa
  (*Preterit: onitlapipitzoh*)
suckle *iv.* chichi (*Preterit: onichichic*)
sudden *adj.* atenemachtih
suddenly *adv.* ateimachica, atenemachpan
suffer *iv.* tlapanohua (*Preterit: onitlapanouh*); tonehua
  (*Preterit: onitonehuac and onitoneuh*)
suffering *n.* tlapanoliztli
suffix *n.* tlahtollamiliztli
suffocate *iv.* iihyomiqui (*Preterit: oniihyomic*);
  reflex. v. iihyotzacua (*Preterit: oninihyotzauc*)
suffocating *adj.* teiihyotzacuani
suffocation *n.* teiihyo
sugar *n.* tlazopeliloni
sugar cane *n.* ohuatl
sugar cane juice *n.* ohuaatl
suicide *n.* nemictiliztli; **commit ~** *reflex. v.* momictia
  (*Preterit: oninomictih*)
suitable *adj.* tlamelauhcachihuani
sulfur *n.* tlequihquiztlalli
summer *n.* tonallan, xopaniztempa; **during ~** tonalco,
  tonallan
summit *n.* monamicyan, tlacpaccayotl
sun *n.* tonatiuh
sunburned *adj.* tonalmicqui
sunflower *n.* chimalxochitl
sunken *adj.* pachtic
sunny *impers. v.* tona (*Preterit: otonac*)
sunset *n.* aqui in tonatiuh, calaqui in tonatiuh
superstition *n.* neteomatiliztli
superstitious *adj.* neteomatini, neteomatqui
supper *n.* cochcayotl

supplement *n.* tlaaxiltiliztli; *tv.* axiltia (*Preterit: onitlaaxiltih*)

support *n.* tlachicahualtiliztli, tlatzitzquiliztli, tlanapaloliztli;
tv. tzitzquia (*Preterit: onitlatiztizquih*),
napaloa (*Preterit: onitlanapaloh*),
quitzquia (*Preterit: onitlaquitzquih*)

surface *n.* ixmaniliztli

surgeon *n.* texoxotlani, tlama, tlamatqui, tlahmah,
tlahmatqui

surgery *n.* texoxotlaliliztli

surname *n.* nenotzaloni, notzalli, ontetocaitl, ontocaitl

surprise *n.* neizahuiliztli; *tv.* ateimachitica ahci
(*Preterit: ateimachitica onicahcic*)

suspect *n.* itech chicotlamachoni; *iv.* chicotlamati
(*Preterit: onichicotlamat*)

suspense *n.* netzotzonaliztli, motzotzonaliztli

suspicion *n.* chicoyotl, chicotlamatiliztli, ayuhnematiliztli

suspicious *adj.* chicotlamatini, ayuhmomatini

svelte *adj.* piaztic

swallow *n.* cuicuitzcatl; *tv.* toloa (*Preterit: onitlatoloh*)

swamp *n.* ahnepanolli, zoquiatl

swear *iv.* tlalcua (*Preterit: onitlalcuah*), teoixpan nelihtoa
(*Preterit: teoixpan onelihtoh*)

swear in vain *iv.* tlapictennamiqui (*Preterit: onitlapoctennamic*)

sweat *n.* itonilli, tzotl, tzoyotl; *iv.* itoni (*Preterit: niiton*),
itonia (*Preterit: oniitonih*)

sweep *iv.* tlachpana (*Preterit: onitlachpan*)

sweet *adj.* necuhtic, tzopelic

sweet potato *n.* xiuhcamohtli

sweet water *n.* yecatl

sweetness *n.* necuhtiliztli, tzopelicayotl

swell *impers. v.* pozahui (*Preterit: opozauh*), pozahua
(*Preterit: opozahuac*)

swelling *n.* pozahuiliztli, nanahuatl
swim *iv.* tlamaneloa (*Preterit: onitlamaneloh*), mahuitequi
   (*Preterit: onitlmahuitec*)
swimmer *n.* tlamaneloani
swimming pool *n.* tlamaneloloyan
swindle *tv.* teixcuepa (*Preterit: oniteixcuep*)
swollen *adj.* pozactic, pozahuac
swoon *iv.* zotlahua (*Preterit: onizotlahuac*)
sword *n.* tepuzmacuahuitl, matepuztli
symbol *n.* nenehuiloni
symbolize *iv.* nenehuia (*Preterit: oninenehuih*)
symphony *n.* centlapitzaliztli
symptom *n.* cocoliznexiloni
syrup *n.* necuhpathli, ohuatl, necuhtli;
   cane ~ *n.* ohuanecuhtli; **corn ~** *n.* ohuanecuhtli

T

table *n.* ahcopechtli, cuauhtlapechtli
tadpole *n.* atepocatl, atolocatl
tail *n.* cuitlapilli
tailor *n.* tlahtzonqui, tlahtzomani
tailor shop *n.* tlahtzomaloyan
take *tv.* ana (*Preterit: onican*), cui (*Preterit: oniccuic*)
take off one's shoes *reflex. v.* caccopina
   (*Preterit: oninocacopin*)
take out *tv.* quixtia (*Preterit: onitlaquextih*)
take revenge *reflex. v.* tzoncui (*Preterit: oninotzoncuic*)
talent *n.* tlachializtli
talk with *tv.* nonotza (*Preterit: onitenonotz*)
talkative *adj.* papal, popoloc, teneh tlahtoleh
tall *adj.* cuauhtic, cuahcuauhtic, huecapantic

tamale *n.* tamalli; **make ~** *tv.* tamalchihua
  (*Preterit: onitamalchiuh*), *iv.* tamaloa (*Preterit: onitamaloh*)
tamarind *n.* cuauhmochitl, cuemochitl
tambourine *n.* ehuahuehuetl
tangle *tv.* pazaloa (*Preterit: onitlapazaloh*); *n.* tlapazolotl
taper *tv.* yacapitzahua (*Preterit: onitlayacapitzahuac*),
  yacahuitzoa (*Preterit: onitlayacahuitzoh*)
tapered *adj.* yacahuitztic, yacapitzahuac, yacapitzactic
taepworm *n.* cuitlacoatl
tardiness *n.* huehcahualiztli
tariff *n.* hualpatiuhtli
taste *n.* huelicayotl, hueliliztli, tlapalolizlti;
  tv. paloa (*Preterit: onitlapaloh*),
  huelicamati (*Preterit: onic-huelicamat*)
tasty *adj.* huelic, hueltic, tzopelic
tattletale *n.* ichtacapitzani, ichtacateilhuini
taut *adj.* tilinqui, tilictic, tilintoc
tax *n.* tequitl, tlacalaquilli
tea *n.* atlapozonilli
teach *tv.* machtia (*Preterit: onitemachtih*)
teacher *n.* temachtiani, temachtihqui
teaching *n.* nemachtiliztli, tlanextiliztli
tear *n.* ixayotl
teeth *n.* tlantli; **front ~** tlanixcuatl
telegram *n.* tepuzicpatemachiltiliztli,
  tepuzicpateiximachtiloni
telegraph *n.* tepuzicpamacuecuetzoloni
telegraph office *n.* tepuzicpamacuecuetzoloyan
telephone *n.* huehca tlahtolli, quiquiztozcapanahuiloni,
  tenonotzaloni, tlanonotzaloni
telephone call *n.* quiquiztozcapanahuilli;
  make a ~ *iv.* quiquiztozcapanahuia
  (*Preterit: oniquiquiztozcapanahuih*)

telephone number *n.* tlahtoltlapohualmachiyutl, ipohual
   tlanonotzaloni, tlanonotzalontlapohualli, pohualiztli
   itlanonotzaloni
telephone office *n.* quiquiztozcapanahuiloyan,
   tecciztozcapanahuiloyan
telephone operator *n.* quiquiztozcapanauhqui
telescope *n.* nehuehcatlahicaloni, tehuiloixtli
television *n.* huehca tlachializtli, huehca tlachializtepuztli
tell *tv.* pohua (*Preterit: onitlapouh*)
tell jokes *tv.* xochhuia (*Preterit: onitexochhuih*)
temperature *n.* tetotoncaimachiyoca
temple *n.* teocalli, teopantli (*worship*); canahuacantli (*head*)
temporarily *adv.* tepantlayecohuaca
temporary *adj.* tepantlayecohuani
temptation *n.* teneyeyecoltiliztli
ten *num.* mahtlactli
tenant *n.* motlanehuiani
tender *adj.* celic, piltic
tenderness *n.* celticayotl
tense *n.* cahuitl (*time*); *adj.* tilinqui, tilictic, tilintoc
termite *n.* cuauhocuilin
terrace *n.* tlapanco, tohpolli
terrible *adj.* cencatlahuelli
terrifying *adj.* cecepatic
territory *n.* necallotiloyan
terror *n.* tenemauhyotl
test *n.* yecolli (*general*); tlamachtilyehyecoliztli (*student*);
   tv. yecoa (*Preterit: onitlayecoh*), ixyehyecoa
   (*Preterit: onitlayehyecoh*)
testament *n.* miccanecahualiztli, nemiquiznenahuatiliztli
testicle *n.* atetl, yoyomoctli, tzintomapilcac
testify *tv.* neltilia (*Preterit: onitlaneltilih*)
testimony *n.* tlaneltiliztli

thank *tv.* tlazohcamati (*Preterit:* onictlazohcamat)

thank you *interj.* tlazohcamati

that *pron.* inon

the *art.* in

theater box *n.* tlapechneittaloni

theater *n.* ixehuaniliztli, tepantlayeyecalhuiloyan

theft *n.* ichtequiliztli

their *poss.* im–, in–

themselves *reflex. pron.* mo–

then *adv.* niman, ihcuaquinon, in ihcuac

theologian *n.* teotlamatini

theology *n.* teotlamatiliztli

there *adv.* ompa, uncan

there will be *iv.* onyez, yez

therefore *conj.* anca

thermometer *n.* atonahuiztamchihualoni,
  totoniliztamachihualoni

thesis *n.* tetlatzohuilililiztli

they *pers. pron.* yehhuantin, yehhuan, yehuantin, yehuan

thick *adj.* chamahuac, tzintomahuac (*at the base*)

thick centered *adj.* yollochamahuac

thicken *iv.* tlatetzahua (*Preterit:* onitlatetzahuac)

thicket *n.* milpazolli

thief *n.* ichtecqui, tetlacuicuiliani

thigh *n.* metztli, maxatl, maxactli

thimble *n.* tepuztlatzumaloni

thin *adj.* canahuac, piltic, pitzahuac, cuauhpitztic,
  tzinpitzahuac (*at the base*); **be ~** *iv.* pitzahua
  (*Preterit:* onipitzahuac); **become ~** *iv.* caxahua
  (*Preterit:* onicaxahuac)

thing *n.* tlamantli

think *reflex. v.* yolmaxiltia (*Preterit:* oninoyolmaxiltih);
  tv. nemilia (*Preterit:* onitlanemilih)

thinker *n.* moquexquitzahuiani
thirst *n.* amiquiliztli, amiquiztli
thirsty *adj.* amiquini; **be ~** *iv.* amiqui (*Preterit: onamic*)
thirteen *num.* matlactli onei
this *pron.* inin
thistle *n.* tlapatl
thorn *n.* huitztli, ahuatl
though *adv.* immanel, intlanel
thought *n.* tlalnamiquiliztli
thoughtless *adj.* tlaixtomahuac
thoughtlessly *adv.* ilihuiz
thoughtlessness *n.* tlaixtomahualiztli
thread *n.* icpatl, ichtli
threat *n.* temahmauhtiliztli
threaten *tv.* mamauhtia (*Preterit: onitemamauhtih*),
    miquiztlalhuia (*Preterit: onitemiquiztlalhuih*)
three *num.* yei
threshold *n.* tlaixcuahuitl
throat *n.* cocohtli, tozcatl, tozquitl
throat infection *n.* zahuactli
throne *n.* tlahtocaicpalli, tlahtocayeyantli
throng *n.* miectlacatl
throw *tv.* tlaza (*Preterit: onitlatlaz*)
throw down *tv.* tlaza (*Preterit: onitlatlaz*)
thumb *n.* huey mapilli, mapiltecuhtli
thunder *n.* tlatecuintli
thus *adv.* yuhqui
tibia *n.* tlanitztli
tick *n.* mazaatemitl (*parasite*), pepeyoctli (*parasite*), ixcauhtli
    (*parasite*)
ticket *n.* amatlahcuilotontli
tickle *tv.* quehqueloa (*Preterit: ontequehqueloh*)

ticklish *adj.* quehqueleh; **be ~** *iv.* cuecueyoca
  (*Preterit: onicuecueyocac*)
ticklishness *n.* cuecueyoctli, quehquelli
tide *n.* acueyotl
tie *tv.* ilpia (*Preterit: onitlalpix*)
tight *adj.* tilinqui, tilictic, tilintoc
tighten *tv.* tilinia (*Preterit: onitlatilinih*); *iv.* tilini
  (*Preterit: onitilin*)
tilde *n.* tlatliltzicuiniliztli
tile *n.* tlaxiuhzaloloni
tile roof *n.* tapalcatlapantli
time *n.* cahuitl; *adv.* **it is ~** yeh imman, immani, yeh oncan;
  at the right ~ *adv.* imonequiyan; **~ of death** *n.* miquian,
  miquiztentli
timekeeper *n.* cahuitamachihuani
timid *adj.* pinotic
tin *n.* amochitl
tinder *n.* tlexotlaltiloni
tinsel *n.* teocuitlaamatl
tip *n.* yacatl
tire *n.* oltemalacatl
tired *adj.* ciciammicqui; **be ~** *iv.* ciahui (*Preterit: oniciauh*)
title *n.* amoxmachiotl, tlatocayotl
toad *n.* tamazolin, tamazollin, caca
toast *tv.* icequi (*Preterit: onitlacec*)
toasted *adj.* tlacetli
toasted corn chip *n.* totopochtli
tobacco *n.* picietl, tlachichinalli
tobacco flower *n.* yexochitl
tobacco leaf *n.* picihyatl
today *adv.* axcan
toe *n.* xopilli
toenail *n.* xopiliztitl, xopiliztetl, iztetl

together *adv.* cepantin, netloc, nehuan
toilet *n.* cuitlacalli
toilet paper *n.* tzinpohpoalamatl
tolerance *n.* yolloyamancayotl, tlayollotepitzhuiliztli
tolerant *adj.* moyollotepitztiliani
tolerate *tv.* oquichhuia (*Preterit: onitlaoquichhuih*);
    reflex. v. yollotepitztilia (*Preterit: oninoyollotepitztilih*)
tomato *n.* tomatl, xitomatl
tomb *n.* miccapetlacalli, mihcapetlacalli, tepetlacalli
tombstone *n.* miccatetl
tomorrow *adv.* moztla
tomorrow afternoon *adv.* moztla teotlac
tongs *n.* tepuztlaanoni
tongue *n.* nenepilli
tonsil *n.* quechtlatlahualli, quechtlatlaollotl
too *adv.* no
too much *adv.* zazan
tool *n.* tepuztlatlatquitl
tooth *n.* tlantli, coatlantli (*canine*)
tooth decay *n.* tlancualoliztli, tlampalanaliztli
toothbrush *n.* netlampohpoaloni, netlammatiloloni,
    tlantlachichiconi
toothpick *n.* netlancuihcuihuani, netlanyectiloni
top *n.* monamicyan, tlacpaccayotl
topic *n.* netlahtolpehpechtiliztli
torch *n.* cuauhocotl, ocopilli (*made of pine branches*), ocotl
torn *adj.* coyauhqui
tornado *n.* mixcoatl
torso *n.* tlactli
tortilla *n.* tlaxcalli; **make tortillas** tlaxcalchihua
    (*Preterit: onitlaxcalchiuh*), tlaxalmana
    (*Preterit: onitlaxcalman*); *iv.* tlaxcaloa (*onitlaxcaloh*)
tortilla stand *n.* tlaxcalnamacoyan

toss and turn *reflex. v.* mocuecueptinemi
    (*Preterit: oninocuecueptinen*)
total *n.* tlacempohualiztli
totter *reflex. v.* occampa olinia (*Preterit: occampa ninolinih*)
toward *prep.* huic, –copa
towel *n.* nemapopohualoni
town *n.* altepetl, atl tepetl, chinamitl
town crier *n.* tecpoyotl, tzatzani
towrope *n.* huey mecatl
toy *n.* chayelahuiltiloni, pepetotl
trace *n.* necauhcayotl
track *n.* nemachiyohtiloni
trade *n.* tlapaliliztli; *tv.* tlapatla (*Preterit: onitlapatlac*)
tradition *n.* tlahtollotl, tlamanitiliztli
trail *n.* ohpitzactli, ohtli; mazaohtli (*animal*)
train *n.* tepuzcoatl, tepuzocuilin, tepuztlahuilanalli
train station *n.* tepuzocuilquixohuayan
training *n.* nemachtiliztli
traitor *n.* necoc yaotl
trample *tv.* quequeza (*Preterit: onitlaquequez*)
tranquil *adj.* motlaliani, motlalih
tranquility *n.* tlacaconemiliztli
transfer *n.* necuanaliztli
translate *tv.* tlahtolcuepa (*Preterit: onitlatolcuep*);
    ~ **into Nahuatl** *tv.* nahuatlahtolcuepa (*Preterit:*
    onicnahuatlahtolcuep); ~ **into Spanish**
    tv. caxtillantlahtolcuepa (*Preterit: oniccaxtillantlahtolcuep*)
translation *n.* tlahtolcuepaliztli, tlacueptli tlahtolli
transparency *n.* tehuilticayotl
transparent *adj.* naltonac, tehuiltic, naltoctic;
    be ~ *iv.* (*Preterit: onaltonac*)
transport *tv.* zaca (*Preterit: onitlazacac*), zazaca
    (*Preterit: onitlazazacac*)

trap *n.* tlapehualli
trash *n.* tlahzolli, tlahzollalli
travel *iv.* ohtoca (*Preterit: oniohtocac*); *n.* ohtlatocaliztli
traveler *n.* nehnemini, nehnenqui, yani
treasure *n.* teocuitlacayotl
treasurer *n.* teocuitlapixqui
treasury *n.* teocuitlapixcoyan, teocuitlapixcalli
treaty *n.* nenahualiztli
tree *n.* cuahuitl, tetepontli
tree trunk *n.* cuauhtlactli, cuauhtzontetl
tree with fruit *n.* xocoyoh
tremble *iv.* cuetlani (*Preterit: onicuetlan*)
trench *n.* cuemitl
triangle *n.* yexcampa
tribunal *n.* tlacacoyan
trick *n.* nemachtli
trim *tv.* xipehua (*Preterit: onitlaxipeuh*)
trip *n.* nehnemiliztli
triplets *n.* tenamaztli
triumph *n.* tepanahuiliztli
trough *n.* mazatlacualtiloyan, mazacualoyan,
    cahuahtlacualoyan
trout *n.* xiomichin
trowel *n.* tenextlazaloloni, tlaaquiltetl
truce *n.* neyaocehuiliztli
true *adj.* nelli, neltic, melahuac
truly *adv.* nel
trumpet *n.* tepuzquiquiztli/tecciztli (*conch*)
trumpeter *n.* tepuzquiquizoani/tepuzquiquizpitzani
trumpline *n.* mecapalli
trunk *n.* tetepontli
trust *n.* temachtli, temachyotl
truth *n.* neltiliztli

tub *n.* apazyahualli, hueyapaztli

tuberculosis *n.* huaccatlatlaxiztli, tetzauhcocoliztli;
     having ~ *adj.* tetzauhcocolizoh

tuft *n.* papachtli

tumble *iv.* xitini (*Preterit: onixitin*)

tumor *n.* palancapozahualiztli, pozahuacayotl, xoxalli

tune *tv.* caccualtilia (*Preterit: onitlacaccualtilih*), tectema
     (*Preterit: onitlatecten*)

tuner *n.* tlacaccualtiliani (*person*), tlacaccualtililoni (*device*),
     tlatectemaloni

tuning *n.* tlacaccualtiliztli

Turk *n.* Tolquian chaneh

Turkey *n.* Tolquian

Turkish *n.* Tolquiantlahtolli (*language*)

turkey *n.* huexolotl, huehxolotl

turkey stew *n.* totollaapozonilli

turn *n.* cuepcayotl

turn back *iv.* tzinquiza (*Preterit: onitzinquiz*), iloti
     (*Preterit: onilot*)

turn over *tv.* cuecuepa (*Preterit: ontilacuecuep*)

turnover *n.* tlaoyotl

turpentine *n.* tzotl

turquoise *n.* xihuitl, teoxihuitl (*fine*), tzitzitl (*used in
     mosaics*), xipalli, xiuhtomolli; *adj.* xiuhpaltic

turtle *n.* ayotl

turtledove *n.* cocohtli

tutor *n.* tlacazcaltiani, tlacahuapauhqui, tlacazcaltih

tweezers *n.* neixcuamotzompihuani, tepuzcuacualoni

twelve *num.* mahtlactli omome

twenty *num.* cempohualli

twin *n.* coatl

twist *tv.* malina (*Preterit: onitlamalin*)

twisted *adj.* colihtic, coltic, malinqui

two *num.* ome
two-faced *adj.* omeyolloh
type *n.* tlacopinalli (*kind*); *tv.* tepuztlahcuiloa
    (*Preterit: onitepuztlahcuiloh*)
typewriter *n.* tepuztlahcuiloloni
typhoon *n.* ehecamalacotl, yehcamalacotl
typist *n.* tepuztlahcuiloh

U

ugliness *n.* ahmo tlacalnexiliztli
ugly *adj.* ahmo cualneci
ulcer *n.* palaxtli
umbilical cord *n.* xicmecayotl
umbrella *n.* atlapachoni
unanimity *n.* tlahtolcentlalilli, tlahtolnamiquiliztli
unanimous *adj.* tlahtolnamic; **be ~** mocentlalia in totlahtol
    (*Preterit: omocentlalih in totlahtol*)
unanimously *adv.* tlahtolcentlaliztica, tlahtolnamiquiliztica
uncle *n.* tlahtli, tlacpaicniuhtli (*a parent's brother*)
uncleanliness *n.* catzactiliztli
uncooked *adj.* ayahmo icuhci, ayamo huicci
uncover *tv.* tlapoa (*Preterit: onitlahtlapoh*), tlapohua
    (*Preterit: onitlahtlapouh*)
uncultivated land *n.* zacaixtlahuatl
undecided *adj.* cototzic
underarm *n.* ciyacatl, ciacatl, zecactli
underarm odor *n.* chipahyayaliztli
underbrush *n.* milpazolli
understand *tv.* yeccaqui (*Preterit: onitlayeccac*);
    ~ correctly *tv.* melahuacacaqui
    (*Preterit: onitlamelahuacacac*);
    ~ well *tv.* nalquizcacaqui (*Preterit: onitlanalquizcacac*)

understanding *n.* ahcihcamatiliztli, tlaixaxiliztli
understood *adj.* tlacactli
undertaker *n.* miccaquimiloani
uneasiness *n.* teamanaliztli
unending *adj.* aictlanqui
unforgivable *adj.* ahtlapopolhuilloh
unfortunate *adj.* nenquizani, nenquizqui
unfortunately *adv.* nenquizaliztica
unhappy *adj.* nenquizani; **be ~** nenquiza (*Preterit: oninenquiz*)
unhealthful *adj.* ahpahtihuani
uniformity *n.* nenneuhcayotl
union *n.* cetiliztli
United States *n.* Cepanca Tlahtohcayotl, Tlahtohcayotl
    in Cepanca
unity *n.* cetiliztli, necetiliztli
universal *adj.* nohhuianyoh
universally *adv.* nohhuianyotica
universe *n.* cemanahuatl
university *n.* calmecac, telpochcalli
unjust *adj.* ahmo cualli, ahmo melahuac
unjustly *adv.* ahmelahualiztica
unmarried *adj.* ahnamiqeh
unoccupied *adj.* cacticac
unravel *tv.* caxania (*Preterit: onitlacaxanih*)
unreliable *adj.* yolnentic
unroll *tv.* toma (*Preterit: onitlaton*)
unsanitary *adj.* ahpahtihuani
unskilled laborer *n.* tlaquehualli
unsociable *adj.* temauhcaittani
unstable *adj.* yolnentic
untie *tv.* caxania (*Preterit: onitlacaxanih*); tohtoma
    (*Preterit: onitlatohton*)

until *adv.* ixquichca, ixquichcauh
unwind *tv.* toma (*Preterit: onitlaton*)
up *adv.* ahco, pani, tlacpac, tlehco
upholster *tv.* tilmahtlazaloa (*Preterit: onitilmahtlazaloh*)
upholsterer *n.* tilmahtlazaloani
upholstery *n.* tilmahtlazalolli
upright *adj.* ixmelactic
uprising *n.* tehuicpanehualli
uproar *n.* chachalaquiztli
upset *adj.* pozonqui
upside down *adv.* ixtlahpach
upward *adv.* ahcohuic
urban *adj.* coyotl
urethra *n.* acayotl, axixpiztli
urge *n.* tlanenequiliztli
urinal *n.* axixcomitl, cuitlacomitl, neaxixaloyan
urinate *reflex. v.* axixa (*Preterit: oninaxix*); *iv.* tlapiazohua
    (*Preterit: onitlapiazouh*)
urine *n.* axixtli, tlapiaztli
urn *tv.* petlacalli
usable *adj.* aaquiloni, aaquilloh
use *tv.* aaquia (*Preterit: ontlaaquih*), xexelaquia
    (*Peterit: onitlaxexelaquih*); ~ **for first time**
    tv. chalia (*Preterit: onitlachalih*),
    yancuilia (*Preterit: ontlayancuilih*)
useful *adj.* aaquilli, tlaxexelaquilli
usefulness *n.* aaquillotl, tlaxexelaquillotl

V

vacant *adj.* cacticac
vacation *n.* tlacehuilizpan, nemachtilizcehuillotl (*school*)
vaccinate *tv.* pahmatzopinia (*Preterit: onitepahmatzopinih*)

vaccination *n.* tlatzopiniliztli, tlapahmatzopiniliztli
vacuum cleaner *n.* tepuztlacuihcuiloni
vagabond *n.* nehnenqui
vagina *n.* cihuanacayotl, cihuatl iacayo
vain *adj.* ahuillahtoani, chachamahuani, mopouhqui;
    adv. **in ~** nen, nempanca, zan nenca
valid *adj.* nahuatillapaltli
validity *n.* nahuatillapaltiliztli
valley *n.* atlahuitl, atlauhtli, atlauhxomolli, teotlalli, tepeihtic
valuable *adj.* tlazohtli, cencapatiyoh
value *n.* patiyotl
vampire *n.* teyollocuani
vanilla *n.* tlilxochitl, cuauhmecaexotl
vanity *n.* chachamahualiztli
vapor *n.* apoctli, ihpotoctli, pocyotl, tlalli ipocyoh
variable *adj.* yollocuecuepqui
various *adj.* nepapan
vassal *n.* temacehual
vegetable *n.* quilitl, xiuhtlacualli, quiltonilli
vegetable patch *n.* quilmilli
vegetable salad *n.* xiuhtlacualli
vegetable soup *n.* quilatl
vegetarian dish *n.* quilmolli
vein *n.* cocoyotl, ecayotl, ezcocohtli
vendor *n.* tlanamacac
venerate *tv.* yectenehua (*Preterit: onitlayecteneuh*)
venereal disease *n.* tlacahzolnanahuatl, nanahuatl;
    have ~ *iv.* nanahuati (*Preterit: oninahuatic*)
venison *n.* mazanacatl
venom *n.* coaiztlactli (*snake*)
ventilate *tv.* ehecatia (*Preterit: onitlaehecatih*)
ventilation *n.* tlaehecatiliztli, tlayehyecatiliztli, yehyecatiliztli
ventilator *n.* tlaehecatiloni, tlaehecahuiloni

verb *n.* tlachihualiztlahtolli, aitiliztlahtolli, tlachichualiztli
verifiable *adj.* neltililoni
verification *n.* neltiliztli, neltiloni
verify *tv.* neltilia (*Preterit: onicneltilih*)
very *adv.* cenca, huel
very bad *adj.* cencatlahuelli
very early *adv.* oc yohuahtzinco, oc ihuahtzinco
very well *adv.* cenca cualli
vest *n.* xicolli
vestige *n.* nellimachiyotl
vestment *n.* teopixcatlatquitl
veterinarian *n.* yolcapahmatini, yolcapahtiani
veterinary medicine *n.* yolcapahmatiliztli
vibrate *iv.* papatlaca (*Preterit: onipapatlacac*)
vice *n.* ahuilquizaliztli, teuhtli tlahzolli
victim *n.* netlahahualmicqui
victory *n.* tepololiztli, tlatlanilzitli
view *n.* tlachializtli, tlachialoni; *tv.* tlachia (*Preterit: onitlachix*)
vigil *n.* tlapializtli
village *n.* altepemaitl
vine *n.* xocomecatl, temecatl
vinegar *n.* vino xococ
vineyard *n.* xocomecamilli
violence *n.* tlacamazayotl, tetlachihualtiliztli
violent *n.* tlacamazatl
virginity *n.* huelichpochotl, ichpochyotl
virile *adj.* oquichnacayoh
virility *n.* oquichyollohtli
virtue *n.* cualtiliztli, yectiliztli
virtuous *adj.* cualli iyollo, yectli iyollo, cualnemiliceh
visible *adj.* ittoni, ihtoni, itztoc
vision *n.* tlachializtli
visit *n.* onteittaliztli, teittaliztli

visitor *n.* onteittani

vocabulary *n.* tlahtoltecpanaliztli, tlahtoltecpantli, tlacontemaliztlahtolli

vocation *n.* teyolnotzaloni

voice *n.* tozcatl, tozquitl

volcanic rock *n.* tezontli

volume *n.* ixquichin

voluminous *adj.* ixquichic

voluntarily *adv.* cealiztica

vomit *n.* nehzotlaliztli, tlaihzotlalli;
   reflex. v. ihzotia (*Preterit: ninihzotih*);
   reflex. v. ihzotla (*Preterit: oninihzotlac*),
   xochtia (*Preterit: onixochtih*)

vow *n.* nehtolli, nehtoltiliztli

vowel *n.* icelticaquiztli

vulgar *adj.* ahtlacatlahtoani

vulture *n.* cozcacuauhtli, tzohpilotl

vulva *n.* maxactli, tepilli

W

wafer *n.* yoltextlaxcalli

wage *n.* patiuhtli, patiyotl

waist *n.* pitzahuayan, topitzahuayan, tlahcoyan

wait *tv.* chia (*Preterit: onitechix*)

waiter *n.* tetlacualtiani

waiver *reflex. v.* omeyollohua (*Preterit: oninomeyollohuac*)

wake *iv.* cochehua (*Preterit: oninococheuh*), ihza
   (*Preterit: onihzac*); *tv.* cochehua (*Preterit: onitecocheuh*)

walk *iv.* nehnemi (*Preterit: oninehnen*)

wall *n.* tenamitl, tepantli

walnut tree *n.* michpahtli

want *tv.* nequi (*Preterit: onitlanec*)

war *n.* mitl chimalli, yaoyotl; *tv.* **make ~** yaochichua
 (*Preterit: oniteyaochiuh*); **weapons of ~** yaotlatquitl

war song *n.* yaocuicatl

wardrobe *n.* cihuatlatlatquitl (*female*)

warehouse *n.* tlapialoyan

warn *iv.* xoneca (*Preterit: onixonexcac*)

warped *adj.* pachtic

warrior *n.* yaoquizqui

wart *n.* michinix, tzocatl

was *iv.* catca

wash *tv.* paca (*Preterit: onitlapacac*)

wash bowl *n.* nematequilcaxitl, nematequiloni

wash one's hands *reflex. v.* matequia (*Preterit: oninomatequih*)

washing machine *n.* iceltlaquempapaconi

wasp *n.* tetocani (*yellow*), tlaletzalli, tlaletzatl (*brown*)

waste *tv.* nenquixtia (*Preterit: onitlanenquixtih*),
 tlanenpoloa (*Preterit: onitlanenpoloh*),
 tlahzolchihua (*Preterit: onitlahzolchiuh*)

watch *tv.* pia (*Preterit: onitlalpix*)

water *n.* atl; (**to**) **~** *tv.* ahuilia (*Preterit: onitlaahuilih*), atequia
 (*Preterit: onitlaatequih*)

water down *tv.* ayotia (*Preterit: onitlayotih*)

water flower *n.* atenxochitl

water level *n.* atezcaittaloni

water source *n.* ameyalli

water vapor *n.* apoctli

watercress *n.* atzanalquilitl, atezquilitl

waterfall *n.* apipiloyac

waterspout *n.* ehecamalacotl, yehcamalacotl

watery *adj.* ayoh

wave *n.* acueyotl, amimilli

wavy *adj.* acuenyoh

wax *n.* xicohcuitlatl
we *pron.* tehhuan, tehhuantin, ti–
weak *adj.* zotlahuac
weaken *reflex. v.* zotlahua (*Preterit: oninozotlahuac*)
weakness *n.* zotlahualiztli
wealth *n.* miec axcaitl, miec tlatquitl, netlamachtilli
wealthy *adj.* axcahuah, hueyaxcahuah, tlatquihuah
weapon *n.* tlahuitztli, yaotlatquitl
weasel *n.* cozahtli, cozamatl
weave *iv.* ihquiti (*Preterit: onihquit*), tzahua (*Preterit: onitzauh*)
wedding *n.* nemanepanoliztli
wedge *n.* tepuztlatlilli
weed *n.* zacahuitztli, quilitl; **place full of weeds** xiuhtlah
week *n.* chicueyilhuitl
weigh *tv.* nenehuilia (*Preterit: onitlanenehuilih*), pexohuia
     (*Preterit: onitlapexohuih*), tamachihua
     (*Preterit: onitlatamachiuh*)
weight *n.* etiliztli
weld *iv.* tepuzaloa (*Preterit: onitepuzaloh*)
well *n.* atlacomolli atlacuihuayan; *adv.* cualli ic, huel, yec;
     feel ~ *iv.* huelmati (*Preterit: onihuelma*)
welt *n.* tatapalihuiztli
west *n.* cihuatlampa, tonatiuh icalaquiyan
western *adj.* tonatiuh icalaquiyancayotl
wet *adj.* pahpaltic, paltic
wet one's bed *iv.* cochtlapiazohua (*Preterit: onicochtlapiazouh*)
wharf *n.* acaltecoyan
what *interr. pron.* tle, tlein
wheel *n.* amalacachtli, temalacatl, yahualli
when *adv.* ihcuac, iquin, in y
when? *interr. adv.* quemman, itquin, ic, iquin
whenever *adv.* zaciquin
where *adv.* can, campa, canin

which *interr. pron.* catleh, catlehhuatl, cahtli

while *adv.* nonca, noca; **in a short ~** zan cualcan, zan cuel;
   conj. in oquic

whim *n.* tlenenequiliztli

whip *n.* mecahuiteconi, temecahuiteconi

whirlpool *n.* axictli

whirlwind *n.* huey ehecatl, huey yehyecatl

whisper *reflex. v* ichtacanonotza (*Preterit: oninichtacanonotz*)

whistle *n.* chichtli, mapihpichtli; *iv.* mapihpichoa
   (*Preterit: onimapihpichoh*)

white *adj.* iztac, iztactic

white bean *n.* iztaquetl

white hair *n.* tzoniztalli

white-haired *adj.* tzoniztac

whitefish *n.* amilotl

who *pron.* ac, aquin

whole *adj.* cenquizqui, centetl, motquitini

wholly *adv.* cenquizca

whore *n.* ahuiani, cihuacuecuech, motzinnamacani

whorehouse *n.* ahuiancalli, netzinnamacoyan

whoring *adj.* motetzincohuani

why *adv.* tleca, tleica, tle ipampa?

why not? *adv.* tle inic ahmo, tleica ahmo?

wick *n.* icpatlahuiloni

wide *adj.* coyahuac, coahualli, patlac patlactic (*very*),
   patlahuac, patlachtli

wideness *n.* coyahualiztli

widow *n.* oquichmicqui, oquichmihqui, icnocihuatl

widower *n.* cihuamicqui, icnooquichtli; **become a ~**
   iv. cihuamiqui (*Preterit: onicihuamic*)

wife *n.* tecihuauh, tenamic

wig *n.* tzoncalli

wild cat *n.* ixtlacmiztli

wild dog *n.* tepeitzcuintli
wild duck *n.* zolcanauhtli
wilderness *n.* cuauhtlah
will *n.* cealiztli, tlanequiliztli, tlatzonquizcanequiliztli
willow *n.* huexotl
win *tv.* tlani (*Preterit: onitlatlan*)
wind *n.* ehecatl
window *n.* tlachialoyan, tlanexillotl, tlanextilli
windpipe *n.* cocotl, cocohtli
wine *n.* octli
wing *n.* aztli
wink *tv.* teixnotza (*Preterit: oniteixnotz*), teixtlahtoa
    (*Preterit: oniteixtlahtoh*)
winter *n.* cecuizpan
wire *n.* tepuzicpatl
wisdom *n.* tlamachilizlti, tlilli tlapalli, tlaixmatiliztli
wise person *n.* tlamatini
wisely *adv.* mimatca
wish *n.* tlanequiliztli
wit *n.* texochtiliztli
witch *n.* nahualli
with *prep.* ica, ica
with me *adv.* nohuan
with pleasure *adv.* ica paquiliztli, paquiliztica
with us *adv.* tohuan
with you *adv.* mohuan (*Sing.*), amohuan (*Plural*)
wither *iv.* cuetlahuia (*Preterit: onicuetlahuiac,*
    onicuetlahuix), tonalhuaqui (*Preterit: otonalhuac*),
    xolochahui (*Peterit: onixolochauh*)
withered *adj.* cuetlauhqui, cuetlahuic
without *prep.* in ahtle, in ayac
without reason *adv.* zazan

witness *n.* tlaixpancaittani, tlaneltilih, tlaneltiliani;
    tv. ixpancaitta (*Preterit: onitlaixpancaittac*)
wittiness *n.* texochtiliztli, texochtilizzotl
witty *adj.* texochtiani, tehuehuetzquitiani
wolf *n.* cuetlachtli
woman *n.* cihuatl, zohuatl
womanizer *n.* cihuatlahueliloc
womb *n.* nanyotl, xillantli
wonderful *adj.* tlamahuizoltic
woo *tv.* teyolahcocui (*Preterit: oniteyolahcocuic*),
    teyolehua (*Preterit: oniteyoleuh*),
    teyollotlapana (*Preterit: oniteyollotlpan*)
wood *n.* cuahuitl; cuauhnacayotl (*of a tree*)
wooden flute *n.* cuauhtlapitzalli
wooden spoon *n.* xomahtli, xomalli
woodpecker *n.* cuauhchohchopihtli, cuauhquequex
woodsman *n.* cuauhtlacatl
woodwork *n.* cuauhtlacentemaliztli
wool *n.* tomitl
word *n.* tlahtolli
worldliness *n.* tlalticpaccayotl
worldly *adj.* tlacticpaccayotl
work *n.* tequitl; *iv.* tequipanoa (*Preterit: ontequipanoh*),
    tequiti (*Preterit: onitequit*)
work in vain *iv.* nenquiza (*Preterit: oninenquiz*)
work plan *n.* amatequitl
work season *n.* tequipan
worker *n.* tequini, tequitqui, tequipanoani
workshop *n.* tequitiloyan, tlachichiuhcan
world *n.* cemanahuac, cemanahuatl
worm *n.* ocuilin, payatl, cinocuilin (*corn*), cuachocuilin
    (*cloth eating*)

worry *iv.* nentlamati (*Preterit: oninentlamat*), tequipachoa
    (*Preterit: onitequipachoh*)
worse *adj.* cenca ahcualli, oc hualca inic ahcualli
worship *n.* neteotiliztli; *reflex. v.* teotia (*Preterit: oninotlateotih*)
worst *adj.* cencatlahuelli
wound *n.* tlahuitectli, tlatectli; (**to**) ~ *tv.* tehuitequi
    (*Preterit: onitehuitec*)
wrap *tv.* piquia (*Preterit: onitlapiquih*), quimiloa
    (*Preterit: onitlaquimiloh*)
wrapping *n.* quimilli, piccatl
wrestler *n.* momaiztlacoani
wretchedness *n.* tzotzocayotl
wring *iv.* ahuatza (*Preterit: onahuatz*), *tv.* patzca
    (*Preterit: onitlapatzcac*)
wrinkle *n.* xolochticayotl; *tv.* xolochoa (*Preterit:*
    onitlaxolochoh); *iv.* xolochahui (*Peterit: onixolochauh*);
    ~ **at the face** *iv.* ixxolochahui (*Preterit: nixxolochauh*)
wrinkled *adj.* xolochtic, xolochtli
wrist *n.* maquechtli
write *tv.* tlahcuiloa (*Preterit: onitlahcuiloh*)
writing *n.* tlahcuilolli, tlilli tlapalli

Y

yam *n.* camohtli
yawn *n.* cochcamachalizlti; *iv.* cochcamachaloa
    (*Preterit: onicochcamachaloh*)
year *n.* xihuitl
yearning *n.* neteelehuiliztiliztli
yeast *n.* xocotextli
yell *iv.* tzahtzi (*Preterit: onitzahtzic*)
yellow *adj.* cozauhqui, coztic
yes *adv.* quemah, quemahcatzin (*reverential*)

yesterday *n.* yalhua
yet *adv.* nohmah
you *pron.* teh, tehhuatl, ti–(*Sing.*); amehhuantin,
   am–/an– (*Plural*)
young *adj.* xochtic (*very, not speaking yet*)
young man *n.* telpochtli (*Plural: telpopochtin*), telpocatl,
   tlapaltzintli
your *poss.* mo– (*Sing.*); amo– (*Plural*)
yourself *reflex.* timo–
yourselves *reflex.* ammo–
youth *n.* telpochcayotl
yucca *n.* cuauhcamohtli, iczotl

Z
zapote fruit *n.* tzapotl
zoo *n.* yolcatlamatilli, yolcatzacualli

Reference

Everyday Words and Phrases

Please.
Nimitztlatlauhtia.
nee-meets-tlä-tlouh-tee-yä

Thank you.
Tlazohcamati.
tlä-so-kä-mä-tee

You are welcome.
Ahmitla.
äh-mee-tlä

Excuse me.
Moixpantzinco.
mo-eesh-pän-seen-ko

Excuse me.
Xinechtlapohpolhui.
shee-nech-tlä-poh-pol-wee

Be well.
Ma xipactinemi
mä-shee-päk-tee-ně-mee

Good.
Cualli.
kwäl-lee

Yes.
Quemah.
kĕ-mäh

No.
Ahmo.
äh-mo

Numbers

1	ce
2	ome
3	ei/yei
4	nahui
5	macuilli
6	chicuace
7	chicome
8	chicuei
9	chicunahui
10	mahtlactli
11	mahtlactli once/mahtlactli huan ce/mahtlacce
12	mahtlactli omome/mahtlactli huan ome/ mahtlacome
13	mahtlactli omei/mahtlactli huan yei/ mahtlacyei

14	mahtlactli onnahui/mahtlactli huan nahui/ mahtlacnahui
15	caxtolli
16	caxtolli once/caxtolli huan ce/caxtolce
17	caxtolli omome/caxtolli huan ome/caxtolome
18	caxtolli omei/caxtolli huan yei/caxtolyei
19	caxtolli onnahui/caxtolli huan nahui/ caxtolnahui
20	cempohualli
21	cempohualli once/cempohualli huan ce/ cempohualce
22	cempohualli omome/cempohualli huan ome/ cempohualome
23	cempohualli omei/cempohualli huan yei/ cempohualyei
24	cempohualli onnahui/cempohualli huan nahui/ cempohualnahui
25	cempohualli ommacuilli/cempohualli huan macuilli/cempohualmacuilli
26	cempohualli onchicuace/cempohualli huan chicuace/cempohualchicuace
27	cempohualli onchicome/cempohualli huan chicome/cempohualchicome
28	cempohualli onchicuei/cempohualli huan chicuei/cempohualchicuei
29	cempohualli onchicunahui/cempohualli huan chicunahui/cempohualchicunahui
30	cempohualli ommahtlactli/cempohualli huan mahtlactli/cempohualmahtlactli

31	cempohualli ommahtlactli once/cempohualli huan mahtlactli huan ce/ cempohualmahtlacce
35	cempohualli oncaxtolli/cempohualli huan caxtolli/cempohualcaxtolli
36	cempohualli oncaxtolli once/cempohualli huan caxtolli huan ce/cempohualcaxtolce
40	ompohualli
50	ompohualli ommahtlactli/ompohualli huan mahtlactli
60	epohualli
70	epohualli ommahtlactli/epohualli huan mahtlactli
80	nauhpohualli/nappohualli
90	nauhpohualli ommahtlactli/nauhpohualli huan mahtlactli
100	macuilpohualli
200	mahtlacpohualli
300	caxtolpohualli
400	centzontli/cetztontli
500	centzontli ommacuilpohualli/cetzontli huan macuilpohualli
600	centzontli ommahtlacpohualli/cetzontli huan mahtlacpohualli
700	centzontli oncaxtolpohualli/cetzontli huan caxtolpohualli
800	ontzontli/ometzontli

900	ontzontli ommacuilpohualli/ometzontli huan macuilpohualli
1,000	ontzontli ommahtlacpohualli/ometzontli huan mahtlacpohualli
2,000	macuiltzontli
4,000	mahtlactzontli
8,000	cenxiquipilli
16,000	onxiquipilli
80,000	mahtlacxiquipilli
160,000	cempohualxiquipilli
320,000	ompohualxiquipilli

Ordinals

1st	inic ce
2nd	inic ome
3rd	inic ei
4th	inic nahui
5th	inic macuilli
6th	inic chicuace
7th	inic chicome
8th	inic chicuei
9th	inic chicunahui
10th	inic mahtlactli
11th	inic mahtlactli huan ce
15th	inic caxtolli
20th	inic cempohualli

Parts of the Body

ankle	**quequeyolli**
anus	**tzintli/tzoyotl**
arm	**maitl, matzotzopaztli**
back	**cuitlapantli/tepotzli/teputztli**
back hair	**ahcoltzontli**
beard	**tentzontli/camatzontli**
biceps	**ahcolnacayotl**
big toe	**tohueixopil/xopiltecuhtli**
bladder	**axixcomitl**
blood	**eztli**
body	**tonacayo**
bone	**omitl**
brain	**cuatextli/cuayollotl**
breast	**chichihualli**
buttock	**tzintamalli/tzintlantli/tonacayocan**
calf	**cotztetl/cotztli**
callus	**chacayolli/caczolli** (*feet*)
cheek	**camapantli/cantli**
chest	**elpantli**
chin	**tenchalli**
clitoris	**zacapilli**
colon	**cuitlaxcoltomactli**
ear	**nacaztli**
elbow	**molicpitl**
entrails	**eltzaccatl**
excrement	**cuitlatl**
eye	**ixtli/ixtololohtli/ixtelolohtli**

eyeball	**ixtetl**
eyebrow	**ixcuamulli/ixtohmitl**
eyelash	**tocochia**
eyelid	**ixtentli**
face	**ixtli**
face flesh	**ixnacatl**
facial hair	**camatzontli**
facial skin	**ixehuatl**
finger	**mahpilli**
fingernail	**iztetl**
fist	**mapichtli**
flesh	**nacayotl**
foot	**icxitl**
forehead	**ixcuaitl**
front teeth	**tlanixcuatl**
gums	**quehtolli**
hair	**tzontli**
hand	**maitl**
head	**cuaitl/tzontecomatl**
hip	**cuappantli/nacayocantli**
incisors	**coatlantli**
intestine	**cuitlaxcolli**
jaw	**camachalli**
jawbone	**camachalcuauhyotl**
joint	**huihuilteccantli/zazaliuhyantli**
kidney	**yoyomoctli**
knee	**tetepontli/tlancuaitl**
knuckle	**cecepoctli**
lap	**cuexantli/cuixantli**
left hand	**opochmaitl**

leg	**xotl**
leg hair	**metztzontli**
leg nerve	**metztlalhuatl**
lip	**tentli**
liver	**elli**
male genitalia	**oquichnacayotl**
menstruation	**cihuacocolli**
middle finger	**mapilhueyacatl**
molar	**tlancochtli**
mouth	**camatl**
mucus	**yacacuitatl**
muscle	**acoltetl**
nape	**quechcochtetl, quechcochtli**
navel	**xictli**
neck	**quechtli**
nerve	**tlalhuatl**
nose	**yacatl**
nose hair	**yacatzontli**
palate	**camatapalli/copactli**
palm	**macpalli**
penis	**tepolli/tepulli**
pinkie	**mapiltontli/mapilxocoyotl**
placenta	**cihuatlahyelli**
prepuce	**xipintli**
pupil	**ixnenetl**
rheum	**ixcuitlatl**
rib	**omicicuilli**
right hand	**mayeccantli/mayectli/yecmaitl**
saliva	**iztlactli/chihchitl**
scalp	**cauehuayotl**

scrotum	**atexicolli/aloyotl**
semen	**xinachyotl**
shin	**tetepontli/tlanitztli**
shoulder	**ahcolli**
shoulder blade	**ahcolchimalli**
skeleton	**miccuahuitl/mihcacuahuitl**
skin	**ehuatl**
skull	**cuacacalaccantli/cuaxicalli**
small toe	**xopilxocoyotl**
sperm	**xinachyotl**
spleen	**elcomalli**
stomach	**ihtitl**
tear	**ixayotl**
teeth	**tlantli**
temple	**canahuacantli**
testicle	**atetl/chiquiztli/yoyomoctli**
thigh	**maxatl/maxactli/ metztli**
throat	**tozcatl**
thumb	**hueymapilli**
tibia	**tlanitztli**
toe	**xopilli**
toe nail	**xopiliztitl**
tongue	**nenepilli**
torso	**tlactli**
urethra	**acayotl/axixpiztli**
urine	**axixtli/tlapiaztli**
vagina	**cihuatl iacayo/cihuanacayotl**
waist	**topitzahuayan**
womb	**xillantli**
wrist	**maquechtli**

Family

aunt	**ahuitl**
brother (*older*)	**teachcauh**
brother (*younger*)	**teiccauh**
brother-in-law (*man's*)	**textli**
brother-in-law (*woman's*)	**huepulli**
child	**conetl/pilli**
daughter	**cihuaconetl/cihuapilli**
daughter-in-law	**cihuamontli**
father	**tahtli**
father-in-law	**montahtli**
grandchild	**ixhuiuhtli**
granddaughter	**ixhuiuhtli**
grandfather	**colli**
grandmother	**cihtli**
grandson	**ixhuiuhtli**
great granddaughter	**icuhtontli**
great grandfather	**achtontli**
great grandmother	**piptontli**
great grandson	**icuhtontli**
husband	**namictli/teoquichhui**
mother	**nantli**
mother-in-law	**monnantli**
nephew	**machtli**
niece	**machtli**
relative	**notehuanyolqui**
sister (*older*)	**hueltiuhtli**
sister (*younger*)	**teicuh**

sister-in-law (*man's*)	**huepulli**
sister-in-law (*woman's*)	**huezhuaztli**
son	**oquichconetl/oquichpilli**
son-in-law	**montli**
stepfather	**tlacpatahtli**
stepmother	**tlacpanantli**
uncle	**tlahtli**
wife	**tecihuauh**

Cardinal Points

east	**tlauhcampa/tonayampa/ tonayan**
north	**mictlampa**
south	**huitztlampa**
west	**cihuatlampa**

Day

afternoon	**teotlac**
day after tomorrow	**huiptla**
day before yesterday	**ye ohuiptla**
evening	**yohualli**
midday	**nepantla tonalli/ nepantla tonatiuh/ tlahcotonalli/tlahcotonatiuh**
midnight	**yohualnepantla**
morning	**tlaneci/yohuahtzinco**

night	**yohualli**
night before last	**yalhua/yalhua yohualli/ yalhua yohuac**
today	**axcan**
tomorrow	**moztla**
yesterday	**yalhua**

Names of Days

Contemporary Nahuatl combines the suffix *–tica* (with, in) or the preposition *ipan* (in) with the names of the days in Spanish. Day names are not capitalized. In addition, names of days are sometimes designated ordinally (starting with Sunday) as 1st day of the week, 2nd day of the week, etc.

Monday	**lunestica/ipan lunes/ometonalli ipan chicomilhuitl**
Tuesday	**martestica/ipan martes/yeitonalli ipan chicomilhuitl**
Wednesday	**miércolestica/ipan miércoles/nahuitonalli ipan chicomilhuitl**
Thursday	**juevestica/ipan jueves/macuiltonalli ipan chicomilhuitl**
Friday	**viernestica/ipan viernes/chicuacetonalli ipan chicomilhuitl**
Saturday	**sábadotica/ipan sábado/chicometonalli ipan chicomilhuitl**
Sunday	**domingotica/ipan domingo/cetonalli ipan chicomilhuitl**

The indigenous Nahuatl calendar had twenty days. These were combined with a number (1–13) as in the following examples: ce cipactli (*1-crocodile*), ome ehecatl (*2-wind*), yei calli (*3-house*), etc.

cipactli (*crocodile*)	ozomahtli (*monkey*)
ehecatl (*wind*)	malinalli (*twisted grass, hay*)
calli (*house*)	acatl (*reed*)
cuetzpalin (*lizard*)	ocelotl (*jaguar*)
coatl (*snake, twin*)	cuauhtli (*eagle*)
miquiztli (*death*)	cozcacuauhtli (*vulture*)
mazatl (*deer*)	olin (*movement*)
tochtli (*rabbit*)	tecpatl (*flint*)
atl (*water*)	quiahuitl (*rain*)
itzcuintli (*dog*)	xochitl (*flower*)

Names of Months

Names of months are expressed as the first month (January), the second month (February), etc. The preposition *ipan* (in) is also combined with the names of the months in Spanish. Month names are not capitalized.

January	**inic ce metztli/ipan enero**
February	**inic ome metztli/ipan febrero**
March	**inic yei metztli/ipan marzo**
April	**inic nahui metztli/ipan abril**
May	**inic macuilli metztli/ipan mayo**
June	**inic chicuace metztli/ipan junio**

July	**inic chicome metztli/ipan julio**
August	**inic chichuei metztli/ipan agosto**
September	**inic chicunahui metztli/ipan septiembre**
October	**inic mahtlactli metztli/ipan octubre**
November	**inic mahtlactli once metztli/november**
December	**inic mahtlactli omome metztli/ipan diciembre**

The indigenous calendar had 18 months (*metztli*) consisting of 20 days. Five empty days (*nemontemi*) were added to complete the cycle of the year (*xihuitl*).

atlacahualo	xocotl huetztli
tlacaxipehualiztli	ochpaniztli
tozoztontli	teotlehco
huey tozoztli	tepeilhuitl
toxcatl	quecholli
etzalcualiztli	panquetzaliztli
tecuilhuitontli	atemoztli
huey tecuilhuitl	tititl
tlaxochimaco	izcalli

Seasons

autumn	**tonalco**
spring	**xopan/xopantlah**
summer	**tonallan/xopaniztempan**
winter	**cecuizpan**

Animals & Insects

animal	**yolcatl**
ant	**azcatl**
anteater	**aztacoyotl**
bat	**quimichpatlan/tzinacantli**
bee	**pipiolin/xicohtli**
beetle	**pinacatl**
bird	**tototl**
blackbird	**tzanatl**
bluebird	**xiuhtototl**
boar	**coyametl**
bobcat	**ocotochin**
bull/cow	**cuacuahueh**
butterfly	**papalotl**
calf	**cuacuahuehconetl**
cat	**mizton**
caterpillar	**chiahuitl**
catfish	**coamichin**
centipede	**centummayeh**
chameleon	**cuemitl/tapayaxin**
chick	**piotl**
chicken	**cuanaca**
chipmunk	**motohtli**
cockroach	**calayotl**
cocoon	**cochiopitl/tecilli**
coyote	**coyotl**
crab	**atecuicihtli/tecuicihtli**
cricket	**chopilin**

crocodile	**cipactli**
deer	**mazatl**
dove	**huilotl**
duck	**canauhtli**
eagle	**cuauhtli**
earthworm	**tlalocuilin**
eel	**coamichin**
falcon	**huactli/tlohtli**
fawn	**mazaconetl**
fish	**michin**
flea	**tecpin**
fly	**zayolin**
fox	**capizcayotl/cuectli**
frog	**cueyatl**
gander	**atlatlalacatl/concanauhtli/ zoquicanauhtli**
goat	**cuacuauhtentzoneh**
goldfinch	**tzocuil**
goose	**atlatlalacatl/concanauhtli/ zoquicanauhtli**
gopher	**tuzan**
grasshopper	**chapulin**
hairless Mexican dog	**xoloitzcuintli**
hawk	**tlohtli**
heron	**aztatl**
horse	**cahuayo**
horsefly	**temolin**
hummingbird	**huitzilin**
iguana	**cuahuito**
insect	**yolcatzintli**

jaguar	**ocelotl/tecuani**
lamb	**ichcatl**
lizard	**cuetzpalin**
macaw	**alo**
maggot	**nacaocuilin**
maguey worm	**meocuilin**
monkey	**ozomahtli**
mosquito	**moyotl/yoyoliton**
mountain lion	**miztli**
mouse	**quimichin**
mule	**yolitl**
opossum	**tlacuatzin**
oriole	**xochitototl**
owl	**tecolotl**
oyster	**eptli**
parakeet	**quiltototl**
parrot	**cochotl**
partridge	**tepezolin**
peccary	**coyametl**
pig	**pitzotl**
puma	**miztli**
quail	**zolin**
quetzal bird	**quetzaltototl**
rabbit	**tochin/tochtli**
racoon	**mapachin/mapachtli**
rat	**huizacotl**
raven	**cacalotl**
roadrunner	**poxacuatl**
rooster	**cuanaca**
scorpion	**colotl/acaltetepon**
sea turtle	**ayotectli**

shrimp	**chacalin**
skunk	**epatl**
snail	**cilin**
snake	**coatl**
sparrow	**molotl/teocaltototl**
spider	**tocatl**
squirrel	**chechelotl/chachalotl/**
	motohtli/techalotl
stork	**aztatl**
swallow	**cuicuitzcatl**
tadpole	**atepocatl**
tick	**mazaatemitl/pepeyoctli**
toad	**tamazolin**
turkey (*hen*)	**totolin**
turkey (*tom*)	**huexolotl/huehxolotl**
turtle	**ayotl**
vulture	**tzohpilotl**
wasp	**tetocani**
weasel	**coyahtli**
whitefish	**amilotl**
wolf	**cuetlachtli**
woodpecker	**cuauhchochopihtli**
worm	**ocuilin**

School Terms

blackboard	**huapaltlahcuilolhuaztli**
book	**amoxtli**
homework	**caltequitl**

library	**amoxcalli**
notebook	**izhuaamoxtli**
number	**tlapohualmachiotl**
paper	**amatl**
pen	**tlahcuiloloni/totolacatl**
pencil	**teconalli**
reading	**amapohualiztli**
school	**nemachtiloyan**
student	**momachtiani**
teacher	**temachtiani**
writing	**tlahcuilolli**

Flowers

lily	**omixochitl**
magnolia	**yolloxochitl**
marigold	**cempohualxochitl**
poinsettia	**cuitlaxochitl**
sunflower	**chimalxochitl**

Colors

black	**tliltic**
blue	**texoticyapalli**
gray	**nextic**
green	**quiltic/xoxoctic**
navy blue	**yahuitl**
orange	**xochipalli**

pink	**tlaztalehualli**
polychrome	**cuicuiltic**
red	**chiltic**
white	**iztac**
yellow	**cozauhqui/coztic**

Plants & Fruits

banana	**xochihcualli, zapalotl**
cabbage	**coloix**
grape	**caxapo/xocomecayollotl**
green bean	**exotl**
peanut	**cacahuatl**
pine nut	**ococenyollohtli**
pineapple	**matzahtli**
pinto bean	**zoletl**
plum	**xocotl**
potato	**papas**
prickly pear	**nochtli**
pumpkin	**ayohtli**
pumpkin seed	**ayohachtli**
squash	**tlalayohtli**
vegetable	**quilitl**

Language

adjective	**tocahcencahquetl**
adverb	**tlachihualcencahquetl**

affirmation	**tlaneltililiztli**
comma	**tlahuazancoliuhqui**
conjugation	**tetocapatlachihualnepanoliztli**
conjunction	**tlanechicoltiquetl**
future tense	**tlen panoz**
negative	**ahnecuitiliztli**
noun	**tocaitl**
parenthesis	**yahualmachiotl/** **yahualmachiotlahcuilolli**
past tense	**opanoc cahuitl**
period	**tliltetl**
present tense	**axcan cahuitl**
pronoun	**tetocapatlaquetl**
question mark	**tlatlanilmachiotl**
quotation mark	**tetlahtolmachiotl**
tense	**cahuitl**
verb	**tlachihualiztli**
vocabulary	**tlahtoltecpantli**

Spanish and Latin American Interest Titles ...

Emergency Spanish Phrasebook
80 pages • 4½ x 7½ • 0-7818-0977-0 • $5.95pb • (460)

Spanish-English/English-Spanish Practical Dictionary
35,000 entries • 338 pages • 5 x 8 • 0-7818-0179-6 • $9.95pb • (211)

Spanish-English/English-Spanish Dictionary & Phrasebook
2,000 entries • 250 pages • 3¾ x 7 • 0-7818-0773-5 • $11.95pb • (261)

Hippocrene Children's Illustrated Spanish Dictionary
English-Spanish/Spanish-English
500 entries • 94 pages • 8 x 11 • 0-7818-0889-8 • $11.95pb • (181)

Spanish-English/English-Spanish Concise Dictionary
(Latin American)
8,000 entries • 500 pages • 4 x 6 • 0-7818-0261-X • $11.95pb • (258)

Spanish Learner's Dictionary
14,000 entries • 300 pages • 4 x 6 • 0-7818-0937-1 • $14.95pb • (386)

Beginner's Spanish
313 pages • 5½ x 8½ • 0-7818-0840-5 • $14.95pb • (225)

Mastering Advanced Spanish
326 pages • 5 x 8 • 0-7818-0081-1 • $14.95pb • (413)
2 cassettes: ca. 2 hours • 0-7818-0089-7 • $12.95 • (426)

Spanish Grammar
224 pages • 5 x 8 • 0-87052-893-9 • $12.95pb • (273)

Spanish Verbs: Ser and Estar
220 pages • 5 x 8 • 0-7818-0024-2 • $8.95pb • (292)

Dictionary of Latin American Phrases and Expressions
1,900 entries • 178 pages • 5½ x 8½ • 0-7818-0865-0 • $14.95pb • (286)

Dictionary of 1,000 Spanish Proverbs: Bilingual
131 pages • 5 x 8 • 0-7818-0412-4 • $11.95pb • (254)

Spanish Proverbs, Idioms and Slang
350 pages • 6 x 9 • 0-7818-0675-5 • $14.95pb • (760)

Mexico: An Illustrated History
150 pages • 5 x 7 • 50 illus. • 0-7818-0690-9 • $11.95pb • (585)

Tikal: An Illustrated History of the Ancient Maya Capital
271 pages • 6 x 9 • 50 b/w photos/illus./maps • 0-7818-0853-7 •
$14.95pb • (101)

Treasury of Spanish Love Poems, Quotations and Proverbs: Bilingual
128 pages • 5 x 7 • 0-7818-0358-6 • $11.95hc • (589)
2 cassettes: ca. 2 hours • 0-7818-0365-9 • $12.95 • (584)

Treasury of Spanish Love Short Stories in Spanish and English
157 pages • 5 x 7 • 0-7818-0298-9 • $11.95hc • (604)

Folk Tales from Chile
121 pages • 5 x 8 • 15 illus. • 0-7818-0712-3 • $12.50hc • (785)

Indigenous North and Central American Language Titles from Hippocrene . . .

Colloquial Navajo: A Dictionary
Robert W. Young and William Morgan

A useful reference, this book addresses the inadequacy of literal translation when working with idioms by offering interpretations based on the general meaning of a phrase rather than the individual words that comprise the expressions.
10,000 entries • 461 pages • 5 x 7 • 0-7818-0278-4 • $16.95pb • (282)

Dictionary of Maya Hieroglyphs
John Montgomery

This authoritative work is the first visual dictionary of Maya Glyphs published since the script's complete decipherment, offering a much-needed, comprehensive catalog of 1,100 secured glyphs. Each entry includes the illustrated glyph, its phonetic transcription, Mayan equivalent, part of speech and meaning. Multiple indices cross-reference the glyphs with their English and Spanish translations, subject, visual components, T-numbers, and other criteria.
1,100 entries • 200 pages • 6 x 9 • b/w line drawings • 0-7818-0862-6 • $19.95pb • (337)

How to Read Maya Hieroglyphs
John Montgomery

The Ancient Maya Civilization of Mesoamerica was one of five in the history of the world to invent an original, functional writing system. Maya scribes documented the history of their civilization in hieroglyphic script, yet by the nineteenth century there was not a single person left who could read this pictorial writing.

The first of its kind, this comprehensive guide to deciphering Maya hieroglyphs contains a complete outline of the writing, presenting individual signs and their meanings, the script's grammatical structure and content, and explanations of the sophisticated Maya calendrical and mathematical systems. Clear visual examples of the glyphs drawn by the author illustrate the text, as well as diagrams, maps, and photographs.

225 pages • 6 x 9 • b/w and color illus. • 0-7818-0861-8 • $24.00hc • (332)

Navajo-English Dictionary
Leone Wall & William Morgan

This guide to the Navajo language, which is now spoken by more than 200,000 people in the Southwestern United States, is ideal for students, anthropologists, and Dineh. A detailed section on how to pronounce Navajo words accompanies the more than 9,000 entries included in this (one-way) dictionary.

9,000 entries • 166 pages • 5½ x 8½ • 0-7818-0247-4 • $11.95pb • (223)

Yoeme-English/English-Yoeme Standard Dictionary
Felipe S. Molina, Herminia Valenzuela, David L. Shaul

This unique guide to one of the indigenous languages of the Southwestern United States and Mexico is the first dictionary of Yoeme ever published. It includes over 8,000 entries with informative facts about the Yaqui culture. It also features an introduction to the Yoeme alphabet and spelling, a concise guide to Yoeme word and sentence structure and sentence complexity.

11,200 entries • 351 pages • 5½ x 8½ • 0-7818-0663-X • $16.95pb • (713)

Zapotec-English/English-Zapotec (Isthmus) Concise Dictionary
A. Scott Britton

Isthmus Zapotec, one of at least six known varieties of Zapotec, claims the largest number of speakers in the Zapotecean family. It is spoken in Oaxaca, in Mexico's Isthmus of Tehuantepec, and in the state's capital city, Oaxaca de Juárez. This is the first dictionary of Isthmus Zapotec to be published in English. In addition to over 5,000 entries—with etymological notes given when entry words derive from Spanish—the dictionary contains detailed yet concise section covering spelling and pronunciation, as well as the major points of Isthmus Zapotec Grammar.

5,000 entries • 250 pages • 4 x 6 • 0-7818-1010-8 • $14.95pb • (217)